A CONCISE HISTORY OF
THE ARMENIAN PEOPLE

Other Books by George Bournoutian

Eastern Armenia in the Last Decades of Persian Rule:
　　1807-1828 (out of print)

The Khanate of Erevan under Qajar Rule, 1795-1828

A History of Qarabagh (Karabagh) (out of print)

A History of the Armenian People,
　　　I: From Prehistory to 1500 AD (out of print)
A History of the Armenian People
　　　II: From 1500 to the Present (out of print)

Armenians and Russia, 1626-1796

Russia and the Armenians of Transcaucasia, 1797-1889

The Chronicle of Abraham of Crete

Abraham of Erevan: History of the Wars, 1721-1738

The Journal of Zak'aria of Agulis

A Concise History of the Armenian People

(From Ancient Times to the Present)

Second Edition

George A. Bournoutian

MAZDA PUBLISHERS, Inc.
2003

The publication of this volume was made possible by grants from
Iranica Institute, Irvine, California and a number of individual donors

Mazda Publishers, Inc.
Academic publishers since 1980
P.O. Box 2603
Costa Mesa, California 92628 U.S.A.
www.mazdapub.com

Library of Congress Cataloging-in-Publication Data

Bournoutian, George A.
A Concise History of the Armenian People/ George Bournoutian.
p.cm.
Includes bibliographical references and index.
ISBN: 1-56859-141-1
(Softcover, alk. paper)

1. Armenian—History. 2. Armenians—History. I. Title.
DS175.B65 2002
909'.0491992—dc21
2002021898

10 9 8 7 6 5 4 3 2

To my brother David

Barekamê amēn aten kê sirē
U eghbayrê neghut'ean atenowan
hamar tsnats' ē

A friend loves you at all times,
But a brother is born to share adversity

(Proverbs: 17. 17)

CONTENTS

Part II: From Foreign Rule to Independence

Preface to the Second Edition

Between 1992 and 1994, at the suggestion of Louise Manoogian Simone, the President of the Armenian General Benevolent Union, I composed a two-volume study, *A History of the Armenian People*. The purpose of the work was to enable Armenians to view their past objectively and to familiarize non-Armenians with the history of an ancient people who had lost most of their historic territory and were scattered around the globe.

Lecture tours sponsored by the AGBU, as well as the assistance of Armenian leaders such as Raffy and Vicki Hovanessian and Hrant Bardakjian brought the book to the attention of the Armenian communities in the US, Canada and Australia and the first printing was soon sold out. Second and third printings appeared between 1995 and 1997 and eventually some 10,000 copies were printed.

The study, the first comprehensive survey of the history of the Armenians from ancient times to the early 1990s in English, was soon adopted as a required text or used as a basis for lectures by instructors and professors of Armenian history. Historians and geographers made use of the maps, imitated the format, copied the timelines, and borrowed the ideas and interpretations.

Dwindling supplies, the absence of relevant material in some chapters, the need for additional maps, time-lines, plates, and a more comprehensive bibliography and index, as well as the current political importance of the region encouraged me to prepare a concise and more scholarly edition. I have not only added much new data for the Armenian diaspora, but have also included additional information on the significant events which have occurred in the region during the closing years of the twentieth century and the dawn of the new millennium.

I have examined the history of Armenia and its people in relation to that of the rest of the world. The timelines and the maps will help the reader to correlate Armenian history with that of other nations. The present work contains some fresh interpretations of traditional views of Armenian history. Its main purpose is to familiarize Armenians and non-Armenians with a people and culture that is absent from most history courses and texts. The work does not address every issue of the extremely complicated history of the Armenians, but rather focuses on the political and socioeconomic history while glossing over the arts and literature.

Acknowledgements

Hrag Vartanian spent countless hours preparing the maps, tables, and plates. In addition, he designed the cover. I am truly indebted to his generosity and friendship. The Dean of Arts and Science, the Provost of Iona College, the Committee of Rank and Tenure, and the Faculty Travel and Research Committee granted the much-needed sabbatical and the research/travel funds. The staff at the Iona Faculty Computer Resource Center, as well as the staff at the Mazda Academic Press helped with the formatting. Raffy and Vicki Hovanessian, Jean-Marie Atamian, Karnik and Jill Boyajian, Andrew Shahinian, and Michael Ansour demonstrated their friendship and their support of Armenian Studies by providing generous subsidies to cover part of the publication costs. Finally, my wife Ani, helped edit the various drafts. I am, of course, responsible for any flaws that remain.

George Bournoutian
Professor of History
Iona College
New Rochelle, New York

Explanatory Notes

Dating System

In an effort to provide a global perspective and eliminate a seeming Christian or Western bias, some college texts have decided to substitute B.C.E. (Before the Common Era) for B.C. (Before Christ) and C.E. (Common Era) for A.D. (*Anno Domini*). I have retained the B.C. and A.D. designations in the text, but have used B.C.E. and C.E. in the timelines. It is important to note, however, that various cultures have different calendars. The Armenian Church calendar, for example, differs by 551 years from the calendar used in the Western world today. Chinese, Hebrew, Arab, Iranian, and pre-Revolutionary Russian calendars, among others, also differ from our calendar. To simplify matters, all dates have been converted to the dating system used in the West.

It should be noted that there are no exact dates for some historical occurrences or reigns of some rulers in ancient times. In such cases an approximate date or circa, abbreviated as c., is used. All dates following the names of kings or catholicoi refer to their reigns; in all other cases they refer to life span.

Geographical Terms

Another attempt to correct any Eurocentric bias has been to alter some, but not all, commonly used geographical terms. Thus instead of Middle East, Near East, or the Levant, some historians now use the more accurate term, Western Asia; Far East or the Orient has sometimes been replaced by East Asia; the Indian subcontinent is referred to as South Asia; Transcaucasia is occasionally called the eastern Caucasus. The concept has not been universally accepted and I shall, therefore, retain traditional geographical terms or, in some instances, as they are currently used in the news media. The term Middle East, therefore, includes the present day territories of Iran, Egypt, Syria, Turkey, Lebanon, Iraq, Jordan, Palestine, Kuwait, Saudi Arabia, Yemen, and the various Gulf States. Asia Minor or Anatolia refers to the territory of present-day Turkey. Western

Armenia refers to the eastern part of present-day Turkey, while eastern Armenia refers to the present-day Armenia plus parts of Azerbaijan and Georgia. Transcaucasia refers to the present-day republics of Armenia, Georgia, and Azerbaijan. Mesopotamia refers to the territory of present-day Iraq. The Balkans refers to the present-day states of Greece, Albania, Bulgaria, Romania and Yugoslavia. The Levant encompasses mainly Lebanon and parts of the coastal lands of Syria. The term Azerbaijan, used prior to the twentieth century, refers to Persian Azerbaijan, or the territory in northwestern Iran south of the Arax River.

Transliteration

To conform to the spoken language in the Republic of Armenia, Armenian words, with minor exceptions, have been transliterated according to sounds of Eastern Armenian. The Persian words are transliterated according to the sounds of modern Persian. A simplified transliteration system with no diacritical marks or ligatures has been utilized in both instances. Some of the foreign names and terms, particularly those included in the *Webster's Unabridged Dictionary*, have been Anglicized, while others have retained their original form. Finally, the romanized version, if any, of Armenian names or variations of common names will appear in parentheses.

Reference Sources

In addition to the sources listed in the bibliographical guide, I have consulted the following world history texts, encyclopedias, and atlases for the chronology and the preparation of the timelines and maps.

History Texts
The Cambridge Ancient History
The Cambridge Medieval History
The Cambridge Modern History
The Cambridge History of Iran
The Cambridge History of Islam
A. M. Craig, W. A. Graham, D. Kagan eds., *The Heritage of World Civilizations*
B. Esler, The Human Venture: *A World History from Prehistory to the Present*

R. L. Greaves, R. Zaller, eds., *Civilizations of the World*
J. P. McKay, B. D. Hill, J. Buckler eds., *A History of World Societies*
W. H. McNeill, *A History of the Human Community*
P. L. Ralph, R. E. Lerner, E. M. Burns eds., *World Civilizations*
L. S. Stavrianos, *A Global History*
J. Upshur, J. Terry, J. Holoka eds., *World History*
T. W. Wallbank, A. M. Taylor eds., *Civilizations Past and Present*
R. W. Winks, C. Brinton eds., *A History of Civilization*

Encyclopedias

Encyclopaedia Iranica
The Columbia History of the World
An Encyclopedia of World History
Soviet Armenian Encyclopedia
The Timetables of History
Encyclopaedia of Islam (both editions)
Great Soviet Encyclopedia
The Oxford Dictionary of Byzantium

Atlases

Historical Atlas of Armenia
Hammond Historical Atlas of the World
The Penguin Atlas of Ancient History
The Penguin Atlas of Medieval History
The Penguin Atlas of Modern History
The Penguin Atlas of Recent History
The Penguin Atlas of Diasporas
Historical Atlas of Iran
An Atlas of Russian and East European History
Soviet Armenian Atlas
Anchor Atlas of World History
Grosser Historischer Weltatlas

Part I

From Independence to Foreign Rule
(Ancient Times to AD 1500)

Introduction

In their 3000-year history, the Armenians have rarely played the role of aggressor; rather, they have excelled in agriculture, arts and crafts, and trade. Armenians have produced unique architectural monuments, sculptures, illuminated manuscripts, literature, and philosophical and legal tracts. Moreover, a number of important philosophical and scientific works from other cultures have survived only in their Armenian translations. In addition, the Armenians, because of their location and participation in international trade, have contributed to the cultural and scientific development of both the East and the West. College graduates and even teachers, however, know very little about the Armenians or their history. Historians have traditionally concentrated their research on the record of conquerors that dominated or destroyed other nations. Thus, despite their accomplishments, the Armenians have been given less space in general history texts than the Mongols or the Vikings.

To be sure, the history of Armenia is a difficult one to reconstruct. Sources written before the invention of the Armenian alphabet in the fifth century A.D. require a familiarity with Aramaic, Greek, Middle Persian and Syriac. Later sources demand the knowledge of Arabic, Latin, Georgian, Turkish, Modern Persian, Mongolian, Russian, French, and German, as well as classical and modern Armenian. The numerous invasions of and earthquakes in Armenia have no doubt destroyed valuable historical evidence. Furthermore, the divisions of historic Armenia among modern neighboring states have made archival and archeological research a sensitive, and often difficult, task. Moreover, the systematic application of modern historical research techniques to the study of Armenian history is but a recent phenomenon.

Armenia is one of the few small nations that have managed to survive repeated invasions, destruction, and persecutions. The Armenians have been described through the centuries as adaptable, resilient, enterprising and steadfast. How they managed to survive while larger and more powerful states disappeared, and how, at the same time, they were able to make significant contributions to world civilizations, is the amazing history of the Armenian people.

1

Highlands and Crossroads
The Land of Armenia

ARMENIA is a landlocked mountainous plateau that rises to an average of 3,000 to 7,000 feet above sea level. It extends to the Anatolian plateau in the west, the Iranian plateau in the southwest, the plains of the South Caucasus in the north, and the Karadagh Mountains and the Moghan Steppe in the south and the southeast. The Armenian highlands stretch roughly between 38°and 48°longitude East, and 37°and 41°latitude North, with a total area of some 130,000 square miles. In present-day terms, historic Armenia comprises most of eastern Turkey, the northeastern corner of Iran, parts of the Azerbaijan and Georgian Republics, as well as the entire territory of the Armenian Republic.

Armenia is defined by a number of natural boundaries. The Kur (Kura) and Arax (Araxes) Rivers separate the Armenian highlands in the east from the lowlands that adjoin the Caspian Sea. The Pontus Mountains, which connect to the Lesser Caucasus mountain chain, separate Armenia from the Black Sea and Georgia and form the northern boundary. The Taurus Mountains, which join the upper Zagros Mountains and the Iranian Plateau, form the southern boundary of Armenia and separate it from Syria, Kurdistan and Iran. The western boundary of Armenia has generally been between the western Euphrates River and the northern stretch of the Anti-Taurus Mountains. Armenians also established communities east of the Kur, as far as the Caspian Sea, and states west of the Euphrates, as far as Cilicia, on the Mediterranean Sea.

Some fifty million years ago, the geological structure of Armenia went through many phases, creating great mountains and high, now-inactive, volcanic peaks throughout the plateau. The larger peak of Mount Ararat (16,946 feet), Mount Sipan (14,540 feet),

Mount Aragats (13,410 feet), the smaller peak of Mount Ararat (12,839 feet), and Mount Bingöl (10,770 feet), from which the Arax and the Euphrates Rivers originate, are some examples. A number of mountain chains and highlands within Armenia including Zeitun, Sasun, Karabagh, Siunik, Vardenis, Areguni, Sevan, Gegham, Pambak, and the Armenian Chain divide the plateau into distinct regions, a phenomenon that has resulted in significant political and historical ramifications (see map 1). Tufa, limestone, basalt, quartz, and obsidian form the main composition of the terrain. The mountains also supply abundant deposits of mineral ores, including copper, iron and zinc, lead, silver, and gold. There are also large salt mines as well as borax, obsidian and volcanic tufa stone used for construction.

The many mountains are the source of numerous un-navigable rivers, which have created deep gorges, ravines and waterfalls. Of these, the longest is the Arax River, which starts in the mountains of western Armenia and, after joining the Kur River, empties into the Caspian Sea. The Arax flows through and fertilizes the plain of Ararat—the site of major Armenian cities like Armavir, Yervandashat, Artashat, Yerevan, Dvin, Ani, Nakhichevan and Vagharshapat. The second important river is the Euphrates, which is divided into the western and eastern branches. Both flow westward and then turn south toward Mesopotamia. The Euphrates was the ancient boundary dividing what became Greater and Lesser Armenia. The Kur and the Tigris and their tributaries flow briefly through Armenia. Two other rivers, the Akhurian, a tributary of the Arax and the Hrazdan, which flows from Lake Sevan, provide water to an otherwise parched and rocky landscape devoid of forests. Minor rivers in the west and the north flow into the Kur or Lake Sevan.

A number of lakes are situated in the Armenian highlands, the most important of which is Lake Van in present-day Turkey. The deepest lake, Van's waters are charged with borax and hence undrinkable. Lake Sevan, which is the highest in elevation (some 6,300 feet above sea level), is in the present-day Armenian Republic. Lake Urmia (Urmiyeh/Rezaiyeh), in present-day Iran, is the shallowest and extremely salty. A number of lesser lakes also exist in western Armenia (see map 1).

Armenia lies in the temperate zone and has a variety of climates. In general, winters are long and can be severe, while summers are usually short and very hot. Some of the plains, because of their lower altitudes, are better suited for agriculture, and have fostered population centers throughout the centuries. The variety of temperatures has enabled the land to support a great diversity of *flora* and *fauna* common to Western Asia and Transcaucasia.

The generally dry Armenian climate has necessitated artificial irrigation throughout history. In fact, the soil, which is volcanic, is quite fertile and, with sufficient water, is capable of intensive farming. Farming is prevalent in the lower altitudes, while sheep and goat herding dominates the highlands.

Although Armenians have been known as artisans and merchants, the majority of Armenians, until modern times, were engaged primarily in agriculture. In addition to cereal crops, Armenia grew vegetables, various oil seeds, and especially fruit. Armenian fruit has been famous from ancient times, with the pomegranate and apricot, referred to by the Romans as the *Armenian plum*, being the most renowned.

Lying on the Anatolian fault, the Armenian Plateau is subject to seismic tremors. Major earthquakes have been recorded there since the ninth century, some of which have destroyed entire cities. The most recent earthquake in the region, on December 7, 1988, killed some 25,000 people and leveled numerous communities.

Geography has determined the history of most nations and nowhere is this truer than in Armenia. Unlike Japan, which has rarely faced invasions, Armenia's unique position as a corridor between Asia and Europe frequently attracted invaders and resulted in long periods of foreign domination. Assyrians, Scythians, Greeks, Romans, Persians, Arabs, Kurds, Turks, Mongols, Turkmen and Russians have all left their impact on the land and the people. Armenia's geographical position, however, enabled its people to prosper materially and enhance culturally. In fact, Armenia has served as a major highway for merchants since ancient times. In return, Armenians became the conduit that enabled Europe to learn from Asia (during the ancient and medieval periods) and for Asia to borrow European technology (in modern times).

Many of Armenia's small and large neighbors have disappeared from history, but Armenia and its people have managed to survive. Ironically, the same landscape, which invited foreign invasions and encouraged the rise of autonomous nobles, was also partially responsible for preserving its identity. The numerous mountains, which divided Armenia into valleys, prevented it from achieving a united state under a strong centralized ruler during much of its history. This very fact has been a blessing in disguise. For unlike a highly centralized state, such as Assyria, whose entire culture vanished with the collapse of its capital city, Armenia's lack of political unity meant the survival of its culture even when its kings were deposed and its capital cities were destroyed.

2

Ara and Semiramis
Urartu, the First Kingdom in Armenia
(c. 870-585 BC)

T
HE TERRITORY of historic Armenia, together with Mesopotamia, was one of the earliest regions to possess incipient
agriculture—a stage in history when man began to replace the
hunting and food gathering of the Old and Middle Stone Ages with
the food producing of the New Stone Age period. Soon after, the
use of copper began in the region and for the next two millennia remained confined to Anatolia, Transcaucasia, Mesopotamia and
Egypt. By 3000 BC the Mesopotamians had developed bronze, an
alloy of copper and tin, which was soon adopted by the inhabitants
of the Caucasus as well. Settlements, agriculture, and the use of
metal utensils made Transcaucasia and Asia Minor not only one of
the cradles of civilization but gave it wealth and made it attractive to
invaders.

Between 3000 and 1500 BC Indo-European tribes, who had concentrated around the Aral, Caspian and Black Sea regions learned
the art of making iron and began to move into the older and richer
regions of the ancient world. The Indo-European Iranians from Asia
and the Indo-European Hittites from Europe entered Transcaucasia
and Asia Minor, respectively. The Iranians possibly confronted the
indigenous Caucasian groups such as the Hurrians, the Kassites and
the Mitanni, introduced new words and deities and created hybrid
cultures. Simultaneously, the Hittites established a kingdom in Asia
Minor, which, by 1300 BC, had developed into an empire stretching
to the Euphrates River.

At the same time, the Semitic Assyrians had established a kingdom in the south and slowly began to intermingle with or replace
the older Semitic cultures of Mesopotamia. The local Caucasian and

Anatolian people formed alliances with the Indo-European groups and established new federations who traded with or fought the Hittites and Assyrians. Records from the Hittite king Suppiluliumas (c.1388-1347 BC) and the famous Assyrian ruler Tiglath-Pileser I (c.1115-1077 BC) mention the Hayasa, Arme-Shupria, Uruatri (Urartu) and other federations (see map 2). By 1200 BC the Hittite Empire had collapsed and was possibly replaced by the Phrygians, while the Assyrian Kingdom had gone into a period of hibernation.

The Origins of Urartu

The absence of a dominant state in western Asia, after the collapse of the Hittite Empire in the thirteenth century BC, allowed the Uraratians, who were probably of Hurrian stock, to absorb various local and Indo-European tribes in the Armenian plateau and to create a new federation. The dawn of the Iron Age around 1100 BC, in the region and the threat from neighboring Assyria were apparently responsible for the unification of parts of Anatolia and Transcaucasia under Urartian leadership. By the ninth century BC, the Urartians, who called themselves Biainili, had formed the first kingdom in what later became Armenia.

The period of the kingdom of Urartu (c.870-585 BC) referred to by some historians as the Kingdom of Van, witnessed a number of new developments around the world. Greece emerged from its dark ages and gave birth to Athens and Sparta. The Iliad and the Odyssey were composed and the Doric architectural style was developed. Zoroaster began to preach his message in Persia (Iran). Egypt lost its ancient glory and was dominated by Libyans, Nubians, Assyrians, and finally the Kush of Ethiopia. In India, the Upanishads were written, Hinduism emerged, and the caste system was formulated. Feudalism developed in China, while the Olmec civilization flourished in Mexico.

Urartu as the Rival of Assyria

The formation of Urartu also corresponded with the resurgence of the Assyrian Kingdom in the ninth century BC In fact much of the data on Urartu comes from this neighbor and adversary. The first mention of the Urartian Kingdom is by the Assyrian king Ashur-Nasirpal (c.884-859 BC), who campaigned there. For the next three centuries, Assyria and Urartu fought each other, with Assyria having limited success but never managing totally to subjugate its neighbor. Urartu was ultimately responsible for halting the Assyrian expansion into Anatolia, northern Persia, and Transcaucasia. One may view the history of the Kingdom of Urartu as part of the struggle between the new Indo-Europeans and the Semites. In some regions, the two united to form new states; in others, cultural, linguistic, and religious differences resulted in long conflicts. With the exception of China, the entire Eurasian world witnessed a period of great transition. In the end, the Indo-Europeans became dominant and created the classical civilizations of Greece, Persia, and India.

The first Urartian king, mentioned by the Assyrian ruler, Shalmaneser III (c.860-825 BC), was Aramu who ruled in the first half of the ninth century BC and who expanded his domain into Media. While Aramu is credited for organizing a united kingdom, Sarduri I (c.845-825 BC) is credited for establishing a dynasty that would last until the sixth century BC. His first act was to build the capital city of Tushpa (present-day Van), on the eastern shore of Lake Van. The height of Urartian power was formed during the reigns of Ishpuini (c.825-810 BC), Menua (c.810-785 BC), Argishti I (c. 785-753 BC) and his son Sarduri II (c.753-735 BC). The brief decline of Assyria at the end of the ninth century assured Urartu's dominance of the region.

By the eighth century BC the kingdom of Urartu stretched from the Euphrates in the west, the Caspian lowlands in the east, the shores of Lake Urmia in the south, and the Caucasus in the north—that is, the territory that would later be called Greater Armenia. The Assyrians during their numerous campaigns recorded small cities, forts and many Urartian settlements. Menua constructed large irrigation canals, some of which are still in use today. Vineyards, orchards and various grains were also planted, and Urartu became a food-producing region.

The availability of copper and iron and the early knowledge of metallurgy enabled artisans to produce bronze and iron weapons and other objects for war and trade. The result of all this activity was an increase in population. It was at this time that the city of Musasir, west of Lake Urmia, was conquered by the Urartians and was made the religious center of the kingdom. The Urartians managed to defeat Assyria in a number of wars, took booty and prisoners, and extended their domination over northern Syria. The Urartians built a number of forts to defend their kingdom from nomadic and Assyrian invasions. Argishti I founded the two most important bastions.

In 782 BC, on the plain of Ararat, he built the Erebuni (Arin Berd) fortress. This was the predecessor of the present-day city of Yerevan, making it one of the oldest continuously inhabited urban centers in the world. In 775 BC, west of Yerevan, on the bank of the Arax River, he constructed Argishtihinili (Armavir). (See map 3).

The reigns of Tiglath-Pileser III (c.745-727 BC) and Sargon II (c.722-705 BC) not only halted Assyria's decline but transformed it into a new empire which managed to penetrate much of Urartu, destroy and loot its cities, and take prisoners. Sargon employed a network of spies who reported on his northern neighbor. Some of these reports have survived, enabling historians to piece together some of the events that occurred. They state that the Urartian rulers had to fight both the Assyrians and the Cimmerians, who were invading from the north. By 714 BC, both of the invaders had destroyed parts of Urartu, forcing King Rusa I (c.735-714 BC) to commit suicide. Urartu had acted as a buffer zone for the Cimmerian invaders, however, and when it was weakened, the Cimmerians poured into Anatolia and Syria, and attacked Assyria.

Decline of Urartu

The seventh century BC witnessed the gradual rise of a new Babylonian state, and a minor revival in Egypt, as well as the emergence of Indo-European power centers in Persia. Urartu and Assyria, both in decline, made peace with each other and tried to cope with the Cimmerians and the Scythians, new nomadic invaders who had penetrated the region from passes in the Caucasus. The Urartian kings Argishti II (c.714-685 BC) and Rusa II (c.685-645 BC) paid tribute to Assyria and concentrated on repelling the nomads.

The last powerful Assyrian king was Ashur-Banipal II (c. 668-624 BC). He tried to reclaim the greatness of Assyria by destroying the kingdom of Elam in western Persia, an action that allowed the rise of Elam's neighbor, Media. Simultaneously, a minor revival occurred in Urartu, and Argishti and Rusa built the great fortress of Teishebaini (Karmir Blur) on a hill north of Erebuni to store the royal treasury and to serve as a safe haven from the Scythians.

The history of the last years of the Urartian kingdom is unclear. A number of leaders rose amidst internal and external conflicts. Among those was Erimena, who may have been an Armenian and who probably formed alliances with neighboring tribes. Erimena led a rebellion against the Urartian leadership, an action which, combined with renewed Scythian attacks, must have considerably weakened the kingdom. At the same time, the decline of both Urartu and Assyria enabled the Medes to emerge as a new force. Around 670 BC the Medes built their capital at Ecbatana and occupied parts of Persia. They and Babylonians combined forces to end the Assyrian hegemony in Mesopotamia. In 612 BC they sacked Nineveh, the Assyrian capital, and by 610 BC the Assyrian Empire ceased to exist.

The Medes and the Babylonians divided the Assyrian Empire and its satellite states. The Babylonians formed the New Babylonian Kingdom by taking the lands west of the Tigris River, all the way to the Mediterranean Sea. The Medes expanded to the regions east of the Tigris and invaded Urartu. They seem either to have subjugated Urartu, or to have made tribute arrangements with the dominant group, which by then was probably the Armenian (see chapter 3). In any case, somewhere between 605 and 585 BC the Urartian federation became a tributary of the Median Empire.

Urartian Culture

During their three centuries of existence the Urartians built canals, palaces, cities and fortresses, some of which have been excavated in modern times. In addition, they created tools, weapons, jewelry and pottery, fragments of which have been preserved and are on display in the museums of Armenia and in the Hermitage Museum in St. Petersburg, Russia. The Urartian pantheon included indigenous, Indo-European, and Assyrian gods. *Khaldi* was the main god and god of war; *Teishebaini* was the god of thunder; and *Shivini* represented the sun god. Horses were important both in the economy and the military, and the image of the horse was represented on Urartian shields. Assyrian and Etruscan influences are to be found in Urartian art, demonstrating the extent of trade in the ancient world. Urartian bronzes and iron-works such as cauldrons, candelabra, and decorative shields were prized and have been found throughout the Transcaucasian and Greek worlds. Although at first much was copied from Assyria and the Hittites, a distinctive Urartian style soon emerged, a synthesis of many other art forms, which can be seen in the palace wall decorations at the Erebuni complex in Yerevan. Urartian inscriptions in Vannic cuneiform replaced Assyrian cuneiform, which had replaced earlier Urartian pictograms. This wedge-shaped script had more than five hundred forms, many of which had multiple meanings. Trade and war had made Urartu wealthy, for the records describe the great riches taken by the Scythians and Assyrians in their campaigns against Urartu.

Unlike Assyria, which was relatively intolerant and depended solely on its military might, Urartu borrowed from other cultures and engaged in trade and diplomacy. Assyria prided itself on its centralized bureaucracy, but once that center was sacked, the Assyrian Empire disintegrated. The Urartian confederation, a largely decentralized and tolerant state, however, managed to survive. The new leadership, composed of Armenians, adopted these characteristics.

More than a thousand years later, when Armenian historians began to record the history of their nation; the existence of Urartu was unknown to them. The great Armenian historian Movses Khorenatsi (Moses of Khoren), making use of oral traditions and Greek sources transformed Aramu, the first ruler of Urartu into the legendary Armenian king, *Ara the Handsome*. The Assyrians were personified by the evil, yet enticing, Queen *Semiramis* (Shammur-Amat c.810-805 BC), who lusted after Ara and caused his death. Although Aramu and Shammur-Amat were not contemporaries, the struggle between their two states was symbolized in the narrative of Moses of Khoren. Ironically, the cuneiform fragments recording the greatness of the Urartian kingdom stood mute before their historical descendants, who could no longer interpret them. Urartu, like most ancient civilizations, disappeared under the layers of classical and medieval civilizations, to be rediscovered only in the nineteenth and twentieth centuries.

3

From the Ark to Archeology
The Origins of the Armenian People

A S WITH MANY ancient peoples, the origins of the Armenians contain elements of myth and unresolved scholarly arguments. The explanations can be grouped into three versions: The Greek, the Armenian and recent scholarly versions.

The Greek Versions

Although some Greek sources maintain that Armenia was named after or founded by Armenus the Thessalian, one of Jason's Argonauts, Greek historians, all writing long after the appearance of the Armenians, but well before the written works of Armenian chroniclers, have left a number of historical explanations as to the origins of the Armenian people. Two of the most quoted versions are by Herodotus and Strabo. According to the fifth-century BC historian, Herodotus, the Armenians had originally lived in Thrace from where they crossed into Phrygia in Asia Minor. They first settled in Phrygia and then gradually moved west of the Euphrates River to what became Armenia. Their language resembled that of the Phrygians while their names and dress was close to the Medes.

According to the historian and geographer Strabo, who wrote at the end of the first century BC, Armenians came from two directions, one group from the west, or Phrygia, and the other from the south, or the Zagros region. In other words, according to the ancient Greeks, the Armenians were not the original inhabitants of the region. They appear to have arrived sometime between the Phrygian migration to Asia Minor following the collapse of the Hittite Empire in the thirteenth century BC and the Cimmerian invasion of Urartu in the eighth century BC. The decline of Urartu allowed the Armenians to establish themselves as the primary occupants of the region. Xenophon, who passed through Armenia in 401 BC, recorded that, by his time, the Armenians had absorbed most of the local inhabitants.

The Traditional Armenian Version

According to the earliest Armenian accounts, written sometime between the fifth and eighth centuries AD, the Armenian people are the descendants of Japheth, a son of Noah. After the ark had landed on Mt. Ararat, Noah's family settled first in Armenia and, generations later, moved south to the land of Babylon. The leader of the Armenians, Haik, a descendant of Japheth, unhappy with the tyranny and evil in Babylon, rebelled and decided to return to the land of the ark. The evil Bel, leader of the Babylonians, pursued Haik. In the ensuing war, good conquered evil when Haik killed Bel and created the Armenian nation. Haik became the first Armenian ruler and his sons continued to lead the Armenians until King Paruir, a descendent of Haik, formed the first kingdom of Armenia and had to face the mighty Assyrian foe.

This legend, probably as old as Mesopotamian legends, including that of *Gilgamesh*, not only blends historical facts with fable but manages also to place the Armenians in a prominent position within the biblical tradition. Noah, after all, was "the second Adam," his descendants chosen and blessed by God to repopulate the earth. Armenians, like the Jews, thus had a special calling to fight the evil Babylonians and to live in accordance to the laws of God. The periodic floods in Mesopotamia must have left vivid memories for the people living in Western Asia. Numerous invasions into the region, particularly that of Assyria, and Assyria's clashes with the pre-Armenian rulers, must have been etched into the folklore of the local Caucasian and Indo-European inhabitants. It is not surprising therefore that between AD 440 and 840 early Armenian historians, such as Moses of Khoren, who did not have our historical and archeological data, recorded the oral tradition by substituting Babylon for Assyria and the Haik dynasty for the Urartian rulers in Armenia. The aim was not accuracy but rather a sure place for the Armenians in the history of Christianity, a religion that the Armenians had by then embraced wholeheartedly.

Recent Scholarly Versions

Modern archeological finds in the Caucasus and Anatolia have presented sketchy and incomplete versions of the possible origins of the Armenians. Until the 1980s, scholars unanimously agreed that the Armenians were an Indo-European group who either came into the area with the proto-Iranians from the Aral Sea region or arrived from the Balkans with the Phrygians after the fall of the Hittites. Some scholars maintain that *Hay* or *Hai* (pronounced *high*) the Armenian word for "Armenian," is derived from *Hai-yos* (Hattian). Hence, the Armenians, during their migration over Hittite lands, adopted the name of that empire. Others maintain that the Armeno-Phrygians crossed into Asia Minor, took the name Muskhi and concentrated in the Arme-Shupria region east of the Euphrates River where non-Indo-European words became part of their vocabulary. They stayed in the region until the Cimmero-Scythian invasions altered the power structure. The Armenians then managed to consolidate their rule over Urartu and, in time, assimilated most of its original inhabitants to form the Armenian nation. Therefore, Armenia and Armenians, the Perso-Greek name for the Armenians, derives from *Arme-Shupria*.

More recent scholarship offers yet another possibility, that the Armenians were not later immigrants but were part of the original inhabitants of the region. Although this notion has gained some credibility (based on new archeological finds in Armenia) in the last two decades, there remain a number of unresolved questions: What was the spoken language of the early Armenians? Are the Armenians members of a non-Indo-European, Caucasian-speaking group who later adopted an Indo-European dialect, or are they, as many believe, one of the native Indo-European speaking groups?

A number of linguists maintain that the Armenians, whom they identify with the Hayasa, together with the Hurrians, Kassites and others, were indigenous Anatolian or Caucasian people who lived in the region until the arrival of the Indo-Europeans. The Armenians adopted some of the vocabulary of these Indo-European arrivals. This explains why Armenian is a unique branch of the Indo-European language tree and may well explain the origin of the word *Hayastan* ("Armenia" in the Armenian language). As evidence these scholars point to Hurrian suffixes, the absence of gender and other linguistic data. Archeologists add that the images of Armenians on a number of sixth-century Persian monuments depict racial characteristics similar to those of other people of the Caucasus.

Other scholars, also relying on linguistic evidence, believe that Indo-European languages may have originated in the Caucasus and that the Armenians, as a result of pressure from large empires such as the Hittite and Assyrian, merged with neighboring tribes and adopted some of the Semitic and Kartvelian vocabulary and legends. They eventually formed a federation called Nairi, which became part of the united state of Urartu. The decline and fall of Urartu allowed the Armenian component to achieve predominance and by the sixth century BC, establish a separate entity, which the Greeks and Persians, the new major powers of the ancient world, called Armenia.

Further linguistic and archeological studies may one day explain the exact origins of the Indo-Europeans and that of the Armenian people. Presently, western historians continue to maintain that Armenians arrived from Thrace and Phrygia, while academics from Armenia, especially after the recent archeological finds which indicate that western Transcaucasia had the earliest humanoids, argue in favor of the new explanation; that is, Armenians are the native inhabitants of historic Armenia.

4

From Satraps to Kings
The Yervandunis, the First Armenian Autonomous Rulers
(c. 585-189 BC)

T HE FOUR centuries that spanned the end of the Urartian kingdom and the beginning of the Armenian kingdom under the Artashesian (Artaxiad) dynasty were formative years not only for the Armenians, but also for a number of peoples and cultures of the time. Many of today's religions, languages, arts, philosophies, and legal systems evolved during this period, which witnessed the dominance of the Indo-Europeans and the flowering of the Classical Age in Eurasia.

In the Middle East, the first great Persian or Iranian Empire, which for the next two centuries controlled much of that region, as well as Central Asia and Egypt, replaced the empire of the Medes. In Europe, Classical Greece witnessed its golden age and the rise of city-states, as well as their decline and eventual conquest by Philip of Macedon. Alexander the Great conquered a large part of the civilized world, defeated the Persian Empire, and introduced Hellenism into Asia and North Africa. Rome founded its republic, consolidated its power on the Italian peninsula, fought Carthage, absorbed the Greece of Alexander's successors, and challenged their power in Asia and Africa. The Mauryan Empire united India, and Buddhism, Jainism, and Hinduism, spread throughout South Asia. In East Asia, during the Chou and Ch'in (Qin) dynasties, China began its unification behind the Great Wall, under the philosophical and social guidance of Confucianism, Taoism, Legalism and the *Book of Changes*. The Olmec culture continued to flourish in Mexico, while in sub-Saharan Africa, city-states began to emerge.

Until a few decades ago, it was believed that the first Armenian dynasty appeared only at the beginning of the second century BC.

There is new evidence, however, of an earlier family, the Yervand-uni (Orontid/Eruandid/Yervandian), who ruled in Armenia as governors appointed by the Medes and Persians. After the fall of the Persian Empire to Alexander the Great, the Yervanduni governors began to act autonomously.

Although some believe the Yervandunis were of Urartian origin, their background is unknown. They were probably linked, either by blood or marriage, to the Persian royal family. It is possible that, if not Armenian themselves, the Yervandunis eventually intermarried with Armenians. The term Yervanduni is derived from Yervand, the name of at least four governors. Not much else is known about the Yervandunis. Successive dynasties and invasions have obliterated most of the culture of Armenia in that period. However, in Nemrud Dagh, Turkey, a commemorative monument of the first century BC, erected by a ruler of Commagene, who was related to the Yervand-unis, mentions a number of his Yervanduni ancestors who had ruled Armenia.

The Medes and Armenia

As stated, the Medes, together with the Babylonians, had crushed and divided much of the Assyrian Empire by 610 BC. The New Babylonian kingdom lasted less than a century. Its most famous ruler was Nebuchednezzar, who conquered Jerusalem and took many Jews as slaves, thus beginning their Babylonian captivity. The Medes, in the meanwhile, went on to annex parts of Urartu and Mesopotamia and, by 585 BC, had become a major power. The Medes appointed local governors to maintain control over their large territory, which included Elam, Cappadocia, Parthia, and Persia, as well as Urartu/Armenia. A Yervanduni family member administered this last province.

The Persian Empire and the Armenians

By the mid-sixth century BC, a number of these vassal groups, the Yervandunis among them, had rebelled against the Medes, under the leadership of Cyrus the Great of Persia. By 553 BC Cyrus had over-thrown the Medes and had founded the Achaemenid dynasty. Cyrus and his son, Cambyses, then conquered a territory stretching from India to the Aegean and Mediterranean Seas, including Armenia and Egypt. In the process the Persians freed the Jews from their Babylonian captivity and permitted the reconstruction of the temple of Jerusalem. It was Darius I (the Great), another member of the Achaemenid family, however, who forged this multinational territory into the great Persian Empire, which lasted until Alexander the Great defeated it in 331 BC.

Little is known about the Armenians during this period, though they probably still shared land and military power with the other groups inhabiting the former Urartian kingdom. Tradition has it that while hostage at the Median court Cyrus befriended another hostage, the Armenian prince, Tigran-Yervand, and thus established good relations between the Armenians and the Persians, which soon enabled the Armenians to govern all of the former Urartian State.

In any case, by the late sixth century BC, Armenian power and cultural dominance had increased significantly. In fact, after only three generations following the fall of Urartu, the Armenians were sufficiently important to be included among the major provinces or satrapies and peoples listed on the Behistun carving, a monument designed in c.520 BC to commemorate Darius' achievements and conquests. This is the first time that the name Armenia (inscribed as *Armina*) appears in recorded history. Although, as stated, the Armenians refer to themselves as *Hai*, non-Armenians adopted the Persian and Greek (the latter referring to Armenians as *Armenioi*) terms.

There is evidence that Darius later conducted a number of campaigns against the Armenians, who had rebelled against his new taxes. He may have appointed a Persian or another Armenian family as the new satraps rather than the Yervandunis, for there is no mention of them as provincial governors until the next century.

Darius organized his empire into twenty-three *satrapies* (provinces) and placed trusted family members or friends as *satraps* or governors of these provinces (see map 4). Armenia is listed as the 10th *satrapy* in the Persian inscriptions at Naqsh-e Rostam. In the fifth century Herodotus mentions Armenians occupying the 13th *satrapy*, while the remnants of the Urartians (Alarodians) lived in the 18th *satrapy*. Armenians soon became the dominant force and subjugated or assimilated the other groups.

The Yervandunis, the First Armenian Rulers

The Persian Empire was soon linked by a royal road, which connected Susa in central Persia with Sardis in western Asia Minor. The road had rest stops for royal messengers and travelers; fifteen of these stations, stretching across some 150 miles, passed through southern Armenia (see map 4). Although the Armenians had to pay a large annual tribute in silver and horses, as well as contribute contingents to the imperial army, their inclusion in the empire and the communications made possible by the royal road, enabled them to gradually consolidate much of the former Urartian lands. The Achaemenids were tolerant, and as long as peace was maintained and tribute paid, they allowed their subject peoples, including the Armenians, to follow local customs and worship their own deities.

From the late fifth century BC onward, Armenia was left to its satraps and generally existed peacefully within the Persian Empire until the end of the Achaemenid dynasty. Armenians served in the Persian army in the Greek and other campaigns during the fifth and fourth centuries BC and were among the Persian forces of Darius III defending Persia against Alexander the Great.

The main source on Armenia in this period is the *Anabasis* ("The March Up-Country") by the Greek historian Xenophon. Xenophon was among the Greek troops who had entered Persia in 401 BC to intervene on behalf of a candidate in a disputed succession. Unfortunately for the Greeks, their candidate was defeated prior to their arrival and they were forced to retreat through Armenia (see map 4). Xenophon mentions a Yervand, the son-in-law of the Persian king Artaxerxes I, ruling in the eastern parts of Armenia. He records that the region had an Armenian as well as a non-Armenian population, which remained isolated in the highlands. The latter were probably some of the Urartians (Alarodians) who had resisted assimilation. Some historians claim that they are the ancestors of the present-day Kurds. (Other historians maintain that the Kurds are the descendants of the ancient Medes).

Xenophon also mentions Tiribazus, the governor of the western parts of Armenia and a personal friend of the Persian king, who alone had the honor of assisting the king in mounting his horse. In Xenophon's description of the land itself, he does not mention the existence of any major cities, but records that the region was made up of villages with fortified houses above ground, as well as underground winter quarters. A large portion of the population spoke

Armenian, while the people of the hills had their own dialect. The satrap worked with the clan elders, who mediated between the people and the provincial administration. The population was mainly engaged in agriculture and raising livestock, including the famed Armenian horses, thousands of which were sent as annual tribute to Persia. Xenophon reports that there was plenty of food, including a variety of meats, vegetables, breads, oils, and wines. He also describes a kind of beer drunk with what resembled a straw, one of the early mention of this drink in recorded history. Armenians are depicted as short and stocky with straight dark hair, dark eyes, and prominent noses. In a relief at Persepolis the Armenians are depicted presenting a horse and other tribute. They are dressed much like the Medes of that time, with long hair tied at the back of their necks, and with tunics down to the knees, worn over pants tied at the ankles. Aramaic, the language of the imperial administration, was introduced into Armenia, where, for centuries, it continued to be used in official documents. Old Persian cuneiform, meanwhile, was used in most inscriptions.

Xenophon mentions that he used a Persian interpreter to converse with Armenians and in some of the Armenian villages they responded in Persian. Evidently the knowledge of Persian had spread among the Armenians. The influence of Persia on the Armenian language is evident in the thousands of Persian words, which remain in the Armenian language until today. The Armenians soon adopted the Persian social structure and the Zoroastrian pantheon. These included *Aramazd*, the creator of heaven and earth; *Mihr*, the god of light; *Astghik*, the goddess of love; *Vahagn*, the god of war; *Tir*, the god of the arts and sciences; and *Anahit*, the goddess of fertility and wisdom. The cult of *Mithra*, as well as other cults and religious beliefs which were prevalent in the Persian Empire, slowly made inroads in Armenia as well. The many temples of *Anahit* in Armenia and festivals dedicated to her indicate that this Zoroastrian goddess had become a particular favorite among the Armenians and that she served as their protector. Despite the degree of Median and Persian influences, however, an Armenian cultural identity, influenced by local traditions, gradually took shape.

With the decline of the Achaemenids, some of the satrapies began to assert their autonomy. By the mid-fourth century BC, the Yervandunis had united much of Armenia into a single province, established close marriage alliances with their western neighbor,

Commagene, and had, in effect, created an autonomous unit within the Persian Empire.

Alexander the Great and Hellenism

During these two centuries, the Persians repeatedly tried to control the Greek mainland, a struggle that Herodotus has recorded in his history of the Persian Wars. Although never successful, Persia threatened Greece by supplying contending Greek city-states with gold. This threat was eliminated when Alexander the Great crossed into Asia and attacked the Persian Empire. Darius III, the last of the Achaemenids, together with his vassals, including the Armenian sa-trap, another Yervand, tried to defend his empire, but was crushed in the battles of Issus in 333 BC and Gaugamela in 331 BC. According to later Roman historians, the Armenian contingent in these battles was very large. In conquering a good part of the civilized world, Alexander founded new cities and military colonies, and settled Greeks and Macedonians throughout Asia and North Africa (see map 4). Greek culture mixed with that of the indigenous eastern peoples and a Hellenistic culture emerged.

The Seleucids (312-64 BC)

Following the death of Alexander the Great in 323 BC, his Asian and African conquests were soon divided between two of his generals. Seleucus claimed the former Persian Empire and founded the Seleucid dynasty, while Ptolemy took over Egypt and founded the Ptolemaic dynasty (see map 5). While the early Seleucids brought with them the Greek concept of oligarchic city-states, these western ideas were not readily accepted in every part of the former Persian Empire. As Greek culture was essentially an urban one, the Seleucids had to establish new cities in order to attract Greek settlers and administrators. Division and discrimination began to occur between Greeks and non-Greeks. The Seleucids eventually adopted the Persian concept of kingship, while retaining a mostly Hellenistic religion and culture.

Early in their reign, the Seleucids gave up their Indian holdings to Chandragupta Maurya in exchange for 500 elephants to use against their enemies. Fifty years later the Seleucid Empire was reduced further when eastern Persia declared its independence under the Parthians and Central Asia broke away under a Greco-Bactrian dynasty.

Yervanduni Rule in Armenia

Meanwhile, the collapse of the Achaemenid Empire had created an opportunity for the Yervandunis to assert complete independence. Since Alexander never passed through Armenia, and, therefore, left no military presence in the region, the Yervandunis refused tribute to the Greeks. After the death of Alexander, the Armenians maintained this stance towards the governors imposed by the Seleucids. The Yervandunis gained control of the Arax Valley, reached Lake Sevan, and constructed a new capital at Yervandashat, at the confluence of the Arax and Akhurian rivers, to replace Armavir, which had been vulnerable to Seleucid attacks. According to tradition they also built a new religious center at Bagaran, north of Yervandashat, on the left bank of the Akhurian. Although the Yervandunis ruled much of Armenia, they were never able to control the more Hellenized western regions.

By the third century BC three Armenias had emerged: Lesser Armenia or Armenia Minor, northwest of the Euphrates; Greater Armenia or Armenian Major; and Sophene or Cop'k'(Dsopk), in the southwest (see map 6). Lesser Armenia came under Hellenistic influence and occasionally under the political control of either the Seleucids, the rulers of Pontus, or Cappadocia. Greater Armenia, encompassing most of historic Armenia, maintained much of its political autonomy due to its relative geographical isolation, the wars between the Seleucids and their rivals, and the removal of the Seleucid seat of government to Antioch in distant Syria. Sophene, located along the royal road, was at different times, depending on political circumstances, either independent or part of Greater Armenia. The Yervandunis continued to govern Greater Armenia and Sophene, and although a number of Seleucid kings, among them Seleucus I, tried to subdue these areas, they soon accepted the independent status of the Yervandunis.

The Yervanduni family dominance in Armenia came to an end soon after. This occurred when the Seleucids, under Antiochus III (223-187 BC), attempted to revive their empire and to make Armenia a vassal state. An Armenian nobleman, Artashes (Artaxias), who was probably related to the Yervandunis, was encouraged by Antiochus to rebel, and around 200 BC, together with another relative, overthrew the last Yervanduni and laid the foundations of the first Armenian kingdom.

The Yervandunis must be judged as tenacious rulers. They re-sisted Darius I in a number of rebellions, achieved some degree of autonomy during the decline of the Persian Empire, rejected Greek governors, rebuffed the Seleucids, and generally maintained their independence.

Society and Culture

During the two centuries of Seleucid presence, Greek, now the lan-guage of commerce and the arts in the Middle East, periodically replaced Aramaic as the administrative language of Armenia and was frequently spoken by the upper classes. In Armenia, Greek-style temples to Apollo and Artemis were built. Coins with Greek inscription appeared there, as they did all over Asia. Interna-tional commerce passed through Armenia, bringing with it both Eastern and Western culture and science.

Despite the fact that the Greek calendar, law, and religious be-liefs, as well as theater, philosophy, art and architecture, made inroads, Greater Armenia became only partially influenced by Hel-lenism. Persian (Iranian) culture, as well as the Armenian language and customs remained a dominant force. The most important change was the rise of cities, such as Yervandashat, Yervandakert, and Ar-shamashat (Arsamosata), which, later, facilitated the unification of Greater Armenia.

5

Between Roman Legions and Parthian Cavalry
The Artashesians and the Formation of the Armenian Kingdom
(c. 189 BC to AD 10)

T HE LAST TWO centuries before the birth of Christ were a significant era in global civilization. The great Han Dynasty began its more than four hundred-year rule in China and the Yamato clan established the foundations of the first Japanese state. The Ptolemies continued to rule Egypt. Various invaders fragmented the Mauryan Empire in India, and elements of Hellenism were introduced to its northwestern provinces. In Persia, the Parthians, who had emerged in the previous century, formed an empire under the Arsacid dynasty. The most important development in the West was the rise of the Roman Republic, which annihilated the Carthaginians in Africa, conquered Greece and Macedonia, and replaced the Seleucid State in Syria and Asia Minor. The same period witnessed the birth of the first recognized Armenian kingdom and its new strategic importance to the powers that surrounded it.

The Yervandians had, as noted, resisted Seleucid encroachments and kept Greater Armenia independent. The rise of Rome and its push into Greece and Macedonia threatened the Seleucid position in Syria. Antiochus III, the last noteworthy ruler of the line, attempted to restore the Seleucid Empire by halting the advance of the Parthians, who, by the second century BC, had gradually penetrated as far as central Persia. He then sought to extend his sovereignty over the autonomous regions bordering his domains. At the start of the second century BC, Antiochus succeeded in persuading some members of the Yervanduni family to challenge their ruler and to switch their allegiance to the Seleucids. Artashes (Artaxias) and Zareh (Zariadres) accepted his offer, rebelled against the last Yervanduni, received military titles from Antiochus, and established themselves as governors of Armenia. Artashes took control of Yervandashat and all the territory of Greater Armenia, while Zareh took Sophene.

Roman Presence in the East

Feeling secure in the east, Antiochus envisioned a new Hellenistic empire, under the leadership of the Seleucids. He consequently advanced into Macedonia and Greece and attempted to dislodge Roman presence there and expand Seleucid control over the land of Alexander the Great. In 190 BC, however, he was defeated by Rome in the battle of Magnesia, and by the Peace of Apamea (189 BC), lost his possessions in Asia Minor and northwestern Syria. Rome's foothold in Asia was now more secure. Roman presence was to affect the region for the next eight centuries. The Seleucid kingdom, on the other hand, was now squeezed into Syria and Palestine, where it encountered new problems. When Antiochus IV, known as Epiphanes, desecrated the Temple of Jerusalem, the Jews, under the leadership of Judas Maccabeus, revolted in 168 BC, a conflict which preoccupied the Seleucids for the next three years. Taking advantage of this situation, the Parthians took control of Persia and became a new power in the East. Rome fashioned a strategy to further weaken the Seleucids and at the same time protect its own holdings. It encouraged the fragmentation of the former Seleucid Empire in Asia Minor into smaller states, friendly to Rome, which would act as a buffer against any future Parthian advances west of Mesopotamia. Armenia, Cappadocia, Commagene, and Pontus thus emerged as Roman allies, and, after Magnesia and Apamea, were formally recognized by Rome as independent kingdoms.

Artashes and the Foundation of a New Dynasty

Rome recognized Artashes, who claimed relationship to both the Yervanduni and Persian noble houses, as the king of Armenia in 189 or 188 BC. Armenia was now regarded as a sovereign state by both Parthia and Rome. Artashes initiated his rule by conducting a survey of his land. His boundary stones, the first-ever recorded in Armenia, written in Aramaic, have been found in the area of Lake Sevan.

To confirm the new status of his country and to break from the Yervanduni past, Artashes built a new capital city, Artashat (Artaxata), on the left bank of the Arax River near present-day Khorvi-rap. This well-planned Hellenistic city remained the capital of Armenia for the next four hundred years. Statues of various Greek and Persian divinities were brought by Artashes to the new city from the Yervanduni religious center at Bagaran, making Artashat both the political and religious center of the new Armenian king-dom. The size of the city and its great fortifications gave rise to the legend that Hannibal of Carthage had helped in its planning and construction. Although both Strabo and Plutarch reiterate this claim, there is no other evidence to substantiate it. Artashes established an administrative structure and a tax system, and distributed land among his family and faithful retainers. Moreover, he expanded his territory by annexing regions inhabited by the Medes, Caucasian Albanians, and the Iberians (Georgians). His efforts to conquer So-phene from Zareh, however, proved unsuccessful. Lesser Armenia, under the control of Pontus, also remained outside Artashes' do-mains (see map 7).

The Seleucids, who were trying to regain control of the Syrian coast and Mesopotamia, finally subdued the Jews in 165 BC and at-tacked both Parthia and Armenia at the end of Artashes' reign. Artashes was defeated and captured by Antiochus IV but continued to rule in exchange for tribute. Rome, which viewed Armenia and its fellow buffer states as its allies or, more probably, potential vas-sals, was unhappy with the situation in Armenia, but its own domestic problems and its final campaign in Carthage left it too preoccupied to intervene in the affairs of Asia. The Seleucids, in the long run, did not manage to restore their dominance and for the next hundred years ruled only in parts of Syria. The Parthians, however, filled the power vacuum handily and, under the leadership of Mithradates I (171-138 BC), who was an Arsacid, became a major force, adopting both the Persian and Hellenistic culture of their predecessors. They soon established themselves in Mesopotamia and built another capital at Ctesiphon on the Tigris River. Rome, in the meantime, was content to consolidate its position in Asia Minor and gradually extend its influence to the Euphrates River. It was just a matter of time, therefore, before the two new powers would be embroiled in a rivalry that would continue for more than three cen-turies.

For the moment, Rome's lack of involvement left the successors of Artashes, Artavazd I (160-115 BC) and Tigran I (Tigranes) (115-95 BC) subject to the whims of the Parthians. Artavazd was defeated by the Parthians and had to send his nephew as hostage to Ctesiphon. For the rest of that century, as long as Armenia paid tribute and submitted hostages, relations with Parthia were peaceful. The peace fostered trade between China, Rome, and Parthia in the first century BC, which was made possible by the Silk Road. The Parthians realized the importance of Armenia as a major trade emporium, and Artashat became an important stopover for this East-West commerce. The Artashesians established a mint in Armenia to further facilitate trade. Trade and the rise of new cities, further invited Hellenistic influences. At the same time Sophene's expansion to the south and west, helped to bring the two Armenian lands closer together culturally. Greek and Persian remained the languages of the Armenian upper classes, while the masses in both Armenian regions spoke Armenian. Aramaic, with many Persian terms, continued to be the language of administration.

The last century of the pre-Christian era was dominated by power struggles between Rome and Parthia, with both trying to gain control of the fragmented Seleucid territories, as well as Armenia. After destroying Carthage and carrying out a number of domestic reforms, Rome finally set its eyes, once again, on Asia. Roman legions arrived in Syria and forced the local rulers to accept Roman authority. Seeking to secure Asia Minor, Rome gained control of Cappadocia and Commagene. In 96 BC Sulla, the Roman governor of Cilicia, and the representatives of Parthia met to partition the disputed territories in Mesopotamia into zones of influence. Roman actions in Asia, however, antagonized the leader of the Pontic kingdom, Mithradates VI Eupator, a Hellenistic nobleman of Persian descent, who wished to revive the Empire of the Seleucids, and he soon embarked on a mission to liberate Asia Minor and Greece from the Romans.

Meanwhile, the situation in Rome was far from stable. The social reforms of the Gracchi brothers had not been fully implemented, and the non-Romans revolted over the issue of full citizenship. Having conquered a large territory in a short time, Rome was unprepared to administer it. The military and the Senate were vying for power. Republican rule was tested repeatedly as generals, particularly those who had achieved fame and fortune in foreign campaigns, tried to assume control over the state.

Tigran the Great

Following the death of Tigran I of Armenia in 95 BC, his son Ti-gran II, a hostage at Ctesiphon, agreed to cede to Parthia a number of valleys in southeastern Armenia in return for his freedom. Ti-gran's first act after taking power at home was to conquer Sophene and unite the two Armenian regions politically. Thereafter, except for short intervals, Sophene remained part of Greater Armenia. Lesser Armenia, however, continued to remain outside the Arme-nian kingdom and, in fact, would never be under the same ruler as Greater Armenia. Tigran and Mithradates of Pontus realized that Roman and Parthian presence in the region was a constant danger to their own sovereignty. Civil war in Rome and problems over the succession in Parthia, encouraged them to attempt the creation of a third force in the region, a federation led by Pontus and Armenia, which would challenge Parthia and Rome. The alliance was sealed by the marriage of Tigran to the daughter of Mithradates. His east-ern flank secure, Mithradates annexed Cappadocia and the coast of Asia Minor. Parthia and Rome, realizing that this alliance would be detrimental to their own designs, agreed to forgo their differences and to concentrate on eliminating the new threat. This was the first but not the last time that the two powers would plan to partition Armenia and its surrounding regions. Sulla, who like subsequent Roman commanders viewed a successful eastern campaign as an opportunity to gain politically and materially, returned to drive the Pontic ruler out of Cappadocia. In 84 BC he managed to force Mithradates out of Greece and returned to Rome to assume the title of dictator. Mithradates did not give up his quest, however, and for the next ten years kept the Romans occupied by invading Greece and challenging Roman authority in Asia Minor.

With Mithradates keeping the Romans at bay and the western flank secure, Tigran concentrated on the east. The death of the Par-thian king and nomadic invasions of Parthia from Central Asia, allowed Tigran in 90 BC to retake the valleys he had ceded to Par-thia; he then expanded south and took parts of Mesopotamia. By 85 BC Tigran began using the Persian title "King of Kings" and had four viceroys in official attendance. When a group of Syrian nobles invited Tigran to rule, he annexed Commagene, northern Syria, Cilicia and Phoenicia. Tigran's empire thus extended from the Mediterranean to the Caspian Sea, and for a brief period, Armenia was an empire (see map 8).

Antioch, the great Seleucid center and the capital of Syria, became Tigran's headquarters in the Levant. Tigran thus took control of much of the former Seleucid territory west of the Euphrates. To better manage his large empire, however, Tigran built a new capital, Tigranakert (Tigranocerta), and forced immigration of Jews, Arabs, and Greeks from Mesopotamia, Cilicia, and Cappadocia in order to populate it and other new Armenian cities. Tigranakert was a great city with walls reportedly so wide that warehouses and stables could be built inside them. A theater was built in which Greek plays were performed. Parks and hunting grounds surrounded the city. Unfortunately, the remains of Tigranakert have not been found and its site has been debated, although it probably lay somewhere between Tell-Ermen, Amida (present-day Diarbekir), and Martyropolis (present-day Miyafarkin).

With Tigran occupying major Hellenistic centers, Hellenism was no longer on the fringes of Armenia, but penetrated most aspects of Armenian life. Tigran's marriage to Mithradates' daughter and the arrival of many Greeks in his empire, meant that Greek, together with Persian, remained the language of the upper classes, while Armenian continued to be spoken by the masses. Greek theater became the main form of entertainment. Persian influence, however, remained in Tigran's court protocol and in the service required by nobles, neither of which had anything in common with either Greek or Roman traditions.

When Sulla retired from public life in 79 BC, new military commanders sought to advance their standing. The Roman Senate gladly authorized foreign campaigns in order to lessen civil unrest and to end the Mithradatic wars, a thorn in Rome's eastern domains. In 74 BC the Roman general Lucullus invaded Pontus and forced Mithradates to seek refuge in Armenia. Unwilling to break the Armeno-Pontic alliance against Rome, Tigran refused to surrender his father-in-law and faced Roman attacks on Armenia. In 69 BC Lucullus besieged Tigranakert. When the city's inhabitants, a majority of whom were non-Armenians, opened the gates, Tigranakert fell to Roman troops and was looted. Tigran's local governors threw their lot with Rome, and Tigran lost control of Syria and Mesopotamia. Lucullus tried to take Artashat but failed, and unable to form an alliance with Parthia, returned to Rome. Tigran and Mithradates then began the re-conquest of Pontus, northern Syria, and Commagene.

Rome did not surrender its claim, however, and sent Pompey, who defeated Mithradates and forced him to flee eastward. Pompey then advanced toward Armenia. Meanwhile, two of Tigran's sons betrayed him, one joining Pompey, the other the Parthian camp. The Roman presence in Armenia also incensed the Parthians, who wanted to ensure their control of the lands east of the Euphrates. In order to end the Armenian and Roman threats and to regain its territory, Parthia, taking advantage of Armenia's vulnerability, attacked from the east. Tigran resisted the Parthian attacks on Artashat, but when Pompey arrived, he realized the futility of resisting the Romans, and, in 66 BC, agreed to the Peace of Artashat. Pompey, in order to keep Armenia as a friend of Rome and as a buffer against Parthia, left Armenia intact and allowed Tigran to retain the Persian title, "King of Kings." Tigran ruled for another ten years and died in 55 BC. Having resolved the situation in Armenia, Pompey pursued Mithradates, who committed suicide on an island off the coast of the Black Sea. Pompey then reorganized Asia Minor and Syria into Roman provinces and client kingdoms. Furthermore, he terminated the rule of the last Seleucid, probably a pretender, and closed a chapter in the history of the Hellenistic Middle East.

Armenians revere Tigran as their greatest ruler. He fashioned the only Armenian Empire, a state that transformed Armenia from a small nation to a force with which to be reckoned. In their pride, the Armenians have mistakenly attributed nationalistic traits to Tigran. In fact, Tigran spoke Greek and Persian and had little of the modern sense of what it is to be an Armenian. He was a Hellenistic monarch who, at the same time, retained much Persian grandeur at his court. He probably practiced polygamy, as was customary in Asia in this period, and probably executed his rebellious sons. In all of this he was no different than any other contemporary ruler. Tigran's greatness is in his attempt to forge an independent political entity and to break away from the constraints imposed on Armenia by its geography. His early success was primarily due to the prevailing political vacuum and could not have been sustained. Tigran's empire was composed of various peoples who had been forcibly relocated and bore no love for the Armenians. Culturally, a fully Hellenistic and urbanized Syria could probably not have co-existed with the more Persian-influenced and rural Armenia. Finally, Tigran's long reign fostered familial intrigue and the betrayal by his sons. Although Tigran's courage and effort were indeed admirable, the outcome kept Armenia suspended between its stronger neighbors.

Artashesian Armenia after Tigran the Great

Tigran's remaining son, Artavazd II (55-35 BC), began his reign as a friend of Rome but under a very different political climate than had his father. With the demise of the Seleucids and Pompey's victories securing Rome's foothold in the Middle East, Rome's attitude became more that of conqueror than ally. Roman military presence in Syria and its aggressive interference in the affairs of Parthia led the latter to seek new friends in the region. Armenia, an immediate neighbor, located along Parthia's trading route and with its ethnic, linguistic, and cultural ties to Persia, was eventually drawn into the Parthian orbit.

The rivalry among Caesar, Crassus, and Pompey, who were known as the first triumvirate, precluded a consistent Roman policy in Asia. With the success of Julius Caesar's campaigns in Western Europe, the rich Crassus sought glory through a campaign against Parthia. Crassus' request for Armenian assistance placed Artavazd in a difficult situation. The Parthians would obviously view any military cooperation with Rome as a hostile act by Armenia. Rome, however, considered Armenia an ally. Artavazd, according to some sources, advised Crassus not to attack Parthia from the direction of Syria, but rather through Armenia where he could receive supplies and support. Artavazd's strategy seemed to be to aid Rome, but demand in return a Roman military presence to protect Armenia against Parthian retaliation. Crassus, in haste, rejected Artavazd's offer and marched through Syria. Artavazd then shifted his allegiance from Rome to Parthia, either voluntarily, or, according to Plutarch, by force, when the Parthians occupied Armenia. In 53 BC Crassus and the Roman legions were routed in the battle of Carrhae. Crassus was killed, and the Parthians captured the Roman standards. The rapprochement between Armenia and Parthia was sealed by the betrothal of Artavazd's sister to the Parthian heir apparent. According to Roman sources, Artavazd and the Parthian king were watching a Greek play at the wedding celebration when the head of Crassus was presented on a silver platter. Rome now distrusted Armenia, but Caesar's quarrel with Pompey and his involvement with Cleopatra precluded any action to avenge Crassus and to recapture the Roman standards.

Artavazd, in the meantime, made every effort at friendly overtures to Rome, while remaining an ally of Parthia. Following the assassination of Caesar, a second triumvirate emerged in Rome, composed of Mark Antony, Octavian (later, Augustus), and Lepidus. In 41 BC, Mark Antony, urged by Cleopatra, sought to strengthen his position in Rome by recapturing the Roman standards from Parthia. Like Crassus, Antony also demanded the assistance of· Armenia. Artavazd initially cooperated with Antony, but in 36 BC, when Antony's troops suffered a setback, Artavazd welcomed the Romans to winter in Armenia, but refused to commit troops for the war. Antony blamed Artavazd for his defeat, and in 35 BC marched on Artashat and took Artavazd and some members of his family to Egypt, where Artavazd was later executed. Antony commemorated the "vanquishing of Armenia" by minting a coin for the occasion and, in a symbolic act, awarded Armenia to his young son by Cleopatra. Artashes II, a son of Artavazd, fled to Parthia and in 30 BC, with Parthian help, took possession of his country by wiping out the entire Roman garrison. Artashes' death in 20 BC left Armenia open to different internal factions looking either to Augustus, now the Emperor, or to Parthia. A number of Artashesians then ruled in Armenia, including a queen called Erato (whose image appears on a coin) as either Roman or Parthian clients. By around AD 10 the dynasty, after a period of power struggles, that eliminated many a contender, died out. The Roman Empire under Augustus and his immediate successors then controlled Armenia for much of the first half of the first century of the Christian era.

Society and Culture

During the Artashesian period, Hellenism made further inroads into Greater Armenia. Greek equivalents of Perso-Armenian divinities became more common. Zeus replaced *Aramazd*, Hephaestus replaced *Mihr*, Artemis replaced *Anahit*, Hercules replaced *Vahagn*, Aphrodite replaced *Astghik*, and *Tir* replaced Apollo. Artistic trends must have been similar to those found in Commagene, which blended Achaemenid and Greek traditions. Greek priests and cults undoubtedly brought numerous statues to Armenia, of which the bronze head of Aphrodite (though some sources maintain that it represents *Anahit*) is the only surviving example. No painting or architectural monuments have been left from this period. The destruction of Hellenistic culture by both the Sasanids and the early Christians, and the numerous invasions of Armenia, have left few remnants. Despite Greek and Persian influences, Armenians continued to maintain their language and customs, a sign perhaps of nascent self-identity and fear of the assimilation, which had befallen Commagene and Cappadocia.

Most of our information on this period is from numismatic and Roman sources. The latter were not necessarily objective on political matters involving the Armenians. The coins, especially those of Tigran the Great, depict the Armenian crown or tiara, which was unique in its design. The royal diadem was wrapped around a hat-like headgear in the form of a truncated cone decorated with birds on either side of an eight-pointed star; the crown had flaps that fell to the shoulders. The Armenian kings of this period, like most Hellenistic rulers, are depicted beardless. No literature of the period has survived but sources mention that famous Greeks sought refuge in Armenia and that Artavazd had written tragedies, orations, and histories. Greek plays were performed at Tigranakert and Artashat, and a number of Armenians studied in Rome, one of whom, called Tiran, became a friend of Cicero.

Trade formed the principal basis of the economy, especially during the reign of Tigran the Great. Plutarch mentions the great treasury at Tigranakert and the overall wealth of Armenia. There were mints in Tigranakert, Artashat, Damascus, and Antioch. Armenia maintained a standing army and did not employ mercenaries. The majority of the people were peasants, who were probably not fully bound to the soil as yet, but whose status was becoming increasingly serf-like. Land belonged to the king, the nobles, or the village commune. Slavery existed, but was not a significant institution and did not form the basis of the economy. The nobles or *nakharars* made their first appearance in this period. Tigran appointed some as governors of the outlying regions of his empire, while others, like the four great nobles or viceroys, served him at court. A somewhat fragmented administrative structure began to emerge at the end of the Artashesian period, which evolved into a feudal-like system and was to have a major impact on Armenian politics and society for the next fifteen centuries.

The first Armenian dynasty managed to survive for two hundred years and, for a short time, was a major power in the region. Roman involvement in Asia and the extension of its rule to the Euphrates River threatened the nearby capital of Parthia, Ctesiphon. The Parthians were unable to dislodge the Roman presence, and Rome would not relinquish its economic and political assets in the Middle East. The Artashesians first attempted to create a state powerful enough to challenge this dual threat. Its collapse led to an unsuccessful effort to balance relations with the two powers. At the dawn of the Christian era, the independence of the first Armenian kingdom became a casualty of the East-West rivalry in Western Asia.

6

The Arsacid/Arshakuni Dynasty
I
Parthian Body, Roman Crown
The Arsacids in Armenia
(AD 66-252)

THE FINAL FOUR centuries of the Classical Age was a glorious period for world civilizations. In the Americas, the Teotihuacan, Moche, and Mayan Civilizations were formed. In India, the Gupta dynasty ushered in the Indian classical age, spreading it to the far corners of Southeast Asia. In China, the Han dynasty ruled for another two centuries. Its organized administration kept China culturally united, despite political fragmentation and nomadic invasions that lasted for over three centuries. The Yamato clan consolidated its rule over Japan, invaded Korea, and began to adopt some aspects of Chinese culture, including the ideograph script. The greatest changes, however, occurred in Persia and Rome. Although the Parthians managed to rule for another two centuries, they were plagued by nomadic invasions, quarrels among their nobility, epidemics, locusts, and attacks by Rome. In the early third century, they were replaced by a new and more powerful Persian dynasty, the Sasanid. The Sasanid State sought to purge Hellenism and replace it with pre-Alexandrian Persian religion and culture.

Rome, without doubt, left the greatest political and cultural mark on Europe and the Middle East. The Roman Empire, which had replaced the Republic, was responsible for the *pax Romana*, a period of security, order, harmony, flourishing culture, and expanding economy. By the fourth century, Christianity and the rise of the Eastern Roman Empire assured the continuation of the Roman legacy for another millennium. The fate of smaller nations of the region clearly depended on Roman policy, as demonstrated by the Jews, who revolted against Rome and were forced into a two thousand-year diaspora. For the Armenians, the period culminated in the formation of their national religion and language.

Perso-Roman Rivalry in Armenia

Following the death of the Emperor Augustus in AD 16, the Arsacid rulers of Parthia, tried to remove Roman control over Armenia and Mesopotamia. Lesser Armenia, which had gravitated into the Roman orbit during the reign of Augustus, was now firmly in Roman hands. The Romans appointed a number of Armenian and non-Armenian rulers to govern it. The proximity of large Roman forces in the north and west threatened Parthia's security. Roman intrigues, as well as the demand for hostages by the Emperors Tiberius, Caligula, and Claudius, constantly disrupted the internal peace of Parthia. During the next fifty years, therefore, Armenia remained the scene of the conflict between Rome and Parthia. Roman, Iberian (Georgian), or other foreign governors ruled Armenia, while Parthia tried to install its own candidates and urged the Armenian population to rise against Rome. Armenian nobles living in the eastern part of Armenia soon gravitated to the Parthian sphere, while those living in the western part of Armenia continued to look to Roman governors in Syria for protection.

In AD 51, Vologeses I assumed the throne of Parthia and openly challenged Rome by seeking to obtain the throne of Armenia for his younger brother Trdat (Tiridates). The opportunity presented itself when the son of the Iberian king invaded Armenia and captured the fortress of Garni from his uncle, who was the Roman-appointed ruler. The Iberian aggression and looting, combined with Roman mismanagement, not only angered the Armenians but also prompted Vologeses to invade Armenia and capture Artashat and Tigranakert. The arrival of winter, however, forced the Parthians to retreat, and the Iberian prince returned to wreak havoc on the Armenian population, who eventually rebelled against Roman rule altogether. The Parthians were then able to occupy Armenia and install Trdat as king.

In AD 54, Emperor Nero sent General Corbulo to take command of the army in Syria and to reestablish Roman control over Armenia. Corbulo raided those Armenian regions that supported Parthia and encouraged the rulers of Iberia and Commagene to attack Armenia's borderlands. At the same time, the Parthians raided the Roman camps and threatened Roman supporters in Armenia. By AD 59, Vologeses, who had to contain internal revolts in Parthia, as well as to deal with the growing strength of the Kushans in the east, left Trdat unsupported. The Romans invaded Armenia, burning cities and killing and enslaving the population. Corbulo captured Tigranakert and burned the capital city, Artashat, to the ground. Trdat fled to Persia, and Nero appointed Tigranes, a descendant of Herod the Great and the ruler of Lesser Armenia, as King of Armenia.

Corbulo left for Syria, and a new commander, Paetus, was appointed with orders to annex Armenia. The Parthians, having resolved their internal problems, moved to reassert their claims. In AD 62, at Rhandeia, the Parthians surrounded the Romans, who agreed to withdraw from Armenia. Vologeses sent envoys to Nero proposing a compromise whereby Trdat would become King of Greater Armenia, but would receive his crown from Rome. Nero, who had hopes of another military victory by Corbulo, rejected the offer. Nothing came out of the Roman campaigns, however, and a stalemate ensued. Finally in AD 64, again at Rhandeia, Rome accepted the compromise of co-suzerainty. The Armenian kings would henceforth come from the royal Arsacid house of Parthia, while Rome would bestow their authority. Trdat traveled to Rome and was crowned by Nero in great festivities as King of Armenia in AD 66. Nero gave funds to rebuild Artashat, which in his honor was temporarily renamed Neronia. Greater Armenia and Sophene were combined to form the Armenian Arsacid Kingdom. Lesser Armenia remained a Roman vassal ruled by a member of the house of Herod.

The Arsacids in Armenia

In AD 66, Trdat I thus founded the Armenian branch of the Parthian Arsacids, which two centuries later would become an Armenian dynasty, known as the Arshakuni (Arshakian). The chronology of the Arsacid/Arshakuni dynasty is problematic. The Arshakuni kings left no coins (the Arsacids in Armenia were not given the right to mint), a key tool used by historians to date individual reigns. Few sources on this period have survived due to the zealous eradication of Hellenistic culture by the Sasanids, who, as will be noted, had a particular hatred for the Parthian Arsacids and their Armenian kinsmen. The early Armenian Christians destroyed many monuments and records that had survived the Sasanid purges.

The Armenian Arsacids began their reign by rebuilding Armenia. The fortress of Garni was repaired and Trdat's sister added a new temple there. Parthian political, social, and cultural influences became dominant in Armenia. Aside from a threat from the Alans, a people who came down from the Caucasus, and a campaign against Iberia, nothing else is known of the reign of Trdat I. Trade between Asia and Europe revived and enabled Armenia to secure its independence. Although Parthia began its decline in the second century AD, the Roman emperors who followed Nero (Galba to Nerva) honored his agreement concerning Armenia's kings. In AD 72, when the Alans overran Armenia and Parthia, the Emperor Vespasian decided to incorporate Lesser Armenia into the Roman province of Cappadocia and fortify its borders.

It was the Emperor Trajan who broke the Rhandeia compromise and, in 114, when a civil war raged in Parthia, invaded Armenia. His justification was to restore the rightful King of Armenia who had been replaced by a candidate not approved by Rome. Although the unapproved candidate then presented himself, and asked Trajan to crown him, Trajan refused, had him killed and annexed Armenia as a Roman province. For the next three years Trajan remained in the east. By 116, Ctesiphon, the capital of Parthia, had also been captured, and Trajan crowned a new Parthian king, who became a Roman vassal. Rome thus extended its borders beyond the Euphrates and reached the Persian Gulf, the farthest extent of the empire, but the victory was short-lived. Military losses, rebellions, and the death of Trajan in Cilicia in 117 forced the new emperor, Hadrian, to move back to the former Euphrates border. The Rhandeia compromise was restored when another Parthian prince, Vagharsh I (117-140), assumed the throne of Armenia. During his long reign trade and prosperity were restored and the city of Vagharshapat, or present-day Ejmiatsin, was founded.

Social Structure of Arsacid Armenia

The social structure of Armenia, in the meantime, had changed. Trdat and the subsequent Arsacid rulers of Armenia had brought Parthian nobles and family members into Armenia where they had settled on newly created fiefs. Other noble families continued to immigrate to Armenia, especially after the fall of the Arsacids of

Persia. Among these families were the Mamikonians and the Kamsarakans. Greek language, gods, theater, and other aspects of Hellenism were familiar to the upper classes of both Armenia and Parthia. The Parthians nobility thus felt at home and inter-marriages among the aristocracy became common. Persian and Parthian were also spoken, and the Aramaic script gradually gave way to the Parthian script, a derivative of Aramaic. More Persian words found their way into the Armenian vocabulary. Most of the two thousand Persian loan words and derivatives in classical Armenian are from this period and relate mainly to war, hunting, trade, court, and the political structure.

Rome, as noted, occasionally challenged the Parthian choice for the Armenian throne by invading Armenia. The only way to assure continuity of government and to discourage Roman interference was to adopt the Parthian custom of appointing the high ranking nobles to hereditary court and administrative positions and assigning them fiefs in exchange for military service. A loyal nobility was thus formed whose position and lands depended on the Arsacids. Armenia was eventually divided into fifteen provinces. There emerged an elaborate hierarchy headed by the king, who was first among equals, and who ruled the central province of Armenia. Below him were the nobles, known as *nakharars*. The *nakharars'* rights to their lands and titles were inalienable and were inherited through the law of primogeniture. The major *nakharars* could muster up to ten thousand cavalry troops in time of war. A feudal force had thus replaced the standing army of the Artashesids. Four of the *nakharars* were given the title *bdeshkh* (viceroy or margrave), and were granted vast domains and responsibility for guarding the northern and southern borders of Armenia. The remaining ten provinces of Greater Armenia were under the control of other *nakharars* (see map 9). To keep tight control over the *nakharars*, the king, as was later customary in Western feudalism, granted them various posts. The office of coronant, for example, was given to the Bagratuni family; the Mamikonians became the *sparapet*, or commanders of the armed forces; the Gnunis became the *hazarapet*, or officials in charge of taxation and food production. There was also a *mardpet* or royal chamberlain, who was in charge of the king's palace, treasury, and household. The *mardpet* was always a eunuch, implying the existence of a royal harem.

The *nakharars* were not all equal. Another Persian custom, their place or cushion at the royal table indicated their rank. The list of

ranks, called *gahnamak*, obviously varied from time to time. The
sebuhs, or minor princes, came after the *nakharars* and the *azats*, or
the knights, who held small fiefs, formed the cavalry. These four
groups were all exempt from corporal punishment, and, with the exception of the *azats*, from taxes. The rest of the society fell into the
category of *ramik*, which included city dwellers and peasant serfs
(*shinakans*). The *ramik* served as the infantry in time of war and
paid the bulk of the taxes. The artisans and traders, some of who
were foreigners, lived in the cities. The institution of slavery was,
by this time, waning.

The second century of Arsacid rule in Armenia saw the continuation of the Roman-Parthian rivalry and periodic threats from the
Iberians and Alans. The *nakharars*, aided by the mountainous terrain, kept their regions well defended and, together with Parthian
assistance, kept Armenia autonomous. After Vagharsh, a number of
Roman and Persian candidates ruled Armenia. In 186, another Parthian prince named Vagharsh became King of Armenia (Vagharsh
II). In 191 he left Armenia to assume the throne of Persia and
named his son Khosrov as King of Armenia (Khosrov I). Khosrov,
who ruled during the time of the Roman Emperors Septimus
Severus and Caracalla, had to face renewed Roman expansion in
Mesopotamia. Caracalla soon captured Khosrov, and then sent Roman officials to govern Armenia. Neither Rome nor Parthia,
however, expected what followed: the Armenians rose up in arms
and even defeated the Roman general sent to quell them. The Armenian population was by the early third century, apparently tired of
Roman interference in their affairs. More importantly, the Arsacid
rulers who had remained in Armenia for a period of time had become Armenian and considered Armenia their homeland.
Meanwhile, the Armenians, viewing Parthian customs and language
same as theirs and Parthian rule more lenient, favored them over the
Romans. By a new agreement between Rome and Parthia, Khosrov's son, Trdat II (217-252) was crowned King of Armenia.
Following the established tradition, he received his crown from the
Roman emperor, in this case, Macrinus. Trdat II, however, was the
first Arsacid king who was raised in Armenia and who followed his
father as King of Armenia. His long reign, combined with the civil
wars in Rome, not only enabled Armenia to take a respite from
East-West rivalry, but to separate itself from the Persian Arsacids
and establish a fully Armenian branch—the Arshakunis—at the start
of the third century.

II
The Cross and the Quill
The Arshakunis (Arshakians)
(217-428)

The Sasanids and Armenia

Arsacid power in Parthia had begun to wane at the end of the second century. This was because Roman policy in Syria encouraged its military governors to continually interfere in Persian politics in order to undermine the Arsacids, a strategy that was largely successful. A virulent smallpox epidemic added to the general economic drain of warfare, and so weakened the power of the Arsacids that, in 226, Ardeshir, the founder of the Sasanid dynasty, overthrew them. The Sasanid revolution transformed the Middle East and severed Armeno-Persian political and religious ties.

The Sasanids differed in several fundamental respects from their predecessors in Persia, a fact that had significant consequences for Armenia. The Sasanids kept their administration highly centralized and held to the memory of Armenia as part of the Persian kingdom of the Achaemenids. A stronger adversary against Rome than Arsacid Persia had been, Sasanid Persia did not hesitate to violate the agreement of Rhandeia and to act unilaterally regarding Armenia. The Sasanids' fervent promotion of Persian Zoroastrianism as the official religion of the empire meant not only the persecution of other religious sects in Armenia, but the eradication of Hellenistic culture in Persia, and to some extent, in Armenia. No longer able to rely on its Arsacid kinsmen in Persia, Armenia had to depend solely on Rome for protection. Sasanid rule did benefit the Armenians in one respect: Armenia could now install members of its own royal family as kings, creating a truly Armenian dynasty, called the Arshakuni. That the Arshakunis managed to rule under the Sasanids for two centuries is due to their own political skills, intermittent Roman aid, and two events, which united the Armenian people unlike anything before: the establishment of Christianity and the development of the Armenian alphabet.

Trdat II had to rule in the face of this new factor in the Roman-Persian struggle for control of Armenia and Mesopotamia. Armenia cooperated with Rome during the campaigns of Emperor Severus Alexander to forestall Ardeshir's expansion. By 244, however, the situation had changed drastically. The great Sasanid king, Shapur I (240-270), defeated the Roman Emperor Gordian in Mesopotamia. He then made peace with Emperor Philip, who agreed not only to pay a ransom and an annual tribute, but also to renounce Roman protection of Greater Armenia. Sixteen years later, Rome was to be humiliated further by the defeat and capture of Emperor Valerian by Shapur in Carrhae, Syria. In 252 Shapur invaded and occupied Armenia. Trdat II probably fled to Rome at this time, and Shapur incorporated Armenia into the Persian Empire, placing his own son, Hurmazd, on the throne of Armenia. Hurmazd ruled Armenia until his father's death in 270, when he left to assume the Persian throne and was replaced by his brother, Narseh, who ruled parts of Armenia until 293. Persia's strength and direct Sasanid control over Greater Armenia, while interrupting the independent rule of the Arshakunis, did have the benefit of bringing an extended period of peace to Armenia.

Roman fortunes improved after the death of Shapur, and by the end of the third century, Rome, under Diocletian, managed to reassert its influence in the western parts of Greater Armenia and Mesopotamia. A compromise with Persia allowed Rome to revive the Armenian Arshakuni dynasty and to install King Khosrov II, who seems to have ruled in the western provinces of Greater Armenia between 279 and 287. The Sasanids, who continued to view all of Armenia as their domain, plotted against Khosrov and the pro-Roman *nakharars* through the king's brother, who murdered Khosrov, and who, with other pro-Persian Armenians, cooperated with the Sasanids to reassert control over all of Greater Armenia. Khosrov's son, Trdat III, either escaped to Rome or was already in Rome, where, as sons of Rome's other allies, he was being educated in Roman customs. Khosrov's murderer became the ruler of Greater Armenia when, in 293, Narseh left to govern Persia. Trdat, meanwhile, remained at the court of Diocletian until Rome defeated Narseh in 298, and Trdat, backed by a Roman army, reclaimed his murdered father's throne. By the Peace of Nisibis (Mdsbin), Persia and Rome once again agreed to an independent Arshakuni Armenia as a buffer state. The Armenian borders, however, were once again rearranged. Most of Sophene was separated from Greater Armenia.

Its *nakharars* became independent *satraps* and allies of Rome. Lesser Armenia was expanded southward, detached from Cappadocia, and made into a separate province.

Diocletian's abdication, division within the empire, and Constantine's efforts to unify it, kept the Romans occupied during the early years of the fourth century. Armenia was left unprotected at a very crucial period, for the Sasanids had gained another strong king in Shapur II (309-379). Shapur renewed Persian attacks on Armenia and Syria and encouraged Zoroastrian proselytizing in Armenia, bringing the local cults in line with orthodox Zoroastrianism by destroying statues and prohibiting idolatry. It is against this backdrop, during the reign of Trdat III, known as Trdat the Great, that Armenia became the first state to adopt Christianity as its official religion.

Christianity in Armenia

One of the most crucial events in Armenian history was the conversion of Armenia to Christianity. By adopting the new religion in the fourth century, Armenia renounced its Eastern or Persian-influenced past, established a distinct Christian character of its own, and, at times, became identified with the Western world.

The traditional account of the conversion is based on a mixture of facts and fiction recorded a century later by the Armenian chronicler known as Agathangelos. It tells of the wars of an Armenian king, Khosrov (probably Khosrov II), against the Persian Sasanid dynasty and the efforts of Persia to destroy the Armenian Arshakunis. The Persian king employed a traitor named Anak (probably Khosrov's brother) to murder the Armenian king. Promised a reward by the Sasanids, Anak settled in Armenia, befriended Khosrov and murdered him and most of his family. Anak and his family were, in turn, slain by angry Armenian courtiers. Only two boys were saved from death: Khosrov's son Trdat (probably Trdat III), who was taken to Rome, and Anak's son (the future Gregory the Illuminator), who was taken to live with Christians in Cappadocia.

Years later, according to Agathangelos, Trdat, with Roman help returned to Armenia to regain his father's throne. Passing through Caesarea he met the son of Anak, who had been given the name of Gregory by his Christian mentors, and, unaware of his true identity, took him into his service. After regaining Armenia, Trdat, recognizing great abilities in Gregory, raised him in stature at court. Gregory, of course, had already accepted the Christian faith and eschewed pagan ceremonies. Soon rumors of his parentage began to surface, spread by jealous nobles, which lead to his torture and imprisonment in Khorvirap ("deep pit"). Years passed and Trdat, like his godfather Diocletian, continued his persecution of Christians. Among the martyrs of that period were Gayane and Hripsime, two virgins who had refused Trdat's advances and were put to death. According to Agathangelos, Trdat was punished for his sins by turning into a wild boar. No one could cure him of this transformation until his sister, Khosrovidukht, had a dream in which an angel instructed her to release Gregory, who, despite long years in isolation, had, by divine intervention, survived in the pit. Gregory healed the king, who, in 301, proclaimed Christianity the sole state religion, making Armenia the first Christian State. Gregory then traveled to Caesarea to be ordained by the Greek bishop there, an action that would later have serious repercussions for the Armenian Church. Upon his return Gregory baptized the king and all the Armenian nobility, destroyed pagan temples, and in their place erected churches and shrines to the Armenian martyrs. At Vagharshapat, on a spot shown to him by Christ in a vision, he built the great cathedral of Ejmiatsin ("the spot where the Only Begotten Son descended") upon the ruins of the temple of *Anahit*.

This legendary tale was accepted until modern times as accurately describing the forces motivating Armenia to become the first state to adopt Christianity. Like most tales, however, it does not explain the entire story nor gives a correct chronology of events. To understand the reasons for the Christianization of Armenia one should look at political and social developments in Persia, Rome, and Armenia during the previous century. Although available historical data is scarce, scattered, and confusing, it is clear that it was external pressures that gave the Armenian throne the impetus to unite its people behind Christianity.

Christianity, as an underground and forbidden religion, was practiced in the Roman provinces of Palestine and Syria, particularly in the city of Edessa, from where it had spread to southern Armenia as early as the first century. Another Armenian tradition claims that a certain king, Abkar of Edessa, had asked Jesus to come to his kingdom to cure him of an illness. After the Resurrection, the Apostles Thaddeus and Bartholomew went to Edessa to spread Christianity in Syria. Thaddeus then went to Armenia where he preached and was martyred by order of the Armenian king. It is out of this tradition that the Armenian Church claims an apostolic heritage. By the second century, Armenia had a number of underground Christian cells in the southern and western provinces, which had secured the protection of some local nobles. By the third century Christianity was practiced in Armenia, albeit still in a semi-secret manner, along with Hellenistic and pre-Hellenistic beliefs, and another dualistic belief, Manicheanism. According to Eusebius, there was an Armenian bishop called Mushegh, who, in 250, had corresponded with Christians in Alexandria. It is probable that Gregory, who was originally from a Parthian family, came in contact with Christians in Armenia during the second half of the third century.

The situation changed drastically after the Sasanids transformed Zoroastrianism from a religion of the upper classes into the official religion of Persia. An official orthodoxy emerged, fueled by zealous missionary activity, which threatened Armenia's political, as well as religious, identity. In the Roman Empire, on the other hand, overt Christian persecutions had eased with the departure of Diocletian, and Christianity had increased in popularity in Syria and the eastern provinces of the Roman Empire. In 313, Emperor Constantine issued the Edict of Milan, in which he excused Christians from pagan rituals, granted their religion the same tolerance accorded to all others, and restored their confiscated property.

The traditional date of 301 is open to question. It is unlikely that Trdat would go accept a religion abhorred by Diocletian, whose army kept Trdat on the throne. It is more likely that Trdat and some of his officials converted in 301 but did not act openly until after the Edict of Milan. Soon after, probably in 314, and not in 301, the traditionally held date, Armenia was politically ready to become the first nation (it has to be noted that the Ethiopian, Coptic, and Syriac Churches also claim to be the first Christian institutions) to officially adopt Christianity as its state religion. After the Council of Nicea (325) Christianity was accepted as the main religion of the Roman Empire. In 380 Emperor Theodosius adopted Christianity as the sole state religion of the Roman Empire and initiated the second ecumenical council at Constantinople (381).

In Christianity Armenian leaders found a religion both tolerated by their strongest ally and possessing a messianic fervor strong enough to counter Zoroastrianism. Although paganism persisted for some time and even resulted in the martyrdom of a number of Armenian Church leaders, the new Christian religion was forced upon everyone. Hellenistic temples were destroyed and churches were built over them, much as early Roman churches were later built over pagan shrines. Following Gregory's astute dream, the cathedral of Ejmiatsin, as noted, replaced the great temple of *Anahit* in Vaghar-shapat. Christian missionaries spread the new faith throughout Armenia, Georgia and Caucasian Albania. These efforts assured the permanency of Christianity as the religion of Armenia and a deterrent to Persian dualistic beliefs.

Church organization followed the feudal system. The family of Gregory the Illuminator inherited, for a time, the position of the *Catholicos*, or the Supreme Patriarch of the Church. Bishops were chosen from among the *nakharar* families. The lower clergy was included in the *azat* class and received fiefs from bishops in return for service. The bishops and priests served as judges, with the Catholicos as the supreme judge. The Church became a major power in Armenia and helped to create a distinct Armenian identity. Almost a century later, the creation of the Armenian alphabet would further strengthen this sense of identity.

Armenia during the Fourth Century:
The Councils of Nicea and Constantinople

In 325, during the reign of Trdat III, the Emperor Constantine summoned the First Ecumenical Council of the Christian Church to meet at Nicea in Asia Minor. Gregory's son, Aristakes, represented Armenia. The council's main objective was to define the Christian creed and to resolve the controversy between Arius and Bishop Alexander of Alexandria. Arius maintained that Christ was not of the same substance as God, hence not divine, while Alexander, and his successor Athanasius, maintained the doctrine of one substance. While the council rejected Arianism there were some bishops who were unwilling to accept all the decisions of Nicea. Keeping the bishops divided would assure the continuing power of the Emperor over the Church, and so, Constantine and a number of his successors allowed the Arian debate to continue. Armenian kings followed the example of the Roman rulers and clashed repeatedly with the leaders of their own Church. It was not until 381, when the Emperor Theodosius accepted the rulings of the Second Ecumenical Council at Constantinople, which supported Athanasianism that the Armenian and the Greek Churches finally reconciled with their monarchs.

Arshak II

The fourth century was a tumultuous period for Armenia. The seventy year long reign of Shapur II and his attempts to dislodge the Roman presence from Armenia and Mesopotamia ravaged the Armenian economy. The political and socioeconomic condition in Armenia enabled the *nakharars* to play a major role in domestic policy. Some *nakharars* favored Rome, others Persia, while others pursued their own independent course.

As with much of the chronology of the Arshakunis, there is no clear data on the rulers between Trdat III and Arshak II. Khosrov III (known as "Kotak" or "Short") is mentioned in a number of sources as ruling from 330 to 338 and constructing a new capital at Dvin. More is known about the reign of Arshak II. Some historians argue that Arshak II began his reign in 338, although it is more probable that he commenced his rule in 350, after Shapur's third campaign against Rome. Nearly all that is known about Arshak is from Church sources, which, as will be seen, had reasons for painting an unflattering portrait of the ruler. Arshak seems to have been put on the throne as a compromise between the Emperor Constantius II and Shapur. The royal court rarely resided in the new capital city of Dvin during Arshak's reign; rebuilding and reorganization became the first items on his agenda.

Reconstruction and regulation were on the Church's mind as well. The new Catholicos, Nerses I, of the Gregorid house, called the first Armenian Church Council at Ashtishat. As a result, hospitals and orphanages were established, and the practice of pagan and Zoroastrian rituals forbidden. During this period, married men were permitted to join the ranks of the upper clergy, providing that they no longer lived with their wives. In time, however, there developed a two-tiered hierarchy of celibate upper clergy and non-celibate lower clergy.

Arshak, following the example of Roman emperors, maintained a pro-Arian position, and when Nerses objected, Arshak replaced him with a more cooperative Catholicos. He then tried to bring the feudal lords under his control by having those who opposed him killed. Arshak and his followers took refuge in the new city of Arshakavan, which was soon destroyed in a rebellion. The widow Parantsem, whom he married according to some accounts while his first wife was still alive, compounded Arshak's problems. Others accuse him of murdering his first wife in order to marry Parantsem.

Arshak's position was bound to the Roman presence in western Armenia, and as long as Rome managed to resist Shapur, he was secure. When Shapur defeated the Emperor Julian (the Apostate), however, and forced the Emperor Jovian to yield western Armenia in 364, Arshak's fate was sealed. The king and his general Vasak Mamikonian were ordered to Persia where they were blinded, tortured and killed. Parantsem resisted heroically, but she too lost her life, while Arshak's son Pap escaped to Pontus. Shapur sacked a number of Armenian cities, took thousands of prisoners to Persia, and once more made Armenia into a Persian province. Zoroastrian temples were erected, replacing some churches. Two pro-Persian *nakharars*, who were related to the Persian royal house and who had probably converted to Zoroastrianism, were assigned to govern Armenia as Sasanid vassals.

The Partitioning of Armenia

Rome could not tolerate a Persian-dominated Armenia and, in 367, the Emperor Valens, who had become the ruler of the eastern provinces of the Roman Empire, supplied funds and troops to Pap and the Armenian general, Mushegh Mamikonian. The Armeno-Roman force defeated the Persians at Bagavan. Pap asked Catholicos Nerses to return and tried to reconcile with the Church and the *nakharars*, but like Valens and his own father before him, Pap was pro-Arian. Conflict with the Church and the *nakharars* ensued; Nerses was soon murdered and the majority of *nakharars*, including Mushegh Mamikonian, turned against the king. The *nakharars* in Sophene, who had maintained their independence since the Nisibis agreement, abandoned the king and declared the five districts of Sophene, renamed as the Pentarchy or the southern satrapies, as an independent region under the protection of Rome. In 374, Pap was murdered with the acquiescence of Rome. Pap's successor, his nephew, did not rule long and was replaced by the Mamikonian house, whose rule was short-lived. Fortunately for Armenia, Shapur died in 379, while the Roman Empire was soon divided into Western and Eastern (Byzantine) branches (see map 10). The Mamikonians eventually restored the Arshakuni throne to the two young sons of Pap, but retained close ties to the center of power, by marrying them to Mamikonian women.

Arshak III, the younger son of Pap, was forced by pro-Persian *nakharars* to flee in 385 to the western part of the country, and to seek Byzantine protection. The *nakharars* then elevated a pro-Persian Arshakuni prince, Khosrov IV, as the King of Armenia. Tired of a long war, which had resulted in a stalemate, Emperor Theodosius and Shapur III, in 387, decided to partition Armenia. Byzantium received the smaller portion, stretching west of Theodosiopolis (present-day Erzerum) in the north and Martyropolis in the south and including the much-Hellenized Lesser Armenia. Arshak III remained on as king and a vassal of Byzantium. Persia received most of Greater Armenia, including the cities of Artashat and Dvin. Khosrov IV continued as king and vassal of the Sasanids. To further weaken Armenian political and economic power, the Persians stripped Greater Armenia of six of its provinces: Gugark was made part of eastern Georgia, Artsakh and Utik were made part of Caucasian Albania, and Paytakaran, Korjayk, and Persarmenia joined Persia proper (see map 11).

Upon the death of Arshak III, the Byzantines did not appoint another Armenian king and the Arshakuni line in Byzantine Armenia came to an end. Some of Arshak's *nakharars* left for Persian Armenia, the rest became vassals of Byzantium. Greek governors and culture began to make inroads in Byzantine Armenia. In Persian Armenia, Vramshapuh (389-417) succeeded Khosrov IV and installed Sahak, the last Catholicos of the Gregorid line. Vramshapuh is a significant figure in Armenian history, for he is credited with being the motivating force behind the creation of the Armenian alphabet.

The Development of the Armenian Alphabet

The most momentous event of the Arshakuni period was the invention of the Armenian alphabet. Prior to the fifth century, the Armenians used Greek for artistic and cultural expression, Latin and both versions of Middle Persian (Pahlavi) scripts for official communications and inscriptions, and Syriac for their liturgy. Because the majority of Armenians could not read or write Armenia had a rich oral tradition. History was not recorded, but recited from memory and sung by various Armenian and Persian *gusans* or minstrel-poets.

Both the crown and religious leaders of Armenia saw the partition of Armenia as an event of devastating potential. Both realized the perils to an Armenia under Byzantine and Persian administrative and religious control. The fledgling Armenian Church faced other problems as well. On the one hand, the influence of the Syrian Church, whose own liturgy was used by the Armenians, was increasingly encroaching upon the authority of the Armenian Church. The ecumenical councils, on the other hand, foreshadowed the future ecclesiastical domination of Byzantium in the region. Moreover, contrary to popular tradition, Christianity did not take hold of the entire population at once; paganism and Zoroastrianism still commanded many followers and converts.

Both Catholicos Sahak and King Vramshapuh realized that in order to retain any measure of ecclesiastical and political control over a partitioned nation, the unifying factor of the Armenian language would be crucial. They asked Mesrop Mashtots, a learned scholar and clergyman, to create an alphabet, which would distinguish Armenia, linguistically and liturgically, from the powers surrounding it. Mashtots, who was born in the province of Taron, had studied Greek and Syriac, and was employed by the *hazarapet* in the royal secretariat. According to his student, Koriun, who wrote a biography of his master in the mid-fifth century, Mashtots was well versed in secular law and military arts before devoting himself to the religious life. He had traveled all over Armenia and fully recognized the threat of assimilation. Mashtots and a number of his students traveled, examined different alphabets, including samples of earlier attempts at an Armenian alphabet (most prominent the work of a Syrian bishop, Daniel), and consulted calligraphers. Using Greek, Syriac, and letters from other scripts, Mashtots, sometime around the year 400, shaped the thirty-six letters of the Armenian alphabet. To give the new alphabet a divine aura and make it more acceptable, legends were circulated which claimed that the alphabet, like the Ten Commandments, was bestowed on Mashtots in a divine vision. The miracle, however, was the alphabet itself, which represents the many distinct consonant sounds of Armenian and which has remained virtually unchanged for 1600 years. Mashtots' students opened schools throughout the Armenian provinces to teach the new alphabet. Fortunately, the Sasanid monarchs during these years happened to be extremely tolerant, as was Emperor Theodosius II, who permitted Mashtots' pupils to run schools in Byzantine Armenia as well. According to Armenian tradition, Mashtots then went on to develop alphabets for the Georgians and the Caucasian Albanians as well.

Immediately thereafter, Armenians entered upon a period of translating major Christian and philosophical texts into Armenian.

The first work to be translated was, not surprisingly, the Bible. The translation was made from the Syriac and Greek versions and is highly regarded by Biblical scholars. The Catholicos and king enthusiastically supported the efforts of priests and scribes to translate and copy the writings of the early Christian fathers, the canons of Church councils and various liturgical works. Armenians who had studied at Athens, Edessa, Nisibis, and Antioch, and who were familiar with the works of Greek grammar, logic, philosophy, and rhetoric, translated Porphyry, Diodochus, Probus, and other Neo-Platonic philosophers, among others. Aristotle was a particular favorite as demonstrated by the more than three hundred manuscripts of his works in the Armenian archives.

The translators left a legacy for Western civilization as well, as a number of Syriac and Greek texts have been preserved only in their Armenian translations. Among them are: Hippolutus' *Commentaries on the Benediction of Moses*, the complete text of Ephraim's *Commentary on the Diatessaron*, the first part of the *Chronicle* of Eusebius, Timothy Aelurus' (Patriarch of Alexandria) *Refutation of the Definition of the Council of Chalcedon*, and *The Romance of Alexander the Great* by Pseudo-Callisthenes. During the high Middle Ages and the Renaissance, when Western Europe was "rediscovering" the literature and culture of the classical world, these Armenian translations formed an important link to the knowledge of the past.

The Armenian translators began their large output in the fifth century and continued until the second half of the seventh century, when the Arab invasions somewhat slowed their pace. Original works, including histories, were written after the fall of the Arshakunis in 428 and will be discussed in chapter 7.

Trade, Art and Architecture

The only pre-Christian monument surviving from this period is the complex at Garni. The temple, built in the first century AD, was destroyed by an earthquake in 1679 and was restored over two decades ago. Parts of the original fortifications, the Garni fortress and a bath have also been preserved. Garni also provides the only example of the decorative art of the period in the form of a mosaic in the bath depicting sea gods and fish. A number of crude relief and carved heads from tufa, representing unknown Arshakuni kings, are all that is left of the sculptural art of this period. The first churches in Armenia were constructed at Vagharshapat, Ashtishat, and near Lake Sevan. These were single-nave edifices, often built upon the foundations of pagan temples, which had been destroyed by the early Armenian Christians. Some of the temples were simply converted outright by relocating the apse to the traditional eastern side. In the fifth century a number of central-domed cathedrals and domed basilicas began to appear. Few of the early churches constructed in the fourth century have survived. The mother cathedral of Armenia, Ejmiatsin, although dating from this period, was totally rebuilt in the late fifth century and expanded throughout its history. The church of Ereruk, which is also of this period, like other early Armenian churches located on the territory of the Armenian Republic, is being restored; however, those in Turkey, Nakhichevan, Azerbaijan, Iran or Georgia, have, with some exceptions, been left in ruins.

During the Arsacid and Arshakuni periods, trade flourished along the route from Ctesiphon to Armenia and the Black Sea, enabling merchants and artisans to sell their wares in Rome and Persia. The route went from Ctesiphon to Armenia and the Black Sea, and the cities of Artashat, Dvin, Nakhichevan, and Theodosiopolis became major trade centers between India, Iberia, Persia, and Europe. Dvin in particular became an entry port where merchants met to transact business.

After the death of Vramshapuh, the Sasanids installed first, a Persian prince to rule Persian Armenia and later, a son of Vramshapuh, Artashes IV, who ruled until 428 AD. The *nakharars*, preferring to rule themselves, successfully requested the removal of the king and the replacement of Catholicos Sahak. Armenia thus became a land divided between Byzantium and Persia, with no national leader.

Prior to the Sasanids, the Armenian kings, who were related to the Persians, had to deal primarily with Rome. After the Sasanids took over Persia, Armenia once again had to maneuver between the mighty Roman and Persian Empires, resulting in its partition and the termination of its second dynasty. The incessant and violent struggle between Persia and Byzantium and the appearance of the Arabs would subject Armenia to fragmentation and leave it leaderless for over four centuries. But the Armenians had gained three powerful weapons: a new religion, a script, and regional leaders, all of which would enable Armenia to weather the coming storms.

7

Fire Temples and Icons
Armenia Under Persian and Byzantine Rule
(428-640)

T HE MORE THAN two centuries between the collapse of the
second Armenian kingdom and the arrival of the Arabs coincided with the eclipse of the ancient world and the dawn of
the early medieval period. The Western Roman Empire fell and
fragmented, gradually emerging as various kingdoms throughout
Western Europe. The kingdom of Soba rose in Africa. The great Indian Gupta Empire fell to invaders from the north. Buddhism
reached Japan, and China finally restored its imperial order under
the Sui and T'ang dynasties. The Eastern Roman Empire, or Byzantium, continued its struggle against Sasanid Persia in Armenia and
Mesopotamia. The intolerance of the Zoroastrian and Greek hierar-
chies affected the other religious groups who lived in the Middle
East. Furthermore, continual warfare left both Persian and Byzantine resources depleted. Such conditions prepared the ground for the
rise of a new political and religious force, that of the Arabs and Islam.

The spread of Christianity, the invention of the Armenian alphabet, and the growing autonomy of the *nakharars* appeared at an
extremely crucial period. Armenia, now partitioned, would need all
the national identity it could muster to survive the more powerful
cultures, which controlled its destiny. This was especially true by
the mid-fifth century, when the short reigns of the more tolerant Sasanid and Byzantine rulers came to an end. The Persians and the
Byzantines employed different strategies in administering their re-
spective Armenian provinces. During the more than two centuries
following the partition, therefore, the two Armenian regions faced
very different political, religious, and socioeconomic conditions.

Persian Armenia

The Sasanids appointed a governor of the frontier, or *marzpan (marzban)*, to rule Persian Armenia, with its capital at Dvin. The *marzpan* commanded the local garrison and had full authority in administrative, judicial, and even religious matters. He was assisted by a *hazarapet*, who had more authority than the earlier *hazarapets* of the Arshakuni period. A *magpet*, or chief of the magians (Zoroastrian priests), resided at Dvin. Tax officials lived in every district of Armenia and a special supervisor oversaw the Armenian gold mines. Besides being the administrative and religious capital, Dvin also became a center of trade, with both the Persians and Byzantines using Armenia as a passage for their caravans. Weaving, pottery, and jewelry made in Armenia were exported to neighboring regions.

Armenian *nakharars* still controlled many highland areas and for the most part remained autonomous, paying taxes to the Persians and receiving their appointment from the Persian king. A number of prominent *nakharars* were granted the position of *marzpan*, and the *sparapet*, a Mamikonian, continued to lead the *nakharar* military contingents. Sources describe the magnificent residences and jewels and garments worn by the Armenian *marzpan* and other high officials, which duplicated those of Persian counterparts.

Many Christians lived in the Persian Empire, especially in Mesopotamia and western Persia. Once Byzantium assumed the leadership of the Church, however, Christians, even heretic sects, living under Persian rule, were viewed as a threat and were occasionally persecuted. The Persian throne soon began appointing the Armenian Church leadership. The Gregorid house, suspected by both the Persians and *nakharars* of espousing the restoration of the kingdom and a more centralized Armenian government, was removed, and other candidates, including several non-Armenians, were given the title of Catholicos. As a result of Persian control over ecclesiastical affairs, the Church lost contact with the West and became increasingly isolated from its fellow Christian Churches. This isolation was to have serious religious and political consequences in the years that followed.

The Council of Ephesus

In 431, another heresy, Nestorianism, prompted the Christian Church hierarchy to call the Third Ecumenical Council, this time at Ephesus. Nestorius, the Patriarch of Constantinople, believed in the separation of Christ's human and divine natures and started a debate. Although the Council condemned him, the problem continued and two decades later resulted in the first division among the Christians. The Armenian religious hierarchy at Ejmiatsin was still under Persian control at this time and was probably not represented at the Council of Ephesus. Following Ephesus, Nestorians were welcomed in Persia as enemies of Byzantium. The Sasanids, at times, viewed the Armenian Church as part of the Nestorian Church in Persia.

The Vardanank Wars

For the first fifty years following the partition, Armenia was generally left alone in its religious and cultural affairs and held its own Church councils. The situation altered drastically in 439 with the ascension of Yazdgird II to the throne. He and members of his court attempted to impose Zoroastrianism on all of the non-Persian peoples living in his empire. When Armenia resisted, taxes were increased and some *nakharars* were sent to fight Central Asian nomads who threatened Persia. The final blow came when the Persian king dispatched Zoroastrian priests to convert the population. Armenian peasants and especially residents of Dvin were angered at the arrival of Zoroastrian priests who were sent to build a fire temple in the capital. Some of the *nakharars* and churchmen gathered at Artashat in 447 and declared to the king that, although they were faithful to Persia, they were also faithful to their Church. The reaction of another group of *nakharars*, however, was not as strong. A pro-Persian faction sought a dialogue and compromise with their overlords. These were led by the Armenian *marzpan*, Vasak Siuni, whose family had occasionally held the position of viceroy, and who viewed himself as a prince of the Armenian people. His mountainous domain bordered Persia, and his two sons were hostages at Ctesiphon. In opposition to him were most churchmen, a large part of the population, and many other *nakharars*, all led by *sparapet* Vardan Mamikonian.

Resistance to the Persians continued on a minor scale for a decade. By 450 the Armenians were in open rebellion against the

Persians and, together with the Georgians and Caucasian Albanians, who were under similar pressures from Persia defeated a Sasanid army. In search of a stronger ally, the Armenians sought aid from Constantinople. The aid from Byzantium did not materialize and Vasak and his followers continued to oppose the rebellion, which they no doubt viewed as detrimental to their official status as representatives of the Persians. In 451 the main Persian army met the rebels on the plain of Avarayr in Artaz (near present day Maku, Iran). Vardan Mamikonian and his entire army perished, becoming martyrs of the Armenian Church. Vasak Siuni did not join the battle and has been accused of treachery ever since by Church historians. In his own day, however, he, along with the pro-Persian *nakharars*, was held responsible for the insurgency and was imprisoned by the Persians.

The death of Vardan and his stand against more powerful forces elevated him and the rest of the fallen heroes, to the status of religious and national martyrs and gave them an importance that they did not possess in life. Accounts of the battle circulated and helped rally the population against the Persians. Persian persecutions, the arrest of neutral and even loyal *nakharars*, and the execution of a number of churchmen stiffened Armenian resolve and began local Armenian resistance. The Sasanids must have been surprised at the persistence of the Armenians, for Yazdgird soon released many of the *nakharars* and pursued a more lenient policy in Armenia.

During the next two decades, however, the Armenians sought vengeance for the martyrs of Avarayr with a series of rebellions in Armenia and Georgia. Supported by the Armenian Church, the conflict became known as the Vardanank Wars. In 481, the rebels under the leadership of Vahan Mamikonian, took Dvin, the seat of the *marzpanate*, and defeated a Persian army in 482. Disagreements with Georgia led to Armenian losses and forced Vahan Mamikonian to continue his struggle as a guerilla fighter for a year. In the meantime the Sasanids had their own internal problems. They were attacked by nomadic invaders, faced disputes over the succession and had to deal with the heresy of Mazdak and his followers, who espoused communistic and ascetic doctrines. As a result, in 484, peaceful relations were restored when Vahan Mamikonian was named *sparapet* and regained his fief in exchange for the support of a Sasanid candidate to the throne. Armenia was granted freedom of religion and the right to appeal to the Persian court directly, bypassing the *marzpan*. A year later Vahan himself was named *marzpan* and ruled for two decades. Interestingly, the agreement, known in Armenian sources as the Nuvarsak treaty, is not mentioned in Persian sources, indicating that either the Armenian rebellion was considered a minor incident in Persian history or that none of the Persian sources describing it have survived. Nevertheless, Armenians today celebrate Avarayr and Nuvarsak as moral victories. Like the Jewish experience in Masada, the Armenians view the struggle as a symbol of the survival of their religious and cultural identity against overwhelming forces. After the death of Vahan, the next eight Armenian *marzpans* who ruled intermittently continued to face pressures from the Zoroastrians until the Arab invasions.

Following Nuvarsak a period of reconstruction began. Both the *nakharars* and the Church managed to reorganize and rebuild Armenia. Vagharshapat and Dvin were restored. Armenia revived economically as trade once again began to pass to Byzantium. Despite some disruptions during the Perso-Byzantine wars, Armenia's revival continued until the mid-sixth century.

The Council of Chalcedon

In the meantime, the Fourth Ecumenical Council met at Chalcedon in 451. The council decreed that Christ's two natures were not separate as Nestorius claimed, or confused as Eutyches maintained, but united without confusion, change, or division. A number of Eastern Churches, the Coptic and Ethiopian among others, led by the Patriarch of Alexandria, rejected Chalcedon's Dyophysite decrees as a version of Nestorianism, and hence a heresy. They maintained that Christ had only one, divine nature. They became identified as Monophysite Churches. Christian religious leaders, realizing the seriousness of the situation, tried to find a way to reconcile the dissenting groups. In 482 they convinced Emperor Zeno to issue the Act of Union or the *Henoticon*. The Act recognized the religious foundations of the first three ecumenical councils as entirely sufficient. It stated that, "Christ was of the same nature with the Father in the Godhead and of the same nature with us in the manhood." The terms "one nature" or "two natures" were avoided.

Although at first the compromise appeased the leaders of the Monophysitic Churches, the Monophysites and Dyophysites soon rejected it. The Monophysites viewed it as too vague and the Dyophysites saw it as a concession to Monophysitic doctrine. The Armenians, because of the Vardanank struggle and the battle of

Avarayr, which took place in the same year as Chalcedon, did not attend the council. The canons of the council and Zeno's *Henoticon* only gradually arrived in Armenia, in various versions. It was only in the late fifth century, after the Persian threat had subsided, that the Armenian bishops, in 491, gathered in Vagharshapat and rejected the decision of Chalcedon. A few years later (506), in Dvin, they, along with the Georgians and Caucasian Albanians, reiterated their objections. Zeno's *Henoticon* was not rejected, however, and helped to maintain a dialogue between the Armenian and Greek Churches. The decision was a prudent one, as a third of Armenia was still under Byzantine administration. The Armenian Church, at the same time, insisted that it was not Monophysitic, but rather followed its own unique interpretation, which viewed the two natures of Christ as indivisible. Although the humanity of Christ was not emphasized, it was not altogether ignored. Many religious experts classify the Armenian Church as Monophysite. Viewed through strict Monophysite doctrine, however, the Armenians are not true Monophysites; taking a more lenient definition, Armenians come close to holding a Monophysitic doctrine.

Was the decision to reject the Council of Chalcedon political or religious? Probably both. It is likely that the Armenian bishops, witnessing Byzantine control over Western Armenia, feared that the powerful religious hierarchy at Constantinople would eventually engulf their Church. The apostolic tradition of the Armenian Church had long been challenged by the Greeks, who claimed that since the Greek bishop of Caesarea had ordained Gregory the Armenian Church was subordinate to the Patriarch of Constantinople. The Persians, at the same time, were extending tolerance to Nestorians and other heretical Christian groups. By affirming both a unique doctrinal position and their apostolic tradition, the Armenians not only maintained their national Church but also appeased the Persians.

Pressures from Byzantium continued for the next few decades, however, and increased during the reign of the Emperor Justinian. Armenians were finally forced to break with Constantinople. In 552 the Armenian Church adopted its own calendar and in 554, at the second council of Dvin, the Armenian Church considered a complete break from Constantinople, a decision, which by 609 became official and resulted in the establishment of a totally separate Armenian Church.

Byzantine Armenia

The Byzantines gradually tried to transform Byzantine Armenia into a territory resembling the rest of its empire. Lesser Armenia, already under the firm control of the Byzantium military commander, the *Dux Armeniae*, and partially assimilated, was subdivided into the administrative units of Armenia I, with its capital at Sebasteia (Sivas) and Armenia II with its capital at Melitene (Malatya). The western part of Greater Armenia, which had been awarded to Byzantium in the partition of 387, became known as Armenia Interior, where a civilian governor known as the *Comes Armeniae* held a position equivalent to the Persian *marzpan* (see map 11). The Byzantine governor there relied on the few *nakharars* left in the region to gain the cooperation of the population. A number of *nakharars* and princes such as the Mamikonian and Arshakuni families held their own domains but paid taxes and supplied troops to Byzantium.

Until Chalcedon, the Christian Church was unified and Greek remained the literary language of the upper classes. The *nakharars* were left alone and, for the most part, served the imperial administration. The *nakharars* in the southern districts of Armenia Interior, the region of Sophene, now known as the Pentarchy or the southern satrapies, in particular, were viewed as allies and a buffer against Persia, and, as noted, were independent from Byzantine military or administrative control. Persian pressures on their Armenian population also portrayed the Byzantines in a more positive light. These conditions contributed to the gradual assimilation of Lesser Armenia and parts of Byzantine Armenia. There were no challenges to rally the people, no overt threats to their national identity.

The introduction of the alphabet and the subsequent literary and educational activity, however, combined with the independent stand of the Armenian Church, changed the atmosphere. The situation worsened when *nakharars* in the Pentarchy, who had close ties to Constantinople, rebelled in 485. Either the Armenian rebellion and resistance in Persian Armenia motivated these *nakharars* to rebel as well, or they were enticed by promises from Persia. Following the rebellion, Byzantium annexed the Pentarchy and placed it under the same status as the rest of Armenia, to be governed by imperial officials.

Despite having separate administrations, Persian and Byzantine Armenia had numerous channels of communication. Trade from

China and Persia passed through Artashat and Nisibis into Byzantine Armenia. Persian Nestorians maintained a large theological school and translation center at Edessa and Armenians from Persia studied there. Intermarriage between Armenians living on the borders of the two areas was common, and travel, although restricted, was permitted.

Emperor Zeno began the first major changes in Byzantine Armenia. He introduced a number of Roman laws into Armenia Interior, to bring it into line with Armenia I and II, and ordered stricter control of the border. The school at Edessa was closed, forcing its relocation to Nisibis in the Persian Empire. Byzantine spies increased their activities in the border regions, forcing the Persians to restrict travel. The Byzantines especially wished to break the Persian monopoly over Chinese silk, a material in great demand at the imperial court. Byzantium's hostile actions and refusal to pay their share of expenses to guard the passes in the Caucasus against nomadic incursions started new conflicts with Persia.

The wars (503-505 and 524-531) were fought in Byzantine Armenia and Mesopotamia, and although they went against Byzantium, internal problems in Persia hampered them from taking full advantage of Byzantium's weakness. In 531, however, Sasanid Persia resolved its Mazdakite problem by killing Mazdak and his followers, and its succession disputes, when Khosrow I executed all of his own brothers and their male offspring, save one. In 533 Khosrow, known as Anushirvan, finally concluded an "endless peace" with the Emperor Justinian, in which the Byzantines had to pay large sums of gold toward the upkeep of the Caucasian defenses and keep a low offensive profile on its eastern borders.

Byzantine Armenia in the Period of Justinian

Having resolved his war with Persia, Justinian began his reorganization of the empire, initiating major changes in Byzantine Armenia. In 536, he decreed that all the various administrative offices in Armenia were to be abolished and combined under a single military command *(Magister militum per Armeniam)* headquartered at Theodosiopolis. New fortifications separating Byzantium and Persia created a Byzantine Armenia virtually sealed-off from its neighbor. Residents of the two Armenias could no longer intermingle or maintain any degree of unity through commercial or cultural interaction. Justinian divided Byzantine Armenia into four administrative units.

First Armenia (Inner Armenia plus most of the former First Armenia) with its capital at Theodosiopolis. Second Armenia (the rest of the former First Armenia plus additional territory in the northwest) with its capital at Sebasteia. Third Armenia (the former Second Armenia) with its center at Melitene. Fourth Armenia (the Pentarchy or southern satrapies) with Martyropolis as its center (see map 12). Governors and tax collectors resided in each region to assure the incorporation of Byzantine Armenia into the rest of the empire.

The *nakharars* lost their autonomy, and the Byzantines introduced legal measures to assimilate the Armenians as much as possible. Roman law was fully extended to all of Byzantine Armenia, with serious consequences for the *nakharars*. Under Roman law daughters and younger sons could inherit. Thus the Armenian *nakharars*, who had kept their lands intact for generations under the leadership of the eldest male member of the house, or *tanuter*, were now forced to divide them among their children. The *nakharar* lands would eventually be split into powerless smaller holdings. A number of Armenian nobles rebelled, Byzantine officials were murdered, and some *nakharars* even turned to Persia for help. These *nakharars* were either deported to the Balkans or were drafted into the Byzantine bureaucracy. Armenian assimilation, which had begun earlier, continued during the sixth century. Byzantium's armed fortresses on the border, its expansionist policy, and especially its smuggling in the secret of silk production, angered Khosrow. Requests from Armenian *nakharars* in the Byzantine zone encouraged the Persians to start a new war in 540, which dragged on until 562. A fifty-year truce was then established by which Persia would bear the cost of guarding the Caucasian passes but would receive an annual tribute in gold from Byzantium.

Perso-Byzantine Conflicts and the Second Partition of Armenia

The situation for both Armenias had worsened by the last quarter of the sixth century. In 571 the Persian *marzpan* built a fire-temple in Dvin. The Persian Armenians rebelled under the leadership of another Vardan Mamikonian, known as "Red" Vardan and sought the protection of Justin II. The Emperor, who did not wish to pay the large annual tribute in gold to Persia, broke the truce in 572. He offered to aid the Persian Armenians, but when the war turned against Byzantium, Justin abdicated and his successor, in 575, came to terms with Persia in order to retain parts of Mesopotamia. Vardan and a number of Armenian *nakharars* and their retinue fled to Byzantium. This truce did not last either, however, and the two antagonists again fought in Byzantine Armenia. Emperor Maurice (582-602) was more successful in fighting the Persians. He ordered a scorched earth policy on the borders with Persia, creating a vast no-man's land at the expense of both Armenias. The Armenians who had lost their homes in those regions were then deported to Cyprus. Maurice saw a chance to extend Byzantium's borders when Bahram Chubin deposed Khosrow II, known as Parviz, in 591. In the same year, Maurice intervened and helped the Persian prince to regain his throne. Byzantium's newly acquired prominence in the internal affairs of Persia now enabled it not only to annul the annual tribute, but also to receive a large part of Persian Armenia. The boundary between the two sectors now ran from the northeast corner of Lake Van up the Hrazdan River to the northwest corner of Lake Sevan. Dvin remained in the Persian zone but Yerevan fell to the Byzantine side. The additional territories were named Inner, Lower and Deep Armenia.

To complicate matters, the Byzantines renamed their former Armenian holdings. First Armenia became Greater Armenia, Second Armenia remained the same, Third Armenia was renamed First Armenia and the term Third Armenia fell out of use; and Fourth Armenia was referred to as Ioustiniana, and encompassed the Pentarchy as well as additional territory in the north and east (see map 13). Both Maurice and Khosrow carried out a policy of depopulating Armenia and sending its *nakharars* to various parts of their empire to fight in Africa, Central Asia, or the Balkans.

The murder of Maurice and his sons by Phocas in 602 started a new war with Persia. Khosrow II soundly defeated the Byzantines and came within a mile of Constantinople. The war continued after the death of Phocas and the ascendancy of Heraclius in 610. By 620, the Persians had conquered all of Armenia, the Middle East, most of Asia Minor, and had taken the True Cross (on which Jesus was crucified) from Jerusalem to Ctesiphon. The situation in Byzantium was desperate when Emperor Heraclius decided to use his navy to transport troops closer to the Persian lines. The Byzantine offensive of 622 proved successful and by 628 Asia Minor, the Middle East, and Armenia were in Byzantine hands. Khosrow II was killed by his own troops and his son made peace with Heraclius, returned the True Cross, and restored the 591 agreement and borders. From then on, the Sasanids were in no position to threaten Byzantium and rapidly declined.

Heraclius, more than his predecessors, realized the strategic importance of Armenia. In order to concentrate on the now frequent Avar and Slavic raids on the western borders of Byzantium, he required a strong ally and a secure Armenia on his eastern flank. Therefore, he created the position of "prince of Armenia" and chose not a Mamikonian, but a member of a minor *nakharar* family to control the administration of Armenia. The man he chose was Theodore Rshtuni, who was to play a significant role in the next period of Armenian history.

Literature, Learning and Art

The two centuries of devastation, deportation and the disruption of trade affected both Armenias, particularly Byzantine Armenia. It is surprising that artistic, scientific and literary activities not only continued throughout these centuries, but also blossomed.

Architecture found its expression in the numerous churches constructed in this period. Basilican and cruciform central-domed structures were used throughout this period. The cathedrals of St. John in Mastara, Avan, and St. Hripsime, as well as the churches of Odzun, St. Gayane and Aruj are all from this period. A number of architectural historians originally maintained that the Armenians were the first to translate into stone the dome on corner supports. This notion has been replaced by new opinions, which maintain that similar structures were designed in different countries at the same time. Nevertheless, the fact remains that Armenian architectural designs influenced Georgian, Caucasian Albanian, and Balkan church architecture. The main sculpture of this period are a few relief on places of worship, a good example being in the church of Ptghni detailing the founder of the church, an Amatuni *nakharar*, hunting a lion. There are only a few examples of painting, the most important of which is an illustrated gospel that subtly blends Byzantine and Sasanid art into a unique Armenian style.

Political and socioeconomic conditions in Persian Armenia were more favorable for literary activity, but the Byzantine side also contributed with the many Greek philosophical and scientific works, which were translated into Armenian.

In the field of science, seventh-century Armenia produced Anania Shirakatsi (Ananias of Shirak) who studied mathematics with a with a Greek teacher at Trebizond and, upon returning to Armenia, wrote books on arithmetic, chronology, weights and measures, the lunar cycle, geography, and cosmology. His information on the geography of Transcaucasia and Persia, the trade routes, and the weights and measures used in Persia has provided rare and valuable information for historians.

Literature, particularly original Armenian works in history, theology and philosophy, made this period a very important one; indeed the fifth century is referred to as the "Golden Age" of Armenian literature. The earliest historical work was probably that of Pavstos Buzand, whose *History* describes the events of the fourth century up to the partition of Armenia in 387. The author was a great supporter of the Mamikonians and provides valuable information on Persia and Byzantium. His work was either written in the fourth century in Greek and translated into Armenian in the next century, or, written in Armenian during the fifth century. David Anhaght wrote original philosophical treaties, as well as commentaries on Greek philosophical works. Eznik of Koghb wrote his treatise *Against the Sects* in which he refuted Zoroastrianism, Manicheanism, and Gnosticism. The historian Agatangeghos (Agathangelos) wrote the *History of the Conversion of Armenia*; Koriun composed the biography of his teacher, Mesrop Mashtots. The Battle of Avarayr and events from the period of 430 to 465 are chronicled in Eghishe's moving *History of Vardan*. The division of Armenia and the Armenian struggle against Zoroastrianism during the 384-485 period is described in the *History of Lazarus of Parpi* (Ghazar Parpetsi).

The most ambitious work of this period is that of Moses of Khoren, whose *History* begins with the origins of the Armenian people and ends in 440. There has been a lively scholarly debate on Khorenatsi's work, some scholars maintaining that this work could not possibly have been written in the fifth century and was composed some three centuries later, and others arguing that it is indeed from this period. In any event, despite its many chronological inaccuracies, the work is a wealth of information on the early period of Armenian history.

The immense literary and translation activities of this period served as the key ingredient in the rise of national consciousness and in the Armenian struggle against both Persian and Byzantine cultural and religious pressures. Moreover, it prepared the Armenians for an even more important challenge, the Arab invasions and the arrival of Islam.

8

A People of the Book
Armenia under Arab Domination
(640-884)

T HE TWO and a half centuries of Arab occupation of Armenia coincided with the Muslim conquest of the entire Middle East, North Africa, Spain, Sicily, and Cyprus. Europe, after its initial shock at the extent of Muslim successes, finally managed to halt their expansion by defeating the Arabs at Constantinople and Tours. Towards the end of this period, Europe attempted to resurrect the Roman Empire when Charlemagne was crowned as emperor. India saw the height of Sanskrit drama and the period of its finest stone architecture. It resisted initial Muslim attacks from Sind and established the short-lived Harasha kingdom. The T'ang dynasty firmly established itself as the new power in China. Japan, following the Taika Reform Edict, created its imperial government. In the Americas, the Mayan civilization was at its height, and the Tiahuanaco-Huari era began in Peru.

The Arab Invasions of Armenia

The Arab invasions, which began with raids in 640 and culminated in the domination of most of Armenia in the late eighth century, began for the first time to somewhat alter the ethnic composition of Greater Armenia. None of the previous invaders or conquerors had settled in Armenia. Rather, the earlier aggressors had come to loot or to establish political control over the Anatolian or Mesopotamian region, which separated their empires from those of their rivals to the east or to the west. They represented organized and centralized bureaucracies and empires, whose citizens were not willing to abandon their own homes and culture and settle in a foreign land. The

Arabs were different. Their forces were recruited from among many tribes. A number of these received fiefs from the central government and settled in Syria, Mesopotamia, Persia, and Armenia. For the next eight centuries, other nomads such as the Kurds, Turks, Mongols, and Turkmen would follow the Arab example. As they began settling in Armenia, the Armenians, in turn, were killed, converted or emigrated, a situation that significantly affected the history of Armenia in the modern period.

Unlike the speedy conquest of Persia, it took the Arabs half a century to subjugate Armenia. Armenia's mountains and its decentralized and partitioned hierarchy and administration assured pockets of long-standing resistance. The early raids began in 640 and succeeded in capturing Dvin. Theodore Rshtuni, who had been appointed by Emperor Heraclius as prince (*ishkhan*) of Armenia, and who, a year earlier had united Persian and Byzantine Armenian territories into a single entity, resisted further Arab raids for two years. In 644, a larger Arab army beat back an Armeno-Byzantine force. The Byzantines blamed Rshtuni for the defeat and attempted to replace him. At the same time, the Byzantine emperor, taking advantage of the Arab campaigns in Persia and Armenia, tried to impose the decisions of Chalcedon on the Armenian Church. Rshtuni and Catholicos Nerses III, known as the Builder, called a Church council at Dvin and, in 649, rejected these attempts.

The Umayyads and Armenia

In 650, the governor of Syria, Mu'awiyah, sent a large army, which penetrated most of Armenia. Rshtuni defended Vaspurakan and hoped for either Sasanid or Byzantine action against the Arabs. What Rshtuni faced, however, was continued Byzantine demands for acceptance of the canons of Chalcedon as a pre-condition for any assistance and the final collapse of the Sasanid Empire before the Arabs. In 652 Rshtuni, together with a number of *nakharars*, made the fateful decision to make peace with the Arabs.

The agreement with Mu'awiyah was favorable for the Armenians. Armenia was exempted from taxes for a number of years. In time of war Arabs could rely on the Armenian cavalry, which the Arabs agreed to maintain. No Arab governors would be posted to Armenia, and if Byzantium attacked, Arab troops would protect Armenia. Armenians would pay the *jizya* or poll tax, but as "a People of the Book" they were also guaranteed freedom of religion.

Rshtuni thus managed to obtain something from the Muslim ruler, which he had been unable to wrest from the Christian emperor of Byzantium.

The rise of this new force in the Middle East meant significant political changes for Armenia, not all of them to her detriment. With the Sasanid Empire destroyed and the Byzantine Empire pushed back west of the Euphrates, there would be, for the first time in one thousand years, no significant East-West struggle in or over Armenia. Moreover, for the first time since 387 Greater Armenia was united and its people considered a single group by their overlords. Unfortunately this also meant that the Armenian noble families such as the Bagratuni, Mamikonian, Gnuni, Kamsarakan, Artsruni, Amatuni, Siuni, and Rshtuni would struggle among themselves to gain the position of leader of the Armenians.

The treaty between Damascus and Rshtuni angered the Byzantines and their Armenian supporters. The Mamikonians and the Catholicos rejected the pact and joined a Byzantine force in ousting Rshtuni, who sought refuge in the mountains of Siunik. Mu'awiyah dispatched a new army, which then forced the Byzantines to retreat, and reinstated Rshtuni.

The death of Rshtuni in 654, combined with the crisis in the caliphate and the Sunni-Shi'i conflict, presented the Byzantines with a perfect opportunity to put the Mamikonians back in power. Catholicos Nerses returned as well and quickly completed the construction of the church of Zvartnots. But by 661, the struggle for the caliphate was over. The Umayyad family, led by Mu'awiyah, had defeated 'Ali and his followers (the Shi'i) and had established a dynasty. The Umayyads now forced the Catholicos and the Mamikonians to accept Arab suzerainty and to pay an annual tribute in gold in exchange for governing Armenia.

The Byzantines renewed their pressure to subjugate Armenia politically and ecclesiastically. Justinian II and his Khazar allies even invaded Armenia in the late seventh century but were defeated by an Armeno-Arab force. The Arabs had yet not begun to settle in Armenia, which remained largely autonomous for the time being. The Armenians built churches and fortresses. Agriculture expanded and trading increased substantially. Political power alternated between the Mamikonian and the Bagratuni families under Arab suzerainty, while the remaining *nakharars* continued to hold their ancestral lands. Contrary to popular belief, there was no religious persecution by the Muslims during this period. The Catholicos was free to travel and maintained his jurisdiction over the Caucasian Albanian Church, which had tried unsuccessfully to follow the example of the Georgians and unite with the Greek Church.

This peace and prosperity ended in the eighth century. The later Umayyads, and especially their successors, the 'Abbasids, formed large empires that required additional taxes. Taxes were increased throughout the Arab Empire, and centralized control tightened considerably in order to collect them. Continued Khazar and Byzantine incursions into Armenia made it obvious that Armenian leaders could not effectively defend the Armenian borders of the Arab Empire. Armenia was becoming a burden for the Umayyads, who, as stipulated in the agreement of 652, had to pay for the maintenance of the Armenian cavalry. Direct rule there would guarantee greater control and more taxes. In 701, therefore, the Umayyad caliph began the formal annexation of Armenia by sending his brother at the head of a large force.

Both the Byzantines and the Arabs reorganized the Armenian lands under their control. The Byzantines, having lost their domains in Greater Armenia, replaced the First and Second Armenia with military districts called *themes*, the main one of which was called Armeniakon. A general in charge of civil and military affairs headed each *theme*. Troops were recruited locally and were given land in return for their military service. The land could not be sold but, in turn, passed to their sons, who assumed responsibility for military duty. Eventually these *themes* were broken up into smaller ones and remained under the control of Byzantine military governors until the arrival of the Turks. The Umayyads created the province of "al-Arminiya," which included most of Greater Armenia, eastern Georgia, and Caucasian Albania (see map 14). Dvin served as the capital of the region and became the seat of the Muslim governor, or *ostikan*. Arabs installed garrisons in the major cities while Armenian *nakharars* maintained their autonomy under the *ostikan*, with no single family gaining dominance. Islamic law was enforced in Armenia and a number of religious and secular leaders were taken to Damascus as hostages. By 703, the *nakharars*, unhappy with such repressive policies, rebelled and solicited Byzantine help. The rebellion brought an even larger Arab force, which spared the Church, but decimated the ranks of the *nakharars* in a massacre at Nakhichevan.

By 705, the Umayyads, attacked by the Khazars and facing a disgruntled non-Arab Muslim population at home, had eased restrictions and once again permitted the Armenians a degree of autonomy. Some of the *nakharars* fought with the Arabs against the Khazars, and the next two decades was a period of close cooperation between the Arabs and Armenians. The Arabs were particularly lenient toward the Church, which had not participated in the rebellion and which, according to Islamic law, was viewed as the primary leader of the Armenians. This climate enabled the Church, for the first time, to organize the collection of its canons, a milestone in Armenian Church history.

The Paulicians

A primary motivation for the collection of the canons was probably the emergence of the Paulician heresy. The Paulician heresy began in the late sixth century, but gained momentum in the seventh century after the rise of Islam and the weakening of the power of established Churches. The Paulicians were the successors to the early Christian and Manichean non-conformists, who maintained a dualistic doctrine, that is, the belief in the universally antagonistic forces of good and evil. The Paulicians were opposed to the traditional social values of the establishment. They were against procreation, eating meat, holding property, and formed an underground movement, which led armed attacks against Armenian, Arab, and Byzantine religious and secular authorities. By the end of the seventh century, the Paulician movement had spread into parts of Armenia, Persia, and northern Mesopotamia and posed a major threat to civil authorities. In 719, Catholicos John of Odzun, supported by the *nakharars* and the Arabs, convened a council at Dvin at which he publicly ordered the repression of the Paulicians. Similar decrees were enacted at another council in 726. The Paulicians eventually left Armenia and established a republic northwest of the Euphrates where they remained as a thorn in the side of Byzantium. The year 726 also witnessed the start of the century-long debate over icons in the Byzantine Empire, a crisis, which for a time freed the Armenian Church from further interference by the Greek Church.

The 'Abbasids and Armenia

In 750 an event took place in the Muslim world, which brought in a new order and changed its relations with Armenia: the 'Abbasid revolution. Unlike the Umayyads, the 'Abbasids formed a truly Islamic, rather than simply an Arab, Empire. Persians, Turks, and even Christian converts, as well as Arabs could now hold high office. The capital was moved from the Arab center of Damascus to Baghdad, and the administration became more imperial. Fiscal demands increased taxation, which had already been on the rise during the late Umayyad period.

The Armenians took advantage of the confusion in Damascus, staged a minor rebellion, and sought aid from Byzantium against the Arabs. The rivalry between the Mamikonians and the Bagratunis, as well as Byzantium's iconoclastic controversy, thwarted the success of the uprising and the 'Abbasids soon reestablished Arab control over Armenia. Neither the Bagratunis, viewed by the 'Abbasids as pro-Umayyad, nor the Mamikonians, viewed as pro-Byzantine, gained the immediate trust of Baghdad. Reduction of trade, the virtual disappearance of silver, heavy taxes, and the maintenance of the Armenian cavalry, which now fell to the Armenians, forced some Armenian *nakharars*, like the Amatuni, to immigrate to Byzantium. By the third quarter of the eighth century, the Bagratunis, however, had managed to mend relations with the 'Abbasids and had won their recognition as the leaders of the Armenians.

The Mamikonians, the Artsrunis, and the Byzantines were not pleased with this rapprochement and, in 774, incited a rebellion in Armenia in which a number of Arab tax collectors were killed. The Bagratunis cautioned the other *nakharars* against provoking Baghdad. Their advice was ignored, however, and an Armenian force was assembled to face the Arabs. The Armenian defeat at Bagrevand in 775 cost the lives of most of the ruling generation of *nakharars* and critically weakened a number of Armenian houses such as the Rshtuni, Gnuni, and the Mamikonian. In fact, the latter never again played a significant role in the history of Armenia. The Bagratunis, on the other hand, retained and enhanced their position as leaders of the Armenians.

The reign of Harun al-Rashid (786-809) completed the consolidation of the 'Abbasid Empire by the end of the eighth century and signified another major change for Armenia and the Arab world. For the first time, Arab soldiers and merchants were actively encouraged to settle and establish new communities in Arab-held territories, including Armenia. Trade spread Islam to the coastal cities of Africa and south Asia. Baghdad appointed Arab families to rule in or to create colonies in Armenia and other parts of Transcaucasia. Barda'

(Partav), Tiflis, Gandzak, Dvin, Nakhichevan, and Diarbekir (Diyarbakr) became Arab administrative centers, governed by *emirs*. Intermarriages and forced, as well as genuine conversions took place, and some of the Arab clans, such as the Shaybani and Jahhaf, even assimilated into the ranks of the Armenian *nakharars*. The province of *al-Arminiya* was now divided into Armenia, Georgia, and Arran (Caucasian Albania). The Arab *emirs* were no longer temporary governors or commanders of garrisons, but like the Kaysites, who settled near Lake Van, made parts of Armenia their new home. Fortunately for Armenia, these Arab emirates never included a majority of the population, nor were they united.

The death of Harun al-Rashid began the long decline of the caliphate and the central Arab authority. During the decline the emirates acted independently of Baghdad, the *ostikan*, was forced to move from Dvin to Barda' on the easternmost corner of Armenia. This fragmentation of Arab authority provided the opportunity for the resurgence of Bagratuni leadership under Ashot Msaker ["the Meat-Eater"] (790-826).

The Rise of the Bagratunis

At the start of the ninth century, Ashot expanded his domains at the expense of the weakened Mamikonians and Kamsarakans. He clashed with a number of independent *emirs* who had broken with the caliphate and was rewarded by Baghdad with the title of prince of Armenia. His uncle, meanwhile, established the Bagratuni house of Iberia (Georgia). Upon Ashot's death in 826, his oldest son, Bagrat assumed the title of prince of princes, while his younger son was named *sparapet*. In the meantime, in Vaspurakan, the Artsrunis were also creating a power base, while the princes of Siunik made a marriage alliance with Babak, a Mazdakite Persian, who in 816 had rebelled against Baghdad and who had established himself in parts of Artsakh between Arran and Azerbaijan. It is important to note that some Armenian houses allied themselves with Muslims against Baghdad or even other Armenians. The same was true of the Muslims, who would occasionally ally with Armenians against other Muslims. In Baghdad there was internal strife over the succession between al-Ma'mun, the son of a Persian wife of Harun, and al-Amin, the son of a Turkish wife. Al-Ma'mun was eventually the victor and was succeeded by his brother, al-Mu'tasim.

In 836 Afshin, a Muslim Persian commander, was sent by al-Mu'tasim to capture Babak. Afshin promised the Armenians and the Persians a degree of autonomy and tax remissions if they cooperated against Babak. Babak was betrayed and captured one year later. A number of his followers then gathered around another leader, Mazyar, and started a social revolution against the Persian landowners of the Caspian region that had converted to Islam. Afshin, who had gained influence in Azerbaijan, was accused of backing the rebels and, in 841, was killed by the caliph. Eventually a new commander was appointed in Azerbaijan from the Sajid family, a clan that would have a major impact on Armenia. It is at this time that social unrest in Persia spread into Armenia with the appearance of a group of heretics known as the Tondrakians. The Tondrakians appear to have been either remnants of the Paulicians, who had fled Byzantine persecutions after the fall of their republic, followers of Babak, or lower classes of society influenced by either group.

In the meantime, al-Mu'tasim had begun to employ Turkish slaves and mercenaries for his main army. As with the largely German Praetorian Guard that assumed increasing power in Rome, this policy, until the arrival of the Persian Buyids in the early tenth century, resulted in the domination of the caliphate by the Turks. Rivalry among Turkish, Arab, and Persian factions forced al-Mu'tasim, in 836, to move the capital north, to Samarra, on the Tigris' eastern bank, where it remained until 870.

In 847 the Turks installed al-Mutawakkil as the new caliph at Samarra. The new caliph employed the most severe measures to restore the power of the caliphate. The translation of Greek philosophical works was halted, and Jews and Christians were persecuted.

It is against this backdrop that a second major rebellion in Armenia occurred in 850-851, this time against al-Mutawakkil's taxes and repressive policies. A new *ostikan* was sent to Armenia but was refused entry. Instead Bagrat Bagratuni, the son of Ashot Msaker, sent an embassy with the required taxes to the caliph himself, signifying that, although vassals of the caliph, Armenia would keep its autonomous status. The caliph viewed this act as a rebellion. The *ostikan*'s army invaded Armenia but was defeated by Bagrat, who had allied himself with the Artsrunis of Vaspurakan. The caliph then sent a new army. The Artsrunis sent gifts, which were delivered by the mother of the *nakharar* of Vaspurakan, Lady Hripsime, who succeeded in halting the Arab invasion of her domains. Bagrat had to fight alone and was soon captured and sent to Samarra where he was killed (852). The Armenian population then rose up and killed the Arab general, forcing the Arab army out of Bagratuni domains in Taron. The rebellion united most of the *nakharars* against the Muslims. The caliph sent a large army to crush the rebellion and to subdue all the *nakharars* once and for all. Smbat Bagratuni, the brother of Bagrat and the *sparapet*, refused to join the rebels, possibly to signal the caliph that, as the new leader of the Armenians, he was a loyal subject and willing to compromise. Al-Mutawakkil would accept no compromises, however. The Arab army, under the command of the Turkish general Bugha, ravaged Armenia, Georgia and Caucasian Albania. By 853 Bugha captured most of the important *nakharars*, including Smbat Bagratuni, and brought them to Samarra. All of the *nakharars*, with the exception of Smbat, in order to save their lives, agreed to apostatize and were allowed to return home after the death of al-Mutawakkil. Smbat alone refused to convert; he remained in Samarra where he died soon after.

Al-Mutawakkil's campaigns were the last attempt of the caliphate at direct control of Armenia. His murder at the hands of his Turkish troops in 861 hastened the further decline of the 'Abbasids. During the captivity of the *nakharars*, the Arab *emirs* were free to expand their domains. At the same time, Byzantium had finally revived under Basil I (867-886) of the Macedonian dynasty. After their return, the *nakharars*, especially the Bagratuni and Artsruni, continued their struggle against the Arab *emirs*. The major clashes occurred in the southern regions, mainly in Taron, Sasun, Vaspurakan, and Mokk, where the Armenians held their own against the Arabs.

Arts, Literature, Architecture

The two most important Armenian histories of this period are by Bishop Sebeos and Ghevond. Sebeos provides valuable information on Byzantium and Persia in the late sixth and early seventh centuries. He then describes the birth of Islam and the Arab invasions of Persia, Armenia, and the Byzantine Empire to 661. Ghevond's history details the Arab domination of Armenia from 661 to 788. One result of the Armeno-Arab struggles of this period was the birth of the popular oral epic the *Daredevils of Sasun* and its hero, David of Sasun. The story, which was recorded centuries later, depicts the

Bagratunis, led by David, the Rshtunis, in the figure of uncle Toros, and Msr-melik, representing the Muslim leader. Bugha and the Arstrunis are also represented. The victory of David against the stronger forces of the Arabs represents a sort of David and Goliath struggle between good and evil.

In the field of architecture, the church of Zvartnots (644-652) is a perfect example of a niche-buttressed square with four lobes, known as a quatrefoil. Unlike other such structures, Zvartnots had a circular ambulatory with a square chamber outside the circle. Although the church was destroyed in the tenth century, its remains are the primary examples of the sculpture of this period in the form of relief of the workers and planners of the structure. In the field of painting, an illustrated gospel dated 862 and commissioned by the Artsruni family, is noteworthy for its highly stylized manner.

By the late ninth century, following more than two centuries of Arab incursions, Armenians still formed the majority of the population, and the Arab *emirs* had difficulty maintaining their holdings in Armenia. The many mountains and valleys of Armenia controlled by regional *nakharars* served as multiple havens of Armenian autonomy. The son of Smbat, Ashot Bagratuni, became the rallying force and continued to exert pressure on the Arab *emirs*. The prestige of the Bagratunis was on the rise within Armenia and both the weakened caliphate and the emerging Macedonian dynasty in Byzantium realized the value of an Armenian alliance. Conditions were, therefore, right for the emergence of a new Armenian kingdom.

9

A Land of Many Crowns
The Bagratid Dynasty and the Armenian Medieval Kingdoms
(884-1045)

THE ALMOST two centuries of Bagratuni (Bagratid) rule in parts of Greater Armenia coincided with the time when the Carolingian Empire disintegrated, and separate states began to form in England, France, and Germany. Romanesque architecture was developing, and the monastic reforms initiated at Cluny made monasteries vital centers of religious and intellectual life. Europe experienced the height of the Viking raids. The *reconquista* began in Spain, while the Normans prepared to conquer England. Soon after, the Greek Orthodox and Roman Catholic Churches split. Japan and China began the woodblock printing of books. The Sung dynasty ruled in China and in Japan the *bushido* code brought forth the samurai. Lady Murasaki wrote the world's first reputed novel, The *Tale of Genji*. Arab and Persian science reached its zenith with Avicenna. Sufism became a major literary and religious force in the Middle East. The first Russian State was founded in Kiev and was soon after converted to Christianity by missionaries from Byzantium. Islam penetrated sub-Saharan Africa, while the kingdoms of Ghana and Kanem emerged there as well. The Muslims conquered northern India. The Incas settled in the Cuzco valley of Peru, the classical Mayan civilization collapsed, and the Toltecs replaced the Olmecs in Mexico.

The Revival of the Armenian Kingdom

In the last half of the ninth century, Armenia was experiencing a power vacuum. The Byzantines and the 'Abbasids were too preoccupied with internal and external affairs to focus their attention on Armenia, but there were few *nakharar* houses strong enough to take advantage of the situation. Some had left Armenia, while others had died out or were weakened by their own internal feuds. The *apostasy* of the *nakharars* at Samarra, and their eight-year absence from Armenia, further weakened the political structure.

Into this vacuum stepped Ashot Bagratuni, the son of Smbat, the martyr of Samarra. Immediately upon his father's death, he assumed the title of *tanuter* and *sparapet* of the Bagratuni house, and became the rallying point for Armenian resistance against Arab domination.

Ashot was soon able to increase both Bagratuni power and prestige. Between 855 and 862 he expanded his domains by annexing both the Mamikonian and Kamsarakan holdings and through marriage alliances with the Bagratids of Georgia and the Artsrunis of Vaspurakan. Thus, the northern, southern, and western parts of Greater Armenia were either controlled by or allied with the Bagratids. In addition, Ashot made a point of maintaining friendly relations with the lords of Siunik in the east. With the residence of the Catholicos within his borders, Ashot also enjoyed the crucial support of the Church.

Ashot and the later Bagratids faced several internal and external obstacles, however, which prevented them from ever reuniting all of Greater Armenia. The first were the Siunis and the Artsrunis, the only other *nakharar* houses of any strength left in Armenia, who often withheld their support or actively allied against the Bagratids. The second, and more immediate, internal impediments were the Arab *ostikan* and the Arab emirates. The *ostikan* alternated his residence between Barda' and Dvin, thus driving a wedge between the Bagratids on one side and Georgia and Siunik on the other. The emirates occupied the central lands of Greater Armenia between the Bagratids and Artsrunis. Ashot and his successors were thus rarely able to link Armenian-held lands into a united front against the Arabs. Moreover, the important cities of Dvin and Nakhichevan, among others, remained under Arab control for most of the period.

External forces posed a more overt threat to the Bagratids. With the rise of the Macedonian dynasty in Byzantium in the second half of the ninth century, Constantinople once again began to play an intrusive role in the affairs of Armenia. Their common Christianity—and, in the case of the Macedonian emperors, common Armenian ancestry—did little to foster a strong Armeno-Byzantine alliance against the Arabs. Rather, the Byzantines maintained their policy of demanding theological concessions and control of Armenian lands in return for military aid. Moreover, the steady decline of the 'Abbasid caliphate allowed the rise of minor Muslim dynasties on the southern and southeastern borders of Armenia and periodically threatened its security.

Although Ashot transferred his title of *sparapet* to his younger brother, there is little doubt that he maintained full control over the *nakharar* army, which at that time still had some semblance of unity. To further secure his position, Ashot renewed the alliance with Byzantium and, at least officially, approved of a dialogue on Greek Orthodox and Armenian Church unity. The 'Abbasid caliph al-Musta'in saw in the growing power of the Bagratids a possible check to the increasing independence of the Arab emirates. In 862 he conferred on Ashot the title of prince of princes and, according to some historians, the power to levy taxes. Although the title may have included suzerainty over Georgia and other parts of the Caucasus, the presence of the *ostikan* in Barda' meant that, in all probability, Ashot's rule never extended beyond parts of Greater Armenia. The Armenian Church, supported by Ashot, once again assumed jurisdiction over the Caucasian Albanian Church. Ashot was already acknowledged as ruler of Armenia by most of the *nakharars* and the Church when, in 884, the caliph al-Mu'tamid sent him a royal crown. Ashot, the fifth Bagratid prince to bear that name, was thus crowned King Ashot I. Shortly after, the Byzantine emperor, Basil I, in order to maintain his influence on the new dynasty, sent a crown as well. For the moment, Armenia once more possessed a kingdom and a dynasty.

During the next six years Ashot not only extended his political influence over the emirates, but also enabled the Georgian Bagratids to consolidate their control in Iberia (see map 15). Ashot gained control of Dvin but did not move his court there, preferring to remain in his stronghold at Bagaran. This decision had serious consequences, for it periodically left Dvin and the center of Armenia unprotected and, at times, in Arab hands.

Ashot's death, in 890, immediately revealed a number of problems, which were to constantly plague the Bagratids. The five hundred years of partitions and decentralization had resulted in political fragmentation and the loss of a framework for a single state. Furthermore, the large *nakharar* houses had, since the sixth century, broken up into smaller branches that fought among themselves. In addition, Nakhichevan and the Arax valley, which were in Muslim

hands, separated the Siunik lands in the east from the Artsruni territories in the south. Dvin, Tiflis, Nakhichevan, and other cities in the
center thus continued to remain under Arab control. Moreover, the
emirs did not always obey the 'Abbasid caliphs; a problem that at
times aided, and at others, hurt the Armenians and the Bagratids.

After Ashot's death, his son, Smbat I (890-914), assumed the
throne and immediately faced many of the same internal and external problems of his father. Lacking the personal authority of his
father, Smbat could not totally command the Church or the *nakharars*, particularly the Artsrunis; even his uncle refused to recognize
his nephew. The Artsrunis, stating that in the past the Bagratunis
had been no more than the traditional coronants of the Arshakuni
monarchs, now questioned the legitimacy of the Bagratunis as
kings. In the early part of his rule, however, Smbat managed to keep
the support of Byzantium, his Georgian relatives, and the Catholicos, as well as Mohammad, the Sajid ruler of Azerbaijan, who was
the *ostikan*.

Rival Kingdoms in Armenia

The latter part of Smbat's rule was a failure. Mohammad attacked
Armenia. Dvin and Nakhichevan were taken and the Catholicos captured. Smbat managed to conclude a peace agreement with
Mohammad and ransom the Catholicos, who left for the Holy See in
Dvin, which was now in Muslim hands. Although Caucasian Albania remained loyal, Siunik and the Artsrunis at Vaspurakan made a
number of friendly overtures to Mohammad. The latter took advantage of the situation to invade Armenia once again. Smbat's wife
and the royal treasury were captured. In exchange for his wife's release, Smbat was forced to send his eldest son Ashot as hostage, to
give his niece to become one of Mohammad's wives, and to pay
tribute to Mohammad's son, the governor of Dvin. Mohammad then
attacked Vaspurakan and made the Artsrunis his vassals, taking the
brother of the *nakharar* as hostage.

The situation improved for a brief period when the caliph
al-Muktafi, fearing Sajid power, released Armenia from Sajid control. The Siunik and Vaspurakan leaders then quickly renewed their
allegiance to the Bagratids. The picture changed radically, however,
when Mohammad's brother, Yusuf, became the *ostikan* in 901. Taking advantage of the death of Mohammad, Smbat requested direct
vassalage to the caliph thus bypassing the *ostikan*. Yusuf ignored

the caliph's supremacy and invaded Bagratid territory. Baghdad's inaction resulted in an agreement in 903, by which Smbat accepted Yusuf's authority and received a crown for his submission. Smbat's position weakened further when he involved himself in a dispute between a Georgian prince and the Bagratid king of Georgia, as well as in a dispute between the Siunis and the Artsrunis, thus alienating both houses. Taking advantage of the division among the Christians, Yusuf demanded additional taxes beyond the tribute paid by Smbat to Baghdad. To weaken Smbat further, Yusuf, in 908, granted a crown to Gagik Artsruni, creating an autonomous kingdom in the south. Bagratid Armenia was on the road to fragmentation. A year later, the combined Muslim and Artsruni force attacked Smbat's territory and wreaked havoc on the land. Smbat sought aid from Byzantium and the *caliph*, but both were distracted by domestic problems. Yusuf captured and killed Armenian princes, including a son and a nephew of Smbat. To stop the bloodshed, Smbat surrendered, was tortured and crucified.

Smbat's death served a purpose, however. The cruelty of Yusuf towards Smbat and other *nakharars* cost him the support of Gagik Artsruni and other Armenian leaders who now joined Smbat's son Ashot II, known as *erkat* (iron), and drove the Muslims out of most of Greater Armenia. The Georgian Bagratids also came back to the fold, and Ashot II was crowned in 914. Ashot's cousin, however, remained loyal to Yusuf, who installed him as governor of Dvin. Immediately thereafter, the Byzantines, who were troubled by the events in Armenia, offered their assistance in removing the Muslim threat for good. Ashot II went to Constantinople where a Christian union against the common enemy was discussed. In 915 Ashot returned with a Byzantine army, and although he was unable to take Dvin, he extended his influence considerably. Yusuf's rebellion against the *caliph* and his arrest in 919 removed the most dangerous Bagratid foe and at the same time ended the autonomy of Ashot's cousin in Dvin. Gagik Artsruni in Vaspurakan and Ashot II began an era of reconstruction and rebuilding in Greater Armenia.

As noted, a major problem for the Bagratids was the attitude of Byzantium, which occasionally gave aid but demanded political and religious submission in return. Ashot II was not spared either. No sooner had he mended his relations with the new *ostikan* than the Byzantines dispatched forces to destabilize Armenia. In the meantime Yusuf was released from jail, resumed his position of *ostikan*, and began new attacks on his immediate neighbors, Siunik and

Vaspurakan. Ashot and his loyal *nakharars* managed to defeat both the Arabs and the Greeks. The last years of Ashot's rule were peaceful. Ironically, both Ashot and Yusuf died in 929, and a new era began for Armenia when the Sajid interlude in Azerbaijan ended.

Ashot's brother Abas assumed the leadership of the Bagratids in 929 and ruled until 953. The rise of the various Kurdo-Iranian dynasties in Azerbaijan and parts of Armenia, such as the Rawaddids, combined with the constant threat from Byzantium and the Arab *emirs* in Mesopotamia, kept Abas busy. He chose to stay in his own domains and strengthen his defenses from his capital, the fortress of Kars. Gagik of Vaspurakan now became the most powerful Armenian leader. A number of Catholicoi were chosen by him and stayed at his court, mainly because Dvin remained in Muslim hands. Vaspurakan became a major political and cultural center and the island of Aghtamar in Lake Van became the Holy See of Armenia. By the mid-tenth century, thanks to Gagik's efforts, Armenia had restored much of its former political and economic position.

The reign of Ashot III (953-977) began the seventy-year apex of Bagratid rule. Following the death of Gagik of Vaspurakan, Ashot became the undisputed leader of the Armenians. The Catholicos came to Ashot's new capital at Ani and crowned him king. Ashot, in turn, supported the Church and sponsored many new edifices. Ashot made sure that the Caucasian Albanian Church once again accepted the authority of the Armenian Church. He also managed to capture Dvin. Armenia was relatively powerful and united, and when the Byzantine emperor, John Tzimiskes, arrived with an army in 974, he was forced to withdraw. Ashot felt so secure that he granted his brother the fortress of Kars and permitted him to use the title of king. He also gave the region north of Lake Sevan to his son, who soon assumed the title of King of Lori. This pattern was unfortunately repeated in Vaspurakan, which was divided among the heirs of Gagik. By the last quarter of the tenth century Siunik had also become a kingdom (see map 15).

Such proliferation of titles and crowns posed little danger provided that a strong ruler controlled Armenia from Ani. In fact, the granting of titles may have stopped squabbles and satisfied those who otherwise might have plotted against the kingdom, allied with enemies, or rebelled after the death of the king. Problems arose, of course, during the reigns of weak kings or when outside pressures became overwhelming. In addition, bishops in these "kingdoms" occasionally chose to ignore the authority of the Catholicos and styled themselves as Catholicos.

Following the death of Ashot III, his son, Smbat II, assumed the throne and had to deal with his uncle at Kars and the Muslims. Dvin once again changed hands, but Smbat spent his years expanding the city of Ani, which became a major urban center with a cathedral and many churches. With the help of the Georgian Bagratids, Smbat reconciled with his uncle and assumed the leadership of the Armenian Bagratids. The rivalry among the Muslim *emirs* also enabled Smbat to resist Muslim advances and to expand his domains.

Gagik I Bagratuni, not to be confused with Gagik of Vaspurakan, assumed the throne in 990. Vaspurakan was too fragmented to challenge him, and Gagik enjoyed the support or submission of all his clan who ruled in various parts of Armenia, as well as other *nakharars*. Unfortunately Byzantium, under Basil II, took control of western Georgia and was thus close enough to Armenia to cause future intrigue.

The Collapse of the Bagratids

The death of Gagik in 1020 began the rapid decline and collapse of the Bagratids. The potential forces for the destruction of the kingdom were there long before, but had been kept in check by the authority of strong Bagratid rulers. The rivalry between Gagik's sons resulted in the partitioning of the kingdom. All this came at a time when the Turks appeared on the scene, and Basil II was extending his empire by annexing weaker neighbors. The Byzantines had already taken southwestern Armenia when, in 1022, the old king of Vaspurakan, Senekerim, who was childless, willed his kingdom to Basil. The Bagratid king of Ani, Hovhannes-Smbat, feeling insecure, also left his kingdom to Basil. After his death in 1042, the pro-Byzantine faction tried to hand the city over, but Gagik II and his supporters resisted and Ani remained independent. Gagik ruled for three years during which the *emir* of Dvin, the Byzantines, and his kinsmen from Lori fought him. He went to Constantinople to plead his case but was forced to abdicate. Thus, in 1045, the last major Armenian kingdom in historic Armenia came to an end. The Byzantines took Ani, and in 1064 the Bagratid kingdom of Kars was annexed as well. Only two mountainous kingdoms and a principality remained autonomous: the kingdom of Siunik (to 1166), the kingdom of Lori (to ca. 1100) and the principality of Khachen in Karabagh (to ca. 1450).

Armenians in the Byzantine Empire

Armenians had settled in the eastern parts of the Roman Empire prior to the Christian era and had risen to prominent positions. Even the Emperor Heraclius is reputed to have been from Armenian descent. Although Justinian began forcibly transplanting Armenian families to Byzantium, their numbers were very few. Armenians began to enter Byzantium in large numbers in the late sixth century, when Red Vardan Mamikonian, together with his followers, and the Catholicos John II, fled to Constantinople after the unsuccessful rebellion against the Sasanids. Vardan and his retinue reportedly entered the Byzantine army and settled in Pergamum. The reign of Maurice and the second partition of Armenia forcefully removed thousands of Armenians to the Byzantine Empire, a large group of whom settled in Cyprus. In the second half of the seventh century, Armenian Paulicians, driven from their homes in Armenia, settled in Byzantine territory, mainly in Pontus. After the Arab invasions and until the tenth century, more Armenians *nakharars* with their entire families migrated to Byzantium, some settling in Cilicia. The decline and fall of the Bagratid kingdom in the eleventh century brought more *nakharars* to Cilicia, as well as Constantinople and other urban centers of the empire. More would arrive following the later Turko-Mongol invasions. The Armenians were to become an important commercial and administrative force in Constantinople following the fall of Byzantium to the Turks.

Historians consider the Armenians as one of the most influential groups in the multi-national Byzantine Empire. Armenians engaged in trade, administration and farming and they were a dominant element in the army. According to Procopius, there were sixteen generals in Justinian's army alone whose Armenian contingents were known for their valor. Many Armenians held important positions in the army during the eighth through the eleventh centuries. A number of them such as Petronas, Curcuas, and Musele were responsible for Byzantine victories against the Arabs and other invaders. Armenian military leaders were named provincial governors, while others became the power behind the throne and were instrumental in elevating a number of emperors. Not only Hercalius was of Armenian origin, but the Macedonian dynasty, according to most Byzantinists was of Armenian origin as well. The tenure of that dynasty (9th to the 11th centuries) is considered the apex of Armenian dominance in the political and military structure of the empire. Armenians emperors, generals, and military contingents had their greatest military successes against the Arabs, the Slavs, and Bulgars. Ironically, it was this same Armenian dynasty which was chiefly responsible for the breakup of the Bagratid kingdom. However, as will be seen in the next chapter, they were also indirectly responsible for the rise of a new Armenian State in Cilicia.

Armenians played an important role in the intellectual life of Byzantium as well. The director of the University of Constantinople during its height was Leo the Philosopher (also known as Leo the Mathematician). Leo's uncle, John the Grammarian, was another important Armenian scholar.

Trade, Art, Architecture and Learning

The Bagratid kings did not mint any coins. 'Abbasid and Byzantine coins were widely used in Armenia. Armenia at this time exported manufactured goods, silver, copper, iron, arsenic, borax, and salt. Dried fish was exported to Mesopotamia. Falcons were sent as tribute to the caliph, and Armenian horses and mules were highly prized. Armenia had forests, and walnut wood was exported to Baghdad, as were furs and leather goods. Armenian carpets were also in demand at this period, especially those made from goat hair. The textile industry thrived, mainly due to Armenian dyes. The wine-red dye, referred to by the Arabs as *qirmiz*, had been especially valued since antiquity, and was made from the dried shells of the cochineal, an insect that feeds on the roots of a particular plant growing on the slopes of Mount Ararat. In addition, Armenia produced silk in the Artsakh, Siunik, and Ganja regions.

The Bagratid era produced a number of historians: Aristakes Lastivertsi described Armeno-Byzantine relations and the Tondrakian movement of the later Bagratid period, ending his history with a detailed account of the Seljuk invasion of Ani and the Battle of Manzikert (1071). John Mamikonian's *History of Taron* was written in the style of a medieval romance and focuses on the history of the House of the Mamikonians. Catholicos John Draskhanakertetsi (Catholicos Hovhannes V, known as the "historian") wrote a *History of Armenia*. One of the most valuable works (due to the accuracy of its chronology) of this period is Stephen of Taron's

(Stepan Taronetsi, also known as Asoghik) *History*. Thomas Arts-runi's *History of the House of the Artsrunik* details conditions in Vaspurakan during the reign of King Gagik Artsruni. Movses Dask-hurantsi's (some sources refer to him Kaghangatvatsi) *The History of the Caucasian Albanians* is the only existing source in any language on this people, who were eventually assimilated by Armenians, Persians, Arabs, and Turks.

The Bagratid period was the most prolific era of Armenian Church architecture. In fact, most of the surviving churches in present-day Armenia are from this period. The Bagratid kings, wealthy merchants, and *nakharars* supported the construction of numerous of churches in Ani, some of which have survived. The churches on Lake Sevan and the cathedrals of Kars, Argina, and Ani, as well as the monasteries of Marmashen and Khdzkunk, were completed. The construction of the monasteries of Tatev, Sanahin, Haghpat, Geghard, and Makaravank began in this period and continued for the next two centuries. The castle-fortress and church of Amberd and the church of Bdjni are also from this period. One of the most impressive architectural monuments is the Cathedral of Holy Cross in Aghtamar, commissioned by Gagik Artsruni. This jewel of architecture and relief sculpture contains impressive wall paintings representing Adam and Eve, the Annunciation, and the Last Judgement. Other masterpieces of relief sculpture are represented in the numerous *khachkars*, or stone-lace crosses, which began to appear in the ninth century and would reach their zenith in the fourteenth century.

The illuminated manuscripts of this period represent a number of schools. They either stress the decoration at the expense of the human form, or emphasize the natural appearance of the human form, as illustrated in the Ejmiatsin Gospel of 989. The most unique example of manuscript illumination is the Gospel of Moghni, which, used various past and contemporary style and, arrived at a distinct Armenian style. By the eleventh century, Byzantine influence had begun to make inroads in a number of larger miniatures commissioned by the Bagratids, as seen in the Trebizond Gospel at the Mkhitarist Library in Venice and the Gospel of King Gagik of Kars.

The Bagratids, who claimed lineage from the Biblical King David and who occasionally wore turbans and adopted Arab names, restored the Armenian kingdom and, for a time, managed to balance Arab, Byzantine, and internal Armenian pressures. They kept parts of Armenia independent and prevented the establishment of major

Muslim settlements in Armenia. It was the unrelenting intrusive policy of the Byzantines, however, which finally destroyed the Bagratids, as well as the Artsrunis. Ironically, Byzantium's policy toward Armenia contributed to the doom of its own empire, for with the disappearance of the Armenian buffer zone and the inability of the Byzantines to replace the Armenian armies, the way was left open for the Seljuk Turks to penetrate the region (see chapter 11). Ani fell in 1064 and Kars followed a year later. Finally, in 1071, the Seljuks defeated the Byzantine emperor in Manzikert and historic Armenia soon fell under Turkish rule. The Georgian Bagratids, however, continued to flourish and ruled parts of Georgia until the nineteenth century.

10

East Meets West
The Cilician Kingdom of Armenia
(c. 1075-1375)

THE CILICIAN period, culminating in the establishment of a new Armenian kingdom in 1199, represents a unique chapter in the history of the Armenian people. For the first time Armenians created an independent state in lands outside their historic homeland. It is also the first time that Armenians were in a region with direct access to the sea and came into close contact with the emerging nations in Western Europe and the Roman Catholic Church.

Cilicia is a wide plain on the Mediterranean coast of Asia Minor. Surrounded by three mountain chains (the Taurus to the northwest, the Anti-Taurus to the northeast and the Amanus to the east), Cilicia offered a secure enclave, for the narrow mountain passes, most famous of which was the Cilician Gates, were easily defended against invaders. The coastline and the navigable rivers, as well as a number of trade centers made the region ideal for those Armenians who were forced to leave Armenia in the eleventh century.

Armenians in Cilicia

Cilicia had been under Byzantine control since the mid-tenth century. After re-conquering it from the Arabs, the Byzantines had expelled the Muslims and had brought in Christians, especially Armenians from Lesser Armenia, to repopulate the land. Following the Byzantine and Turkish invasions of Armenia, more Armenians arrived in Cilicia, bringing their families and retinues. After the fall of the Bagratid kingdom, the Byzantine Empire assigned a number of Armenian military commanders to Cilicia. The Byzantines gave them the duty of protecting this corridor to the heartland of Byzantium from Turkish and Arab attacks. Having lost their own fiefs, being somewhat distant from the center of Byzantium, and protected by mountains, a number of Armenian lords were able to achieve some level of autonomy.

Among these chieftains, two houses, the Rubenids and Hetumids, emerged as dominant forces and, by the end of the eleventh century, rivaled each other for the control of the plain. The Rubenids, who later claimed to be related to the Bagratunis, challenged Byzantine authority early on and controlled the mountainous region east of the Cilician Gates, with the fortress of Vahka as their headquarters. The Hetumids remained loyal vassals of Byzantium and maintained the fortresses of Lambron and Baberon as their power base. The Rubenids soon sought to extend their control southward to the lower plain with its trade routes and ports. This aggressive policy brought them into conflict with the Hetumids. It is at this time that an event occurred which helped Rubenid ambitions, the arrival of the West European forces of the First Crusade (1096-1099).

The Crusades and the Armenians

The Crusades were an outlet for the political, religious and economic ambitions of the West. In 1010, the Fatimid ruler of Egypt, al-Hakim, abrogated the spirit of the agreement reached in 807 by Harun al-Rashid and Charlemagne, permitting pilgrimages to Christian sites in Jerusalem. Al-Hakim's persecution of Christians and the destruction of many churches, combined with armed conflicts among Muslim adventurers for the control of Syria and Jerusalem, made pilgrimages extremely difficult. The Seljuk conquest of Jerusalem in the late eleventh century actually brought some order, but the years of suffering had left a negative impression in Europe.

In 1095, the Byzantines, who were under attack by the Seljuks, asked Europe for military aid. One of their goals was the restoration of Jerusalem to Christian control. Since the Greek and Roman churches had split in 1054, a crusade into former Byzantine lands would give Rome leverage in any future discussions of terms for a reunion. Byzantium's call, therefore, was too tempting for Pope Urban II to resist. Moreover, the Papacy had been involved in a bitter struggle with the German emperors over the leadership of Christian

Europe. If the pope could gather a large army against the enemies of Christianity, his position would become paramount.

In 1095 in Claremont, France, the pope called for a holy war. The result was the creation of a large army of lords and knights, clerics, and adventurers. Kings trying to establish order found the crusade an outlet to rid themselves of troublesome groups. Younger and landless members of noble families who hoped to gain fiefs in the Middle East embraced the cause, while others sought financial rewards from supplies and commerce. For the pious, the assurance of a plenary papal indulgence was the primary motivation.

Neither the Muslims nor the Byzantines were prepared for such a group of devout Christians, able warriors, and plunderers. The Byzantine emperor immediately punished any looting and reminded the knights that any territory recovered was to revert to his control. The Muslims were distracted by a Shi'i-Sunni struggle between the Fatimids of Egypt and the forces of the Caliph in Baghdad, and by the divisive ambitions of local emirs, who aspired to independent rule. Upon arrival in Cilicia, the corridor to Syria and Jerusalem, the Crusaders sought out Armenians as guides, purveyors of supplies or soldiers.

By 1099 Jerusalem had fallen to the Christians, who massacred the Muslim and Jewish inhabitants. The death of the papal legate left the region in the hands of the feudal barons, who soon carved out the Crusader or Latin states of Tripoli, Edessa, Antioch, and Jerusalem. Neither the Byzantines nor the Arabs were strong enough to resist the newcomers. The Rubenids allied themselves with the Crusaders or "Franks" as they were called by the natives, and soon became the dominant power in Cilicia.

From the very beginning, the Armenian and Crusader leaders had to deal with their own territorial ambitions. Edessa, which was controlled by an Armenian, for example, was taken over by Baldwin, who assumed the title of Count of Edessa. Other minor Armenian, Byzantine and Arab chiefs soon lost their lands to the ambitious crusading lords of Antioch and Tripoli. The Rubenids and the Hetumids remained the only Armenian lords to control their own territories. Taking advantage of the situation, the Rubenids expanded at the expense of the Byzantines. Toros (1102-1129) captured the fortresses of Bardzberd and Anazarba from the Greeks and made it the center of Rubenid rule. His brother, Levon or Leo (1129-1137) expanded the Rubenid domains to the sea. A number of alliances with the Latin rulers, especially with Count Raymond of

Antioch, kept the Rubenid position secure. In 1137, the Byzantine emperor, John Comnenus, after restoring Byzantine power in Serbia and Hungary, invaded Cilician Armenia on the way to Antioch, which was to have been turned over to Byzantium by the Crusaders. The Hetumids cooperated with the emperor in capturing Rubenid fortresses and Antioch. Levon, his wife and two sons, Ruben and Toros, were taken captive to Constantinople, while Count Raymond was left in Antioch as a vassal of Byzantium.

Levon, his wife and Ruben all died in captivity; but Toros (subsequently Toros II) managed to escape. He returned to Cilicia where a few years later he succeeded in restoring Rubenid power. His task was facilitated by the death of John Comnenus in 1143 and by the fall of Edessa to the Zangids, which prompted the unsuccessful Second Crusade in 1147-1149. The Armenians of Edessa escaped to Cilicia and Antioch, and the County of Edessa was divided among the Byzantines and the Muslims. Around this time the fortress of Hromkla (Rum Qalat) located on the Euphrates River, was granted to the Armenian Catholicos by a noblewoman. Despite the fact that for most of that time it was deep in Muslim-held territory, it became the Holy See of the Armenians for the next one hundred years.

Toros II (1144-1169) thus reclaimed his father's domain and, when the Byzantine-Antioch rapprochement suffered a setback, made an alliance with Count Reginald of Antioch. Emperor Manuel Comnenus, however, demanded the submission of Cilicia as a vassal state and invaded the region. Baldwin, now king of Jerusalem and related by marriage to the Byzantine Emperor, mediated and Toros kept his land as a nominal vassal. The rise of the Zangid State and its capture of Damascus under Nur al-Din forced the Christians to abandon their differences and to seek common alliances. Toros managed to keep peace by remaining on good terms with both the Byzantines and the Muslims. He even tried an unsuccessful marriage alliance between the Rubenid and Hetumid houses. His diplomacy and alliances created a strong Rubenid state recognized by the Byzantines and the Latin principalities.

Toros died in 1169 and his brother Mleh, who may have converted to Islam, killed Toros' son, allied himself with Nur al-Din and ruled Rubenid Cilicia. The death of the Zangid chief left Mleh powerless, and he was ousted in favor of Toros' nephew Ruben II (1175-1187). Ruben struggled with the Hetumids and the new Count of Antioch, Bohemond. He was not an able ruler and abdicated in favor of his brother Levon who took over the family fortunes in 1187. Once again external events catapulted the Rubenids into a favorable position.

Saladin, a Kurd who had risen in the service of the Zangids, captured Cairo from the Fatimids in 1171, united it with Syria and established the Ayyubid dynasty. In 1187 he captured Jerusalem and although he spared Christian lives, his action launched the Third Crusade (1189-1192). This crusade, despite efforts of the pope, was primarily a lay and royal affair. The German ruler, Frederick Barbarossa, Richard I (the Lion-Hearted) of England, and Philip II Augustus of France led a great host of knights who managed to capture Acre but failed to retake Jerusalem. Frederick's formidable force disintegrated after he drowned in Cilicia. Saladin's favorable position and the rivalry between Richard and Philip, as well as the eventual departure of the European monarchs, left only the narrow strip of coastal states of Antioch, Tripoli and Tyre in Christian hands. Although the Third Crusade was a failure, one result of this episode was the capture of Cyprus by Richard and its sale to Guy de Lusignan, whose family would later become rulers of Cilician Armenia.

The Emergence of a New Armenian Kingdom

With the Latin states left vulnerable, Cilicia now assumed a new strategic importance, and European secular leaders requested its military and financial assistance to the crusading forces. Levon sought to use the situation to his advantage by seeking a royal crown. There is some evidence to indicate that Frederick Barbarossa had promised a crown to Levon in exchange for his assistance during the Third Crusade. After some correspondence, Levon finally received a crown from Frederick's successor, the German Emperor Henry VI. He was crowned as King Levon I (Leo I) on 6 January 1199 in the Cathedral of Tarsus before the Rubenid, Hetumid, and Crusader nobility. He was anointed by the Catholicos and received the royal insignia from the papal and imperial legate, Conrad, Archbishop of Mainz. A second crown arrived from the Byzantine Emperor as a reminder that Byzantium still viewed Cilicia and its ruler as her vassals.

Levon's coronation began a crisis, which continued throughout the life of the kingdom: the question of religious unity with the Roman Catholic Church. Levon's crown came from the Holy Roman Emperor and was blessed by the pope, whom Western Europe viewed as the head of Christendom. There is no evidence of Levon agreeing to the supremacy of the Roman Church prior to his coronation. After the event, however, he asked the Armenian clergy to make a minor change in the Armenian liturgy and to concede a "special respect" to the pope as the successor of St. Peter. A move towards closer ties with Rome received the support of some of the clergy, such as Bishop Nerses of Lambron, but after the latter's death in 1199, the Armenian clergy rejected any compromise. The rift was to weaken the dynasty and was exploited by both the papacy and the Crusaders.

Levon's elevation to the rank of king and his recognition by Europe put Cilicia on European maps, where it was referred to as "Little Armenia" or "Maritime Armenia." It also enabled Levon to gain the control of the Cilician plain and its ports. He broke the power of the Hetumids, established a new capital at Sis (see map 16), and managed to create a number of important marriage alliances with Cyprus, Antioch and Byzantium. One such alliance, with Antioch, proved problematic. Levon's niece, Alice, had married the son of Bohemond of Antioch, but was soon widowed and left with a son, Raymond-Ruben. Levon planned for an Armenian regent to take over Antioch and unite it with Cilicia after the death of Bohemond. The pope and the emperor initially supported Levon's plan, but the Italian merchants of Antioch and Bohemond's younger son, who ruled Tripoli, objected, and, after a three-year war, ousted the young heir, Raymond-Ruben. Had Levon's plan succeeded, a powerful state would have emerged which might have altered the history of the region.

Such problems notwithstanding, Levon's rule created a kingdom that was to last for almost two centuries. His relationship with the nobility was not based on the Armenian *nakharar* system, but on the Western feudal one of sovereign to vassal. Western feudal law was used to judge cases involving the court and nobility. In fact, the *Assizes of Antioch*, the main code of law used in the Crusader states, has survived only in its Armenian translation. Nobles were knighted in the European tradition, and jousts and tournaments became popular. Latin and French terms of nobility and office replaced Armenian equivalents; for example, *paron* (baron) instead of *nakharar*, and *gonstapl* (constable) rather than *sparapet*. French and Latin became accepted languages at court. Even the Armenian alphabet was extended to accommodate the new sounds of "o" and "f," introduced by European languages. Western feudal dress became the norm, and

French names became common among the courtiers and their wives. Finally, following the European custom of alliances, Armenian noblewomen married into European and Byzantine noble houses. Conversions to Catholicism or the Greek Orthodox faith became common among the nobles. The rest of Armenian society did not imitate these pro-Western tendencies, however. Armenian merchants intermarried far less frequently, and the population at large, led by the Armenian Apostolic Church, was decidedly anti-Western. The Catholicos, with the aid of at least fourteen bishops, supervised the religious affairs of Cilicia from Hromkla. A number of Armenian monasteries were founded as well.

The most notable result of Levon's successful rule was the growth of commerce. Cilicia was a link for several trade routes from Central Asia and the Persian Gulf. Armenian merchants made contact with other traders and opened trading houses in China and Europe. European missionaries recorded that at this time Armenian churches were being built as far away as China. The port of Ayas on the Gulf of Alexandretta became the center of East-West commerce and is mentioned by Marco Polo as the starting point of his trip to China. Its bazaars sold dyes, silk, spices, cotton, wine, raisins, carpets and pearls. Cilician goat-hair cloth, salt, iron, and timber were exported. Levon signed agreements with the Italian City States of Genoa, Venice and Pisa, granting them tax exemptions in exchange for trade. The ports of Tarsus, Adana and Mamistra were soon large cities full of foreign merchants, dominated by the Italians, who according to treaties had their trading establishments, churches and courts. Italian soon became the secondary language of Cilician commerce.

Levon died in 1219, leaving his only child, a daughter named Isabelle or Zabel, as his heir. At Levon's death, the situation in the Middle East was very different from the previous century. The Fourth Crusade (1202-1204), led by the Venetians, had not attacked the Muslims, but had captured and looted Constantinople, considerably weakening the Byzantine Empire. Saladin's dynasty, the Ayyubid, was now a major force in Egypt, prompting the unsuccessful Fifth Crusade (1218-1221). The half-Armenian prince Raymond-Ruben, who had been driven out of Antioch, assumed the throne of Levon with the support of the pope, but was immediately ousted by the Armenian nobles, led by the Hetumids, who saw their chance of assuming control. Zabel was then married to Philip of Antioch with the understanding that he would adopt Armenian customs and become a member of the Armenian Church. Philip, however, disdained Armenian customs and spent most of his time in Antioch. The Armenian nobility decided to end the marriage; Philip was arrested and eventually poisoned. The Hetumid regent, Constantine now arranged the marriage of Zabel to his own son, Hetum. Zabel, who seems to have been fond of Philip, fled the kingdom and even after her marriage to Hetum refused to live with her husband for some time. By 1226, however, the two were crowned at Sis and the Rubenid-Hetumid line was born.

Zabel and Hetum reigned from 1226 to 1252. Their joint reign was commemorated in coins bearing both their images; the second time the image of a woman had appeared on Armenian coinage. After Zabel's death, Hetum continued to rule until 1270, the longest rule of any Cilician king. Hetum's brother, Smbat, served as constable and was an intimate and wise counselor to the king. Although the Ayyubids, and later the Mamluks, as well as the Seljuks, made periodic sorties against Cilicia, the era is known for its flowering of the arts. The most important political event of this period, however, was the arrival of the Mongols in the Middle East.

The Mongols and Cilician Armenia

Genghis Khan, who managed in a short time to conquer a large part of Asia, united the Mongols in 1206. Following his death in 1227, his son and grandson completed the conquest of China and Russia, and entered Eastern Europe, where they defeated Western armies in Poland, Hungary and Germany, and reached the Adriatic Sea. Such an empire was obviously too large and diverse for one ruler, and the Mongols eventually divided their empire into four units. The first group ruled Mongolia, western Siberia, and Central Asia. The second, known as the Ilkhanids, controlled Persia, Armenia, Georgia, and the Middle East. The third, called the Golden Horde, occupied Russia, Ukraine, and parts of Poland, while the fourth moved to China and formed the Yuan dynasty under Kublai Khan, who acted as the leader of the Mongols and did much to promote international trade (see map 17). The Ilkhanids, who were mostly shamanists, fought the Muslim Seljuks and Mamluks in the Middle East. The Papacy, the Crusaders, and the Armenians, therefore, made every effort to gain an alliance with the Ilkhanids and at the same time convert them to Christianity.

Hetum was the first ruler who realized the importance of this new force in the area and sent his brother Smbat to the Mongol center at Karakorum. Smbat met Kublai's brother, Mongke Khan and, in 1247, made an alliance against the Muslims. On his return, Smbat passed through historic Armenia, the first time that any Cilician leader had seen his ancestral homeland. In 1254, Hetum visited Karakorum himself and renewed the alliance. The alliance helped Cilicia initially but, in 1260, the Ilkhanids were defeated by the Mamluks and retreated to Persia. The Mamluks then attacked and devastated Cilicia. In 1269 Hetum abdicated in favor of his son Levon II (1269-1289), who was forced to pay a large annual tribute to the Mamluks. The Mamluks continued their attacks during the reign of his son, Hetum II, and sacked Hromkla in 1292, prompting the Holy See to move to Sis. Hetum's sister married into the Lusignan family of Cyprus, and her children later inherited the Cilician throne. Hetum II, a devout Catholic, sought a closer union with Rome. His efforts did not materialize, and he abdicated first in favor of his brother and later of his nephew, Levon III. Although Cilicia enjoyed a measure of economic prosperity under the Hetumids, the troubled reign of Hetum II caused a sense of political instability in the kingdom at a time when a strong effective leadership was badly needed to deal with the Muslim threat. For it was at this time that the Ilkhanid Mongols adopted Islam, the religion of the majority of their subject people. Hetum, now a Franciscan monk, together with Levon and forty Cilician nobles, made one more attempt at a Mongol alliance against the Mamluks. Upon their arrival at the Ilkhanid headquarters in northern Syria, all forty-two were put to death.

The Collapse of Cilician Armenia

Yet another brother of Hetum, Oshin, assumed the throne and convened the Church councils at Sis in 1307 and Adana in 1316 where a number of Armenian clergy and nobles, hoping to receive military aid from Europe, agreed to conform to Roman liturgical practices and recognize the pope. The Armenian population rose against this decision, and Oshin was poisoned in 1320. His son Levon IV, who was even more strongly pro-Western, was also killed in 1341. There were now no direct descendants of the Rubenid-Hetumid line left, and the throne passed to the Lusignans of Cyprus.

A number of Lusignans, all named Constantine, ruled for brief periods and made concessions to the Mamluks in exchange for short periods of peace. Most were murdered by rivals, or by Armenian leaders suspicious of non-Armenian rulers. The last Cilician king, Levon V (or VI), was crowned at Sis in 1374. He was captured a year later by the Mamluks, who took him to Cairo from where he was ransomed by his European relatives. Levon attempted to revive the Crusader spirit in Europe, but died in France in 1393 and was buried with the kings of France in the church of St. Denis, in Paris. Ironically Levon's title of King of Armenia passed to John I of Cyprus, whose descendants then passed it on to the House of Savoy; they used the title as late as the nineteenth century. The Cilician Armenian nobility left for Byzantium, Armenia and Georgia, while Armenian merchants immigrated to France, Holland, Italy and Poland. A century later Cilicia became part of the Ottoman Empire and its Armenian towns and villages came under Turkish rule.

Arts and Culture

Despite its Armenian majority, Cilicia was home to a variety of peoples, all of who contributed to the richness of Cilician culture. Greeks, Syrian Jacobites, Arabs and Jews lived in the region, each supporting their own religious institutions. Italian merchants and European knights made their home in or frequented the ports of Cilicia. The French language and customs had spread among the Armenian nobility and most of the merchants spoke Italian. European works, including histories, written originally in Latin, found their way into Armenian translations. As noted, the *Assizes of Antioch*, the code of law used in the Crusader states, has survived only in its Armenian translation. A number of original works are significant as well. A noteworthy work on the earlier history of Cilicia is the *Chronicle of Matthew of Edessa* (Matevos Urhaetsi). The *Chronicle* of Constable Smbat, the brother of Hetum I, is the most valuable account of the Cilician Kingdom. His revision of the Armenian law code of Mkhitar Gosh and his account of his trip to the court of the Mongols, are important as well. Hetum, Prince of Cyprus, a nephew of Hetum I, offers another valuable account. Known as the *Little Chronicle* and written in 1307, it contains an historical and geographical survey of Asia, followed by a history of the Mongols, focusing in particular on the conflicts between the Ilkhanids and the Mamluks, and concluding with a plan for a new crusade. Catholicos Nerses, known as Shnorhali (the Gracious), left his *Lamentations on the Fall of Edessa*, as well as many *sharakans* or hymns used in the Armenian mass. Poetry, including poems on love and other secular themes, appeared in the last two centuries of Cilician Armenia. Those of John of Erzinga (Hovhannes Erzingatsi) were written in the early Armenian vernacular, sometimes referred to as Middle Armenian.

What has survived of Cilician architecture resembles Crusader castles and fortresses and copies Byzantine and Western edifices of the period. Although no significant sculpture has survived from Cilicia, reliquary and silver bible bindings from the thirteenth century display the craftsmanship of Cilicia's silversmiths. The glory of the period, however, is undoubtedly its illuminated manuscripts from the twelfth and thirteenth centuries. Humans, animals, flowers and geometric designs are depicted in rich colors and glittering gold. The most renowned are those of Toros Roslin, who used contemporary costumes and naturalism in biblical themes and combined both Asian and European motifs.

There are a number of reasons for the rise and fall of the Armenian Kingdom of Cilicia. The geographical position of Cilicia, the arrival of Armenian feudal families and the temporary weakness of Byzantium permitted the rise of the Rubenids and Hetumids. The coming of the crusades gave the Armenians sufficient political, economic and strategic importance to form first, a principality and later, a kingdom. The failure of successive crusades; division among the Christian forces; the refusal of the Armenian Church to accept Roman suzerainty; the rise of the Ayyubid and Mamluk states; the fall of the last Crusader bastion in 1291; and the conversion of the Ilkhanid Mongols to Islam, contributed to the fall of the Armenian Kingdom. By the fourteenth century, Europe had become involved in its own State-building. The expulsion of the Muslims out of much of Spain spelled the end of the crusading spirit, and Europe largely abandoned its interests in the Christians living in Asia. This was to have major repercussions for the West, for the Ottoman Turks would soon destroy Byzantium and enter Eastern Europe, where they would remain for some four centuries.

The Armenian Community of Jerusalem

One of the consequences of the rise of the Cilician Kingdom was a new prominence for the Armenian secular and religious community of Jerusalem. An Armenian presence in that city can be traced back as far as the first centuries of the Christian era. By the seventh century numerous Armenian monasteries had been built there. After the break with the Greek Orthodox Church, Armenians were subject to discrimination by the city's Byzantine rulers. Following the Arab conquest in 638, control over the Christian holy places of Jerusalem became the avenue to and symbol of power for the city's Armenian and Greek communities. Although the Armenians in Jerusalem numbered fewer than the Greeks, they enjoyed better relations with the Arabs, who saw the Byzantines as their common enemy. The Armenian Church was, therefore, initially granted custodianship of a number of important Christian shrines, although disagreements between the Greek Orthodox and Armenian Churches over their control continued through the years. The arrival of the Crusaders improved the Armenian position considerably and enabled them to acquire a site from the Georgian Church over which they build the cathedral and monastery of St. James and founded the monastic order of the Brotherhood of St. James. St. James became the heart of Jerusalem's Armenian community, providing accommodations for pilgrims and visiting merchants. At the beginning of the fourteenth century, the St. James Brotherhood refused to accept the Latinophile policies of the Catholicosate of Cilicia and proclaimed its leader to be the Armenian Patriarch of Jerusalem and the guardian of the Armenian-controlled Holy Places. The Armenians retained their favored status and were exempted from the *jizya* after the Muslims retook Jerusalem under Saladin. During the Mamluk period the Armenians managed to forestall attempts by the Georgian Orthodox Church to retake the site of St. James, but were forced to share custodianship of parts of the Holy Sepulchre with the Georgian and Greek Churches (see map 18).

11

From Majority to Minority
Armenia under Turkish, Mongol and
Turkmen Domination
(c. 1071-1500)

URING the nearly five hundred years between the arrival of the Turks in Armenia and the establishment of the Safavid dynasty in Persia, Europe made the transition from the Middle Ages to the early Modern Period. In the Middle East, 'Abbasid rule continued for another two centuries. The Caliphate was in decline, however, and various Turkish, Kurdish and Persian military leaders had established their own dynasties. The arrival of the Seljuk Turks resulted in the emergence of a new powerful Islamic state. By the second half of the thirteenth century, the entire situation had changed when the Mongols conquered Baghdad, ending the 'Abbasid Caliphate. Two centuries later, the Turks, under the leadership of the Ottomans, regained power in Anatolia and eventually took Constantinople, toppling the Byzantine Empire.

The same period in Western Europe witnessed changes, which, in the early Modern or post-1500 period, enabled it to assume the military and economic leadership of the world. The rise of trade, cities, and the middle class prepared the ground for representative government. The captivity of the papacy in Avignon, the Hundred Years War, the Black Death, and the War of the Roses weakened the Roman Catholic Church and facilitated the rise of strong monarchies. The Renaissance enabled Europe to discover its Greco-Roman traditions, fostered a spirit of individualism and set the stage for scientific advances and artistic expression. In the meantime, the same centuries saw the gradual re-conquest of Spain, culminating in the fall of Granada in 1492. Ironically, the Ottomans revived the Muslim presence in Europe by penetrating Eastern and

Central Europe. The Mongols terminated the first Russian State. They ruled there for three centuries and passed on some of their sociopolitical institutions to the future Russian State. Both the Ottoman conquests and the Ming dynasty's isolationist policy in China closed the land trade routes with Asia and pushed Europe into the Age of Exploration. With considerable help from Asian technology, Columbus and Vasco de Gama found the Americas and the sea route to India and China.

In Africa, Egypt championed the cause of Islam against the Mongols and the Crusaders. Islam managed to penetrate sub-Saharan regions and became the major religion of North and Central Africa. The kingdoms and states of Mali, Benin, Yoruba, and Songhai flourished until the European penetration, which began when the Portuguese explored the west coast of Africa at the end of this period.

India, which had experienced the Arab invasions of Sind in the early seventh century, was invaded by new Muslim armies, who conquered northern India, established the Sultanate of Delhi, ended the influence of Buddhism and divided India into Muslim and Hindu cultures. In Southeast Asia, the Khmer Empire reached its peak with the completion of Angkor Wat, and Vietnam gained its independence from China.

In China itself, the Sung dynasty lost control of the north to the Chin dynasty. The Mongols soon conquered most of China and established the Yuan dynasty. Kublai Khan adopted Chinese culture, moved his capital to Beijing, and was visited by Marco Polo. The new empire established the *pax Mongolica*, which facilitated East-West trade and the transfer of technology to Western Europe. A century later, the Mongols were driven out of China by the Ming Dynasty, which at first encouraged trade and exploration, but later closed China to all foreigners. In Japan, two successive *shogunates* kept Japan isolated and defended it against Mongol invasions. Finally, in the Americas, the Inca Empire in Peru and the Aztecs in Mexico had blossomed into major organized states.

In contrast, historic Armenia was entering the nadir of its history. The last Armenian dynasty had fallen, and a great number of nobles, soldiers, and artisans had left for Constantinople, Cilicia and Eastern Europe. Furthermore, the next four centuries witnessed the arrival of thousands of nomadic invaders, which would have a major effect on the history of Armenia and the Armenians.

Turks in Armenia

Turkish bands from Central Asia, particularly the Oghuz tribe, had been slowly raiding and settling parts of Azerbaijan, the northern Caucasus, southern Russia, and even northern Asia Minor since the tenth century, without causing much shifts in the population. The Byzantine policy of weakening Armenia by removing its military forces had left the region undefended and had invited marauding Turkish groups to attack southern Armenia. Until the arrival of the Seljuks in the mid-eleventh century, there was no organized Turkish plan to conquer Armenia. Between 1040 and 1045, an Oghuz chief, Toghrul of the Seljuk family, conquered most of Persia and founded an empire. The Seljuks soon faced a problem which confronted all nomadic conquerors after they had settled down in their new territories, namely, how to deal with those in their tribes who wanted to continue to raid and plunder. The Seljuks, fearing the destruction of their new empire, directed the energies of their undisciplined elements to undefended Armenia in the hope of gaining new territory. Thus, for the next two decades Armenia was periodically attacked.

The Armenians and Byzantines fought the invaders, but unfortunately, not together. The Byzantines did not realize the gravity of the situation but, rather, tried to abolish any form of Armenian autonomy and to bring the Armenian Church under the control of Constantinople. At times, Byzantine actions even spurred some Armenians to cooperate with the Turks against the Byzantines. In 1071 the Seljuk army under the command of Alp Arslan defeated and captured the Byzantine Emperor Romanus IV Diogenes. The Byzantines, who had destroyed the Bagratuni Kingdom a few years before, now lost it to the Turks. Many cities were looted, churches destroyed, trade disrupted and some of the population forcibly converted or enslaved. A number of dynasties such as the Danishmendids, Qaramanids, Shah-Armans, and the Seljuks of Rum emerged in Anatolia. The *nakharars* of Artsakh (Karabagh), Siunik (Zangezur), Gugark (Lori), Sasun, and other mountainous regions, however, maintained viable military forces and remained autonomous. A number of *nakharars* left with their families and retinue and established new centers of power in Georgia and Cilicia (see chapter 10). Not all Armenians converted to Islam by force; some Armenian artisans and military men converted voluntarily for economic reasons. Intermarriage between the Turkish and Armenian upper classes also contributed to such conversions. In fact, a number of independent emirs in Anatolia were of Armenian descent. The bulk of the Armenian population, the peasantry, however, remained Christian.

The prestige of the Seljuks reached new heights when they captured Jerusalem and received the title of *sultan* from the Caliph. They soon employed Persian viziers, adopted Persian titles and began to view themselves as monarchs of a centralized state. Armenians and settled Muslims were protected, and trade somewhat revived. By the mid-twelfth century, when new Turkish nomads overthrew the Seljuks in Persia, the situation had changed considerably in favor of the Christians. The crusades had established a strong Christian presence in the Middle East, Georgia was rising as a power in Transcaucasia, the Armenians of Cilicia were creating a viable state, and Byzantium revived under the Comneni emperors. The Turkish groups had also become fragmented into small states scattered in Asia Minor and Transcaucasia.

The period between the decline of the Seljuks and the arrival of the Mongols was a time of revival for the Armenians. The main impetus was the emergence of Georgia and its Bagratuni dynasty, which was of Armenian descent, as the preeminent power in Transcaucasia and eastern Anatolia. The Georgians, under David the Builder (1089-1125), recruited Armenian *nakharars* from the Artsruni, Pahlavuni, Zakarian, Orbelian, and Proshian families, as well as the dispossessed *azat*, who joined the Georgian army to expel the Turks from Armenia. David's successor continued this policy and eventually resettled much of Armenia with these Armenian volunteers. Under Queen Tamar (1184-1213), the Zakarians, who commanded the Armeno-Georgian forces, succeeded in conquering much of Greater Armenia.

The Zakarians ruled Armenia from Ani and Dvin as vassals of the Georgian monarchs (see map 19). Most of the other *nakharars* submitted to Zakarid leadership. The coronation of Leo and the official recognition of the Cilician Armenian Kingdom by Europe in 1199 opened the trade routes from Europe to Asia via Armenia and Georgia and brought new wealth to the region. The Zakarians intermarried into a number of *nakharar* families and, like the Georgian kings, established courts with their own hierarchy. For the first time, new Armenian *nakharars* emerged, men who were not part of the old feudal houses but had risen through military or commercial achievements. They purchased or were assigned lands and became benefactors of cultural and religious institutions. With the

Holy See in Cilicia, new Church leaders emerged in historic Armenia. Artisans lived in the cities, where they received some rights and
established guilds. The peasants, as in the past, remained attached to
the soil and paid most of the taxes. Unfortunately for Armenia and
Georgia, these prosperous days were short-lived. As noted, a new
force made its appearance in world history, a force which not only
ended the Armeno-Georgian interlude, but drastically altered the
history of Russia and the Middle East: the Mongols.

Mongols in Armenia

A decade prior to the major Mongol invasion of Transcaucasia, a
small Mongol force had defeated the Armeno-Georgian army and
had looted the region. In their eastward march, the Mongols had
pushed Turkish tribes westward. Some of the latter then entered
Armenia and used it as a base from which to resist the Mongols. Although the Armenians, Georgians and Muslims succeeded in
ousting the invaders, the loss of life and destruction of property and
crops was severe. It was at this juncture that the main Mongol armies appeared in 1236. The Mongols swiftly conquered the cities;
those who resisted were cruelly punished, while those submitting
were rewarded. News of this spread quickly and resulted in the
submission of all of historic Armenia and parts of Georgia by 1245.
The Muslim rulers of western Armenia were crushed as well.

During the period of consolidation, the shamanistic Mongols did
not impose their taxes or administrative structure on the region. But
in the mid-thirteenth century, they conducted a census and heavily
taxed all the inhabitants, Muslims and Christians. A number of uprisings were put down severely. Armenian and Georgian military
leaders had to serve in the Mongol army, where many of them perished in battle. The Mongols also managed to attract a number of
nakharars to enter their service voluntarily. The most notable were
the Orbelians of Siunik and the Hasan-Jalalians of Artsakh. The
Mongols played the *nakharars* against each other, and occasionally
used Muslims against Christians or vice-versa, to achieve their
goals. In 1258 the Ilkhanid Mongols, under the leadership of Hulagu, sacked Baghdad, ended the 'Abbasid Caliphate and killed
many Muslims. Ironically, this action provoked the anger of another
Mongol group, the Golden Horde, who had conquered Russia, and
some of whose leaders had converted to Islam. Following the defeat

of the Ilkhanid Mongols by the Mamluks in Syria in 1260, the two Mongol groups clashed in the Caucasus.

The Armenian Church was generally spared the havoc of this period. A number of Mongol leaders had become Nestorian Christians and had thus a special sympathy for the Armenians, whom they probably viewed as fellow Monophysites. Armenian monasteries and clergy were periodically exempted from taxes. The Armenian Church leaders cited the privileges granted by the Mongols to gain considerable concessions from the Mongol and Turkmen khans who ruled Armenia during the fourteenth and fifteenth centuries. Armenian merchants were also treated well by the Mongols. The Chinese Mongols encouraged trade and Italian merchants from Venice and Genoa used Cilician or Black Sea ports to conduct a significant trade with China. Caravans were guarded and the Mongols assured them safe passage through Central Asia. Silk, gems and spices were the main exports. Armenian merchants opened trading branches in Beijing, Tabriz, Sultanieh, Bukhara, and Trebizond, as well as in a number of cities in Russia and Italy.

By 1300 the Ilkhanids had accepted Islam, and Armenians were once again treated as infidels. Taxes were increased, Armenians had to wear special badges to identify them as Christians, and large fertile areas were reserved for nomadic tribes, destroying the agricultural economy and forcing starvation and poverty. The collapse of the Ilkhanids in the mid-fourteenth century only worsened the situation. Various tribal groups attacked eastern Armenia, while the Ottomans Turks began their subjugation of western Armenia.

Timur and Turko-Tatars in Armenia

The final blow to the region was left to the last great invader from Central Asia, Lame Timur or, as he is known in the West, Tamerlane. Between 1386 and 1403 Timur, a Turkicized Mongol, and his Turko-Tatar hordes invaded Armenia, devastating cities, destroying crops, killing tens of thousands and enslaving even more. He even fought the Turkmen tribes who had settled in the region, defeated the Golden Horde and delivered a devastating blow to the Ottomans. The destruction was more severe than anything else before and reduced Armenia to rubble. Many cities and villages simply disappeared. Trade ceased completely, and Armenian churchmen, merchants and *nakharars* were put to death. Only the mountainous regions of Artsakh, Gugark, Siunik and Sasun survived the pillage;

some of their inhabitants turning to banditry in order to survive. Timur took many Armenian artisans to Samarkand where they helped to build his great capital city. Although he conquered Delhi, his aim was to loot and not to settle. After Timur's death, his family members ruled in the eastern Caucasus and Central Asia, but a later Timurid, Babur, conquered Delhi in 1526 and began the great Mughal dynasty, which ruled until 1858. Ironically, Armenian merchants were to play a vital role in Indian trade during the Mughal period (see chapter 14).

The Ottomans, Timurids, Shirvanshahs, Aq-Qoyunlu, Qara-Qoyunlu and the few remaining Georgian princes filled the vacuum left by the death of Timur. The Ottomans concentrated their efforts on what was left of the Byzantine Empire. In 1453 Mehmet the Conqueror took Constantinople, and the Ottomans began their rise, culminating in the capture or control of the entire Middle East, most of North Africa and much of Eastern Europe. Only Persia and the eastern parts of Armenia and Georgia eluded them. The Shirvanshahs controlled part of the present-day Republic of Azerbaijan, while the Timurids, their nominal suzerains, had their base in eastern Persia. Historic Armenia fell into the realm of two Turkmen tribes, Qara-Qoyunlu and Aq-Qoyunlu, which had been in the region prior to Timur.

The Qara-Qoyunlu, or Black Sheep, who had Shi'i sympathies, controlled the region east of Lake Van until 1468. The Timurids and the Qara-Qoyunlu fought each other and continued to wreak havoc on Armenia and Georgia. Two Qara-Qoyunlu rulers, Iskandar (1420-1438) and Jihan Shah (1438-1468), who needed the cooperation of the Armenian feudal and religious leaders, had friendly relations with the Armenian Church and *nakharars*. The fall of Cilicia and the decline of the Holy See of Sis thus coincided with the rise of the rise of Armenian secular and religious leaders in eastern Armenia. Following the Council of Florence (1439), where Armenian representatives from Aleppo and the Crimea accepted a union with the Catholic Church (never ratified by the Armenian Church), the clerical leaders in Armenia proper decided to move the Holy See away from Roman influence. Jihan Shah's approval made it possible to call a national assembly in 1441, which decided to move the Holy See back to Ejmiatsin. The move, which was challenged later (major disputes occurred in the seventeenth, nineteenth, and twentieth centuries) by the Cilician religious hierarchy, made

Ejmiatsin, once again, the official religious center of the Armenian people.

The Sunni Aq-Qoyunlu, or White Sheep, controlled all the Armenian lands west of Lake Van to the Euphrates River. They conquered the Qara-Qoyunlu in 1468 and ruled over all of Armenia, Azerbaijan, most of Georgia, and a major part of Persia until the end of the fifteenth century, when they were replaced by the Safavids. The Aq-Qoyunlu under Uzun Hasan (1453-1478) forced the Armenians to wear clothing that distinguished them as Christians and taxed them heavily. Worse conditions arose under Ya'qub (1478-1490), who levied even heavier taxes. Most of the last remaining *nakharars* had their lands confiscated or, in order to save their holdings donated it to the Church as *waqf* or endowment. Some became churchmen while others accumulated whatever capital they could muster and went into trade. A handful of minor nobles or scions of larger houses, such as the princes of Khachen, kept their holdings in the highlands of Karabagh and Siunik. A number of Kurdish tribes from Persia and Syria joined earlier arrivals in Armenia. The economic hardships notwithstanding, the Aq-Qoyunlu restored order, and peace returned to Armenia, enabling the population to recover somewhat before the next round of wars between the Ottomans and the Safavids.

Literature, Learning, and Art

Despite four hundred years of invasions and devastation, Armenians still managed to produce historical and literary works. The major historians of the thirteenth century were Kirakos of Ganja (Kirakos Gandzaketsi) and Vardan Areveltsi. Gandzaketsi was captured by the Mongols and learned their language. His history is a primary source for the Mongol and Zakarid period in Armenia. Arevelsti visited the Mongol court in Central Asia and befriended Hulagu in Persia. Another important historian of this period is Stepanos Orbelian, a bishop and a member of the Siuni family who also visited the Mongol court and who wrote *The History of the Family and the Province of Siunik*. Grigor Akants wrote a history of the Mongols, entitled the *History of the Nation of the Archers*. Finally, Tovma Metsobetsi wrote the *History of Tamerlane and His Successors*, which details the terrible devastation of Armenia by the Turkmen. In the literary arena, Frik, a layman poet, described in the vernacular the sufferings of the people during the Mongol invasions.

One result of the numerous invasions and occupations of Armenia was that Armenians were forced to learn Persian, Turkish, Mongol, Georgian and Uigur, and often acted as interpreters in trade and at court. European travelers mention Armenian translators and middlemen in Central Asia, India, and at the various Mongol courts. Monasteries, as before, served as centers of learning. Tatev and Gladzor, both in Siunik, can be viewed as proto-universities where the arts and sciences, as well as religious studies were taught. These centers were especially active against the inroads of Catholic missionaries. In the fourteenth century, the Dominicans had succeeded in converting a number of Armenian laymen and clergy in Nakhichevan, and had founded the *Fratres Unitores* (in Armenian, *unitork*), an Armenian Catholic branch of the Dominican order. Although the Armenian theologians from Gladzor played an important part in resisting and limiting these Latin influences in Armenia, some Western theological ideas influenced the works of Esayi Nchetsi, Hovhannes Tsortsoretsi, or were translated by Hakob Krnetsi.

These chaotic times did not hinder trade or the construction of churches. One of the trade routes passed through Georgia and northern Armenia to Trebizond, from where it continued to Venice and Genoa. Armenian merchants were active in this trade and accumulated considerable wealth, part of which found its way into donations to monasteries and the construction of churches. The churches of Noravank, Khorakert, Areni, Eghvard and a number of later churches in Ani are of this period. A number of monasteries were completed as well: Sanahin, Hovnannavank, Harijavank, Haghartsin, Spitakavor, Tegher, Kecharis, Goshavank and Geghard. Finally, the Holy See of Gandzasar in Artsakh (Karabagh) was constructed in this period. Relief sculpture in stucco or stone geometric designs, interlacing real and imaginary animals, as had appeared on palaces and churches during the Bagratuni period, now emerged in a more mature form. Silver bindings and reliquaries, especially those commissioned by the Proshian family, evidence the art of silversmiths. The art of making *khachkars*, as noted earlier, reached its peak in this period. Illuminated manuscripts were influenced in their ornamental composition by Cilician works; the Gospel of Haghpat and the Gospel of Gladzor are fine examples from this period.

For over two thousand years Armenia's geographical position and the adaptable nature of its people enabled it to maintain a unique place in the ancient, classical and medieval periods. Armenia produced a number of dynasties, developed its own art and architecture, language and literature, and was one of the first states to adopt Christianity as its official religion, a decision that affected the rest of its history. In a small way Armenia contributed to the Renaissance through the preservation of a number of classical works and in serving as a conduit of goods and ideas from Asia to Europe. Armenian contacts with China may have even aided the transference of some of the technology that gave rise to European supremacy and explorations.

By the end of the medieval period, however, Armenia's political structure had disappeared. The demographic changes which had begun in the eleventh century and which continued uninterrupted until the dawn of the nineteenth century (see Chapters 12, 13, 16) finally resulted in reducing the Armenian population to a minority in parts of their historic homeland.

Time-Lines

1: Pre-History to 1000 BC
2: 1000 BC to 600 BC
3: 600 BC to 200 BC
4: 200 BC to AD 50
5: AD 50 to AD 400
6: AD 400 to AD 600
7: AD 600 to AD 900
8: AD 900 to AD 1100
9: AD 1100 to AD 1300
10: AD 1300 to AD 1500

Maps

1. The Armenian Plateau
2. The Ancient World
3. Urartu (c. 750 BC)
4. The Persian Empire (c. 520 BC)
5. The Hellenistic Empires (c. 300 BC)
6. Yervanduni Armenia (c. 250 BC)
7. Artashesian Armenia (c. 150 BC)
8. Armenian Empire of Tigran II (c. 80 BC)
9. Arsacid Armenia (c. AD 150)
10. The Roman Empire (c. AD 387)
11. First Partition of Armenia (AD 387)
12. Armenia in the Period of Justinian (AD 536)
13. Second Partition of Armenia (AD 591)
14. The Expansion of Islam (c. AD 640-840)
15. Medieval Armenian Kingdoms (c. AD 1000)
16. The Cilician Kingdom of Armenia (c. AD 1200)
17. Armenian Quarter in Jerusalem
18. The Mongol Empires (c. AD 1280)
19. Zakarid Armenia (c. AD 1200)

Plates

1. Twin peaks of Ararat
2. Winged bull, bronze (Urartian period)
3. Figurine of a winged lion with human head (Urartian period)
4. Urartian helmet
5. Monument in Nemrud Dagh, Turkey
6. Behistun Monument, Iran (Achaemenid-Yervanduni period)
7. Bronze head of a Hellenistic deity (Artashesian period)
8. Silver Tertradrachm of Tigran the Great
9. Temple of Garni (Artashesian period)
10. Cathedral of Ejmiatsin (4th century)
11. Church of Ereruk (4-5th centuries)
12. The Armenian Alphabet
13. Cathedral of Mastara (6th century)
14. Church of St. Hripsime (7th century)
15. Monument at Odzun (7th century)
16. Church of St. Gayane (7th century)
17. Cathedral of Zvartnots (remains)(7th century)
18. Capital with eagle, Zvartnots
19. A reconstruction plan for Zvartnots
20. Church at Lake Sevan (9th century)
21. Church of the Holy Cross at Aghtamar (Lake Van)(10th century)
22. David and Goliath, Church of the Holy Cross, Aghtamar
23. Church of the Holy Apostles, Kars (10th century)
24. Cathedral of Ani (10-11th centuries)
25. Church of the Savior, Ani (11th century)
26. Monastery of Khdzkunk (9-11th centuries)
27. Church at the monastery of Sanahin (10-13th centuries)
28. Monastery of Haghpat (10-13th centuries)
29. Monastery of Geghard (12-13th centuries)
30. Monastery of Haghartsin (11-13th centuries)
31. Monastery of Gandzasar, Karabagh (13th century)
32. Khachkar (12-13th centururies)
33. Detail of Coin of Levon I (Cilicia)
34. Tombstone of Levon V (Paris)
35. Fortress of Vahka (Cilicia)
36. Raising of Lazarus, Toros Roslin (Cilicia)(13th century)
37. Armenian Church, Church of the Nativity, Bethlehem

B.C.E.	ARMENIA	FERTILE CRESCENT & EGYPT	CRETE / GREECE	INDIA & CHINA	THE AMERICAS
c.400,000 to 7000	The Old Stone Age (Paleolithic) . Crude tools made from flint and black volcanic rock (obsidian). Evidence of modern man (40,000 B.C.), discovery of fire, hunting and food gathering. Early communal organizations, some along matriarchal lines, develop by 12,000 B.C.. Agricultural experiments with wild grains during the Middle StoneAge (Mesolithic.)				
c.7000 to 3200	The New Stone Age (Neolithic). The end of the last ice-age. Sedentary life begins, tilling the soil, cultivation of plants, domestication of animals, more sophisticated stone tools. After 5,000 B.C., some use of copper during the Copper-Stone Age (Chalcolithic). Nomadic life continues in many regions, agricultural settlements rise in other regions. Some walled villages/towns appear. Beginning of divisions of labor, appearence of textiles, woven baskets and jewelry.				
3200	The Bronze Age.Invention of the wheel, plows with wooden shares, bronze weapons, utensils and tools. Use of animals in agriculture, large-scale irrigation projects and major agricultural developments, rise of cities, writing systems, and recorded history.				
3000	Metal-working in Caucasus (c. 3000)	Sumerian civilization Lunar calendar, early religions, ziggurats, cuneiform script (c. 3200-3000) Egypt unified, first pyramid, hieroglyphics (c. 3[00-2770)		Indus Valley civilization (c. 3000-1600) Early urban civilization in China (c. 3000-1800)	Early pottery in Ecuador (c. 3000)
		Old Kingdom, Egypt (c. 2770-2200)			
2500		Akkadian Empire (c. 2370-2200)		Domestication of horses Silkworm cultivation in China (c. 2500) Mohenjo-Daro and Harappa settlements in India (c. 2500-1500)	
	Hurrians (c. 2300)	Sumerian revival (c. 2200-2000)			
2000		Middle Kingdom, Egypt (c. 2050-1786) Solar calendar Belief of personal immorality in religion			

Table 1: Pre-History to 1000 B.C.

B.C.E.	ARMENIA	FERTILE CRESCENT & EGYPT	CRETE / GREECE	INDIA & CHINA	THE AMERICAS
2000	Guti (c. 2000) Kassites (c. 1900) Indo-European invasions (c. 1700-1500) Mitanni (c. 1600-1400) Federations of Hayasa, Azzi, Arme-Shupria, and Uruatri formed in the region (c. 1300-900)	Old Babylonian Empire (c. 2000-1600) Gilgamesh Epic Horses domesticated Code of Hammurabi (c. 1770) Hyskos invasion/rule of Egypt (c. 1750-1560) New Kingdom, Egypt (c. 1550-1087) Hittite Empire (c. 1500-1200) Phoenicians develop first alphabet Akhenaton's new religion, Egypt (c. 1375) Assyrian Kingdom formed (c. 1300) Moses unites Jews in the worship of Yahweh (c. 1250) Rise of Assyria Shalmaneser I (c. 1274-1245) Collapse of Hittite Empire (c. 1200) Hebrews occupy Canaan Period of Judges (c. 1200-1025) Trojan War (c. 1180) Tiglath-pileser I (c. 1115-1077)	Minoan civilization in Knossos, Crete (c. 2000-1500) Greek Bronze Age (c. 2000-1500) Mycenean civilization in Greece (c. 1600-1200) Mycene dominates Crete (c. 1500-1400) Minoan civilization ends (c. 1400) Trojan War and the collapse of Mycene (c. 1180-1100)	Shang Dynasty in China (c. 1766-1123) Ideograghic script developed in China Aryan invasions of India (c. 1500) Oldest Sanskrit literature in India Early Vedas (Rig Veda) (c. 1500-1000)	Metal-working in Peru (c. 2000) Olmec civilization in San Lorenzo, Mexico (c. 1200-900)
1100 Iron Age		Shalmaneser II (c. 1031-1020) Decline of Assyria (c. 1020-900) United Jewish State (1025-933)	Greek Dark Ages (c. 1100-800)	Chou Dynasty (c. 1100-256)	

Table 1: Pre-History to 1000 B.C.

B.C.E.	ARMENIA	MIDDLE EAST, PERSIA & EGYPT	GREECE & ROME	INDIA, CHINA & JAPAN	SUB-SAHARAN AFRICA & THE AMERICAS
1000	Iron-working in Transcaucasia	Libyan and Nubian rulers in Egypt (c. 1000-700) Kingdom of Israel (933-722) Kingdom of Judah (933-586)	Greek Dark Ages (c. 1100-800)	Chou Dynasty continues (c. 1100-256) Late Vedas (c. 1100-500) Emergence of caste system (c. 1000)	Iron working fosters population centers in Africa Olmec center moved to La Venta in Tabasco, Mexico
900	Urartu emerges as a rival of Assyria Arame (c. 870-845) Sarduri I (c. 845-825) Tushpa built (c. 840) Shalmaneser invades Urartu (841) Ispuini (c. 825-810)	Revival of Assyria (c. 900-745) Ashur-nasirpal (c. 884-859) Shalmaneser III (c. 860-824)			
800	Menua (c. 810-785) Argishti I (c. 785-760) Erebuni built (c. 782) Argistihinili built (c. 775) Apex of Urartu Sarduri II (c. 760-735) Tiglath-pileser invades Urartu (744) Loss of Syria (c. 735) Rusa I (735-714) Cimmerian invasions Sargon's invasion 714 Argishti II (c. 714-685)	Rise of Media Assyria rules parts of Egypt (c. 740-705) Tiglath-pileser III (c. 745-727) Assyrian Empire (c. 750-700) Sargon II (c. 722-705) Cimmerian invasions	Rise of Athens and Sparta (c. 800) Iliad & Odyssey (c. 750) Rome founded (c. 750) Expansion of Greek colonies (c. 750-600) Rise of Greek land-owning class (c. 750 - 600)	Rise of Media (c. 800) Upanishads (c. 800-600) Foundation of Hinduism Feudalism in China (c. 800-250)	Kush Kingdom founded in Africa (c. 800)
700	Scythian invasions Rusa II (c. 685-645) Teishebaini built (c. 650) Erimena (c. 625-615) Decline of Urartu (615-610)	Kushites conquer and unite Egypt (c. 700-525) Ashur-banipal II (c. 688-624) Fall of Elam Zoroaster (c. 650) Rise of Persia (c. 650-550) Fall of Assyria (612-610) New Babylonian Empire (612-539) Medes form empire (612-550)	Age of tyrants in Greece (c. 650-500) Doric architectural style in Greece (c. 650-500) Thales of Miletus (c. 640-546)	Legendary beginning of current line of Japanese emperors (c. 650)	Height of ancient Ethiopian culture Olmec pyramids in Mexico

Table 2: 1000 B.C. to 600 B.C.

B.C.E.	ARMENIA	MIDDLE EAST, PERSIA & EGYPT	GREECE & ROME	INDIA, CHINA & JAPAN	SUB-SAHARAN AFRICA & THE AMERICAS
600	Medes conquer Urartu Yervandunis vassals of Medes (c. 570-550) Yervandunis vassals of Persia (c. 550-530) Revolts in Armenia, Armeno-Persian satraps (c. 530-410)	Kush rule in Egypt Lydians invent coins (c. 600) Height of Median empire (c. 580-550) Babylonian captivity of Jews (586-538) Nebuchadnezzar builds the Hanging Gardens of Babylon, one of the Seven Wonders of the ancient world Persian Achaemenid empire (550-331) End of Babylonian captivity, rebuilding of Temple in Jerusalem (538) Persian conquest of Egypt (525) Darius I (522-486) Behistun monument (c. 520) Royal road built	Solon's reforms in Athens (594) Pythagoras (c. 582-507) Aeschylus (c. 525-456) Roman republic founded (509) Athenian democracy begins (508)	Chou Dynasty to 256 Buddha (c. 563-483) Confucius (c. 551-479) Lao-Tzu (c. 550) Mahavira, founder of Jainism (c. 540-468)	Olmec civilization in La Vente to 400
500		Xerxes I (486-465)	Ionic architectural style in Greece (c. 500-400) Phidias (c. 500-432) Orphic and Eleusinian cults (c. 500-100) Sophocles (c. 496-406) Greco-Persian wars (499-478) Pericles (494-429) Herodotus (c. 484-424) Euripides (c. 480-406) Delian League (479-404) Socrates (c. 469-399) Thucydides (460-400) Hippocrates (c. 460-377) Parthenon (c. 450) Alcibaides (c. 450-404) Aristophanes (c. 445-385) Peloponnesian War (431-404) Plato (c. 426-347)	Use of iron in China (c. 500) Cross-bow and metal tools in China (450)	Nok culture in Africa (c. 500)
400	Yervandunis re-appear as satraps (c. 410)				

Table 3: 600 B.C. to 200 B.C.

B.C.E.	ARMENIA	MIDDLE EAST, PERSIA & EGYPT	GREECE & ROME	INDIA, CHINA & JAPAN	SUB-SAHARAN AFRICA & THE AMERICAS
400	Xenophon in Armenia (401-400) Armenia autonomous (c. 330-300)	Battle of Issus (333) Battle of Gaugamela, end of Persian empire (331) Death of Alexander the Great (323) Seleucid dynasty begins (c. 312)	Corinthian architectural style in Greece (c. 400-300) Aristotle (c. 384-322) Epicurus (c. 342-270) Zeno the Stoic (c. 320-250) Euclid (c. 320-285) Death of Demosthenes (322)	Use of coins in China Indian epics (400-200 A.D.) Magadha Kingdom Nanda dynasty in India Chandragupta and the Mauryan empire (322-185) Rise of Taoism in China The Mahabharata	
300	Greater Armenia ruled by Yervandunis as an independent state (c. 300-200)	Seleucus I (305-281) Ptolemy dynasty in Egypt	Archimedes (c. 287-212) Punic wars between Rome and Carthage (264-146) Rome advances into Greece (215) Polybius (205-118)	Ashoka (c. 270-232) Bhagavad Gita Fall of the Chou dynasty (256) Legalism in China (c. 250) Ch'in dynasty (221-207) Great Wall (c. 220-207) Tomb of First Emperor in Xian (c. 210-200) Han Dynasty (202-220 A.D.) in China I Ching in China	Olmec civilization in Tres Zapotes Early calendars in America
200	End of Yervanduni rule (c. 200)				

Table 3: 600 B.C. to 200 B.C.

B.C.E.	ARMENIA	MIDDLE EAST, PERSIA & EGYPT	GREECE & ROME	INDIA, CHINA & JAPAN	SUB-SAHARAN AFRICA & THE AMERICAS
200	Artashes overthrows Yervanduni rule (c.200) Artashes I (189-160) Artashesian Dynasty (c. 189-10 A.D.) Artavazd I (160-115) Tigran I (115-95)	Ptolemaic rule in Egypt continues Battle of Magnesia, Rome enters Asia (190) Mithradates I of Parthia (171-138) Jewish revolt led by Judas Maccabeus (167-165) End of Seleucid power in Syria (129)	Skeptics (c. 200-100) Rome annexes Greece and Macedon (148) Carthage destroyed (146) Stoicism in Rome (c. 140) Reform of the Gracchi (133-121) Cicero (106-43)	Han dynasty to 220 A.D. Bactrian Rule Hellenism in western India Silk road opens China to Parthia and Rome (c. 104)	Decline of Olmec civilization in Mexico Increase of food production in sub-Saharan Africa
100	Tigran II (95-55) Armenian Empire Lucullus invades Armenia (69-68) Pompey invades Armenia (66) Artavazd II (55-35) Mark Antony invades Armenia (35) Artashes II (30-20) Decline and fall of the Artashesian dynasty	Dead Sea Scrolls (c.100) Lucullus invades Asia Minor (73) Death of Mithradates of Pontus (65) Pompey declares Syria a Roman province (64) Battle of Carrhae (53) Kushans invade eastern Parthia Roman-Parthian conflict in Syria Death of Cleopatra, end of Ptolemaic rule, Egypt a Roman province (30)	Lucretius (98-55) Roman citizenship granted to residents of Italy (90) Sulla in Greece (88-84) Sulla's dictatorship (88-79) Revolt of Spartacus (73-71) Virgil (70-19) Horace (65-8 A.D.) First Triumvirate (60-53) Livy (59-17 A.D.) Death of Crassus (53) Pompey's dictatorship (51-49) Caesar crosses the Rubicon (49) Death of Pompey (48) Caesar's dictatorship (46-44) Death of Caesar (44) Second Triumvirate (43-36) Ovid (43-18 A.D.) Seneca (4 to 65 A. D.) Battle of Actium (31) Death of Antony (30) End of Roman Republic (27) Augustus (27 to 14 A.D.)	Yamato clan forms Japanese state (c. 100) Kushans rule north-western India (c. 25-225 A.D.)	Early Teotihuacan culture in Mexico Early Mayan culture in Central America
C.E.	Roman-Parthian conflict in Armenia		Birth of Christ (c. 4 B.C.) Tiberius (14-37) Pliny the Elder (23-79) Crucifixion (30) St. Paul's missionary activity (35-67) Caligula (37-41) Claudius (41-54)		

Table 4: 200 B.C. to 50 A.D.

C.E.	ARMENIA	MIDDLE EAST & PERSIA	ROME & BYZANTIUM	INDIA, CHINA & JAPAN	SUB-SAHARAN AFRICA & THE AMERICAS
50	Corbulo invades Armenia (58-59) Peace of Rhandeia (64) Arshakuni dynasty (66-248) Trdat I (66-88) Vespasian establishes Roman authority in western Armenia (72)	Vologeses I (51-77) Kushans invade Parthia Jews revolt against Rome (66) Titus ends Jewish state (70) Rome persecutes Jews Jewish diaspora begins	Nero (54-68) Pliny the Younger (c. 62-113) Juvenal (c. 60-140) Trdat crowned in Rome (66) Death of Petronius (66) Tacitus (c. 55-115) Vespasian (69-79) Colosseum built (c. 80) Titus (79-81) Domitian (81-96)	Kushan Empire to 225 in northwestern India Yamato clan rules in Japan Paper invented in China (c. 50) Han dynasty continues its rule in China	Chauvin cult in Peru
100	Trajan invades Armenia (114-116) Vagharsh I (117-144) Vagharshapat built (c. 120-140) Roman-Parthian wars in Armenia (161-163) Vagharsh II (186-198) Khosrov I (198-216)	Roman-Parthian conflict in Mesopotamia (c. 115-211) Jews revolt (116, 132-135) Decline of Parthia Small-pox epidemics (c. 165)	Nerva (96-98) Trajan (98-117) Hadrian (117-138) Pantheon built (c. 120) Cults of Mithra, Cybele and Isis Galen (c. 130-200) Antonius (138-161) Marcus Aurelius (161-180) Small-pox epidemic Commodus (180-192) Severus (193-211)	Emperor Wu (140-186)	Mayan civilization (c. 100)
200	Trdat II (217-252) flees to Rome (252) Sasanid rule in eastern Armenia (c. 260-298) Narseh (272-293) Khosrov II (279-287) rules in western Armenia Khosrov II assassinated Trdat flees to Rome (c. 287) Peace of Nisibis (298) Trdat III (298-330)	Camels first used in Arabian desert (c. 200) Birth of Mani (c. 216) Sasanid dynasty in Persia (c. 224-651) Shapur I (240-270) Death of Mani (271) Narseh (293-302)	End of pax Romana (c. 200) Growth of serfdom (c. 200-500) Economic decline (c. 200-300) Barbarian invasions (c. 200-280) Roman jurisprudence completed (c. 200) Plotinus (Neo-Platonism) 204-270 Caracalla (211-217) Macrinus (217-218) Civil Wars (235-284) Philip the Arab (244-249) Diocletian (284-305)	Buddhism in China (c. 200-500) Fall of Han Dynasty (220) China ruled by various groups (220-589)	Bantu speakers expand through Central Africa (c. 200-900)

Table 5: 50 A.D. to 400 A.D.

C.E.	ARMENIA	MIDDLE EAST & PERSIA	ROME & BYZANTIUM	INDIA, CHINA & JAPAN	SUB-SAHARAN AFRICA & THE AMERICAS
300	Christianity official religion (c. 314) Khosrov III, Dvin founded (c.340) Arshak II (350-368) Parantsem (368-369) Pap (369-374) Arshak III (378-385) in western Armenia (385-390) Khosrov IV in eastern Armenia (385-389) Armenia partitioned (387) Vramshapuh (389-414) Western Armenia under Byzantine rule (c. 390-640)	Shapur II (309-379) Persia persecutes its Christians, Jews and Manicheans	Renewed persecution of Christians (303) Constantine (306-337) Edict of Milan (313) Constantinople founded (c. 315) Council of Nicea (325) Empire under joint rulers (337) St. Augustine (354-430) Julian (361-363) Jovian (363-364) Valens (364-379) rules in the east Theodosius (379-395) Christianity official religion of Roman Empire (380) Council of Constantinople (381) Roman Empire partitioned (395)	Classical period of Hindu civilization (c. 300-800) Gupta Empire (320-467) Indian culture spreads to Southeast Asia Japan invades South Korea (369) Kalidasa (c. 380-450)	Use of camels in African deserts (c. 300-500) Oaxaca Valley civilization in Mexico (c. 300-700) Kingdom of Axum in Ethiopia Spread of Christianity (c. 350) Moche culture in Peru

Table 5: 50 A.D. to 400 A.D.

C.E.	ARMENIA	MIDDLE EAST & PERSIA	ROME & BYZANTIUM	INDIA, CHINA & JAPAN	SUB-SAHARAN AFRICA & THE AMERICAS
400	Alphabet invented (c. 400)	Tolerance for certain Christians in Persia	Pope Innocent I (401-417)	Japan adopts Chinese ideographs (c. 400)	Classical Mayan civilization in Central America (c. 500)
	Artashes IV (422-428)	Bahram V (420-438)	Barbarian invasions (c. 410-470)	Fa-hsien in India (405)	Settlements in Ghana (c. 500)
	End of Arshakuni Dynasty (428)	Yazdgird II (438-457)	Council of Ephesus (431)		Apex of Teotihuacan civilization in Mexico
	Marzpan period (428-638)		Pope Leo I (440-461)		
	Vardanank Wars (c. 440-484)	Peroz (459-484)	Attila in Europe (c. 450)		
	Battle of Avarayr (451)		Council of Chalcedon (451)		
	Nuvarsak agreement (484)	Talmud completed (c. 480)	Fall of Western Roman Empire (476)		
	Armenians reject Chalcedon (491 and 506)	Balash (484-488)	Boethius (c.480-524)	White Huns in north India (c. 480-600)	
		Mazdakism in Persia (c. 490)	Merovingian rule begins (481)		
			Clovis adopts Roman Christianity (496)		
500	Justinian's edicts in Armenia (535-536)	Khosrow I (531-579)	Decline of towns and trade in the West (c. 500-700)	Glass, compass, gunpowder in China (c. 500)	
	Armenian calendar commences (552)	Brief revival of Sasanids	Benedictine order founded (c. 520)	Buddhism in Japan (552)	
	Council of Dvin (554)		Justinian (527-565)		
	Partition of Armenia (591)	Birth of Muhammad the Prophet (c. 570)			
		Khosrow II (591-628)	Maurice (582-602)		
			Pope Gregory I (590-604)		

Table 6: 400 A.D. to 600 A.D.

C.E.	ARMENIA	ISLAMIC MIDDLE EAST	BYZANTIUM & THE WEST	INDIA, CHINA & JAPAN	SUB-SAHARAN AFRICA & THE AMERICAS
600	Break with Orthodox Church (609) Heraclius in Armenia (623-627) Arab invasions and conquest (640-650) Rshtuni-Mu 'awiyah agreement (652)	Hijra—start of Muslim calendar (622) Death of Muhammad (632) Age of the Caliphs (632-661) Muslims conquer Egypt (641) End of the Sasanid empire (651) Sunni-Shi 'i split (656) Umayyad Dynasty (661-750) Mu 'awiyah (661-680) Battle of Karbala (680) Martyrdom of imam Husein	Heraclius (610-641) Decline of the Merovingian Kingdom	Sanskrit drama (c. 600-1000) Stone temple architecture in India (c. 600-1200) T 'ang Dynasty in China (618-907) Hsuan-Tsang in India (629) Taika reform Edict starts Imperial rule in Japan (645)	Tiahuanaco-Huari period in Peru Rise of cities (c. 600) Egyptian and Ethiopian Coptic Churches gain power (c. 650) Slave trade from sub-Saharan Africa to Mediterranean Sea (c. 650-1400)
700	Arabs create the province of Arminiya (700-702) Massacre at Nakhichevan (703) Paulician movement in Armenia Church council at Dvin (719) Church council at Manzikert (725) Armenians rebel against Arab rule (774-775) Rise of the Bagratunis Ashot the Meat-Eater (790-826)	Height of Islamic commerce and industry (c. 700-1300) 'Abbasid Dynasty (750-1258) Harun al-Rashid (786-809)	Agrarian economy in the West (c. 700-1300) Muslims conquer Spain (711) Muslim siege of Constantinople (717) Iconoclasm in Byzantium (726-843) Muslims defeated at Tours (732/733) Boewulf (c. 750) Irish "Book of Kells" (c. 750) Frankish kingdom revived (751) Charlemagne (768-814) Song of Roland	Muslims reach Indus river (712) Nara period—first capital in Japan (710-784) Korea unified Golden age of Chinese poetry Heian period in Japan (794-1185)	Height of Mayan Civilization in Copan, Central America (c. 700) Soba and Dongola states Decline of ancient civilizations in the Americas
800	Tondrakian movement in Armenia (c. 840-850) Armenians rebel against Arab taxes (850-851) Bugha in Armenia (851-853) Samarran captivity (853-861) Ashot Bagratuni Prince of Princes (862-884) Ashot I, King of Armenia (884-890) Smbat I (890-914)	al-Khwarazmi (800-847) al-Amin (809-813) al-Ma 'mun (813-833) Babak's revolt (816) Turkish mercenaries in Baghdad al-Mu 'tasim (833-842) Capital moved from Baghdad to Samarra (836-870) Rise of Afshin (836) al-Mutawakkil (847-861) al-Razi (865-925) al-Mu 'tamid (870-892) al-Kindi (d.870) Rise of Sufism Sajids in Azerbaijan	Carolingian Renaissance (800-850) Height of Byzantine trade and industry (c. 800-1000) Breakup of Carolingian Empire (850-911) Basil I (867-886) Alfred the Great in England (871-899) Height of Viking raids in the West (880-911)	Rise of Japanese culture Flowering of literature Khmer empire in Kampuchea (802)	

Table 7: 600 A.D. to 900 A.D.

C.E.	ARMENIA & GEORGIA	ISLAMIC MIDDLE EAST	BYZANTIUM & THE WEST	INDIA, CHINA & JAPAN	SUB-SAHARAN AFRICA & THE AMERICAS
900	Artsrunis receive crown from Yusuf (908) Ashot II (The Iron) (914-929) Abas (929-953) Ashot III (953-977) Ani becomes capital of Armenia Smbat II (977-990) Gagik I (990-1020)	Rise of Sufism al-Muktafi (902-908) Yusuf (c. 906-929) rules Azerbaijan Sallarids (c. 916-1090) Rawwadids (c. 920-1071) Buyids (932-1062) al-Farabi (d. 950) Shaddadids (c. 951-1174) Ghaznavids (962-1186) Fatimids in Egypt (c. 968-1171) al-Azhar university in Cairo	Cluny founded (910) Reconquista begins in Spain (910) Otto I (The Great) (936-973) Russian state founded in Kiev (c. 950) Basil II (976-1025) Byzantines convert Russians (988) Capetian dynasty in France (989)	Five Dynasties in China (907-960) Wood-block printing widespread in China and Japan Sung Dynasty (960-1279)	Kingdom of Ghana (c. 900-1100) Toltec Empire in Tula, Mexico (c. 900-1200) Collapse of Mayan civilization
1000	King of Vaspurakan wills his kingdom to Byzantium (1022) Hovhannes Smbat (1020-1042) Gagik II (1042-1045) Fall of Ani—end of Bagratunis of Ani (1045) Fall of Kars—end of Bagratunis of Kars (1064) Large Armenian emigration to Byzantium and Cilicia Rise of Rubenid and Hetumid houses in Cilicia (c. 1070-1085) Rise of Zakarids in Armenia and Georgia David the Builder of Georgia (1089-1125)	Avicenna (d. 1037) Seljuks (c. 1038-1194) Seljuks in Baghdad (1055) Danishmandids (1071-1177) Battle of Manzikert (1071) Assassins in Alamut (1090) First Crusade (1096-1099) Crusaders conquer Jerusalem (1099)	Romanesque architecture (c. 1000-1200) Split of Roman and Greek Churches (1054) Normans conquer England (1066) Pope Gregory VII (1073-1085) Struggle between Church and State in the West (1073-1122) Seljuks of Rum (1077-1307) Peter Abelard (1079-1142) St. Bernard of Clairvaux (1090-1153) Crusade preached by Pope Urban II (1095) Comneni emperors (1081-1185)	Turks and Afghans conquer northern India (1022) Feudalism in Japan, code of Bushido Tale of Genji Vietnam independent from China	Kingdom of Kanen in Africa Islam penetrates sub-Saharan and East Africa Incas settle in Cuzco Valley in Andes

Table 8: 900 A.D. to 1100 A.D.

C.E.	(Historic and Cilicia) ARMENIA	ISLAMIC MIDDLE EAST & BYZANTIUM	EUROPE	INDIA, CHINA & JAPAN	SUB-SAHARAN AFRICA & THE AMERICAS
1100	Zakarids rule parts of Armenia as Georgian vassals (c. 1100-1236) Toros I (1102-1129) Levon I (1129-1137) Toros II (1144-1169) Mleh (1170-1175) Ruben II (1175-1187) Queen Tamar of Georgia (1184-1213) Levon II (1187-1199) as King Levon I (1199-1219)	al-Ghazali (d. 1111) Omar Khayyam (d. 1123) Zangids (c. 1127-1222) Second Crusade (1147-1149) Ayyubids in Egypt (1169-1250) Third Crusade (1189-1192) Sa 'di (1193-1292) Averroes (d. 1198)	Revival of towns and trade in the West (c. 1100-1300) Rise of universities in the West (c. 1100-1300) Troubadour poetry in the West (c. 1100-1220) Henry I (England) (1100-1135) Louis IV (France) (1108-1137) Concordat of Worms (1122) Height of Cistercian monasticism (c. 1115-1153) Aristotle translated into Latin (c. 1140-1260) Gothic architecture (c. 1150-1500) Frederick I Barbarossa (Germany) (1152-1190) Henry II (England) (1154-1189) Thomas 'a Becket (d. 1170) Philip Augustus (France) (1180-1223) Windmills invented (c. 1180) Pope Innocent III (1198-1216)	Angkor Wat in Kampuchea (c.1100- 1150) China divided between Sung and Chin Dynasties (1127) Neo-Confucianism (c. 1130-1200) Explosive powder used in China (c. 1150) Genghis Khan in Mongolia and China (c. 1162-1227) Kamakuro Shogunate in Japan (1185-1333) Destruction of Buddhism in India (1192)	Kingdom of Benin (1100-1897) Post-Classical Mayan civilization at Chichen Itza, Central America
1200	Zabel (1219-1223) Zabel and Philip (1223-1225) Zabel and Hetum (1226-1269) Mongols in Armenia (1236-1245) Hetum's alliance with Mongols (1247) Levon II (1269-1289) Hetum II (1289-1293) Holy See moved to Sis (1292)	Maimonides (d. 1204) Fourth Crusade (1202-1204) Fifth Crusade (1218-1221) Mamluks in Egypt (1250-1517) Ilkhanids (1256-1353) Baghdad falls to Mongols End of Abbasid rule (1258) Mongol defeat by Mamluks (1260) Peleologi emperors (1261-1453) Last Crusader state falls to Muslims (1291)	Albigensian Crusade (1208-1213) Franciscan order founded (c. 1210) Roger Bacon (c. 1214-1294) Magna Carta (1215) Fourth Lateran Council (1215) Dominican order founded (1216) St. Thomas Aquinas (1225-1274) Louis IX (St. Louis) (1226-1270) Golden Horde (1226-1502) Edward I (1272-1307) Philip IV (The Fair) (1285-1314) Mechanical clock (c. 1290) Pope Boniface VIII (1294-1303)	Peak of Khmer Empire (c. 1200) Zen Buddhism in Japan (c. 1200) Small-pox innoculation in China (c.1200) Sultanate of Delhi (1206-1526) Mongol conquest of China (c. 1215-1368) Indian culture divided into Hindu and Muslim Kublai Khan (China) (1260-1294) Marco Polo in China (c. 1275-1292) Yuan Dynasty (China) (1279-1368) Japan halts Mongol invasion (1281)	Kingdom of Mali (c. 1200-1450) Decline of Ghana (c. 1224)

Table 9: 1100 A.D. to 1300 A.D.

C.E.	(Historic and Cilicia) ARMENIA	ISLAMIC MIDDLE EAST & BYZANTIUM	EUROPE	INDIA, CHINA & JAPAN	SUB-SAHARAN AFRICA & THE AMERICAS
1300	Council of Sis (1307) Oshin (1307-1320) Council of Adana (1316) Guy de Lusignan (1342-1344) Levon V (1374-1375) Fall of Cilician Armenian Kingdom (1375) Timur's invasions of Armenia (1386-1403)	Ottoman conquests in Anatolia (c. 1300-1395) Murad I (1362-1389) Persian poet Hafiz (d. 1389) Bayazid I (1389-1402)	Petrarch (1304-1374) Avignon papacy (1305-1378) Dante's Divine Comedy (c. 1310) Hundred Years' War (1337-1453) Black Death (1347-1350) Italian Renaissance (c. 1350-1550) Hanseatic League (c. 1350-1450) Boccaccio's Decameron (c.1350) Great Schism (1378-1417) Medici Bank (1397-1494) Chaucer's Canterbury Tales (c. 1390)	Rise of Daimyo in Japan (c. 1300-1500) Ashikage Shogunate in Japan (1336-1573) Ming Dynasty in China (1368-1644) Timur sacks Delhi (1398)	Stone complexes in Zimbabwe (c. 1300) Aztecs arrive in Mexico (c. 1325) University of Timbuktu (c. 1330) Kong Kingdom in Africa (c. 1350)
1400	Holy See returns to Etchmiadzin (1441) Qara-Qoyunlu in Armenia (c. 1380-1468) Aq-Qoyunlu in Armenia (c. 1468-1500)	Timur's invasions of Anatolia (1400-1402) Ibn-Khaldun (d. 1406) Mehmet II (1451-1481) Ottomans capture Constantinople, end of Byzantine rule (1453) Ottoman Empire (1453-1918)	Council of Constance (1414-1417) Hussite revolt (1420-1434) Joan of Arc (active 1429-1431) Council of Basel (1431-1449) Botticelli (1444-1510) Printing press (c. 1450) Leonardo da Vinci (1452-1519) War of the Roses (1455-1485) Ivan III of Russia (1462-1505) Erasmus (c. 1469-1536) Machiavelli (1469-1527) Union of Ferdinand and Isabella (1469) Dürer (1471-1528) Raphael (1483-1520) Martin Luther (1483-1546) Tudor Dynasty in England (1485-1603) Michelangelo (1485-1564) Loyola (1491-1556) Fall of Granada, last Muslim state in Spain (1492)	Muslims establish commercial center at Malacca (c. 1400) Vasco da Gama reaches India (1498) Sikh religious sect founded (1498)	Height of Inca power in Peru (1438-1532) Height of Aztec power in Mexico (c. 1440) Portugese arrive in Benin (c. 1440) Height of Songhai Empire in Africa (1468-1590) Diaz rounds the Cape of Good Hope (1488) Columbus discovers New World (1492)

Table 10: 1300 A.D. to 1500 A.D.

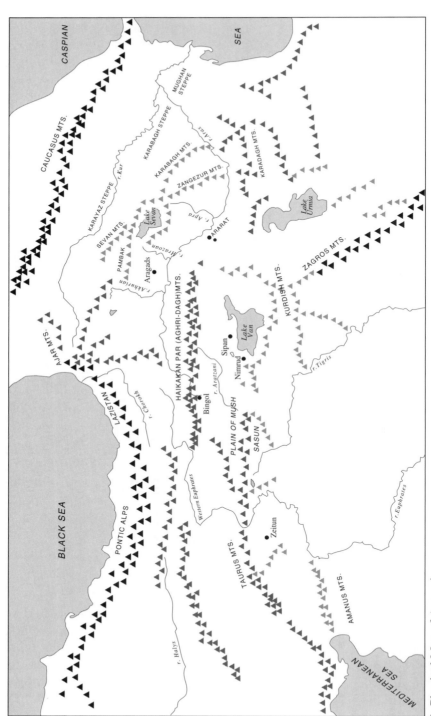

1. Physical Map of Armenia

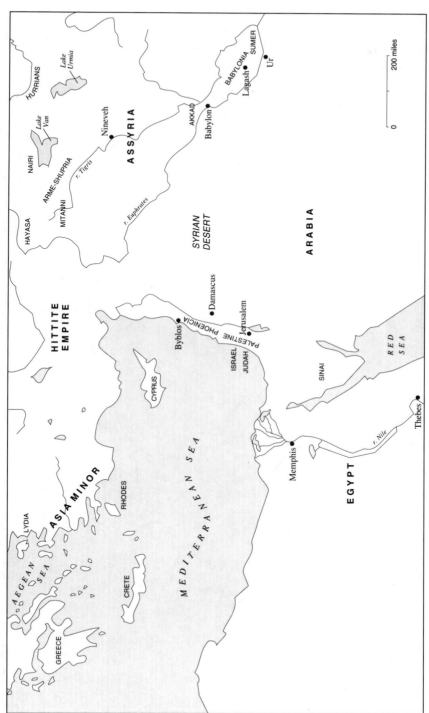

2. The Ancient World

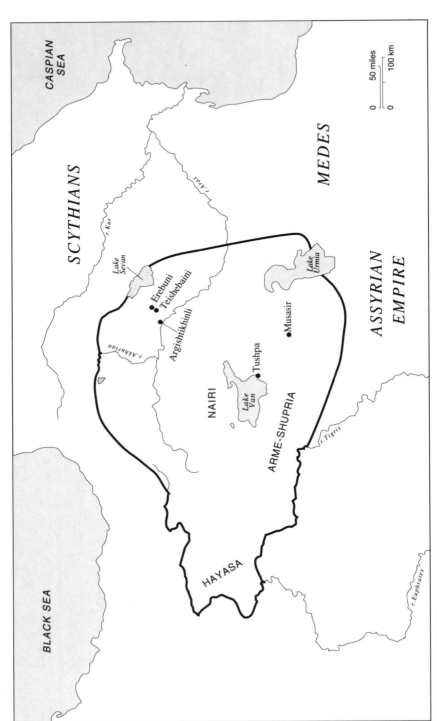

CASPIAN
SEA

SCYTHIANS

MEDES

ASSYRIAN
EMPIRE

BLACK SEA

r. Kur

r. Araxs

Lake
Sevan

Lake
Urmia

Erebuni
Teishebaini

•Musasir

Argishtikhinli

r. Akhurian

Tushpa

Lake
Van

NAIRI

ARME-SHUPRIA

r. Tigris

HAYASA

r. Euphrates

0   50 miles
0   100 km

3. Urartu (c. 750 B.C.)

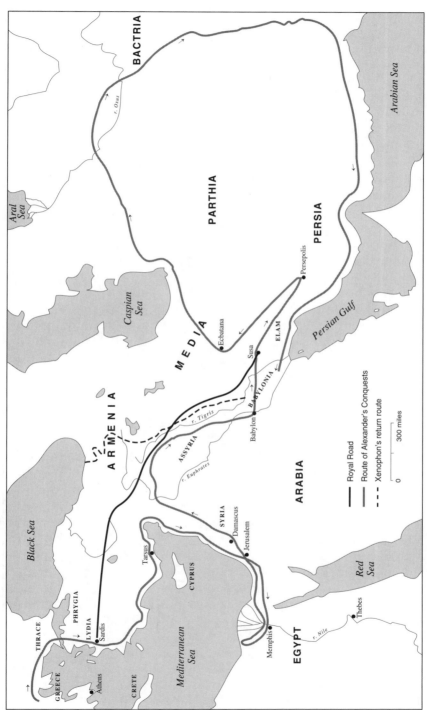

4. The Persian Empire (c. 500–330 B.C.)

Royal Road
Route of Alexander's Conquests
Xenophon's return route

0   300 miles

THRACE
GREECE
Athens
CRETE
PHRYGIA
LYDIA
Sardis
Black Sea
Tarsus
CYPRUS
Mediterranean Sea
SYRIA
Damascus
Jerusalem
ARABIA
Red Sea
EGYPT
Memphis
Thebes
r. Nile
ARMENIA
ASSYRIA
r. Euphrates
r. Tigris
BABYLONIA
Babylon
ELAM
Susa
Caspian Sea
Aral Sea
MEDIA
Ecbatana
Persepolis
PERSIA
Persian Gulf
PARTHIA
BACTRIA
r. Oxus
Arabian Sea

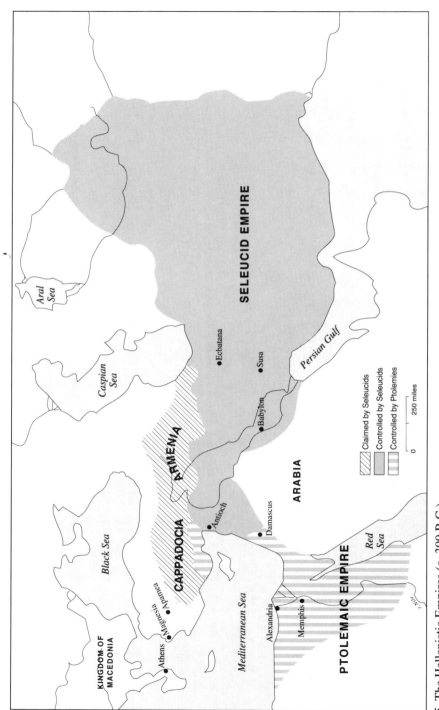

5. The Hellenistic Empires (c. 300 B.C.)

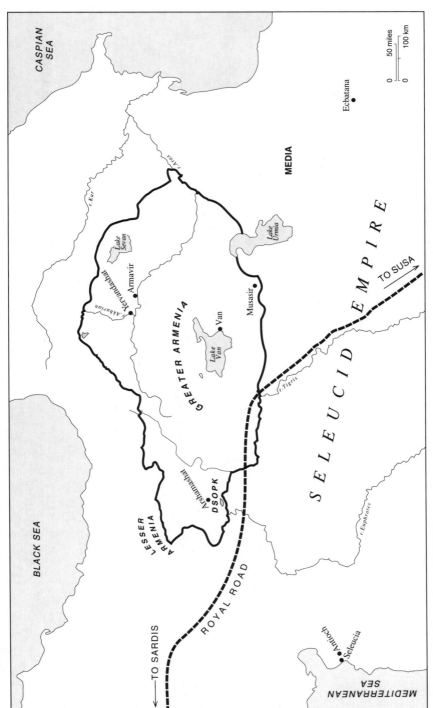

6. Yervanduni Armenia (c. 250 B.C.)

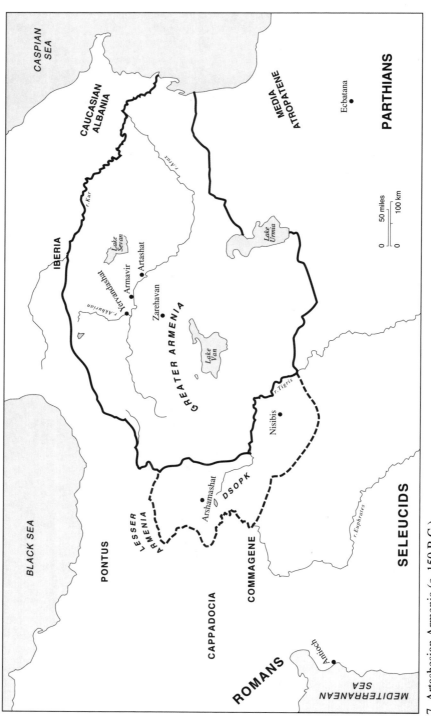

7. Artashesian Armenia (c. 150 B.C.)

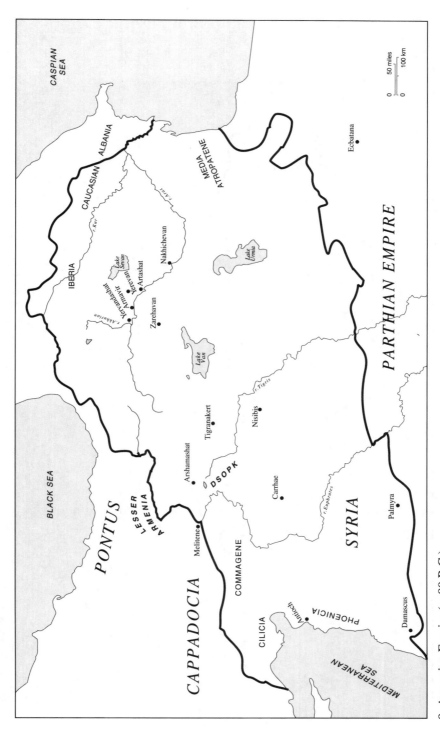

8. Armenian Empire (c. 80 B.C.)

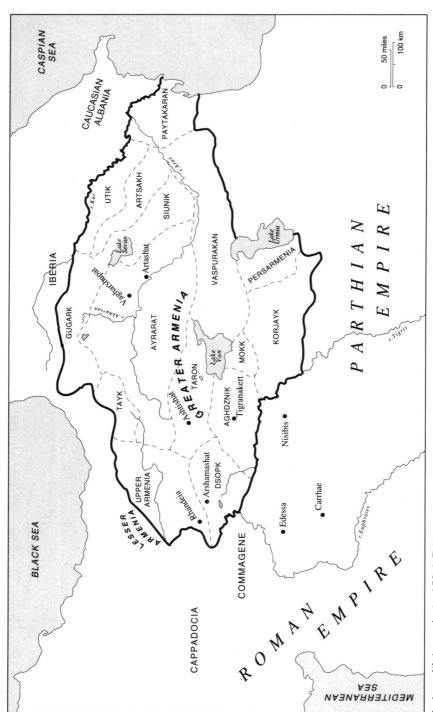

9. Arsacid Armenia (c. 150 A.D.)

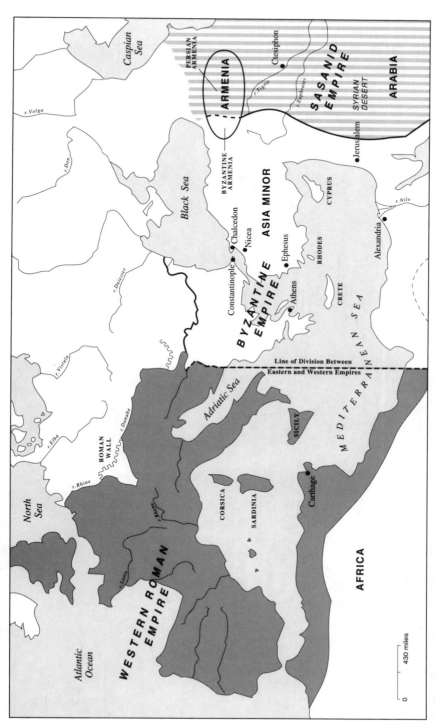

10. The Roman Empire (c. 387 A.D.)

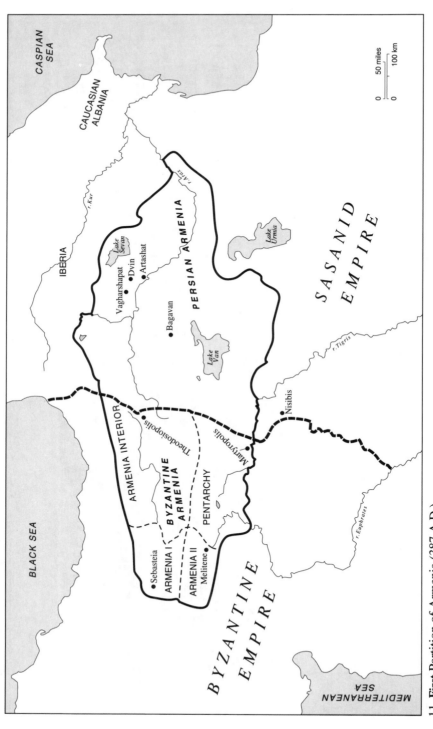

11. **First** Partition of Armenia (387 A.D.)

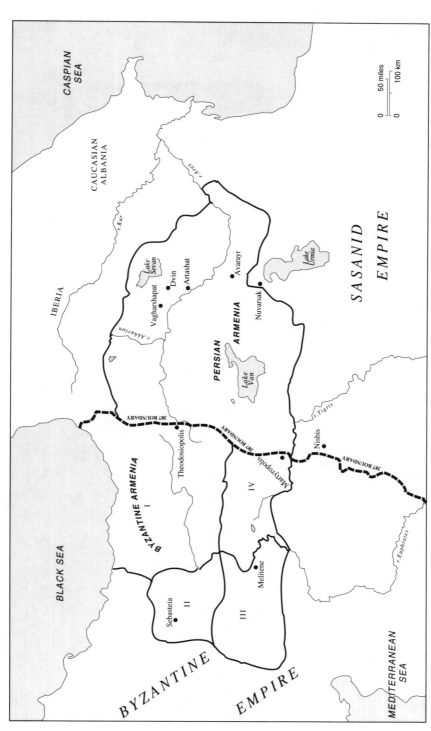

12. Armenia in the Period of Justinian (536 A.D.)

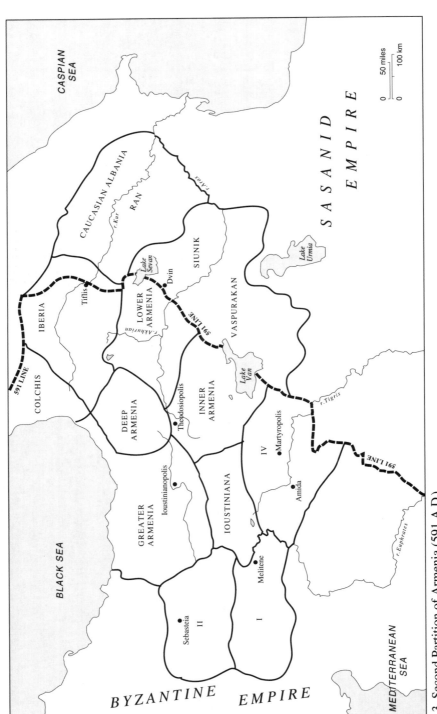

13. Second Partition of Armenia (591 A.D.)

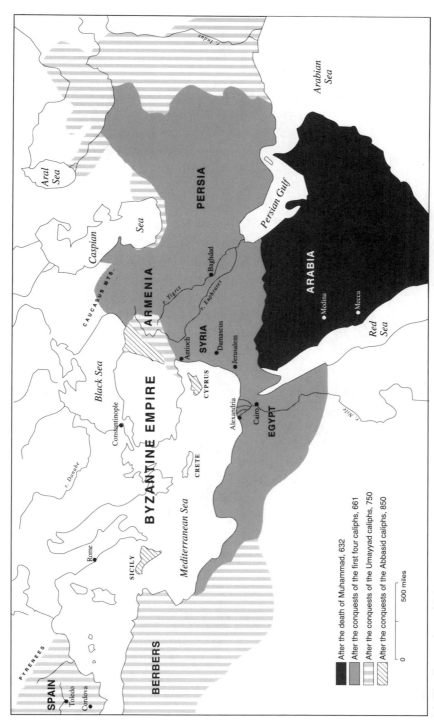

14. The Expansion of Islam

Legend (map key):

After the death of Muhammad, 632
After the conquests of the first four caliphs, 661
After the conquests of the Umayyad caliphs, 750
After the conquests of the Abbasid caliphs, 850

0   500 miles

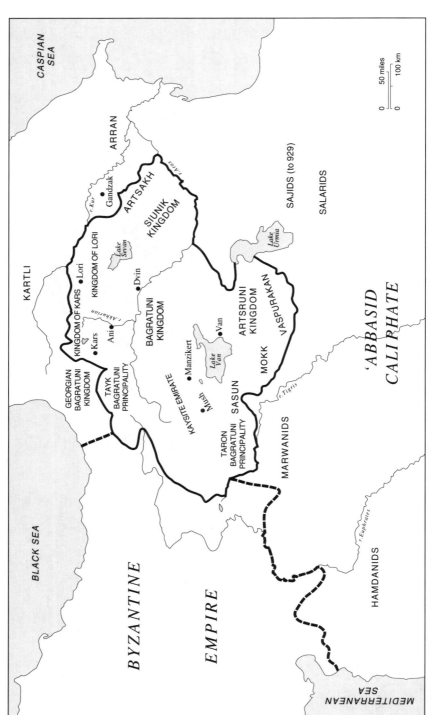

15. The Bagratuni and other Medieval Armenian Kingdoms (c. 1000 A.D.)

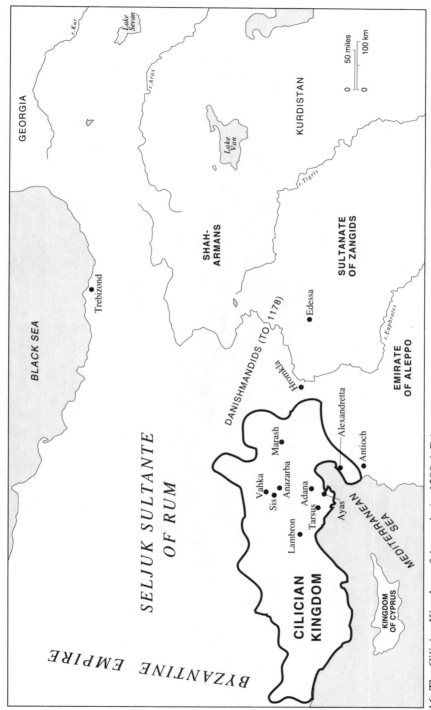

16. The Cilician Kingdom of Armenia (c. 1200 A.D.)

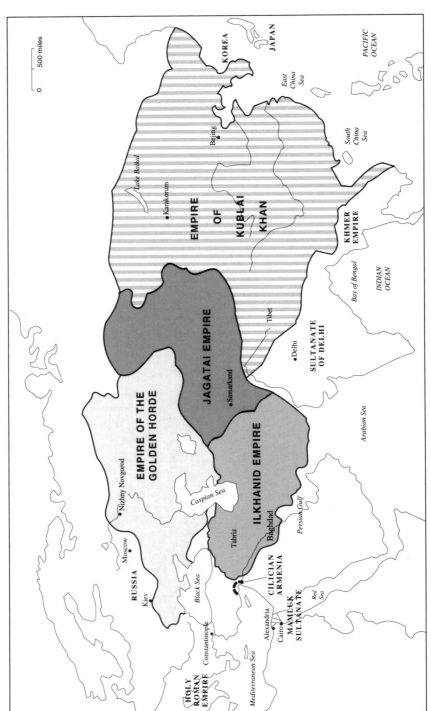

17. The Mongol Empire (c. 1280 A.D.)

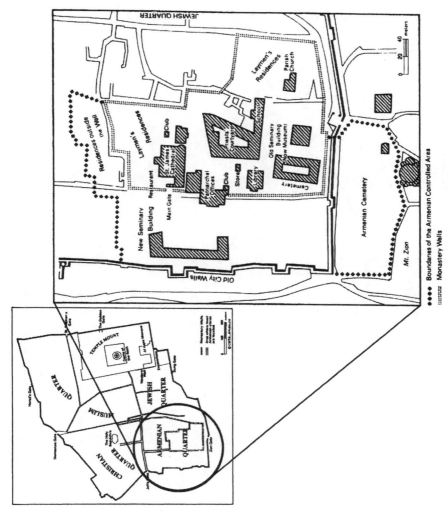

18. Armenian Quarter of Jerusalem

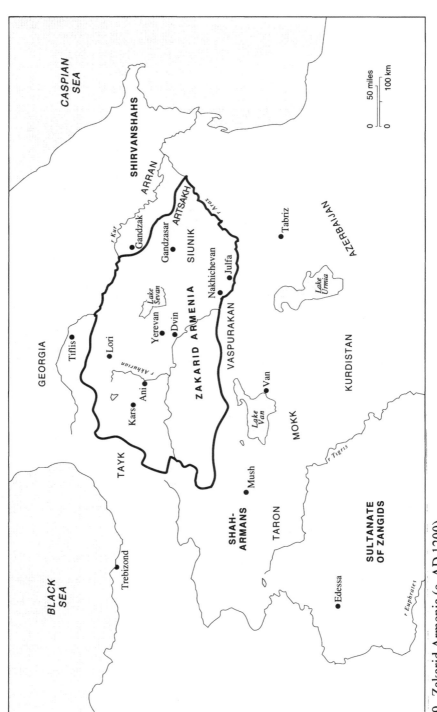

19. Zakarid Armenia (c. AD 1200)

1. Twin peaks of Ararat

2. Winged bull, bronze (Urartian period)

3. Figurine of a winged lion with human head (Urartian period)

4. Urartian helmet

5. Monument in Nemrud Dagh, Turkey

6. Behistun Monument, Iran (Achaemenid-Yervanduni period)

7. Bronze head of a Hellenistic deity
(Artashesid period)

8. Silver Tertradrachm of Tigran the Great

9. Temple of Garni (Artashesid period)

10. Cathedral of Ejmiatsin (4th century)

11. Church of Ereruk (4-5th centuries)

Ա ա	a	Կ կ	k[g]	Ռ ռ	rh
Բ բ	b[p]	Հ հ	h	Ս ս	s
Գ գ	g[k]	Ձ ձ	dz[ts]	Վ վ	v
Դ դ	d[t]	Ղ ղ	gh	Տ տ	t[d]
Ե ե	e	Ճ ճ	ch[j]	Ր ր	r
Զ զ	z	Մ մ	m	Ց ց	ts'
Է է	ē	Յ յ	y	Ւ ւ	w
Ը ը	ě	Ն ն	n	Փ փ	p'
Թ թ	t'	Շ շ	sh	Ք ք	k'
Ժ ժ	zh	Ո ո	o	Օ օ	ō
Ի ի	i	Չ չ	ch'	Ֆ ֆ	f
Լ լ	l	Պ պ	p[b]		
Խ խ	kh	Ջ ջ	j[ch]		
Ծ ծ	ts[dz]				

12. The Armenian Alphabet

13. Cathedral of Mastara (6ᵗʰ century)

14. Church of St. Hripsime (7th century)

15. Monument at Odzun (7th century)

16. Church of St. Gayane (7th century)

17. Cathedral of Zvartnots (remains)(7th century)

18. Capital with eagle, Zvartnots

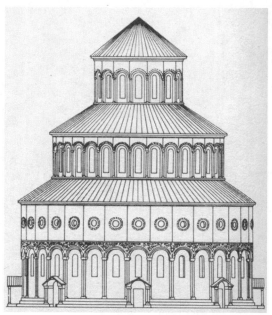

19. A reconstruction plan for Zvartnots

20. Church at Lake Sevan (9th century)

21. Church of the Holy Cross at Aghtamar (Lake Van)(10th century)

22. David and Goliath, Church of the Holy Cross, Aghtamar

23. Church of the Holy Apostles, Kars (10th century)

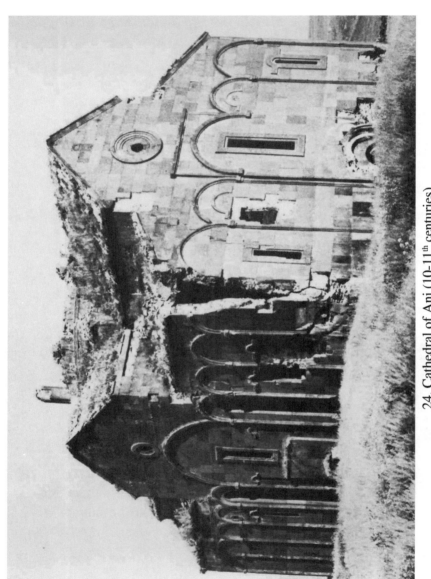

24. Cathedral of Ani (10-11th centuries)

25. Church at Ani (10-11th centuries)

26. Monastery of Khdzkunk (9-11ᵗʰ centuries)

27. Church at the monastery of Sanahin (10-13th centuries)

28. Monastery of Haghpat (10-13th centuries)

29. Monastery of Geghard (12-13th centuries)

30. Monastery of Haghartsin (11-13th centuries)

31. Monastery of Gandzasar, Karabagh (13th century)

32. Khachkar (12-13th centururies)

33. Detail of Coin of Levon I (Cilicia)

34. Tombstone of Levon V (Paris)

35. Fortress of Vahka (Cilicia)

36. Raising of Lazarus, Toros Roslin (Cilicia)(13th century)

37. Armenian Church, Church of the Nativity, Bethlehem

Part II

From Foreign Rule to Independence
(1500—2003)

Introduction to Part II

At the dawn of the early modern period, when the West began to explore a New World and adopted new political ideas, the East entered a gradual period of hibernation and decline. The Ottomans cut off Armenia, which in the past had been at the forefront of cultural exchanges, from the West. Four centuries of nomadic invasions had turned most of Armenia into a leaderless and bleak landscape. Now, a small Christian enclave in a sea of Muslim settlers and nomads, Armenia and its culture—except in a handful of locations in the highlands and the regions of Van and Yerevan—fell into a period of stagnation that lasted until the nineteenth century.

The demographic changes, which took place over the centuries, resulted in the voluntary or forced migration of most of Armenia's talent. It was in the major cities of Europe and Asia that the Armenians maintained much of their national spirit and it was in these diasporas that the revival of Armenian culture and the next chapter of Armenian history would be played out.

The history of the Armenians from the start of the sixteenth century to the present has to focus on two different groups. In the first group are the various Armenian diasporas around the world. These communities, called *spiurk* in Armenian, formed and increased or diminished as a result of invasions, massacres, revolutions, colonialism and nationalism. In the second group are the Armenians, mostly peasants and minor craftsmen, who, led by churchmen and petty lords remained in historic Armenia, which was first partitioned between the Ottomans and Persians and later between the Ottomans and Russians. Although some regions, like Van, Yerevan, Karabagh, Siunik, Sasun, Zeitun, and Mush maintained an Armenian majority into the nineteenth and twentieth centuries, other areas lost most of their Armenian inhabitants. Parts of Russian Armenia eventually evolved into the first independent Armenian Republic (1918-1920), Soviet Armenian Republic (1921-1991) and the present day Independent Armenian Republic (since 1991).

The Armenians in the Ottoman, Persian and Russian empires were in a unique situation. Although some lived in their own historic homeland within these empires, others lived outside, in the major cities of the same empires. Thus Tilfis, New Nakhichevan, Astrakhan, Smyrna, Constantinople, Isfahan, Tabriz, Baku, Moscow, and St. Petersburg contained large and influential Armenian communities. The socioeconomic conditions and the political activities of these Armenians during the eighteenth and nineteenth centuries had a major impact on the largely rural Armenian homeland.

Writing the history of the Armenians in the modern period has to take into account the political divisions among the Armenians following the collapse of the first and second Armenian Republics. The fall of the Soviet Union and the emergence of an independent Armenian State, as well as the question of Karabagh, should also be examined. One also has to review revisionist publications written by Turkish and pro-Turkish authors regarding the Armenian Genocide. Hence, despite its relatively short five centuries (compared to the twenty-five centuries covered in the first part of this study), the second part is longer. There is the simple fact that there are many more sources and data on this period. Objectivity also demands a more thorough examination.

12

Amiras and Sultans
Armenians in the Ottoman Empire
(c. 1460-1876)

DURING the latter part of the fourteenth century and through the fifteenth, Western Europe experienced the Renaissance, succeeded in driving the Muslims out of Spain, and discovered the New World. For the next two centuries Europe would be transformed by the Age of Exploration, the Reformation and Counter-Reformation, the renewed struggle between Church and State, the decline of feudalism, the rise of urban classes and the emergence of centralized nation-states and absolute monarchs. The Muslims and the Chinese were militarily equal or superior to the West. The former had repulsed the crusaders from the Middle East, and were free to rule over Orthodox and Slavic peoples in Asia Minor and Eastern Europe, Christians in the Caucasus, indigenous tribes in North Africa and Hindus in India. The Chinese would hold sway over various peoples in Central and East Asia. Free trade between east and west would give way to a more restricted trade through select channels and companies. While China became isolated and its Ming and Ch'ing dynasties could not pose a threat to the West, the Muslims, in the form of the Ottoman Turks, knocked at the door of Central Europe causing hostility between parts of Europe and the Ottoman Empire for centuries.

In the late middle ages, the Muslim world itself witnessed major transformations. The Mamluks in Egypt, the Ottoman Turks in western Anatolia and the Balkans, the Black and White Sheep tribal confederations in eastern Anatolia and northwestern Iran and the Timurids in northeastern Iran and Central Asia engaged in a power struggle which eventually resulted in the emergence of three powerful Muslim empires: the Ottomans, in Asia Minor, the Arab lands and the Balkans; the Safavids, in Iran, the Caucasus, and parts of Central Asia; and the Mughals, on the Indian subcontinent. In the sixteenth and the early part of the seventeenth centuries, the Ottomans and Safavids fought each other in eastern Anatolia, Transcaucasia, and Mesopotamia. Much of the conflict took place in the Armenian homeland and finally came to an end in 1639, when the two powers ceased their hundred-year hostilities and concluded the Treaty of Zuhab (also known as the Treaty of Qasr-e Shirin). The treaty once again partitioned Armenia, this time into eastern (also known as Persian Armenia) and western (sometimes referred to as Turkish Armenia) sections. The Plain of Shirak became a sort of boundary between the two. Lands west of and including the fortress of Kars fell into Ottoman hands, while territories east of Ani and the Arpachay River became part of Iran. Baghdad and the holy cities of Najaf and Karbala, other centers of contention, ended in the possession of the Ottomans.

Destruction of property, famine, disease, forced conversions and resettlement reduced the population and significantly diminished Armenia's economic viability. Apart from a few princes in Siunik and Lori, the hereditary landowning Armenian nobility virtually disappeared. The Armenian Church submitted to Muslim rule in order to assure its own survival as well as that of its flock. The Ottoman, Safavid and Mughal rulers each dealt differently with their Armenian subjects. The Ottomans and Iranians granted the Church the political as well as the religious leadership of their Armenian subjects. The more tolerant Mughals did not have an established policy but generally left the Armenian secular leaders in charge of their communities. The next four chapters will examine life in these communities, which were scattered in historic Armenia as well as in the various cities of the Ottoman, Iranian and Mughal Empires.

The Armenians of western Asia Minor had emigrated there during the Byzantine era and by the early middle ages had established sizeable communities in a number of cities, particularly Constantinople, where they had achieved military and political importance. By the eleventh century, however, their numbers had decreased in Constantinople and although the Seljuk Turkish invasions of Armenia brought new settlers to that city, the Armenian presence remained insignificant. Sources indicate that Sultan Mehmet II (1444-1446 and 1451-1481) shortly after conquering Constantinople forcibly relocated a large number of Armenians from Anatolia and the Crimea to that city. Such deportations continued through the sixteenth century and significantly increased the Armenian community of the Ottoman capital.

The Armenian Millet

By the late eighteenth century, the Ottomans had fully institutionalized what Arab conquerors had loosely established in the Middle East centuries earlier—that is, organizing the various subject peoples in their empire not into political or racial groups, but into religious communities. The Greeks, the Jews and the Armenians were thus grouped into distinct communities called *millets*, each under the supervision of its own religious leader. Each community eventually restricted itself to its own quarter of Constantinople and other urban centers. Recent scholarship has challenged the notion that the *millet* system emerged as a full-blown institution in the fifteenth century or soon after the fall of Constantinople. It now seems certain that the Ottomans had no consistent policy toward non-Muslims until much later and that the *millet* system evolved gradually. The Ottomans at first dealt with smaller groups of non-Muslims and rarely used the term *millet* until the nineteenth century, when they used it primarily for the Greek, Armenian and Jewish communities.

New scholarship has also cast doubt on the role of Sultan Mehmet II in the creation of the office of the Armenian Patriarch of Constantinople. Tradition has it that in 1461, the Sultan appointed Bishop Hovakim of Bursa as the first Patriarch of the Armenians in the Ottoman Empire. In reality, however, the development of the Armenian Patriarchate of Constantinople appears to have been a more protracted process. Until the first quarter of the sixteenth century, the Holy See of Ejmiatsin was outside the borders of the Ottoman Empire, in adjacent hostile territory. Sultan Mehmet, therefore, recognized the Armenian bishop of Constantinople as the leader of the Armenians of that city and its environs. Subsequently, because the Iranians were tolerant and generous toward the Armenian religious hierarchy, future Ottoman sultans, fearing the influence of pro-Iranian Ejmiatsin over western or Turkish Armenia, not only relocated many Armenians from the interior to Constantinople, but also gave the Armenian bishop special authority. The Ottomans thus hoped to assure Armenian loyalty as well as to weaken Ejmiatsin. Later, other Armenian communities, such as that of Erzerum, established bishoprics with a similar status. The Armenian bishop of Constantinople, therefore, did not initially have authority over all the Armenians of the Ottoman Empire. The Catholicosate of Sis had jurisdiction over the Armenians of Cilicia; that of Aghtamar over the Armenians of Van and its environs and the Patriarchate of Jerusalem over the Armenians of the Arab lands. By the nineteenth century, however, due to the rivalry of the Catholicosates, the rise of an influential Armenian financial elite (the *amiras*), the establishment of schools by Armenian and non-Armenian Catholics and the inclusion of Ejmiatsin within Russian territory, the Armenian archbishop of Constantinople assumed *de facto* authority over all the Apostolic Armenians of the Ottoman Empire. A separate Patriarchate was thus established, with both political and religious prerogatives. The Ottomans, much to their relief, dealt with an Armenian ecclesiastical office that did not have to answer to the Armenian Holy See or any other authority within the Armenian Church. In reality, the Catholicoi at Ejmiatsin, Sis, and Aghtamar, and the Patriarch of Jerusalem exercised higher authority in religious matters; but the political, financial, and geographical position of Constantinople made its Armenian Patriarch a formidable personage indeed.

According to earlier interpretations, the Ottomans, after the fall of Constantinople, divided the Christians into two general groups: the Dyophysites, who were placed under the authority of the Greek Patriarch, and the Monophysites, who were placed under that of the Armenian Patriarch. Thus the various Orthodox Churches in the Balkans, such as the Serbian Church, while retaining some autonomy, fell under the jurisdiction of the Greek Patriarch of Constantinople; and the autonomous Coptic, Ethiopian, and Syrian Jacobite Churches were technically subject to the Armenian Patriarch. This notion has been challenged as well, and it now seems certain that although some attempts were made in that direction, they proved fruitless. In any case, by the late eighteenth century the various Orthodox and Eastern rite Churches had full control over their own religious institutions. In the first half of the nineteenth century, due to the activities of Christian missionaries and pressure from their governments, two new *millets*, the Catholic and the Protestant, emerged as well.

The *millet* was, in effect, self-governing. It was allowed to maintain its own institutions such as schools, charities, and hospitals. It was responsible for law and order and for resolving disputes within the community. The Armenian Patriarch was approved by the sultan and exercised full authority over his people. He had his own court and could dispense civil and ecclesiastical justice throughout his community. He maintained a small police force, as well as a jail. The Turks, who were a minority in parts of their empire, thus managed to keep order by permitting their various conquered ethnic groups to function semi-autonomously and by giving religious leaders greater administrative powers than they had under their own rulers. Armenians and other Christians were still conquered people, however, and were treated as such. Their status, particularly in the hinterlands, was one of *reaya*, which can be best translated as "tribute-paying subjects." For example, the Ottomans, until the eighteenth century, subjected Christian villages, including Armenian, to the *devshirme* or collection of youths who were to be raised as Muslims and enlisted in either the janissary corps (foot-soldiers expert in the use of firearms) or the government administration. The Armenians, like other non-Muslims, were not permitted to bear arms and were, therefore, exempt from military service. They were usually required to pay a poll tax (*jizya*) and their testimony was seldom accepted in Muslim courts. Finally, Armenians in Anatolia had to provide winter quarters for the flocks of the Kurds, nomadic people who were encouraged to move there from their traditional pastures by the Ottomans, or who simply settled in regions abandoned by the Armenians. At its best, during the Ottoman golden age, the *millet* system promised non-Muslims fairer treatment than conquered or non-Christian subjects enjoyed under the Europeans. At its worst, during the decline and fall of the empire, the Christian minorities were subjected to extortion and pogroms.

As the Ottoman sultans lost firm control of Anatolia, and Kurdish raids and Shi'ite revolts created unstable conditions there, more and more Armenian artisans were attracted to Constantinople. A number of later sultans also encouraged Armenians to relocate there and as a result, by the late nineteenth century, the Armenian population in the Ottoman capital reached 250,000. The city had the largest Armenian community in the world and the Armenian Patriarch, by some accounts, became an important and powerful official. But as the Ottoman Empire declined, so did the stability of the office of Patriarch. Although only sixteen Patriarchs occupied the seat from 1461 to 1600, fifty-four held office between 1600 and 1715. As bribery, corruption and nepotism permeated all levels of Ottoman society, the Patriarchate fell under the influence of groups with vested interests.

The Amiras

By the eighteenth century some stability returned to the office of Patriarch. Not coincidentally, there emerged in the same period a powerful group of Armenian bankers and officials known as *amiras* (from the Arabic *amir*, meaning "chief" or "commander"). This unofficial oligarchy managed to gain power by loaning money to viziers, pashas, tax farmers and others who needed to purchase an income-producing position. Some of the wealthiest *amiras* were moneylenders to the sultan and, as such, had great influence at court. As a social elite they were permitted to wear clothes reserved only for Ottoman grandees and to ride horses, both privileges usually denied to non-Muslims. They supported charities and financed the education of many who would later become major Armenian leaders. One historian has identified some 166 *amiras* belonging to 77 different families.

Members of the Duzian, Balian and Dadian *amira* families held, respectively, the positions of director of the imperial mint, chief imperial architect and superintendent of the gunpowder mill. The *amiras* by virtue of their wealth and status at Court had great influence over the affairs of the Armenian *millet* and the election of the Patriarch. The *amiras* often consulted with Armenian merchants and intellectuals, but overall, until the latter part of the nineteenth century, they maintained a control over the Armenian *millet* equal to and often surpassing that of the Patriarch himself.

The Mkhitarists

Although an Armenian printing press was functioning in the Ottoman Empire at the end of the sixteenth century, the two centuries of warfare and the treatment of the Armenians by local lords in Anatolia had created a backward society. Only a few books, all on religion, were published. The earliest concrete evidence of renewed Armenian cultural activity began in the late seventeenth century. The most important Armenian intellectual of the period was Yeremia Chelebi Keomiurjian (1637-1695), who established a short-lived printing press in 1677. His efforts to enlighten the Armenian Church were resisted by the clergy and fostered dissatisfaction among progressive elements, which indirectly led to the establishment of the Mkhitarist order.

Abbot Mkhitar, who was born in Sebastia (Sivas) in 1676, founded this Catholic monastic order. After joining the Armenian Apostolic priesthood, he traveled in western Armenia and was convinced that Armenian education had reached its lowest ebb in his homeland. He sought to establish a religious order that would fulfill the spiritual and intellectual needs of his countrymen. He was rebuked by the Armenian clergy and, after meeting a number of Latin missionaries, felt that the Western Church possessed the necessary tools for his mission. After converting to Catholicism in Aleppo in 1695, Mkhitar founded a new order in Constantinople with ten members on September 8, 1701. Mkhitar maintained that it was possible to adhere to Papal authority and to remain faithful to the Armenian nation. His activities not only angered the Armenian Patriarchate but also were unfavorably viewed by the Latin missionaries, none of whom could accept his dual loyalty. The Mkhitarists were forced to leave for the Morea, in Greece, which at that time was under the control of Venice.

In 1705 the Mkhitarists petitioned Pope Clement XI (1700-1721) to recognize their order. The Vatican, concerned by the rumors circulated by Catholic missionaries trained by the *Propaganda fide*, who accused Mkhitar of tampering with the rites of the Catholic Church, delayed its recognition until 1712. In 1715 the Ottomans took the Morea, destroyed the Mkhitarist monastery, and forced the priests to leave for Venice. The Venetian Senate voted to grant the order the island of San Lazzaro, a former leper refuge, and on September 8, 1717, sixteen years to the day after the founding of the order, the Mkhitarists moved there. In 1718 Mkhitar traveled to Rome to defend his order against continuing rumors. He was successful in convincing the Vatican of his orthodoxy and devoted the rest of his life to religious and intellectual activities. He died at San Lazzaro on April 27, 1749. In 1773 a number of disaffected Mkhitarists fathers left Venice and eventually established a separate branch of the order in 1803 in Trieste. Following Napoleon's invasion of Italy, they fled to Vienna, where they established a new center in 1811.

The Mkhitarists were deeply concerned with preserving Armenian culture as well as with the revival of the study of Armenian history and language. They were able to do more to achieve this end than any other Armenian institution. They translated European classics into Armenian and began writing historical, linguistic, literary and religious works using primary the sources in Latin, Greek and other languages. The efforts of M. Chamchian (1738-1823), G. Avetikian (1751-1827), A. Bagratuni (1790-1866), A. Aytenian (1824-1902), P. Minasian (1799-1866) and Gh. Alishan (1820-1901) produced grammars, dictionaries, histories, plays and numerous philological, geographical and theological works. With financial assistance from Iranian-Armenian and especially Indian-Armenian merchants, the Mkhitarists established schools and produced two periodicals, *Bazmavep* printed in Venice from 1843 onward, and *Handes Amsorya* printed in Vienna beginning in 1887. The Venetian congregation concentrated its efforts on Armenian history and literature, while the priests in Vienna focused theirs on Armenian language and philology. The Mkhitarists not only enabled Europe to learn about the Armenian past, but their labors channeled Western thought to the Armenians in the Ottoman and Russian Empires and played a major role in shaping the Armenian cultural revival of the nineteenth century. Both the Venetian and Viennese Mkhitarist congregations remained active in the twentieth century and reunited into a single order in 2000.

The Eastern Question

From the fifteenth to the seventeenth centuries the Ottomans were the unquestioned masters of a large part of Eastern and Central Europe (see map 20). In the meantime, the Cossacks completed the long process of Slavic colonization of the pasturelands north of the Black Sea and transformed the Don region into a military base from which Russia would expand eastward into the Balkans. The Slavic and Orthodox peoples of Eastern Europe encouraged by the actions of Russian rulers and statesmen, in time began to look to Russia as their liberator from Ottoman rule. In the seventeenth century the Ottoman Empire, which had begun its gradual decline following the death of Sultan Suleiman (1566), suffered a series of defeats by Austria, Poland, and Russia. Some Ottoman officials, especially viziers from the Koprulu family, tried to reverse the tide, but the failure to take Vienna after a two-month siege in 1683 ushered in the end of Ottoman supremacy. By the early eighteenth century the Treaties of Karlowitz (1699) and Passarowitz (1718) resulted in the first major Ottoman territorial losses in Europe. Austria received all of Hungary, Transylvania, Croatia, and Slovenia; Poland obtained

Podolia; and Russia advanced to the Black Sea. The Ottomans were saved from further losses primarily by disagreements among the Europeans and by the support of France.

The eighteenth century witnessed a number of Russo-Turkish wars in which Peter the Great (1689-1725) and, especially, Catherine the Great (1762-1796) succeeded in expanding Russian influence into the Balkans and Transcaucasia. Austria's preoccupation with Prussia, the rising power of Central Europe, hindered its attempt to take advantage of the situation or to stop Russian expansion. The Austrians, despite their fear of Russia's expanding influence in the Balkans, had to cooperate with Catherine for fear that she would ally with Prussia against them. Catherine's first war with the Ottomans (1768-1774) resulted in major victories on land and sea. Maria Theresa (1740-1780) of Austria and Frederick the Great (1740-1786) of Prussia, concerned with Russia's gains, sought to halt its advance and, in 1772, agreed with Russia to partition Poland. Despite pressures from the Germans, Catherine refused to end the war with the Ottomans until 1774, when the Pugachev Revolt in Russia (1772-1774) forced her to conclude a treaty.

The Treaty of Küchük Kaynarca (1774) gave Russia not only a number of forts in the Crimea, as well as free navigation for its trading vessels in the Black Sea, but it made the Crimean Tatars independent from Ottoman suzerainty. More important, however, was the Ottoman promise to grant a larger degree of self-government to people in Moldavia and Wallachia (present-day Romania), permitting Russia to intervene on their behalf. In addition, the Ottomans agreed to protect the Orthodox Christians and not only permitted Russia to build a church in Constantinople, but also gave it extraterritorial privileges as well. The Treaty of Küchük Kaynarca provided the pretext for all future Russian interventions in the Balkans. The Russian interpretation of this treaty gave them the right to champion the cause of Slavic and Orthodox minorities living in the Ottoman Empire. The Ottomans and the Western powers, especially Britain, disagreed. They felt that the treaty gave Russia only the right to a church in Constantinople and that the rest of the clauses dealing with the minorities were extremely vague.

The problem of how to address the rising tide of Balkan nationalism and the rivalry and expansionist designs of Russia and Austria in the region and how to gauge their possible effects on the Ottoman Empire became known as the "Eastern Question." If, as many believed, the "Sick Man of Europe"(as the Ottoman Empire came to be known in the nineteenth century) had to die, how was it to be dismembered without changing the balance of power in Europe and causing an all-out European war? For more than a hundred years, the Eastern Question remained on the mind of politicians, who considered it in every major conference or treaty. The failure to resolve it resulted in the assassination of Archduke Ferdinand of Austria in Sarajevo (1914), which ushered in the First World War and destroyed the Ottoman, Russian, German, and Austro-Hungarian Empires.

Although the Eastern Question primarily involved the Balkans, Britain's vital interests in India, Egypt, and the Persian Gulf forced it to support the Turks against Russian expansion in the Mediterranean. Furthermore, Britain harbored a fear of Russian moves toward Central Asia, which indirectly tied the Eastern Question to the "Great Game," as the Russo-British rivalry in the East was called. All of this political intrigue at times had major repercussions on the fate of the Armenians.

Following the Treaty of Küchük Kaynarca, Austria, hoping to isolate Prussia chose to delay or monitor Russian expansion through a policy of cooperation. In 1781 Catherine and Joseph II of Austria (1780-1790) discussed the "Greek Scheme," by which they hoped to drive the Ottomans out of Europe. According to this plan Austria would annex the western half of the Balkans, while Russia would gain the rest, restoring the Byzantine Empire with Catherine's grandson, Constantine, as the new Emperor at Constantinople.

Catherine annexed the Crimea in 1783 and several years later began her second war with the Ottomans (1787-1792). Austria and Prussia both preoccupied with the French Revolution, then sought to check Catherine's expansion into Eastern Europe. Prussia began to make moves into Poland, and Austria made a separate peace with the Ottomans. Russia was forced to sign the Treaty of Jassy (1792), by which it gained little territory. A year later, in 1793, Russia and Prussia concluded the second partition of Poland, and by 1795 they ended Polish independence with yet a third partition of that country.

The Reforms of Selim III and the Era of Tanzimat (1789-1876)

While the French Revolution shook Europe, some Ottoman leaders, aware of the external threats to their state, began to seriously consider reforming the structure of the once-great empire. Local Muslim lords, or *derebeys*, controlled much of Anatolia. The Chris-

tian population of the Balkans, tired of extortion by Ottoman officials and encouraged by Russia was in constant rebellion. The once-
feared janissary had become an inefficient soldier that conducted
business rather than engaged in war. Together with conservative religious leaders, the janissaries resisted any modernization of the
empire by deposing or killing sultans who favored such a course.

In the same year as the start of the French Revolution, Selim III
(1789-1807) ascended the Ottoman throne. At first he, like some of
his predecessors, felt that the empire could be saved if it reestablished its former discipline. With the exception of modern weapons,
there was no need for modernization; the government had only to
end abuses and inefficiencies. After the Treaty of Jassy, however,
Selim realized that a more thorough reorganization was necessary.
He established a small and effective military force, called the *Ni-
zam-i Cedid* (*New Order* or *New Army*), modeled along European
lines. He also revived the Ottoman navy and established several
modern factories for the manufacture of weapons and gunpowder.
His administrative, financial, and judicial reforms, although partially successful at best, opened the door to Western ideas and
institutions and laid the groundwork for the modernization of Turkey.

By the nineteenth century, the sociopolitical changes introduced
by the Enlightenment and the French Revolution had penetrated the
Ottoman Empire through the introduction of the printing press and
the arrival of European commercial and technical advisors. Ironically, the Christian minorities, especially those in the Balkans, were
the first to benefit from these changes. Their merchants imported the
new ideas into Eastern Europe, while their diaspora encouraged and
financed intellectual and revolutionary activities. Most intellectuals
in the Balkans embraced the cultural nationalism of eighteenth-
century European theorists like Herder and Fichte. Vernaculars replaced the classical languages as the new literary vehicles of the
region. The national consciousness of the ethnic minorities was thus
expressed first through a literary revival and, after the spread of
revolutionary ideas by Napoleon, through uprisings and demands
for autonomy or independence. Some groups, such as the Serbs, the
Greeks, the Romanians, and the Montenegrins, due to Russian political and religious influence, awakened quickly and won
recognition in the first half of the nineteenth century, while others,
like the Bulgarians, Armenians, and Arabs, began their political revivals later in that century. Yet others, such as the Macedonians,

Albanians, and finally the Kurds, voiced their demands only in the early twentieth century.

Napoleon's campaigns in Europe, in the meantime, saved the Ottomans from further Russian or Austrian encroachments. Napoleon's defeat and the Congress of Vienna in 1815 also helped the Ottomans, for the European powers, in a conservative reaction to French revolutionary ideas, agreed to maintain their *status quo* and to quash future revolutions in Europe. As a result, the Austrian and English statesmen, Metternich and Castlereagh, convinced the Russian tsar, Alexander I (1801-1825) not to involve Russia in the Serb revolt (1815-1817) or the early phase of the Greek war of independence, which began in 1821. In the meantime, these revolts, as well as the independent actions of Muhammad 'Ali Pasha, the Ottoman governor-general of Egypt, once and for all demonstrated to the sultans the urgent need for serious reforms in the Ottoman Empire. Although Selim III was killed by reactionary elements, Sultan Mahmud II (1808-1839) finally abolished the janissaries in 1826 and with European help, began to form a completely modern army.

The new Russian tsar, Nicholas I (1825-1855), although a conservative autocrat, was also a defender of Russian Orthodoxy and sympathized with the Balkan Christians. He took a harsher line against the Ottomans and in 1828 began a war against them. A year later, the Treaty of Adrianople (present-day Edirne) not only gave Russia most of western Georgia but also created an autonomous Moldavia and Wallachia. A few months later, in 1830, Russian aid enabled Greece, which had attracted the sympathy of many European liberals, to also achieve its independence. Several years later, Russia increased its influence in the Balkans when it aided the Ottomans against Muhammad 'Ali's invasion of Syria and his move toward Asia Minor. By the Treaty of Unkiar Skelessi (1833), Russia became the protector of the sultan in exchange for closing the Straits (the Bosphorus connecting the Black Sea to the Sea of Marmara, and the Dardanelles connecting the Sea of Marmara to the Aegean Sea) to all foreign warships except those of Russia.

The rest of Europe, led by Britain, could not accept Russian dominance of the region. In order to improve the image of the Turks and at the same time to weaken Russia's role as the protector of the oppressed Balkan Christians, the British convinced the Ottomans to enact reforms. In 1839 the young Sultan Abdul Mejid I (1839-1861), upon the advice of officials who favored Western reforms, issued the *Hatti Sherif-i Gulhane* ("Noble Decree of the Rose

Chamber"), which guaranteed the life, liberty, and property of all his subjects. It promised military and tax reforms, a centralized administration, an assembly of grandees, the establishment of provincial councils, religiously mixed tribunals, and technical colleges. The *Hatt-i Sherif* actually enacted some of these reforms and ushered in the *tanzimat* ("reorganization" or "reform") period, which was to last until 1876.

Although the decrees broke with tradition and were generally opposed by Muslim religious leaders, they were not enacted by legislation but were implemented by the sultan, who could rescind them at will. More importantly, the promise of reforms enabled the Ottomans to counter Russian demands in the Balkans and by 1841, when the Unkiar Skelessi Treaty ran out, the Straits Convention, signed by all European powers, closed the Straits to all foreign warships. This effectively ended Russia's short-lived influence in the Ottoman Empire.

The reforms, overall, were not far-reaching and the Slavic minorities, awakened by cultural revivals and occasionally supported by Russia, continued to demand more concrete changes. The Crimean War (1853-1856), shattered the elusive peace. The war, which ostensibly began as a dispute between the Russians and the French over their protection of the Holy Places in Jerusalem, was in reality the united European challenge to continuing Russian claims arising from the Treaty of Küchük Kaynarca.

Although Russian forces were victorious in Anatolia, their defeats in the Crimea prompted the new tsar, Alexander II (1855-1881), to sue for peace. In the Treaty of Paris (1856) the Ottomans were finally admitted to the "Concert of Europe," while Russia had to return regions captured in western Armenia and had to dismantle its fortifications in the Black Sea. In order to stop future Russian involvement in the affairs of the minorities of the Ottoman Empire, the British, French, and Austrian ambassadors forced Sultan Abdul-Mejid to issue another reform edict, the *Hatti Humayun* ("Imperial Rescript"). The new decree guaranteed Christian subjects security of life, honor, and property and abolished the poll tax. In addition it drastically curbed the civil power of the heads of the *millets*, an action that was to have a major impact on the Armenian community. Full freedom of conscience was also guaranteed and every civil office was open to all citizens. Christians became eligible for military service, but with the option of purchasing exemptions. Once again the reforms benefited the major urban centers and had little or no effect on the conditions in the provinces.

The Armenian Cultural Revival

By the nineteenth century, European historians, archaeologists, and even artists had begun to develop a deep interest in eastern cultures. Babylonian, Egyptian, Iranian, Greek, Chinese, and Armenian culture attracted French, German, and English followers. Orientalism became a vogue and travelers visited the Middle East, producing many illustrated volumes on their experiences. The activities of the Mkhitarists facilitated the study of Armenian history and language in Europe. The English poet Lord Byron studied Armenian with them in Venice. Scholars such as Langlois, Brosset, and Hübschmann not only wrote studies on Armenian history and language, but Hübschmann determined that Armenian was a separate branch of the Indo-European language tree.

In the meantime, the Armenian intellectual class in Smyrna and the religious hierarchy in Constantinople, reacting to and influenced by Mkhitarist and Jesuit activities, the writings of the Madras circle (see chapter 14), and the reforms initiated by Selim III, had established half a dozen schools, two hospitals, and ten new presses that published numerous religious and secular works. Many of these projects were financed by the *amiras*.

In addition, the Armenians founded the Mesropian College in Smyrna, which attracted teachers like Stepan Voskanian, who imbued a whole generation of intellectuals with French literary thought. A graduate of the college was the translator, novelist, and journalist Matteos Mamurian (1830-1901), who, after studying in Paris opened a school in Smyrna in 1851, and, in 1871, became the editor of the monthly periodical, *Arevelian Mamul*. The works of Scott, Goethe and Dumas influenced Armenian writers such as Mamurian, Dzerents (1922-1888) and Diusap (c. 1841-1901). Their work emulated the romantic nationalism of their European counterparts. The result of all this activity was the *zartonk*, a renaissance or cultural awakening, of the Armenians in Ottoman Turkey.

The reforms of 1839 enabled the appearance in 1840 of the first vernacular periodical, *Dawn of Ararat*, which was published in Smyrna. By the second half of the nineteenth century, many Armenian writers, ignoring the admonitions of the Church and the conservative hierarchy, adopted the spoken vernacular of Constantinople and developed the modern western Armenian language spoken today in most of the Middle East, Europe and the Americas. A kind of rivalry emerged between Smyrna, where the Armenian literary revival had started, and Constantinople, whose more cosmopolitan atmosphere attracted Smyrna's intellectuals. In 1852 the Dedeyan family established a new press in Smyrna, which within three decades had published some 200 Armenian translations of French, English and German romantic writers, who, in turn, influenced modern Armenian authors such as Petros Turian (1851-1872). Classical tragedies were translated into Armenian, as well, and performed in the first theater established in Constantinople under the direction of the poet Mkrtich Beshiktashlian (1828-1868).

The press played a crucial role in the Armenian cultural revival. Armenians founded the first newspaper published in Ottoman Turkey in 1812. Between 1840 and 1866, fourteen Armenian periodicals were established in Constantinople. Most noted among these were *Masis*, edited by Garabed Utudjian; *Bee*, edited by Harutiun Svajian; and *Fatherland*, edited by Arpiar Arpiarian (1851-1908). The most influential journals in western Armenia were *The Eagle of Vaspurakan* and *The Eagle of Taron*, published by the future Catholicos, Khrimian, in Van and Mush respectively. In the second half of the nineteenth century these periodicals, some of which had become dailies, played a major role in the political awakening of the Armenian masses living in Anatolia.

Other forces served to awaken the Armenian spirit as well. Although early Catholic missionary activities had faced stiff resistance from the Armenian Church, by the nineteenth century reforms had weakened the position of the *millet* chiefs. European states had gained major concessions and influence in the Ottoman Empire. French and Italian missionaries, as well as English and American evangelists, opened missions and schools, including institutions of higher learning, in Ottoman Turkey. Having little success in converting the Muslims, they concentrated their efforts on Armenians and other Christians. Although most Armenians remained within the mother Church and simply took advantage of the education offered by the missionaries, they were nevertheless influenced by Western progressive ideas. The number of Armenian Catholics grew after French influence and resulted in the formation of the Armenian Catholic *millet* in 1831.

American evangelical missionaries arrived in the early nineteenth century. They began by printing the Bible in the vernacular and in Turkish, written with Armenian characters. They sent over able and committed individuals such as Eli Smith, one of the first two Americans ever to visit Armenia (1830-1831), and William Goodell, who opened schools in every major city of Anatolia and Cilicia; and by mid-century had made over 8,000 Armenian converts. In 1847, American and British pressures created the Armenian Evangelical *millet*. The establishment of these *millet*s gave Catholic and Evangelical Armenians (some two to three percent of the Armenian population) opportunities not only to pursue their higher education at home or abroad, or to emigrate to Europe and the United States, but, at times, to enjoy the diplomatic protection of their European co-religionists.

Armenian schools played a key role in the Armenian awakening, as well. The reforms of Selim III removed the restrictions placed on public education. A small number of elementary parochial schools opened in Constantinople between 1790-1800. Schools for girls opened after 1820.

Challenges from the Catholic and Evangelical missionaries forced the Armenian Church to open many more schools, including an upper-level academy *Jemaran* in Constantinople in 1839. By mid-century, thanks to the *tanzimat*, Constantinople alone had close to 5,000 students attending some forty schools and two colleges. Levies on the community, particularly on the wealthy, supported these schools, which were practically free, and made it possible for some two-dozen students to receive scholarships to study in France each year. On their return these students spread European ideas by teaching, writing, or publishing newspapers. By the end of the *tanzimat* era (1876), elementary and secondary schools had spread to the six western Armenian *vilayets* or provinces of Van, Bitlis, Erzerum, Diarbekir, Kharput and Sivas (see map 21). Five centuries after the fall of the last Armenian kingdom in 1375, the Armenians finally had the tools to begin a political revival. Political movements in Russia and the last Russo-Turkish war of the nineteenth century were to present a unique opportunity in that direction.

The Armenian National Constitution

Unlike the Christians in the Balkans, the Armenians did not rebel or agitate against the Sublime Porte (the official residence of the grand vizier and the seat of government was called *Bab Ali* (Sublime Porte, or Porte) and were favored by the Ottomans, who viewed them as the "loyal" *millet*. By the mid-nineteenth century, the Armenian community in Constantinople and Smyrna was socially and economically stratified. After Greek independence in 1830, all Greeks in the empire were suspect and the Armenians replaced them in many positions, further enhancing the power of *amiras*. Armenian merchants, as well as the *amiras*, had also amassed a good deal of wealth and many had become agents for European firms, trading spices, jewels, carpets, fabrics, glassware, amber, weapons, dried fruit, and fur with Italy, the Netherlands, France, Iran, India, and Russia. The Armenian middle class consisted of artisans and craftsmen who were grouped into *esnaf* or guilds. Some one hundred Armenian guilds, with approximately 40,000 members, were recorded by the mid-nineteenth century. Not all the Armenians of Constantinople and Smyrna were well to do, however. The resettlement of tens of thousands of Muslim refugees from the Balkans and the Caucasus had led to deteriorating living conditions in the eastern provinces of Anatolia. By 1860 some 20,000 Armenian migrant workers, or *pandukht* in Armenian, had flocked to the two cities, where they lived in crowded dwellings, performed menial jobs, and died from disease and neglect. Many more arrived by the end of the century.

Since the *tanzimat* guaranteed individual rights and equality before the law, Armenian liberals who demanded changes finally challenged the authority of the Patriarch and the *amiras*. Less influential merchants, intellectuals (some of whose education the *amiras* themselves had financed) craftsmen, and even some of the common workers began to demand an end to their oligarchic rule. In 1838 some of the active guild members rebelled against the *amiras* and demanded a voice in affairs of the community. The division became so serious that the Patriarchate and the Ottoman government had to intervene, and in 1841 the guilds achieved a major victory when a committee of twenty-four merchants and craftsmen was established to assist the *amiras* in administering the finances of the Armenian Apostolic *millet*. By 1847 two more bodies, a religious council of fourteen clerics and a civil council of twenty laymen, began to supervise the affairs of the community. Councils for education, economic, and judicial affairs soon emerged as well. In 1848 the *amiras* tried to reassert their control by forcing the resignation of a popular Patriarch. Armenians of Constantinople rose in protest and elected another popular cleric. The Ottomans provided the final stimulus for change. In 1856 the *Hatt-i Humayun*, as stated, officially decreed that the subject communities could have a representative government chosen from among their lay and religious members. The power of the Armenian Patriarch, as the sole spokesman for the Armenian Apostolic *millet*, was waning.

Each religious community was to prepare a self-governing document and submit it to the Sublime Porte. The Armenians were the first minority group to submit a draft in 1857 and a revised document in 1859. The *amiras* and the conservative clerics rejected both. Finally a compromise was achieved and on May 24, 1860, a constitutional assembly of religious and lay members of the Armenian *millet* approved the Armenian National Constitution, or *azgayin sahmanadrutiyun*, to be implemented by an elected council. Although the council argued with the Patriarchate of Jerusalem over the latter's authority and jurisdiction and had some problem getting the document ratified by the Porte, by March 1863 a slightly revised document became a part of Ottoman law as it related to the Armenian *millet*.

The constitution was the work of a new type of Armenian: young men who had visited Europe or who had been trained in European institutions and who had been affected by the liberal and constitutional ideas of the late eighteenth and the early nineteenth centuries. The document laid out six principles outlining the individual's and the community's rights and obligations towards each other. If the individual was to pay his share of taxes, perform services and obey the administrative council, he could expect an education for his children, preservation of his traditions and his Church, and security for his community. The constitution had ninety-nine articles, which covered the religious and civil affairs of the community on all levels. The national council was to have one hundred and forty representatives from Armenians throughout the empire: twenty clerics and eighty laymen from Constantinople and forty from other major urban centers. Most of the Armenians from the six provinces, that is, western Armenia, were neither involved in nor affected by this undertaking. The council participated in the election of the Patriarchs of Constantinople and Jerusalem—although their role in the election of the latter was questioned. They also participated in the election of the catholicos at Ejmiatsin. The Catholicosates of Sis and Aghtamar, contrary to earlier assumptions of the council, were not answerable to it. It should be noted that the Porte continued to reserve the right to confirm the Patriarch and refused to officially guarantee the individual or collective rights of the Armenians, an issue that was to come up some two decades later.

By 1865, the activities of the Christians and the easing of censorship initiated by the *tanzimat* had also resulted in the emergence of a group of Turkish intellectuals known as the "Young Ottomans." Most of them had studied in France, had been influenced by European liberalism, and sought a constitutional government. Young Armenians, all children of the well to do, also formed intellectual and political circles in Europe. Like their Russian counterparts (see chapter 16), they would remain in Europe and would conduct anti-government activities in self-exile. They also would eventually form political parties with nationalistic aspirations.

13

Khojas, Meliks and Shahs
Armenians in Iran
(1501-1896)

P RIOR TO THE third century AD, Iran (Persia) had more influence on Armenia's culture than anyone else. Intermarriage
among the Iranian and Armenian nobility was common. The
two peoples shared many religious, political, and linguistic elements
and traditions and, at one time, even shared the same dynasty. Sa-
sanian policies and the Armenian conversion to Christianity, in the
fourth century, however, alienated the Armenians from Zoroastrian
Iran and oriented them toward the West.

The Arab conquests, which ended the Iranian Empire and the
conversion of Iran to Islam in the seventh century, culturally separated the Armenians even further from their neighbor. In the
eleventh century, the Seljuk Turks drove thousands of Armenians to
Iranian Azerbaijan, where some were sold as slaves, while others
worked as artisans and merchants. The Mongol conquest of Iran in
the thirteenth century enabled the Armenians, who were treated fa-
vorably by the victors, to play a major role in the international trade
among the Caspian, Black, and Mediterranean seas. Armenian merchants and artisans settled in the Iranian cities bordering historic
Armenia. Sultanieh, Marand, Khoi, Salmas, Maku, Maraghe, Urmia,
and especially Tabriz, the Mongol center in Iranian Azerbaijan, all
had, according to Marco Polo, large Armenian populations.

Ottoman-Safavid Rivalry

Tamerlane's invasion at the end of the fourteenth century and the
wars between the Black and White Sheep Turkmen dynasties in the
fifteenth century had a devastating effect on the population of historic Armenia. The later part of the fifteenth century witnessed the

weakening of the White Sheep and the attempts of the Ottoman Sultan, Bayazid II (1481-1512), to take advantage of the situation and to extend his domains eastward into Armenia and northwestern Iran. At the dawn of the sixteenth century, however, Iran was unified under a new dynasty, the Safavids (1501-1732) and after some nine centuries once again acquired the sense of nationhood, which has continued into the present.

The Safavids assumed importance during the early fourteenth century when Sheikh Safi al-Din established his Sufi order in Iranian Azerbaijan. A century later, the order, now known as the Safavi, had assumed a wholly Shi'i character and began gathering support among the Turkmen tribes of northwestern Iran and eastern Anatolia. The order obtained the support of a number of major Turkic tribes, who called themselves the *kizilbash* or "red heads" (from the red caps that they wore). By 1501 the Safavid leader Isma'il seized parts of Transcaucasia from the White Sheep and declared himself Shah. Ten years later he managed to gain control over Iran, historic Armenia, and much of eastern Transcaucasia, and founded a theocratic dynasty that not only claimed to be descended from 'Ali, the son-in-law of the Prophet Muhammad, but that also portrayed the shahs as reincarnations of the Shi'i imams or saints. Shi'ism thus became and remains the state religion of Iran.

The emergence of the Safavids and the rise of Shi'ism in eastern Anatolia were major threats to the Ottomans, whose claim to the caliphate and the leadership of the Muslim world was challenged by the new Iranian dynasty. In 1514 Sultan Selim I (1512-1520) crossed the Euphrates River and for the first time entered historic Armenia. Shah Isma'il was not ready to fight the Ottomans and withdrew his forces, burning many villages en route to forestall the advancing Ottoman army. Thousands of Armenians were forced to leave their land. The Ottomans pushed deep into Armenia and on August 23, 1514, at the Battle of Chaldiran, destroyed the Iranian army through their superior numbers and artillery. Although Selim captured Tabriz, the administrative center of the Safavids, he had to withdraw a week later, as Ottoman military leaders refused to winter in Tabriz or to pursue the enemy into the Iranian highlands. This pattern was to be repeated a number of times, particularly during the reign of Shah Tahmasp I (1524-1576), who also pursued a scorched-earth policy when he had to face the mighty Sultan Suleiman the Magnificent (1520-1566). The harsh Armenian climate and difficulties in transportation from and communications with Constantinople made it possible for the Safavids to repeatedly survive such defeats. Although the Safavids managed to recover Tabriz, Iran relinquished most of eastern Anatolia. The first peace agreement between the two powers in 1555 left the western parts of historic Armenia in Ottoman hands, while the eastern parts ended up under Iranian control. Realizing the vulnerability of Tabriz, Tahmasp moved the capital south to Qazvin. The uncertain situation over Tahmasp's succession encouraged the Ottomans to invade Armenia again in 1578 and to continue their campaign until 1590, taking most of Transcaucasia and once again occupying Tabriz.

Caught in the middle of these warring powers, some Armenians were deported by the Ottomans to Constantinople from Tabriz, Karabagh, and Nakhichevan and others, by the Iranians, to Iranian Azerbaijan from Van. To replace them, Sultan Selim and his successors settled Kurdish tribes in Armenia, a policy that continued into the seventeenth century. Indo-European speakers like the Armenians, the Kurds were Muslims who were divided into Sunni, Shi'i, and Yezidi sects. They were a nomadic people who were exempt from cash taxation, but had to present a quota of their herds and guard the border regions. Their settlement in historic Armenia was to create a major problem later for the Armenians when the state was powerless to control the Kurds or, conversely, when it actually used them against the Armenians. The protracted Ottoman-Safavid war and the resulting forced migrations depopulated parts of historic Armenia, and the Kurdish settlement changed its social and ethnic balance.

The Great Migration

It was Shah 'Abbas the Great (1587-1629) who left the greatest imprint on the Iranian Armenian community. Recognizing the comparative weakness of the Iranian army, he quickly concluded a treaty with the Ottomans in 1590, ceding eastern Armenia and parts of Iranian Azerbaijan. He then began the formation of a new force, recruiting Georgian and Armenian mercenaries and converts as sharpshooters, and, with European help, fashioned artillery and started the basis of a modern army. He moved his capital from Qazvin to Isfahan, a safer location. Isfahan was also closer to Baghdad, the soft underbelly of the Ottoman Empire.

By the start of the seventeenth century 'Abbas felt strong enough to break the peace he had made with the Ottomans in 1590. In the autumn of 1603 the Shah advanced to retake Iranian Azerbaijan and to force the Ottomans out of Transcaucasia as well. He succeeded in taking the cities of Tabriz, Marand, Ordubad, Akulis, and the province of Nakhichevan, which eluded the town of Julfa. The Shah was greeted as a liberator by the Armenians, who could no longer endure heavy Ottoman taxes, and the Shi'i Muslims, who were tired of religious persecutions. The Armenian merchants of Julfa, who had been engaged in international trade for some time, were especially happy with the Iranian capture of Julfa. According to one primary source, the Sunnis of Nakhichevan province were killed and the Safavid army razed their villages. The same source adds that 'Abbas deported the Armenian merchants of Julfa to Iran at this time in order to prevent the region from regaining its economic viability. All other contemporary sources, however, indicate that only the main fortress of Nakhichevan was destroyed in 1603 and that the Armenian population was not moved until 1604.

In November 1603, 'Abbas laid siege to the fortress of Yerevan, a formidable bastion constructed by the Ottomans. The siege lasted over seven months and resulted in the conscription of over 10,000 local Armenians and Muslims, which, in turn, spelled an economic and demographic decline of that province. In the summer of 1604, at the news of an Ottoman counteroffensive, 'Abbas laid waste much of the territory between Kars and Ani and deported its Armenians and Muslims into Iranian Azerbaijan. 'Abbas was sure that the Ottomans would not launch an attack so close to winter and according to some sources, demobilized most of his army in the fall. The Ottomans, however, did advance, catching the Shah unprepared. Orders went out from 'Abbas to forcibly remove the entire population residing in the regions of Bayazid, Van, and Nakhichevan and to carry out a scorched-earth policy.

According to primary sources, some 250,000 to 300,000 Armenians were removed from the region between 1604 and 1605. Thousands died crossing the Arax River. Many of the Armenians were eventually settled in Iranian Azerbaijan, where other Armenians had settled earlier. Some ended up in the Mazandaran region and in the cities of Sultanieh, Qazvin, Mashhad, Hamadan and Shiraz. The wealthy Armenians of Julfa were brought to the Safavid capital of Isfahan. The Julfa community was accorded special care and seems to have suffered less in their migration. They were settled across the banks of the Zayandeh Rud and in 1605 a town called New Julfa (Nor Jugha) was constructed especially for them. Persian

masons, together with Armenian craftsmen, built the new settlement. Many churches were constructed, thirteen of which survive
today Armenians had rights which were denied other minorities.
They elected their own mayor, or (*kalantar*), rang church bells, had
public religious processions established their own courts, and had
no restrictions on clothing or the production of wine. No Muslims
could reside in New Julfa. The Armenia mayor was given one of the
shah's royal seals in order to bypass bureaucratic tangles and had jurisdiction over the two-dozen Armenian villages around Isfahan. He
collected and paid to the throne a poll tax in gold, which was gathered from each adult male. In time, the Armenian population of
New Julfa and the surrounding villages grew to some 50,000. Here
they were granted trading privileges and a monopoly on the silk
trade, which transformed the community into a rich and influential
one and New Julfa into a main center of trade between Iran and
Europe. Interest-free loans were granted to the Armenians to start
businesses and light industries.

Soon the Armenians, who enjoyed the shah's protection, handled
a major part of Iran's trade with Europe, Russia, and India. The
New Julfa merchants formed trading companies, which competed
with the Levant, East India, and Muscovy companies, and established businesses in Kabul, Herat, Qandahar, Marseilles, Venice,
Genoa, Moscow and Amsterdam, and in cities of Sweden, Poland,
Germany, India, China, Indonesia, and the Philippines. 'Abbas
would spend time in New Julfa at the houses of the most successful
merchants, known as *khojas* or notables, whom the silk monopoly
had made extremely prosperous. Sources describe their fabulous
houses, decorated with Oriental and Western artwork, with tables
set with gold utensils. The Armenians paid a set fee for each bale of
silk and most of their profits remained in Iran. Ottoman profits from
overseas trade fell and the Persian Gulf became a center of trade
with Western ports.

The military decline of the Ottoman Empire encouraged the
West to establish new contacts in the East. Western diplomats, visi-
tors, and merchants were dispatched to Iran and most were housed
in New Julfa. The Armenian merchants' contacts with the West
made them a conduit through which the shah was able to secure diplomatic and commercial alliances against the Ottomans.

The Armenians of New Julfa became a unique part of the diaspora in other ways as well. They formed a separate ecclesiastical
unit under their own bishop, appointed by Ejmiatsin, which had ju-

risdiction over all Armenians of Iran and Iraq. New Julfa soon became a cultural center. A school was opened not only for the sons of the *khojas* but also for some of the talented boys from less prominent Armenian families. The future catholicos, Hakob Jughaetsi (1655-1680), as well as a number of historians and translators were among its graduates. One graduate, a priest, was sent to Italy to learn the art of printing and brought back the first printing press in Iran. The first book printed in Iran, in any language, was an Armenian translation of the book of Psalms, produced in 1638. Manuscript illuminators developed a distinct New Julfa style, beginning in the first half of the seventeenth century, with the work of Mesrop of Khizan, originally from Armenia. A few artists even began to copy European works brought to New Julfa by the *khojas*. Prior to 1600, Armenian merchants had for some five hundred years conveyed Eastern technology to Europe. From the seventeenth century onwards, beginning with the New Julfa merchants, the Armenians were one of primary channels for the introduction of Western technology and culture to Western Asia.

European sources of the seventeenth century portray 'Abbas as a great benefactor of the Armenians, who secured them from the Turks and who made them wealthy in New Julfa. Armenian historians of the time, however, such as Arakel of Tabriz, view Shah 'Abbas' deportations and the Turko-Iranian conflict in Armenia as a major catastrophe, during which the land and the people suffered terribly, with the resulting depopulation making the Armenians a minority in part of their historic land. 'Abbas' policies did indeed have varying short-term effects, in the long term however the forced deportations established the basis for the Armenian diaspora in Iran and India, communities, which as we will see were to play an important role in the Armenian cultural and political revival of the nineteenth century.

One of the intangible benefits of Armenian economic power in Iran was the transformation of the Armenian self-image and national consciousness. After centuries of foreign rule, Armenians were granted equal and at times greater privileges than Muslims. This increased prestige extended to the Church as well, and enabled the leaders at Ejmiatsin to regain some control over outlying dioceses and communities and to establish ties with the Patriarchs of Constantinople and Jerusalem. This new status also allowed a number of Armenian secular leaders to achieve recognition and to rally support. This was particularly true of the lords, or *meliks*, of Karabagh and Siunik who, under the patronage of the shahs, the Church, and the Armenian merchants, retained and expanded their ancestral fiefdoms in Karabagh. The *meliks* were the last scions of Armenian nobility in eastern Armenia. They lived in mountainous regions and usually paid tribute directly to the shahs. Unlike the Church leaders, they lacked unity and had to contend with Muslim rulers, who viewed any landed and armed Christian nobility as a threat. Their autonomy and occasional defiance, however, attracted some popular support and together with some Armenian merchants and clerics, initiated the Armenian emancipation movement.

Eastern Armenia (1639-1804)

The Treaty of Zuhab partitioned historic Armenia in 1639 between the Ottomans, who took western Armenia, and the Safavids, who took eastern Armenia. Eastern Armenia was itself divided into the Beglarbegi of Chukhur Sa'd (the regions of Yerevan and Nakhichevan), and the Beglarbegi of Karabagh (the regions of Karabagh-Siunik and Ganja). The first was thus composed of sections from the historic Armenian provinces of Ayrarat, Gugark, and Vaspurakan; the second from Artsakh, Siunik, and Utik (see map 22). Administered by khans, mostly from the Qajar clan, the regions were under the supervision of a governor-general stationed in the city of Tabriz, in Iranian Azerbaijan. The Beglarbegi of Chukhur Sa'd was especially important, for its main city, Yerevan, was a center of Iranian defense against the Ottomans.

Although 'Abbas protected the Armenians of New Julfa and prevented the Catholic missionaries from making major inroads in the community, his death and the eventual decline of the Safavids in the second half of the seventeenth century forced some of the *khojas* to emigrate to India and Italy, where they established branches of their trading houses. The absence of an Iranian merchant marine meant that the Armenian merchants of New Julfa, over time, could not keep up with the large English or Dutch joint-stock venture companies such as the East India Company, which, by the mid-eighteenth century had taken over much of the trade of the region. By the beginning of the eighteenth century, growing Shi'i intolerance and new laws unfavorable to the Armenians also created a difficult situation for the *khojas*, and more of them emigrated to Russia, India, the Middle East, and Western Europe. Insecurity at home also meant that Armenians would look to Catholic Europe and especially

Orthodox Russia for protection or even deliverance. The fall of the Safavids and the Afghan occupation of Isfahan and New Julfa in 1722 marked the end of the influence of the *khojas*, but did not end the Armenian presence in Iran. Large Armenian communities remained in Isfahan, New Julfa, and a number of Iranian cities.

The fall of the Safavids encouraged Peter the Great to invade the Caspian coastal regions, while the Ottomans broke the peace of Zuhab and invaded eastern Armenia and eastern Georgia in 1723. In two years' time the Ottomans were in control of the entire region, save for Karabagh and Siunik, where Armenian *meliks* under the leadership of Avan Yuzbashi, David Bek, and Mkhitar Sparapet held them off for nearly a decade. The Ottomans installed garrisons in Tiflis (present-day Tbilisi), Nakhichevan, Ganja, and Yerevan. The fortress of Yerevan was repaired and served as the administrative headquarters of the Ottoman military-governor of eastern Armenia.

By 1736 a new ruler, Nader Shah (1736-1747) and a new dynasty, the Afshars, had restored order in Iran, had convinced the Russians to withdraw and had pushed the Ottomans back to the boundaries of 1639. Rewarding the Armenian *meliks* for their stand against the Ottomans, the Shah exempted them from tribute and recognized their autonomy. Catholicos Abraham Kretatsi (1734-1737), who had befriended the Shah, was a guest of honor at Nader's coronation. The new Shah not only visited Ejmiatsin but also reconfirmed its tax-exempt status. Nader removed a number of Turkic tribes from eastern Armenia, especially Karabagh, and divided the region into four khanates: Yerevan, Nakhichevan, Ganja, and Karabagh (see map 23).

Nader's assassination in 1747 unleashed a fifteen-year period of chaos in eastern Armenia. The exiled Turkic tribes returned and led by the Javanshir clan established a strong presence in the plains of Karabagh. The highlands of Karabagh, composed of the five districts of Gulistan, Khachen, Jraberd, Varanda, and Dizak, as well as a number of districts in Siunik (the later Mountainous Karabagh and Zangezur), as noted, were controlled by Armenian *meliks*. The region had its own See in Gandzasar. The lowlands, stretching to the Kur River, were populated by Turkic and Kurdish confederations. By allying themselves with Melik Shahnazarian of Varanda, Panah Khan Javanshir and his son Ibrahim Khan managed to gain a foothold in a part of the exclusively Armenian stronghold of Mountainous Karabagh.

By 1762 another ruler and dynasty, Karim Khan Zand (1750-1779), took control of most of Iran and was recognized as their suzerain by the khans of eastern Armenia. His seat of power was in southern Iran, however, and Transcaucasia was left to Ibrahim Khan of Karabagh and King Erekle II (1762-1798) of eastern Georgia, both of who divided parts of eastern Armenia into zones of influence. The death of Karim Khan in 1779 started another fifteen-year conflict among Ibrahim, Erekle, the khans of Yerevan and Ganja and the Armenian *meliks*. More Armenians emigrated from the khanates of Yerevan and Karabagh to Russia and Georgia. Tiflis, the main city of eastern Georgia, became a major Armenian center.

Russia's annexation of the Crimea and its 1783 Treaty of Georgievsk with Erekle once again involved Russia in Transcaucasian affairs. The khans of the region rushed to make their own separate peace agreements with each other and with Georgia, Russia, or Iran. Iran, in the meantime, was in the throes of another dynastic struggle. By 1790, Aqa Mohammad Khan, the leader of the Qajar clan, had subdued all other pretenders to the throne and now swore to restore the territory of the former Safavids. Most of the khans of eastern Armenia soon submitted, but Erekle of Georgia, relying on Russian protection, refused. Aqa Mohammad invaded Georgia, sacked Tiflis in 1795, and on his return was crowned Shah (1796).

To restore Russian prestige, Catherine the Great declared war on Iran and sent an army to Transcaucasia. Her death, shortly after, put an end to that campaign, however. Aqa Mohammad soon contemplated the removal of the Christian population from eastern Georgia and eastern Armenia. His new campaign began in Karabagh, where he was assassinated in 1797. Aqa Mohammad Khan, who had been castrated by the enemies of his clan in his youth, was succeeded by his nephew, Fath 'Ali Shah Qajar. At the dawn of the nineteenth century, the new Shah had to face a third and final Russian incursion.

Socioeconomic Conditions in Eastern Armenia (17th to 19th centuries)

During the seventeenth century the Safavids transformed Iran's economy. A number of towns in eastern Armenia, located on the trade routes between Asia and Europe, served as depots for goods from India, China, and Iran, which, in turn, found their way to the markets of Russia, the Ottoman Empire, and Western Europe. Well-maintained, safe roads, uniform tariffs and comfortable caravansaries aided in the transfer of merchandise. Eastern Armenia itself exported wheat and silk from Karabagh and dried fruit, salt, hides, and copper from Yerevan. The large nomadic population supplied wool and Caucasian carpets and rugs woven by Armenians and Turkish craftsmen, which were valued for their colors and design.

The population of eastern Armenia prior to the Russian conquest consisted of a Muslim majority and an Armenian minority (although the Armenians had a majority in some districts). The Muslims were divided into Persians, who formed much of the administration and part of the army; the settled and semi-settled Turkish tribal groups, who were either engaged in farming or formed the balance of the army; and the Kurds, who led a traditional nomadic existence and who formed a part of the Iranian cavalry. Although the Armenians were engaged in trade and formed the majority of the craftsmen, most of them were farmers.

The khans were responsible for the defense and the collection of taxes and were usually the sole authority in their khanates. They themselves were exempt from taxes and received lands from the crown in recognition of service. When the central government was weak or had collapsed, the khans tended to become the hereditary owners of their domains. Tax collectors, accountants, scribes, police officers, judges and other officials managed the administration. Various property taxes and a rigid land tenure system supplied the revenues and compensated the administrative officials. Corveé, or forced labor, was mandatory for most peasants. The Armenian villages were supervised by their elders or belonged to the Church as endowed and charitable tax-exempt property, or *waqf*. Their own elders (*kadkhoda*) supervised the Muslim villages. Since eastern Armenia was a dry region, irrigation played a crucial part in the life of the inhabitants. Canals, some stretching twenty miles, were common, and officials in charge of irrigation followed a rigid set of rules to supply all farmers with water.

Large villages farmed communally, while large clans generally farmed small settlements. Agricultural lands followed a primitive two-field rotation system; half the plot planted, half left fallow. Oxen and wooden plows were used, and manure was used both as a fertilizer and as a fuel. Honey, nuts, millet, barley, and various oil seeds were the major crops. Cochineal insects, the source of the famed Armenian red dye, were highly prized. Gardens and orchards were especially abundant and produced a large variety of fruit, especially grapes, and vegetables. Since the peasants surrendered much of their harvest as taxes to the state or the lord, life was frugal. Rice, meat and high-quality wheat were reserved for holidays. Yogurt, cheese, and bread baked in clay ovens, accompanied by greens and vegetables, were the main diet. Few people had beds; most slept on mats and used wooden utensils.

Family life was patriarchal. Men worked in the fields or pastures, while women, supervised by the oldest female (*tantikin*), threshed the grain, spun wool, and made carpets. The oldest male (*agha*, *tanmetz*, or *tanuter*) headed the clan and had the final word on most matters. Sons inherited, while daughters generally received a dowry. Just like their Muslim counterparts, Armenian women rarely spoke in the presence of men or strangers, covered their faces, and were secluded. Apart from religion and customs concerning marriage and divorce, there were few differences between Muslims and Armenians. Both groups equally shared age-old habits, prejudices and superstitions.

Armenians in Nineteenth-Century Iran

In 1801, Russia annexed eastern Georgia and began its final penetration of Transcaucasia. In 1804 Russia started the First Russo-Persian War (1804-1813) and a year later, with the assistance of the Armenians of Karabagh, had captured half of eastern Armenia. The chaotic political and socioeconomic conditions of the previous century and the departure of many Armenians to Georgia hurt the economy of Yerevan, the center of the Iranian defense of Transcaucasia. Iranians, in order to save the rest of eastern Armenia, heavily subsidized the region and appointed a capable governor, Hosein Qoli Khan, to administer it. The khan, together with the Iranian crown prince, 'Abbas Mirza, initiated a number of administrative and military reforms and, aided by Napoleon's campaigns in Europe, managed for two decades to thwart Russian designs on the remaining territories in eastern Armenia. In the end, superior Russian forces conquered all the lands north of the Arax River during the Second Russo-Persian War (1826-1828). Transcaucasia became part of the Russian Empire, and the fate of eastern Armenia, henceforth known as Russian Armenia, was inextricably tied to that of Russia (see map 24). Some 30,000 Armenians left northern Iran and settled in Russia (see chapter 16).

The Armenian community in Iran revived in the second half of the nineteenth century, thanks to commercial ties with Armenian merchants in Russia and to the benevolence of the Qajar shahs. New Julfa re-emerged as well and its cathedral-monastery complex of the Holy Savior organized an excellent library. The first Armenian periodical and a history of the Armenians of New Julfa were published in 1880. The Armenian school in New Julfa received a state subsidy, Armenian clergy and churches were exempted from taxes, and confiscated Church property was returned. Armenian merchants opened new trading houses in the Caspian and Persian Gulf regions and traded with Russia, India, and Europe. Dried fruit, leather, and carpets were exported, and machinery, glassware and cloth were imported. Royal sponsorship brought Armenians to Tehran, where, taking advantage of their linguistic abilities and foreign contacts, Nasr al-Din Shah (1848-1896) used them as envoys to Europe. Some of them, like Mirza Malkum Khan, David Khan Melik Shahnazar, and Hovhannes Khan Masehian were responsible for the introduction of Freemasonry, Western political thought, and technological innovations into Iran. Armenian tailors and jewelers introduced European fashions, and Armenian photographers were among the first in that profession. Armenians were also among the first Western-style painters and musicians. By the end of the nineteenth century there were some 100,000 Armenians living in a dozen cities in Iran (see map 25). The Armenians in Iranian Azerbaijan were soon exposed to the national and political ideas of the Armenians in Transcaucasia and, as will be seen, were to play a significant role in the history of twentieth-century Iran.

14

From the Mughals to the Raj
Armenians in the Indian Subcontinent
(c. 1550-1858)

THE ARMENIAN community of India has a special place in the history of the Armenian diaspora. Although not large, the community's wealth and national aspirations had a significant impact on the Armenian cultural awakening. At the same time, the rise and decline of the community is a perfect example of the effects of internal, external, political and economic forces on the survival of a diaspora community.

Although some Armenian merchants had conducted trade with India as early as the eighth century and are credited with locating the tomb of St. Thomas, the Apostle, it was the benevolent policies of the Mughal Emperor Akbar (1556-1605) that encouraged Armenian traders to settle there. Akbar trusted and favored the Armenians and appointed them to a number of high administrative positions, including the post of chief justice, which he bestowed upon the Armenian called Abdul Hai. One of Akbar's wives, Maryam Begum, was Armenian. The first Armenian church in India was built in 1562 in Agra, the main center of the Mughal dynasty. One of Hai's grandsons, named Mirza Zul-Qarnain, grew up in the royal household, attained the position of governor and later served Emperor Jahangir.

The largest Armenian influx came in the seventeenth century when New Julfa merchants opened commercial branches in various Indian cities. Several of these merchants attained prominence and served as agents of the Iranian court. The Mughal Shahs, Jahangir (1605-1627) and Jahan (1628-1657) continued the benevolent policies of their predecessor, attracting more Armenians to India. The Armenians imported woolen cloth, amber, Venetian glassware, mirrors, guns, swords and clocks. They exported spices, pearls, precious stones and cotton. The jute trade was almost totally in the hands of the Armenians of Bengal who concentrated in the Armenian sector of Dhaka (the capital of present-day Bangladesh), where they built a very large church. Indian Armenians became an important link in the trade among South Asia, Iran, and Europe, and like their New Julfa counterparts were granted privileges and religious freedom by their Muslim overlords.

Armenians had their own quarter in Agra, where they operated a caravansary and had their own cemetery. As Christians, Armenians were asked to act as hosts or interpreters for various European envoys who arrived in India. A number of Europeans who settled in India married Armenian women. The community increased in size, wealth and importance throughout the seventeenth century. Armenian trade centers were eventually established in a dozen cities of the empire including Surat, Delhi, Chinsurah, Lucknow, Dhaka, Saidabad, Heydarabad, Benares, Lahore (in present-day Pakistan), Calcutta, Madras and Bombay (see map 26). Armenian churches were eventually constructed in Surat, Chinsurah, Dhaka, Calcutta, Madras, and Bombay; some of these churches survive to this day. The Armenian churches of India maintained regular contact with the Holy See at Ejmiatsin. Armenians carved out their own neighborhoods and a number of places in these cities still bear the name "Armenian Street, " Armenian Quarter," or "Armenian Port."

Armenians do not seem to have faced any major problems during the reign of Aurengzeb, also known as Alamgir (1658-1707), who, unlike his traditionally tolerant predecessors, adopted extreme anti-Hindu and a number of anti-Christian measures. Iran's anti-Christian policies at the start of the eighteenth century were far worse and drove a number of Armenian merchant houses to their familial associates in India. The intolerance of the late Mughals had a long-term consequence for Indian Armenian merchants, however, for it encouraged the Hindus to cooperate with the British and hastened the subsequent British colonization of India and full control of its trading activities.

The British established their presence in Surat at the start of the seventeenth century. The Armenians, who had utilized British shipping in their trade activities and had contacts with various British companies, became intermediaries between them and a number of Indian rulers. In 1661 the British gained Bombay as part of the dowry of the Infanta (crown princess) of Portugal, who had married the English king, Charles II. Realizing the importance of Armenians in Indian trade, the British invited them to settle there. In 1688, the British East India Company and Khoja Panos Kalantar, representing the Armenian merchants in India, signed a formal agreement, which diverted trade from the traditional routes to the new British-dominated sea-lanes of the Persian Gulf and the Cape of Good Hope. In 1715, Armenians helped the British to establish themselves in Bengal and to make Calcutta the new commercial center of that region. The British aided in the construction of Armenian churches, and, like the Mughals, employed Armenians in their civil administration and permitted Armenians to trade throughout their territories in South Asia. Armenians became active in the legal, medical and military services, and even became expert gunsmiths. By the eighteenth century Bombay, Calcutta, and Madras emerged as the new centers of Armenian activities, with large churches and a school in Calcutta.

Armenians not only served the Mughals but a number of independent rajas in India, as well as various grandees in Burma and Malaysia. Armenian traders constructed a number of churches In Burma and Malaysia in the seventeenth century. Armenian merchants in Java and Sumatra (present-day Indonesia) engaged in the spice trade and became quite wealthy. A community of some 2,000 Armenians in Indonesia is recorded in Java and Sumatra by the seventeenth century. They built schools and churches in Batavia (present-day Jakarta) and Surabaya. The Surabaya church survives to this day. The arrival of the Dutch in the area in the first half of the seventeenth century altered the economic prominence of the Armenians there, and they were reduced to functionaries and shopkeepers under Dutch colonial rule. Armenian merchants also settled in the Philippines and were the only foreigners allowed to continue trading after the Spaniards conquered the region in the sixteenth century. By the nineteenth century a large number of them had relocated to Indonesia.

Although the arrival of the British in South Asia adversely affected Armenian trade monopolies, it brought the Armenians into contact with British education and political systems, and imbued them with the ideas of parliamentary rule and other tenets of English political tradition. Influenced by English liberalism, Armenian leaders of Calcutta and Madras initiated an Armenian national revival in the second half of the eighteenth century. Joseph Emin, an Indian Armenian whose family had migrated from Iran, became convinced that superior strategy and weapons had enabled the Europeans, especially the British, to take control of large parts of Asia. He studied in England, joined the British army, and was befriended by English liberals such as Edmund Burke. He visited Armenia in 1760 and was amazed by the passivity of the Armenians and their religious leaders, who seemed to accept their subjugation as the will of God.

Emin returned to England and, realizing that the British were not interested in helping the Armenians went to Russia in late 1761. He visited Moscow and St. Petersburg, traveled to eastern Armenia and Georgia, and remained in the region throughout the 1760s, trying to convince the Russians that a united Armeno-Georgian army financed by Indian Armenian merchants and under the leadership of Russia could free the Caucasus from Muslim control. Emin also advocated the establishment of modern schools and administrative reforms in the Caucasus to further this goal. Emin met with Russian officials, with the Georgian king Erekle II, and with the Armenian Catholicos Simeon (1763-1780). Emin's ideas were poorly received. The Russians were not ready for liberal reforms and were too busy fighting the Ottomans to consider military assistance. The Armenian catholicos and Erekle insisted on more concrete assurances before embarking on a rebellion against their Muslim overlords (see chapter 16).

Emin left the region at the end of 1768 and returned to Calcutta in early 1770. He did not abandon his dream, however, and a few years later, when Catherine had inflicted severe defeats on the Ottomans, he traveled to Madras, where he convinced the Armenian merchants to pledge a huge sum in gold for the creation of an Armenian army. He then went to New Julfa to gather funds from the khojas, who, facing an uncertain future in war torn Iran, were more willing to contribute to his plan of liberating Armenia. Once again, his efforts were fruitless and in 1783 he returned to India, where he died in 1809.

Indian Armenian merchants financed the establishment of the first printing press in Ejmiatsin in the latter half of the eighteenth century and, as we have seen, sponsored the educational and printing efforts of the Mkhitarists in Venice. At the same time, a group of Armenians from Iran established a political union in Madras and were responsible for printing the first Armenian political pamphlets. These works codified the agenda initiated by Joseph Emin to liberate the Armenians from Muslim rule and to establish a democratic and independent state based on the principles of the Enlightenment. The leaders of this group, Shahamir Shahamirian (1723-1797), his two sons Hakob and Eghiazar, and their teacher, Movses Baghramian, the latter of whom had worked with Emin in Russia, were not freedom fighters, but liberals, who wished to promote and spread their ideas through the power of the printing press.

In 1771, Hakob Shahamirian established a printing press in Madras. Between 1772 and 1789 he published three political documents written by his father and teacher, *A New Pamphlet Called Exhortations*, *The Snare of Glory*, *A Booklet of Counsel*. These works are significant for, although the authors had deep religious beliefs, these were very secular works and differed considerably from previous Armenian political writings. For the first time Armenians expressed a wish for individual and collective equality and freedom for both physical and intellectual endeavors.

The Snare of Glory was a particularly important document. It detailed 521 tenets for the constitution of an independent Armenian republic. The new state would have mandatory education for girls as well as boys, an elected parliament, a tax collection and judicial system, and, most importantly, would be governed not by kings, but by natural and divine laws. These laws were to be formulated by the rational spirit and promulgated by the elected representatives of the citizens. Citing the Roman Republic, Shahamirian advocated a social contract between the government and the governed.

Although this document predates both the American and French revolutions and their constitutions, it took many of its ideas from the late seventeenth-century English revolution, known as the Glorious Revolution, and from the fervor of the Enlightenment, particularly Jean Jacques Rousseau's *Social Contract* of 1762. By the end of the eighteenth century the first Armenian periodical, *Monitor (Azdarar)*, appeared in Madras, where it was published for two years (1794-1796) under the efforts of an Armenian priest from Iran, Harutiun Shmavonian. The concept of the rights of man and the notion of self-determination were thus introduced to a segment of the Armenian public. During the early nineteenth century, these ideas found their way to the Armenian communities in Europe, Russia, and the Ottoman Empire. The Mkhitarist order in Venice, the Armenian meliks of Karabagh, as well as Hovsep Arghutian (Iosif Argutinskii), prelate of the Armenians in Russia and the Lazarian (Lazarev) merchant family of Moscow all had contacts with the Madras group and were influenced by their ideas (see chapter 16).

The nineteenth century witnessed a new attitude on the part of the British. Although England had secured its predominance in India following the 1763 Treaty of Paris, the French had retained their economic and cultural centers in India. Napoleon's invasion of Egypt created a general Francophobia and the desire to rid India of all French influences. At the same time, the British governor-general, Lord Richard Wellesley, whose older brother was to become Duke of Wellington, was determined to rid India of its native rulers and to make the entire subcontinent subject to the British Empire. During his tenure (1798-1805) he began the process that continued through the first half of the nineteenth century and eventually subordinated the various provinces of India. In the meantime the British expanded their influence into Burma, Punjab, and Afghanistan. The prominence of the Armenian community of Madras was soon eclipsed by the Calcutta community, which established their own printing press in 1797 and opened another school in 1798. By 1818, an Armenian weekly, the *Mirror of Calcutta*, was being printed. New presses in Calcutta published European authors in Armenian translations, and, in 1821 an Armenian college was established in Calcutta. However, despite the efforts of newcomers from Iran, especially Mesrop Taghiatian, who started a journal called *Patriot*, the Armenians had soon to accept the Anglicization of their community. By the mid-nineteenth century ten Armenian journals were published in India. Armenians also published the first Persian language book outside Iran in Madras.

By the mid-nineteenth century the introduction of railroad and telegraph—as well as challenges to Indian traditions and encroachments against a number of independent principalities by the new governor-general, the Marquess of Dalhousie—had angered many natives. In 1857 the British introduced a new rifle that used cartridges smeared with pig and cow fat. The British ignored the fact that Islam prohibited eating any part of a pig and that cows were sacred to the Hindus. Before inserting the ammunition into the guns, the native troops (*sepoys*) were required to bite the tip off the cartridges. A rebellion known as the Sepoy Mutiny erupted all over India; a number of British soldiers and their families were killed. Armenian merchants, who were viewed as associates of the British, lost property in the looting of European businesses, especially in Calcutta.

In 1858 the British government took complete control of India and made it a crown colony. Their rule called the Raj, continued until 1947 and brought with it a new order. British businessmen and administrators flooded India. Indians were trained to work under

British supervision and Armenians lost their economic edge. The Armenian community in Calcutta was the only one to remain viable, thanks mainly to a cooperative formed by a number of merchants that competed with the British. The Armenian College, church, clubs, and philanthropic organizations managed to keep 1,000 Armenians in Calcutta by the end of the nineteenth century.

Armenians from other parts of India, however, lost their economic advantages and began to emigrate in the second half of the nineteenth century. Some joined their families and associates in Burma, Malaysia, or Indonesia. In Burma (Myanmar), Armenians obtained the monopoly of a number of oilfields and opened shipbuilding and shipping enterprises. An Armenian called Captain Manouk became a well-known seafarer and was decorated by the Burmese government. Armenians eventually purchased the famed Strand Hotel in Rangoon and opened businesses and hotels in Malaysia, as well. Singapore became a major Armenian center when the British made it one of the focal points of their colonial administration. By the mid-nineteenth century Armenians from India had built the first Christian church, an Armenian center, and were publishing a periodical in Singapore.

Some Indian Armenians immigrated to China, where Armenian merchants had settled earlier. An Armenian church had been built in 1307 in Canton. Armenian merchants and artisans also settled in Shanghai, and some, like Hovhannes Ghazarian, studied Chinese culture. His translation of the Bible from Armenian into Chinese is well respected by scholars. A number of Armenian merchants settled in Hong Kong and Macao. Paul Chater, an Armenian, took part in the planning of the Hong Kong harbor and another Armenian, Khachik Asvadzadarian, was one of the founders of Hong Kong University.

By the end of the nineteenth century, European colonial governments in South and East Asia had appointed their own officials, bureaucrats and merchants to manage the regions. Armenians, who had earlier played a key role, lost their influence and their numbers began to dwindle.

15

Protected Minorities
Armenian Communities in the Arab World and Ethiopia
(From the Middle Ages through the Nineteenth Century)

A RMENIANS have been part of the Middle East from the
very beginning of their history. They came into the region as
citizens of the Persian Empire, traded and settled there during the Hellenistic and Roman periods, and were, at times, forcibly
moved within the area during the Byzantine era. The rise of Islam
and Muslim conquests introduced a new order, for in a Muslim
state, the individual's place in society is determined primarily by his
religion. All non-Muslims, including the Armenians, were included
among the *dhimmis*, the protected and tolerated minorities, who had
a subordinate status and to had to pay a special poll tax, but who
were exempt from military service.

After the Ottomans conquered the Arab lands, Armenian enclaves were established throughout the region. The Ottoman rule of
the Arab lands was at times tenuous and the Armenian communities
developed somewhat differently from those in Ottoman-controlled
Eastern Europe or Anatolia. In addition, the arrival of the French
and the British, in the nineteenth century, had a significant impact
on the Armenians in the Arab lands.

The Armenian Communities of Egypt and Ethiopia

Armenians had trade relations with Egypt from ancient times; some
Armenians settled in Alexandria during the Hellenistic periiod.
Egyptian Copts, who preferred the anti-Chalcedonian Armenians to
the Greeks, welcomed the Armenians. There is little information
about Armenians in Egypt just after the Arab conquest, apart from a
seventh-century description of a unit of five hundred Armenian
troops under the command of an Armenian officer. A certain Vartan

Rumi is credited with building a covered bazaar (*Souk el-vartan*) in Fustat, or old Cairo. By the ninth century there is mention of an Armenian governor, 'Ali ibn Yahya Abul-Hasan al-Armani.

The Armenian community grew and gained prominence under the Fatimid dynasty (969-1117), a period during which the Arabs maintained generally peaceful relations with Byzantium and cooperated with them against the Turkish threat in Syria and Anatolia. In fact, except for the early part of the reign of Caliph al-Hakim (996-1021), Christians and Jews were comparatively well treated in Egypt. The Fatimids controlled Greater Syria, thus they neighbored the lands ruled by the Armenian Bagratunis. Armenian merchants and soldiers made their way to Cairo, and a number of Armenian viziers, the most famous of whom, Badr al-Jamali (1070-1094), is mentioned by Arab sources. Some of these Armenian viziers were slaves who had converted to Islam and who had climbed into the ranks of the Egyptian hierarchy. Badr al-Jamali's son, Avdal, succeeded him (1094-1121). The two supported the arts and sciences by building libraries and observatories. Another Armenian, Bahram al-Armani (Vahram Pahlavuni), who was related to the great churchman, Nerses Shnorhali of Cilicia, held the post of commander of the army, as well as vizier. Armenian architects built several gates along the ramparts of Cairo. Cilicia and the Fatimid State had commercial and political ties with each other, and the Fatimids recruited Armenian soldiers from Cilicia. Cilician Armenian merchants and artisans settled in Cairo and Alexandria. Estimates place some 30,000 Armenians in Egypt during the height of Fatimid rule.

Ayyubid rule in Egypt (1169-1250) was not favorable to the Armenians, who were viewed as allies of the deposed Fatimids and friends of the Crusaders. The founder of the Ayyubids and the champion of Islam against the Crusaders, Saladin (1169-1193), despite having a number of Armenians in his service, was nevertheless especially harsh toward the Armenians, causing many of them to leave for Cilicia and Ethiopia.

The condition of the Egyptian Armenians worsened during Mamluk times (1250-1517). The Mamluks treated all Christians unfavorably, attacking Cilicia and the remaining Crusader states that had survived Ayyubid assaults. Armenian slaves were brought from Cilicia and Syria as prisoners of war. Christian children were brought from Russia and Armenia as slaves and enlisted in the Mamluk army. In one attack on Hromkla, some 30,000 Armenians were taken as prisoners and slaves. The Mamluks also enslaved Armenians from Cyprus.

Following the Ottoman conquest of Egypt in 1517, the condition of the Armenian community deteriorated further. By the seventeenth century, however, Ottoman military successes and stability in the region increased trade and brought a few Armenian merchants and artisans from Aleppo and Constantinople. The period of growth was brief. By the end of the eighteenth century most Armenian churches in Egypt were in ruins, and the few Armenian families remaining there had to use Coptic churches for their services. There is evidence of Armenians being engaged in menial jobs and living in the poorer sections of Cairo.

Armenian fortunes improved during the viceroyalty of Muhammad 'Ali Pasha and his son Ibrahim Pasha, in the first half of the nineteenth century. Merchants and craftsmen from the Morea, Asia Minor, and Greater Syria gravitated to Cairo and Alexandria, where Western ideas were gaining influence and where educational, economic and military reforms were carried out by the progressive viceroys. Armenian goldsmiths, tailors, and shoemakers were sought after, and Armenians were among the new merchant classes that increased their fortunes in this period.

The Nubarian family—who were originally from Karabagh and who had settled in Smyrna and Cairo—and the Yusufian and Tcherakian families became the most prominent. The most noted member of the Nubarian family was Nubar. He had studied in Europe and, in 1842, at the age of sixteen, was invited to Egypt by his maternal uncle Boghos Bey, who was a government official in charge of commerce and foreign affairs. Nubar became secretary to his uncle and, after the latter's death in 1844, was given the title of *bey* and became a secretary of Muhammad 'Ali. After the death of Ibrahim Pasha, Nubar served 'Abbas and Said Pashas in their negotiations with France and England. Nubar met with the British statesman, George Canning, and was sent to London by the viceroy to discuss Anglo-Egyptian relations with Lord Palmerston in 1851. It was during the reign of Isma'il (1863-1879) that Nubar's fortunes and those of the Egyptian Armenians rose to new heights.

Recognizing Nubar's talents, Isma'il elevated him to the rank of pasha granted him diplomatic status, and dispatched him on a number of missions. In 1867 Isma'il secured from the Ottoman Sultan the title of *khedive* and hereditary succession for his descendants. Egypt, although technically under Ottoman rule, became virtually independent, and began to expand into Ethiopia and the Sudan. Such ventures, as well as the building of the Suez Canal, soon put Egyptian finances under the control of European creditors and by the end of the century resulted in the British protectorate of the country. Nubar Pasha served the two *khedives* that succeeded Isma'il; he was thrice prime minister of Egypt and carried out a number of important social, agricultural, and judicial reforms. Disliked by some Egyptians as pro-Western, Nubar was in fact pro-Egyptian. He not only established mixed tribunals, but also opposed the sale of Suez Canal shares to the British and clashed with foreign officials when they began to interfere in the administration of Egypt. Intrigues by the British Foreign Office forced his dismissal in 1888. He returned as Prime Minister in 1894 and served the government for another year.

Armenian bankers, merchants, artisans and agriculturists, such as Hovhannes Yusufian, prospered in Egypt during the second half of the nineteenth century and Armenian churches, schools, and community centers were built in Cairo and Alexandria, where close to 50,000 Armenians lived. Although favored by the Europeans, Armenians by and large remained loyal to the ruling family of Egypt and were a major force in that country's modernization.

Armenians had traded with Ethiopia from the first century AD. Armenians began to settle there, however, during the Arab invasions of the Middle East in the seventh century. The Armenian community of Ethiopia continued to be connected to the Arab world, both economically and culturally. The Ethiopian Church, following the Coptic Church of Egypt, also welcomed the Armenians for their anti-Chalcedonian stand. They established good relations with the Ethiopian royal family and some were raised to high posts. The Ethiopian Church, in particular, was grateful to the Armenian Church for permitting them to hold services in the Armenian-controlled churches in Jerusalem. By the sixteenth century an Ethiopian Armenian named Matevos was an envoy to Portugal and another named Murad negotiated agreements in the Netherlands on behalf of the Ethiopians.

In 1875 additional immigrants arrived from the Middle East. A number of them served as regional governors and worked as officials in a number of Western embassies. Most Ethiopian Armenians were engaged in trade, importing metals and exporting hides and coffee. An Armenian church and school were built in Addis Ababa, the Ethiopian capital. In time there was some intermarriage between

Armenians and Ethiopians and a number of black Armenians resulted from those unions.

The Armenian Communities of Greater Syria and Mesopotamia

The Armenian communities of Greater Syria and Mesopotamia date
back to the pre-Christian era. Armenian lands bordered the region
and Armenian merchants frequented Syria during Achaemenid
times and continued to do so in the Hellenistic period, especially
during the Seleucid era, when many Armenians settled in Antioch.
During the reign of Tigran II, part of Syria was under Armenian
rule. Armenian administrators, artisans, and merchants settled in
Greater Syria, where they continued to live after Rome retook the
area. Armenians resided in the cities of Antioch, Edessa (present-
day Urfa) and Amida (present-day Diarbekir), and attended a number of institutions of higher learning. Armenian sources state that
Mesrop Mashtots and several of his students went to Edessa and
Amida in search of a model for the Armenian alphabet.

The beginnings of the Armenian diaspora in Greater Syria can be
traced with more certainty, however, to the sixth century. In
539/540, and again in 544, the Iranian king, Khosrow, having defeated the Byzantines, settled some Armenians—along with the
Nestorians—in Edessa and Antioch as a buffer against the Byzantines. A number of Byzantine Armenians, unhappy with that state's
policy towards them, immigrated to Greater Syria. The Byzantines,
who wanted to weaken the Armenian nobility, forced others there.

The Arab conquests and the establishment of the caliphate in
Damascus brought the Armenians in Syria under the rule of the
Umayyads. In general, the relations of the Arab rulers with princes
and nobles in Armenia determined the living conditions of the Armenians of Greater Syria. Armenians fared better overall under the
Umayyads than they did later under the 'Abbasids. At the same
time, the Byzantines began to resettle their rebellious Armenian
subjects on their borders with Syria. This policy was facilitated
when the Byzantines captured the northern part of Syria in the ninth
century. Beginning in the tenth century, Byzantium settled more
Armenians in the region as a buffer against the Arabs. The fall of
the Bagratunis brought more Armenians there and resulted in the
formation of Cilician Armenia.

During the Crusades, Syria was divided under successive
Fatimid, Crusader, and Ayyubid rule, with the Armenians living un-

der different Christian and Muslim rulers. They settled in various cities, built a number of churches, and were engaged as small merchants and artisans. In the thirteenth century, the Armenians of Cilicia, hoping for a more powerful state, joined the Mongols and attacked the Mamluk forces in Syria. Although initially successful, the Mamluks defeated the Armeno-Mongol armies in 1260, and Syria was united with Egypt. By the fourteenth century the decline of the Ilkhanids, or the Mongol rulers in the Middle East, and their conversion to Islam enabled the Mamluks to capture Cilicia and the remaining Crusader states.

Those Armenians who remained in the region settled primarily in the northwest, particularly in Alexandretta and Aleppo. There were small Armenian enclaves in Antioch, Damascus, Latakia, Beirut and Musa Dagh (Jabal Musa or Musa-Ler). The establishment of the regional Catholicosate of Cilicia at Sis in 1446 added prestige to the community. Aleppo, located on the trade routes between east and west, became the main Armenian center in Syria. The remaining Armenian communities of Syria suffered under Mamluk rule. Prisoners and slaves were taken to Cairo and many Armenians were forced to immigrate to Western Europe or Constantinople.

The Ottoman conquest brought stability and growth of trade, which was evident most of all in Aleppo. From the sixteenth to the nineteenth centuries Armenian immigrants arrived in Aleppo from Marash, Zeitun, Sasun, Erzerum, and Erzinjan. A number of churches were constructed in Aleppo during this period. The Franco-Ottoman treaty of 1535 and other agreements with various European states opened the region to trade and missionary activity. The Europeans gained extra-territorial rights and traded under the protection of their consuls through native Christian and Jewish middlemen. The merchants of Julfa played a prominent role in Aleppo and controlled most of the silk trade. After their move to New Julfa, they continued a part of their trade via Aleppo. The Ottomans established a mint in Aleppo and, in the seventeenth century, a number of Armenians served as its superintendent. Armenians and Jews were the primary moneychangers in that city as well.

The decline of New Julfa, the Napoleonic wars, the campaigns of Muhammad 'Ali Pasha and Ibrahim Pasha in Syria and the opening of the Suez Canal all affected the Armenians of Greater Syria. Although the economy of Aleppo declined, Armenian merchants there retained some of their economic power. By the end of the nineteenth century the city once again revived, thanks to the commercial and banking activities of the Armenians of Constantinople. Armenian schools and cultural centers opened in Aleppo and the city gained new Armenian residents.

The Armenians of Damascus, in contrast, did not form an important commercial base, but were primarily shopkeepers and artisans. The Armenians of Antioch, Alexandretta, Homs, Latakia, Kessab, and Musa Dagh included few merchants; rather they were primarily engaged in agriculture and crafts. A number of villages in the region were populated solely by Armenians. Here they cultivated tobacco and produced oil from laurel leaves.

There were also small Armenian communities in Mesopotamia, the area later known as Iraq. Armenians concentrated in Baghdad, Mosul, and Basra, and built several churches. These communities, as will be seen, gained new immigrants in the first half of the twentieth century.

The Armenian community of Lebanon was formed after the fall of Cilicia, when Armenians settled in Tripoli and Sidon. Lebanon was unique in that it was controlled by Druze and Maronite lords, who, at times, sought to free themselves from direct Ottoman rule. In 1736 the Maronite Church united with Rome and opened its territories to Greek, Armenian, and Syrian refugees, particularly those who had converted to Catholicism. Catholic Armenians, who were persecuted by the Armenian Church in the Ottoman Empire, began to settle in Lebanon. In 1742, the Vatican established an Armenian Catholic Patriarchate there. The religious strife between Druzes and Maronites ended in massacres of the Christians, which in turn prompted the French to send forces to Lebanon in 1861. The European powers forced the Ottomans to accept a special status for Lebanon as an autonomous region under a Christian governor-general. This agreement provided some stability to the region, which benefited the Armenians; two Armenians, both Catholics, later served as governors-general. By the end of the nineteenth century Beirut was attracting Armenians belonging to the Armenian Apostolic Church, who were fleeing religious and political persecutions in Anatolia.

The history of the Armenian community of Jerusalem up to the middle ages has been discussed earlier. The community fell under Mamluk rule and suffered to the same extent as all the other Armenian centers in this region. Ottoman rule began in 1517 and continued until the end of World War I. The Armenians were drawn into arguments between the Catholic Church (supported by France) and the Orthodox Church (supported by Russia) regarding their rights to the Holy Places. The Ottomans exploited this situation, and although at times, the Ottomans supported the Armenian Patriarchate, in the long run, the Armenians lost some of their historic prerogatives to Catholic and Orthodox incursions.

The Armenians had both lay and clerical residents in the city and the monastery of St. James served as the educational and cultural center for both. The Armenian population of Jerusalem was never large, however, and seems to have decreased after the Ottoman conquest. The community revived somewhat in the nineteenth century, when a seminary was established in 1843. The economic gains of the Armenians of Egypt and Syria, and the rise of the Armenian *amiras* in Constantinople in the nineteenth century, enabled the wealthy Armenians to support the Armenian Patriarchate of Jerusalem. It aided the Armenians to maintain their historical custodianship of the houses of Annas and Caiaphas and their shared custodianship of the Church of the Holy Sepulcher, the tomb of Mary at Gethsemane, the Church of the Ascension and the Church of the Nativity. After the Greek Orthodox and Roman Catholic Churches, Armenians rank third in their jurisdiction over the Holy Places of Jerusalem. Beginning in 1866, donations from Armenian *amiras* also sponsored the publication in Jerusalem of the monthly periodical, *Sion*.

The majority of the Armenian communities in the Arab lands (see map 27) were in a state of decline by the end of the nineteenth century. Few realized that historic Armenia and the Armenians who remained there would have to endure yet another catastrophe. The events of the closing years of that century and the early decades of the next century made the death and destruction caused by previous invasions of Armenia pale by comparison. It brought thousands of new Armenian immigrants to the Middle East, where thanks to Arab hospitality they began a new chapter in the saga of the Armenian people.

16

Promises of Deliverance
Armenians in the Russian Empire
(c. 1550-1828)

A RMENIANS had contacts with Kievan Russia as early as
the tenth century, but their presence in Moscow is recorded
only at the close of the fourteenth century. From the fifteenth century onward there is evidence of the activities of Armenian merchants and artisans. Armenians were one of several ethnic
groups that the Mongols of the Golden Horde used as traders, emis-
saries, and tax collectors. They thus began traveling in the
Caucasus, the Crimea, and especially along the Volga River, where
they settled in various cities of that region.

When Ivan the Terrible defeated the Mongols and took Kazan, in
1552, and Astrakhan, in 1556, there was already a sizable group of
Armenians in both cities. By the end of the century, the Russians
had reached the Caucasus and had established colonies along the
Terek River. During the seventeenth century, Armenians and Georgians petitioned the Christian Russians to expand their presence into
Transcaucasia. The Muslim tribesmen of Daghestan, however,
routed the Russian armies and the Russians soon retired beyond the
Terek.

This military defeat did not adversely affect trade or the part that
the Armenians played in it. Russian control of the area's water-
ways—the Caspian and North seas and the Volga River—created
stable overland routes between Europe and Asia, which were less
costly than the sea-lanes controlled by European ships. Armenian
traders made good use of these cheaper routes. The favorable situation of the Armenian community in Iran encouraged and fostered
the exporting of Asian goods to Russia and the rest of Europe and
the importing of Western goods to Russia, Iran, India, and the Ottoman Empire. Armenians set up trading stations—not communities

in the true sense—in Kazan, Novgorod, Astrakhan, Smolensk, Niz-hni-Novgorod, Arkhangelsk, and Moscow. Astrakhan became the focal point of this trade and by 1639 an Armenian community began to take shape there.

The genesis of the large Armenian community in modern Russia began in 1660, when Armenian merchants from New Julfa, repre-senting Armenian traders in Iran and India, sought to increase their trading activities with Russia. They presented Tsar Alexei Mik-hailovich (1645-1676) with the famous Almazi or Diamond Throne (currently on display in the Kremlin's Armory Museum) and other rare gifts. A treaty between the Armenian merchants and the Rus-sian ruler was eventually concluded in 1667. The agreement granted the Armenians a monopoly on selling specific Persian merchandise, primarily silk, in Russia. By the late seventeenth century, the Arme-nians had built a tanning factory in Moscow.

Opportunities for Armenians in Russia soon expanded beyond trade. Armenians found employment in the Russian diplomatic ser-vice and the Russian court employed a number of Armenian artists. Such security and support from the state created several Armenian centers by the eighteenth century. In 1716 the Armenian Church in Russia, due partly to Russian political goals, was granted formal recognition and a prelacy with its center in Astrakhan was estab-lished. Armenians were exempted from military service, were permitted to construct their own churches, to practice their religion, to build schools, and to establish printing presses. These opportuni-ties would eventually foster the building of a new leadership and a new spirit which, after centuries of conquest and degradation, would lead to hopes and plans for political emancipation.

Peter the Great and the Armenians

By the mid-sixteenth century, a number of Catholicoi at Ejmiatsin had initiated missions to Europe to urge Western rulers to free Ar-menia from the warring Safavids and Ottomans, going so far as to consider a union with Rome. Although Shah 'Abbas and his imme-diate successors considerably improved the conditions of the Armenians, by the late seventeenth century, as we have seen, the economic and political privileges of Armenians in Iran had begun to deteriorate. In 1677 Catholicos Hakob Jughaetsi called a secret meeting of the Karabagh *meliks* and the leading clerics of eastern Armenia. He proposed to head a delegation to Europe to seek aid in freeing Armenia from Muslim rule. The death of the Catholicos en route ended the project, but one of the delegates, Israel Ori, the son of a *melik* of Siunik, continued on to Europe on his own. He proceeded to Venice and then France, where he remained for several years as a merchant and sometime mercenary. He eventually married and entered the service of Prince Johann Wilhelm of the Palatinate. Ori took the initiative of offering the crown of a restored Armenian kingdom to the prince. In return, the prince gave Ori letters addressed to the king of Georgia and the Armenian *meliks* of Karabagh. Ori returned to Karabagh in 1699.

Although he was met with skepticism and received no encouragement from the new Catholicos, Ori was nevertheless backed by a number of *meliks*. He returned to Europe, where Johann Wilhelm dispatched him to his overlord, the Holy Roman Emperor Leopold, in Vienna. The Emperor showed some interest in Ori's project but pointed out that little could be accomplished without the cooperation of Russia, whose territory had to be crossed in order to reach Armenia.

The ever-persistent Ori continued on to Russia and in 1701 managed to receive an audience with Peter the Great (1682-1725). Peter, who had his own plans for the Caucasus, promised that Russia would be willing to aid in the proposed plan, once it had concluded its war against Sweden. In the meantime, Ori entered Peter's service and was appointed his envoy to the court of Iran. Ori was dispatched to Isfahan to assess the chaotic conditions in Iran and possibly to gain the cooperation of Iranian Armenians in his plans. Ori spent two years in Iran (1709-1711) without any major success in this effort. In 1711, he was on his way back to St. Petersburg when he died in Astrakhan and was buried in the Armenian church there. Ori was the first, but certainly not the last, advocate for the liberation of Armenia from Muslim rule. Other strong-willed and self-appointed individuals, both secular and religious, would play roles in rallying the Armenians and in drawing the attention of European powers to the plight of their people.

Meanwhile, the collapse of the Safavids and the murder of a number of Russian merchants in the Caucasus gave Peter, who had just concluded his war with Sweden, the pretext for invading Transcaucasia. Russian troops once again crossed the Terek in 1722, conquering the Caspian littoral. Armenians from Georgia, Iran, and Karabagh joined Peter's campaign and formed Armenian squadrons. The Ottomans, fearful of a Russian presence along their eastern borders, protested and, after realizing that Russia concentrated its expansion efforts along the Caspian, broke the 1639 treaty with Iran and invaded eastern Armenia and Georgia in 1723. Although Peter gave asylum to both Christian groups in Russia, Armenian and Georgian pleas went unanswered, for Peter did not want to risk a war with the Turks and came to an agreement with them in 1724. Ironically, according to its terms Russia would take over predominantly Muslim-populated eastern Transcaucasia, while the Ottomans would take control over predominantly Christian-populated western Transcaucasia, or eastern Armenia and Georgia. The Armenians were thus left without Russia's promised support and were forced to rely on their own forces. Peter's death in 1725 ended Russian interest in the region and his successors pulled back across the Terek River.

The Turks had little trouble taking over fortresses in Yerevan, Nakhichevan, Ganja, and Georgia, as well as most of Iranian Azerbaijan. But the Armenian *meliks* of Karabagh and Siunik (as noted in chapter 13) managed to set up formidable defenses from their mountain forts and maintained their autonomy until Nader Shah forced the Turks out of the region in 1735. Nader also negotiated the Russian withdrawal from Transcaucasia and for the next fifty years Russia kept out of that region. Although Empress Anna of Russia continued her nation's policy of encouraging Armenians to settle in their realm, practice their religion, and enjoy royal protection, Empress Elizabeth policy of Russification halted the construction of Armenian churches in Moscow and St. Petersburg.

Catherine the Great and the Armenians

The reign of Catherine the Great (1762-1796) witnessed a major revival in Armeno-Russian relations and the growth of the Armenian communities (see map 28). In 1763, Catherine recognized the Armenians in Russia and their prelate as a separate religious community. After her war with the Ottomans (1768-1774), Catherine relocated the Armenian community of the Crimea to a new settlement along the Don River in 1779. A year later she asked, Archbishop Argutinskii, the Armenian prelate in Russia to build a town for the Armenian immigrants. The settlement, known as Nor, or New Nakhichevan (now within present-day Rostov-on-Don), became a major Armenian center with six churches, a theater, a school. Following the Russo-Turkish War of 1787-1792, Catherine ordered Potemkin to build the town of Grigoriopol in Bessarabia (later Moldavia) to settle the Armenian refugees from eastern Romania. Armenians had their own churches and were given much autonomy. They were free to follow their own traditions and had their own city councils. Catherine's benevolent policies towards the Russian Armenians enabled a number of them to achieve high positions. One of the families who prospered was the wealthy Lazarevs (Lazarians), who founded the Lazarev Institute of Oriental Languages in Moscow (currently the Armenian Embassy in Russia). Catherine permitted the construction of Armenian churches in Moscow and St. Petersburg and enabled Armenians to rise to high diplomatic, military, and administrative positions in the nineteenth century.

Catherine's interest in the Caucasus and her victories against the Ottomans encouraged Georgians and Armenian leaders, such as Joseph Emin and the meliks of Karabagh, to place, once again, their hopes in Russia and to promise financial and military cooperation in exchange for autonomy under Russian protection.

Meanwhile, difficult conditions in Iran and Transcaucasia brought Armenian refugees into Georgia and Russia. By 1783, the weakness of the Ottomans, new civil unrest in Iran, renewed petitions from Armenian and Georgian leaders, and the prompting of Catherine's advisors, Potemkin and Archbishop Iosif Argutinskii, the prelate of the Armenians in Russia, convinced Catherine to act. In that year, she annexed the Crimea and concluded the Treaty of Georgievsk, placing eastern Georgia under the protection of Russia. The treaty frightened the Muslim khans of the Caucasus and they scrambled to make their own agreements with Russia or Georgia. Agha Mohammad Qajar, who was in the process of consolidating his power in Iran, reminded the Georgians of their vassalage to Iran. Catherine ignored Agha Mohammad Khan's threats and Georgian fears of Persian attack, as she was convinced that the "eunuch" was merely boasting.

In 1795, Aqa Mohammad Khan attacked Georgia and sacked Tiflis taking some 15,000 Georgian and Armenian prisoners as slaves. The Persians killed a large number of Christians, including priests. Among the casualties was the famous Armenian minstrel, Sayat Nova, whose grave is in one of the Armenian churches in Tbilisi. Shocked by the sacking of the capital of a Russian protectorate, Catherine ordered the Russian army to cross the Terek once again. Russian troops were well advanced into Transcaucasia when Cath-

erine died and her son Paul, disagreeing with the policy of his
mother and disliking her favorite generals, recalled the Russian
forces.

Russo-Persian Wars and the Conquest of Eastern Armenia

At the start of the nineteenth century, Russia, for the third and last
time since the reign of Peter the Great began to move beyond the
Caucasus Mountains. In 1801 it annexed Georgia, which had been
under Russian protection since 1783 but which was technically under the suzerainty of Iran. In 1804, under the pretext that Ganja
belonged to the Georgians, Russia invaded that *khanate* and sparked
the First Russo-Persian War (1804-1813). General Tsitsianov, the
Russian commander, received help from the Armenians of Ganja
and Karabagh, who had been waiting for years for the Russian arrival. By 1805 half of eastern Armenia was in Russian hands.
Tsitsianov was not successful in taking Yerevan, however, and Napoleon's adventures in Europe soon diverted Russia from the
Caucasian front. Iran signed the short-lived treaty of Finkenstein
(1807) with France, which brought French officers to Iran to train a
new army. The Russians tried and failed to take Yerevan again in
1808. A stalemate then ensued until 1812.

In the meantime, more Armenians from Yerevan left for Tiflis,
and the Armenian population, whose numbers had gradually increased during the latter part of the eighteenth and the early part of
the nineteenth century, achieved a plurality in that city. With the exception of the Tiflis community, the influential Armenian leadership
within the Russian Empire was all outside the Caucasus, in Astrakhan, New Nakhichevan, Moscow, and St. Petersburg, as well as the
now-Russian regions of the Crimea, Ukraine, and Poland.

Having concluded the peace of Bucharest (1812) with the Ottomans and having repelled Napoleon, the Russians concentrated in
earnest on the Caucasus, and, in 1813, defeated the Iranian armies in
several battles. The Treaty of Gulistan in that year awarded the
khanates of Karabagh, Ganja, Shirvan, Shakki, Kuba, Baku, and
Talesh (see map 24) to Russia. By controlling Karabagh and Ganja,
Russia became master of half of eastern Armenia. The Armenian
leaders, however, did not take advantage of their position and the
favorable situation to press St. Petersburg to create a separate administrative unit out of Ganja and Karabagh. Rather, in the wake of
Russia's wresting of one half of eastern Armenia, the Russian Ar-

menian leadership's main concern was liberating the other half, that is, the khanates of Nakhichevan and Yerevan, which included Ejmiatsin, the religious focal point for many Russian Armenians. No one could predict that by the time the remainder of eastern Armenia would be annexed to Russia, earlier administrative configurations would have already incorporated Ganja into Georgia, and Karabagh, with its sizable Armenian population, within the Caspian, or Muslim, Province.

The new khan of Yerevan, Hosein Khan Qajar, as we have seen, tried to reverse past abuses and succeeded in gaining the support of some of the Armenian population. However, by the second decade of the nineteenth century Armeno-Persian relations in Yerevan had deteriorated and the Catholicos had left Ejmiatsin for Georgia. Moreover, neither Iran nor Russia was content with the Gulistan treaty. The Russians planned to expand further, the Persians hoped to regain their losses, and some Armenian leaders, led by archbishop Nerses of Ashtarak, who had left Ejmiatsin for Tiflis in 1814, actively campaigned for the resumption of hostilities and the liberation of the rest of eastern Armenia.

Taking advantage of the death of Tsar Alexander I and the Decembrist uprising in Russia (1825), the Persians invaded Karabagh in the beginning of 1826 and began the Second Russo-Persian War (1826-1828). Having caught the Russians off-guard, the Persians scored a number of initial victories. The local Muslims rose against the Russians, while the Armenian population stood fast by the outnumbered Russian garrisons. Armenian volunteer brigades were formed in Georgia and Karabagh and, under a newly designed Armenian flag, joined the Russian forces. Nicholas I, the new tsar, appointed another commander, Ivan Paskevich, who arrived with reinforcements and artillery. Within a year the Russians had captured 'Abbasabad, Ordubad, Sardarabad, Nakhichevan, and Yerevan. When the Russians crossed the Arax and approached Tabriz, the capital of Iranian Azerbaijan, the Shah sued for peace and agreed to the treaty of Turkmenchai (1828). The khanates of Yerevan and Nakhichevan—or much of the rest of eastern Armenia—now became part of Russia and the Arax River became the border between Iran and Armenia (see map 24). The treaty also awarded Russia an indemnity of twenty million rubles, exclusive naval rights in the Caspian Sea, and other economic and political prerogatives in Iran, which bound the Qajar dynasty to Russian whims.

The Formation of a Russian Armenian Province

At the conclusion of the war a number of influential Armenians and Russians, such as Archbishop Nerses of Ashtarak, the wealthy Russian-Armenian merchant Christopher Lazarev, Count Argutinskii-Dolgorukii, and the writer and statesman Alexander Griboedov, advocated the establishment of an "Armenian Province." They felt that the role of the Armenian volunteers during the war had been significant and that Armeno-Russian historical ties proved that the Armenians were one group upon whom the Russians could truly rely. They began an immediate campaign for the restoration of an Armenian homeland under the supervision of the Church and the protection of Russia. The major problem, however, was the fact that a large part of the Armenian population had, in the last three centuries left eastern Armenia and the Armenians had become a minority in the Yerevan region. To resolve this, the Armenian leaders, and their Russian supporters, set about to convince the Russian commanders and diplomats to include as a condition in their negotiations with Iran the repatriation of those Armenians who had been forcibly taken to Iran at the time of Shah 'Abbas.

This idea vas formally incorporated into article XV of the Treaty of Turkmenchai, which allowed for a specific period of population transfers across the Arax River. Eventually over 30,000 Armenians returned to eastern Armenia, the majority settling in the Russian Armenian Province, which was officially formed in 1828 from the combined territories of the khanates of Yerevan and Nakhichevan (see map 29). A year later the Russians concluded the Russo-Turkish War of 1828-1829. The Treaty of Adrianople (1829) awarded Russia the territories of Akhalkalak and Akhaltsikh in western Georgia, both of which had sizeable Armenian populations. Although the Russians had occupied a large part of western Armenia, the treaty forced the return of almost all of it. Some 20,000 Armenians from western Armenia left Kars, Ardahan, Bayazid, and Erzerum, and arrived in Yerevan, Nakhichevan and Tiflis. In the meantime nearly 50,000 Persians, Kurds, and Turks left eastern Armenia for Iran, and the Ottoman Empire. A good number of Armenians also returned to Yerevan, Ganja, and Karabagh from their temporary exile in Georgia, and thus, after two centuries, the Armenian population of the Armenian Province slightly surpassed that of the Muslims. The city of Yerevan, however, retained its large Muslim population until the early twentieth century. These migrations began a trend, which was resumed after the Crimean War as well as after the final Russo-Ottoman conflict in the last quarter of that century. It finally created a solid Armenian majority in a part of the Armenian homeland, a situation that was soon to have great political significance.

17

Between Orthodoxy and Catholicism
Armenian Dispersion in Eastern and Western Europe
(From the Late Middle Ages through the Nineteenth Century)

MOST OF THE European diaspora communities were formed when deteriorating conditions in historic Armenia and the fall of the Cilician kingdom forced the Armenians to leave their homelands in large numbers. Those European Armenian communities with earlier origins became even larger and assumed new importance. The several centuries following the fall of the last Armenian kingdom were not, contrary to popular belief, the "dark ages"—certainly not for Armenian arts and sciences. As in the Middle East, unique works of art and scholarship were produced in the European diaspora. Moreover, some European-Armenians also played a role in the later political and intellectual resurgence of the Armenian people and their eventual road to independence.

ARMENIAN COMMUNITIES IN EASTERN EUROPE

The Eastern European communities were formed when the Armenians in the Byzantine Empire, who had formed the first major diaspora, began to leave that area in the medieval period. They were joined by emigrants from historic Armenia and formed half a dozen major communities, some of which have survived into the present.

The Armenian Community of Cyprus

Armenian merchants from Byzantium had established a minor presence in Cyprus in the fifth century. In 578, however, the Byzantine general Maurice, who later became emperor, forcibly relocated many Armenians to Cyprus during his pacification of Byzantine Armenia. This created the core of the Armenian community on that island as well as in Greece. Cyprus came under the rule of the Arab caliphate from 648-958 (except for the short-lived Byzantine control of 868-874). In 958 the Byzantines recaptured Cyprus and replaced most of its Muslim population with Greeks and Armenians. In fact, a number of Byzantine Armenians became military-governors of the island.

The Cilician kingdom of Armenia opened commercial contacts with the Armenians of Cyprus, whose numbers grew. By the twelfth century, the Armenian population there was large enough to require the creation of a separate *theme*, under its own administrator. The importance of the community is demonstrated by the fact that its bishop attended the Church Council of 1179 in Hromkla, Cilicia. The sack of Cyprus by Richard the Lionhearted during the Third Crusade does not seem to have affected the Armenian community. It continued its commercial activities with both Cilicia and Europe. Armenian merchants and artisans concentrated in the cities of Limassol, Famagusta, Nicosia, and Paphos. Closer ties between Cilicia and Cyprus were established during the reign of the Lusignans, a Cypriot Crusader family of French origins, who had earlier intermarried into Cilician nobility and gained the throne of Cilicia in the mid-fourteenth century. Dissatisfaction with Roman Catholic influence in Cilicia, Mamluk attacks, the fall of Cilicia, and subsequent repressive Mamluk policies brought many Armenians to Cyprus. By the first quarter of the fifteenth century some 50,000 are estimated to have resided there.

In 1426 the Mamluks captured Cyprus, causing terrible damage to the Armenian community and taking some 5,000 prisoners to Cairo as slaves. Better days arrived when the Venetians conquered the island in 1489 and the Venetian senate recognized the rights of the Armenians to administer their own separate community. In 1570 the Ottomans captured Cyprus, and although conditions did not change drastically at the beginning, they began to deteriorate in the seventeenth and especially the eighteenth century. Armenians began to emigrate from the island to more secure places, particularly Greece and Italy.

The Armenian Community of the Crimea

One of the largest and longest-lived Armenian communities of the diaspora was that settled by the Byzantines in the Crimea. The Crimean community was composed at first of Armenian soldiers and their families, who, starting in the eighth century, were stationed there in the service of the Byzantine State. By the eleventh century, following the fall of Ani and the Seljuk Turkish invasions of Armenia, the community was enlarged by Armenian immigrants from Armenia proper and from Constantinople, the latter group facing persecution from the Greek Orthodox Church of Byzantium. Greek and Italian commercial activities had made the Crimea a major trading center with Europe, thus particularly appealing to Armenian merchants. Kaffa, also known as Theodosiopolis (modern Feodossia), became the major Armenian commercial and cultural center in the Crimea.

The Mongol invasion of the region in 1239 had little effect on these merchants; they simply paid their taxes to the Golden Horde, or the Mongols, who had settled in Russia, and continued their commercial enterprises. During the second half of the thirteenth century, the Genoese concluded a number of agreements with the Mongols and Byzantines and gained trading monopolies, which gave them virtual control over parts of the Black Sea. Armenian merchants found the Crimean trade lucrative and more Armenians, including those uprooted from Ani by the Mongols, settled in that region. By the fourteenth century, a number of Armenian churches, including a Catholic one, were already functioning there. As a result of the fall of Cilicia, the invasions of Armenia by the last major Turkic conqueror, Timur (Tamerlane), and the Ottoman-Safavid conflict, even more Armenians settled in the region. It is estimated that over 300,000 Armenian peasants, merchants, artisans, soldiers, and several nobles made their way to the Crimean peninsula, establishing new centers in Karasubazar (present-day Belogorsk), Kazarat, Akmechit (present-day Simferopol), Bakhchesarai, and Odabazar (present-day Armiansk) among others. Kaffa alone had over forty Armenian churches, the foremost being the monastery of St. Sargis. So strong was the Armenian presence in the Crimea that by the first half of the fifteenth century, the area was sometimes referred to by Europeans as "Maritime Armenia."

In Kaffa and Kazarat the Armenians had their own quarters, chose their own officials, and managed to maintain their culture. Crimea became a major center of Armenian art. The artist Nikoghos, who continued the tradition of the great Cilician illuminator Toros Roslin, produced unique illuminated manuscripts. Although the Armenians spoke their own language, they conducted business in Italian, Greek, and most often, Kipchak Turkish, the language of the Turko-Mongols (Tatars). Armeno-Kipchak, written in Armenian script, remained one of the primary languages of Armenian merchants in parts of Eastern Europe until the seventeenth century.

Neither the Catholic Genoese nor the Muslim Tatars forced or actively encouraged Armenians to convert. The Armenian community of the Crimea was given its own prelacy and the town of Surkhat, with its Holy-Cross Monastery, became a bishopric. One of the most significant legacies of the Crimean community was the voice gained by artisans and farmers in the late fifteenth century in the election of their prelates. This development later contributed to the nineteenth-century political climate in Constantinople, where the descendants of Crimean Armenians would demand the participation of the artisans and workers in the election of that city's Armenian Patriarch.

In 1475 the Ottomans attacked the Crimea, putting an end to Genoese control. A Tatar khanate, subordinate to the Ottoman Sultan, emerged in 1478, and Armenian dominance diminished thereafter. Some Armenian churches were converted to mosques; executions and forced conversions occurred as well. Many Armenians fled to other parts of Eastern Europe, primarily to Ukraine and Poland, where they bolstered the small Armenian communities which were already there; others were taken captive by the Ottomans and joined the growing Armenian community in Constantinople. A revival of the community did occur, however, in the seventeenth century when new immigrants, fleeing the resumption of Ottoman-Safavid wars in eastern Anatolia, settled in the Crimea. Armenian historians David and Martiros of Crimea and Khachatur of Kaffa chronicled the history of the Crimean Armenians in the seventeenth century.

In 1778, some 12,000 Crimean Armenians migrated to Russia as a result of the treaty of Küchük Kaynarca (1774) forcing the Ottomans to accept the independence of the Tatar khanate of the Crimea. After 1774 the region fell under Russian influence and in order to cripple the Crimean economy, Catherine the Great encouraged its remaining Greek and Armenian merchants to migrate to Russia before she annexed the Crimea in 1783. The Armenians were permitted to establish their own center of New Nakhichevan, in memory of the community in historic Armenia that many of their ancestors had fled a century earlier. The Armenians of New Nakhichevan, as noted, were to play a significant role in the intellectual development of the Armenians of Transcaucasia in the nineteenth century (see chapters 16, 19).

The Armenian Communities of Poland

The Armenian communities of Poland were primarily located in the eastern part of that kingdom, that is, in regions that are at present part of Ukraine. The ancestors of some of the Armenian merchants and mercenaries who eventually settled in Poland first arrived in what historians refer to as Kievan Russia in the tenth century. Following the Seljuk invasions of Armenia in the eleventh century, more immigrants arrived in Kiev. In that same century the first important Armenian colony was established in the city of Kamenets-Podolsk. During the same period, Armenians from Ani immigrated to Red Ruthenia, which later became part of Poland. The Mongol invasions in the thirteenth century brought even more Armenians into Kiev. The Mongol sacking of Kiev in 1240 soon forced many more Armenians to relocate to Poland, where they settled in the regions of Galicia, Podolia, Volhynia and in the city of Lvov or Lemberg, which by 1303 became the second most important Polish-Armenian center with its own church. Armenian troops defended Kamenets-Podolsk against the Mongols and an Armenian church was constructed there in the mid-thirteenth century. A hundred years later, Armenians from the lower Volga region increased the size of the community there.

In 1340, the King of Poland, Casimir the Great, occupied Galicia and Volhynia and, recognizing the Armenians' contribution to commerce, granted them the right to observe their own laws and traditions. A cathedral, still standing, was built in Lvov in 1363. By the fifteenth century more Armenians arrived in eastern Poland from Cilicia and from the Crimea and, during the Iranian-Ottoman wars of the sixteenth and seventeenth centuries, others joined them from historic Armenia.

Armenians had their own guilds in Poland and were considered by the Poles to be excellent artisans. Armenian jewelers, painters, and weavers were especially well regarded. Their merchants played a major role in the trade with Russia, Iran, and the Ottoman Empire. Many Armenian trading houses in Lvov had branches in Moscow, Isfahan, and Constantinople. The large number of Armenians all over Poland (Lvov, Kamenets-Podolsk, Balta, Var, Berejni, Broti, Virmeni, Korodenka, Dubno, Zamosk, Bajkov, Stoutianitsa, Stanislaw, Dismenitsa, and Wladimir) necessitated the creation of a separate Armenian Diocese.

Although there have been estimates of over 300,000 Armenians in Poland at the height of the community, the actual numbers were probably less (some 200,000). Armenians had their own elected officials and judges (12 individuals) and established their own courts in Lvov and Kamenets-Podolsk, which utilized the late thirteenth-century law code of Mkhitar Gosh. The documents of the Armenian courts were written in Kipchak Turkish, which continued to remain the language of business, and Polish, both transcribed in the Armenian script. An Armenian printing press was established in Lvov in 1616 and the first play written in Armenian was performed there in 1668. Polish Armenians even joined the army and an Armenian battalion participated in the lifting of the siege of Vienna in 1683. Polish Armenian intellectuals such as Stepanos Lehatsi and Stepanos Roshka, wrote historical, theological, and grammatical works. Lvov attracted Armenian priests from the homeland who, in the seventeenth century, came to study at its seminary and copy manuscripts at its scriptorium and upon their return, transferred Western ideas to lay and religious leaders in historic Armenia. Armenian merchants were active in Lvov and 22 out of the 38 trading houses belonged to the Armenians.

By the third decade of the seventeenth century, the Polish Armenians felt the effects of the Catholic Counter-Reformation. The Catholic Church established a seminary in Lvov to prepare young Armenian Catholic priests, who, with the approval of the Polish crown, soon replaced the older priests of the Armenian Apostolic Church. Armenian lay leaders began to convert to Catholicism as well. Since the lay members controlled all Church property, their conversion meant the gradual assimilation of the Armenians and their Church into Polish society. By 1629 the Polish prelacy, under the leadership of Archbishop Nicholas Torosewicz, accepted the supremacy of Rome but maintained its ties and, according to some historians, allegiance, to Ejmiatsin until 1635. The ordination of young Armenian Catholic priests in 1664, however, eventually resulted in a complete union with Rome. In 1689 Archbishop Vardan Hunanian severed all contacts with the Holy See of Ejmiatsin. Armenian merchants lost their power and by the end of that century there were only two Armenian trading houses in Lvov. The community declined thereafter for other reasons as well. The Turkish takeover of Podolia in 1672 led to a general economic decline, which in turn resulted in an Armenian immigration to Constantinople and a number of cities in present-day Romania and Bulgaria.

The final blow was Catherine the Great's occupation of eastern Poland during the first partition of Poland in 1784 and her occupation of Podolia in 1793. This act cut off the Armenians of Poland from Lvov, which had been given to Austria and was renamed Lemberg. These events resulted in the decline and the eventual demise of the community. In fact, by 1820, there were only 100 Armenian families left in Lvov and even less in the other Polish towns.

The Armenian Communities of Bulgaria, Romania, and Hungary

The Armenian community of Bulgaria began when Byzantine emperors such as Justinian (527-565) and Maurice (582-602) relocated a number of Armenian lords and their followers to Thrace and Macedonia in order to weaken Armenian power in western Armenia and to create a buffer zone against the nomadic invaders in the Balkans. Armenian Paulicians and other immigrants soon joined this initial group of Armenian immigrants and by the eleventh century a significant Armenian element emerged in Bulgaria, especially in Burgas, Sofia, and Philippopolis (present-day Plovdiv), where a prelacy was established. The Armenians were mainly engaged in trade and eventually formed communities in Burgas, Varna, and Sofia. Between 1363 and 1393 the Ottomans conquered Bulgaria and the Armenians there were later included in the Armenian *millet*.

New arrivals from historic Armenia came during the Perso-Turkish wars of the sixteenth century. Following the Counter-Reformation, Armenians from Poland who had refused to convert to Catholicism came to Bulgaria where, ironically the Ottoman *millet* system permitted them to practice their own form of Christianity. After 1878, deteriorating political and socioeconomic conditions in Turkey and Bulgaria's recent autonomy attracted more Armenians there.

The community of Romania was formed as a result of immigrations from the lower Volga into Moldavia, Wallachia, and Bukovina in the fourteenth century. Here, too, churches were built and a prelacy was established in Moldavia. The fall of Constantinople (1453) and Kaffa (1475) brought more Armenians to Romanian lands. The Armenians in Bukovina and Moldavia had to endure invasions by Poland and the Ottoman, Russian, and Austro-Hungarian Empires. In 1654 religious persecutions and economic difficulties forced some to Transylvania. The Armenians in Wallachia fared better. They concentrated on the trade between the Ottomans and northern

Europe and by the early seventeenth century had built a church in Bucharest. The Armenians retained their language and religion and participated in the political and cultural life of Romania.

The treaty of Adrianople (1829) awarded Bessarabia to Russia. Armenians in Bessarabia then made contacts with the influential Armenian community in Russia and gained their own prelate soon after. Armenians in the rest of Romania benefited from the various reforms carried out by the governors of these Danubian principalities. Unlike Bulgaria, Romania, backed by Russia, gained its autonomy in the first half of the nineteenth century. Armenian churches and monasteries flourished, and Armenian schools, newspapers, and journals were published in large numbers. The Armenians in Romania became more affluent than their counterparts in Bulgaria and participated in the political and cultural life of their adopted land.

Although there is evidence of Armenians in Hungary as early as the tenth century, the main influx arrived in Transylvania, then part of Hungary, in the sixteenth century, following religious intolerance in Moldavia. A second wave of immigrants came following the tax increases in Moldavia during the seventeenth century. The Armenians joined the Hungarians against the Ottomans and, after the unification of Hungary, were given internal autonomy and the right to conduct commercial activities. They were also allowed to elect their own judges and to have their own courts. The Transylvanian cities of Gherla, also called Armenopolis, and Elizabethopolis (present-day Dumbraveni) were the main Armenian centers where some 20,000 Armenians engaged in leather works, candle making, and trade.

The Armenians of Hungary were forced to convert to Catholicism when the Hapsburgs took over Transylvania at the start of the eighteenth century. The Armenian Catholic bishops of Lvov, now under Austrian rule, took control of the Armenian churches in Transylvania. The Apostolic Armenians in Hungary were thus cut off both from Russia and from the rest of the Balkans and, lacking the religious protection of the *millet* system, converted to Catholicism. The Hungarian Armenians, however, managed to establish a separate bishopric and, with the help of the Mkhitarist order of Venice, operated a school and maintained some autonomy as Armenian Catholics.

The Hungarian Armenians involved themselves in the political life of Hungary and participated in the 1848 revolution against the

Hapsburgs. After crushing the rebellion, the Hapsburgs punished the Armenian leadership by executing two Armenian generals (the third escaped to Argentina), abolishing the bishopric, and demanding considerable war reparations. The Armenians of Hungary lost the right to have schools and soon forgot their own language, which, in turn, discouraged new immigrants and resulted in the total assimilation of the Armenians of Hungary.

ARMENIAN COMMUNITIES IN WESTERN EUROPE

The Armenian communities in Western Europe have their earliest origins in the sixth century. The main influx of Armenians, however, came there during the Crusades and the Cilician period, from the eleventh to the fourteenth centuries, and once again during the seventeenth century when, as we have seen, Armenian merchants from Iran established trading houses in various cities of Western Europe.

The Armenian Communities of Italy

Armenians arrived in Italy as part of the army of the Byzantine Empire during the sixth century. Armenian generals, together with Armenian contingents, fought in Sicily during the seventh century under the leadership of Emperor Constance. Two Armenian bishops from Italy even attended the Lateran Council of 649. The main Armenian communities of Italy, however, were formed in the thirteenth century, primarily as a result of the trade treaty negotiated by King Leo I of Cilicia with the Italian city-states of Genoa and Venice in 1201 and with Pisa in 1216. The Armenian and Italian merchants, who were acquainted through the Black Sea trade, now engaged in large-scale trade in the Mediterranean. Soon small Armenian communities grew in Rome, Venice, Genoa, Ancona, Lugano, Mantua, and Pisa. The Mamluk incursions into Cilicia and the decline of that kingdom, combined with Turkish advances in Asia Minor, brought more Armenians to Western Europe, especially Italy. The significant inroads made by the Latin Church among the Armenian nobility and merchants of Cilicia, plus these two groups' knowledge of French and Italian, made Western Europe in general, and Italy in particular, a logical choice for emigration and eased their transition to a Western society.

The fall of Cilicia in 1375 brought a large flood of Armenian refugees to Italy via Cyprus. According to the historian Ghevond Alishan, some 30,000 Armenians were living in Italy by the first quarter of the fifteenth century. Venice, where a street and bridge were named after the Armenians, became their main center. "Armenian houses" (*case degli Armeni*), hostels where Armenian merchants and artisans congregated, were established in various Italian cities. A number of Armenian churches, among them the Church of the Holy-Cross in Venice, were also constructed. Since Italy was not a united state and each Italian city-state operated independently, the Armenian communities in these various cities followed suit—they functioned as individual units and did not develop a collective Italian Armenian identity.

The Armenians of Venice can take credit for the printing of the first books in Armenian. In 1512 Hakob Meghapart printed two volumes, a prayer book and a ceremonial calendar (*Urbatagirk* and *Parzatumar*). Soon various scientific books were printed as well and, by the second half of the eighteenth century, Italy became a center for the publication of Armenian secular books. The art of Armenian printing moved from Italy in the second half of the sixteenth century, when Abkar Tokhatetsi left Rome due to the harsh policies of Pope Pius V (1566-1572) against non-Catholic Armenians, and set up his press in Constantinople, the first in any language in the Ottoman Empire.

During the sixteenth century, the Italian communities increased in size due to the arrival of silk merchants from Julfa in Nakhichevan. They increased even further in the seventeenth century, however, when Shah 'Abbas, who had transferred Armenian merchants from Julfa to New Julfa, sent an official delegation to Venice in 1607 to purchase various goods. In 1610 the Shah sent the Armenian merchant Khoja Safar as his envoy to conclude trade and alliance treaties against the Turks. Khoja Safar visited Venice, Rome, and Florence and returned with commercial and military agreements. Armenians soon controlled the silk trade between Iran and Italy, and were given tax-exempt status in a number of Italian cities. Iranian Armenians in Venice were concentrated around the Church of St. Mary of Formosa located on a street that became known as Julfa Street. Armenian merchants soon left their traditional hostels and began to purchase individual houses.

By the seventeenth century a large stone church was constructed in Venice, where by then some 2,000 Armenians resided. Perugia, Ancona, Siena, Milan, and Ferrara also gained Armenian residents.

Several Armenian churches, named after St. Gregory, were built in Naples, Nardo, and Livorno. Catholicism was a strong force in Italy and most Armenians converted to the Roman Church. By the late seventeenth and early eighteenth centuries, when Armenian fortunes in Iran declined, a number of prominent *khojas* moved to Venice. Most important of these were the Shahumians (1650-1757), the Martirosians (1690-1737), the Sharimanians (1697-1800), and Noradungians (1717-1757). Armenian merchants from Poland, France, and Russia also set up trading houses in Venice. A number of Armenian sailors and artisans settled in Italian ports as well.

The end of the Venetian Republic forced many Armenians to leave and by the nineteenth century only a dozen Armenian families were left in that great city. The most significant event in the history of the Armenians in Venice was the relocation of the Mkhitarist order to Venice, described earlier. Thanks to the generosity of wealthy Armenian merchants from India, the Mkhitarists established two colleges, one in Venice (Murad Raphaelian) and the other in Padua (later transferred to Paris and then to Sèvres). The activity of the Mkhitarists assured a continued Armenian presence in Venice.

The Armenian Communities of France

Armenian trade contacts with France began as early as the seventh century and increased during the tenth century. A number of Armenians were reportedly among the envoys sent by the 'Abbasid Caliph Harun at-Rashid to the court of Charlemagne in 807. The Byzantines also sent Armenian envoys to France. In the ninth century a number of Armenian Paulicians arrived via Dalmatia and Italy to France where they may possibly have had some influence on the rise of the later Albigensian movement in the south. After the fall of Ani in the eleventh century many Armenians fled to Europe and established a community in France as well. Armeno-French contacts were sporadic, however, until the Crusades. The Crusades and subsequent trade between France and Cilicia brought not only commercial, but also military agreements, as well as inter-marriages between Armenian and French merchants and nobles, from the twelfth to the fourteenth centuries. French merchants received special privileges from King Oshin of Cilicia in 1314 by which they paid a custom duty of only two-percent. French ships and merchants made stops at Ayas, Tarsus, Mersin, and Sis, and Armenians visited French ports. The French brought mirrors, soap, and beeswax, while

Armenians brought silk and other oriental luxury items to Marseilles, Narbonne, and Nîmes. After the fall of Cilicia numerous Armenian merchants relocated to French cities including the city of Avignon. In 1389 the last Armenian king of Cilicia, Leo V, after being ransomed from Egypt, came to France and tried to mediate between the French and the English. He encouraged them to abandon their own conflict (the Hundred Years' War) and to start a new crusade to liberate the Christians in the Middle East. Nothing came out of that and he died on November 29, 1393. Of French descend and related to French kings, Leo was buried in St. Denis in Paris, the resting-place of French monarchs.

Armenian artisans and builders also came to France. An Armenian architect built the early ninth century Church of Germigny des Prés in Orleans, the oldest Carolingian church in France. The church evinces both Armenian and Visigothic architectural styles. In 1453, after the fall of Constantinople, a number of Armenians arrived in Paris and Marseilles. By the seventeenth century Armenian *khojas* from Iran initiated new trade with France. The great ministers of France, Richelieu, Mazarin, and Colbert, recognized the importance of Armenian merchants and encouraged them to settle in Marseilles. By 1622 Armenian merchants were competing so well that their French counterparts complained and forced the government to restrict Armenian goods, forbidding French ships to carry them. Silk was restricted, and taking French gold and silver coins out of the country was forbidden. Armenian merchants complained to Shah 'Abbas, who send a letter with Antoine Armeni, a commercial agent appointed by France, to Louis XIII in 1629, resulting in the revocation of some of these restrictions. By the 1660s, Colbert, despite objections from the French merchants of Marseilles, revoked most of the restrictions. An avenue, named rue Armeni, still exists in Marseilles.

Armenians opened businesses inland, in Paris and Lyon, as well as in the ports of Nice (then part of Savoy) and Toulouse. An Armenian from Nakhichevan, Hovhannes Altoun (Jean Altin) introduced madder, a plant from whose roots a red dye (alizarin) is produced, to the cloth dyers of Avignon in the mid-eighteenth century. Until the introduction of synthetic alizarin, the Rhone valley was a major center of the production of this dye. As in Italy, the Armenian community set up a printing press in France, producing an Armenian-Latin dictionary in the 1630's. The famous Armenian printer, Voskan Vardapet, who had already relocated from Amsterdam to Livorno, came to Marseilles and, beginning in 1673, printed some thirty books in Armenian. Armenians continued immigrating to France during the eighteenth and especially in the nineteenth century, when some Armenians from the Ottoman Empire and the Arab lands settled there. Catholic influence upon the Armenians was strong in France and, in time, most of these Armenians converted.

The Armenian Community of the Netherlands

There is evidence of Armenians in the Low Countries that is, Belgium, Holland, and Luxembourg, beginning in the eleventh century. Trade became active, however, in the thirteenth and fourteenth centuries, when Dutch and Flemish merchants arrived in Cilicia and Armenian trading houses opened in the Low Countries. Armenians brought in carpets, dyes, cotton, and spices, concentrating their trade in the city of Bruges, specifically at the St. Donal Church Square, where they traded their goods for woolen cloth, Russian furs, Spanish oil, and other items brought from the four-corners of Europe.

After the fall of Cilicia, Armenian refugees arrived in Bruges where they were supported by a number of Flemish Christian charities. In 1478 Armenians built a large hostel in Bruges, which became the "Armenian Hospice." By the end of that century Armenians began to move to Amsterdam, the new center of commerce in the region. Dutch sources record Armenian merchants selling pearls and diamonds there in the second half of the sixteenth century. Armenian commerce in Amsterdam received a major boost when Armenian merchants from Iran began trading in Western Europe in the first half of the seventeenth century. Dutch merchants went to Isfahan and some even settled in New Julfa, while Armenians opened trading houses in Amsterdam.

Although the first Armenian book was printed in Venice (1512), the first Armenian printing house was established in Amsterdam. Voskan Vardapet printed the first Armenian Bible in 1666 in that city. The Dutch were Protestant and more tolerant than the Catholic states and other Armenian books were printed in Amsterdam during the second half of the seventeenth century. The press fell into debt, however, and in the first part of the eighteenth century was sold to the Mkhitarists of Venice. Armenians from Amsterdam also introduced the first printing press to Iran.

In 1612, after the conclusion of a trade treaty between the Turks and the Dutch, Armenian merchants from the Ottoman Empire arrived in Amsterdam as well. As in the rest of Europe, Silk was the primary item traded by the Armenians there and they continued to control the Dutch silk trade until the mid-eighteenth century. According to Dutch sources there were some 500 Armenians living in Amsterdam, concentrated in the Monnikenstraat, Dykstraat, and Keiserstraat streets and selling their wares in the Qoster ("Eastern") Market.

In 1713-1714 the Armenians constructed an Armenian Church in Amsterdam and received permission from Ejmiatsin to have their own priest. A number of Armenian merchants were wealthy enough to have their own ships flying the Dutch colors and to be escorted by armed frigates on their journeys to Smyrna. A hundred years later, however, due to various European conflicts, particularly the blockade enforced during the Napoleonic wars, as well as the rise of English trading companies, the Armenian community had lost its economic power in the Netherlands. By the early nineteenth century, the Armenian church of Amsterdam was closed down and eventually sold to a Catholic religious order.

By the end of the nineteenth century most of the Armenian communities in Europe (see map 30) had reached the low ebb of their social and economic influence. No one could predict that the cataclysms of 1895-1896 and 1915-1922 would bring new, and very different, Armenian immigrants to the shores of Eastern and Western Europe.

18

The Armenian Question and Its Final Solution
Armenians in Ottoman Turkey
(1876-1918)

THE REFORMS initiated by Selim III, which culminated in the "Imperial Rescript" of 1856, had not resolved the socio-economic and political troubles of Ottoman Turkey. Although the urban population in Constantinople had benefited from the new safeguards, the majority of the inhabitants, that is the peasants, were not affected. Yet, the Armenians were the only large Christian group who, despite a cultural revival, had not sought autonomy or separation from the Ottomans. In the Balkans, with the exception of the Bulgarians, most of the other major national groups had already gained autonomy or independence. The Armenians, however, only longed for a stable and fair government. There were a number of reasons for the behavior of the loyal *millet*. More than a thousand years of invasions, Armenian emigrations, and the settlement of Turkish and Kurdish tribes in Anatolia, had resulted in the fact that Armenians had but a Christian plurality in some places and a majority in only a handful of districts of western Armenia. Thus, unlike the Arabs or the Christians of the Balkans, Armenians did not constitute a majority in their homeland. More importantly, the Armenian leadership consisted of urban merchants, who did not reside in historic Armenia, among the still-dissatisfied peasants. By the mid-nineteenth century, almost all of these leaders lived in Constantinople, Smyrna, Cairo, Alexandria, Aleppo, Tiflis, Baku, New Nakhichevan, Moscow, St. Petersburg, or other urban centers of Europe and Asia. They not only were far removed geographically from the Armenian workers and peasants, but also had little in common with them. With the exception of a few mountainous enclaves, Armenians in the interior had no military leaders or noblemen to rally the population. The Armenian urban elite was generally respected by the states they lived in and, in fact, found working with the ruling power advantageous to their socioeconomic well being. With the exception of Ejmiatsin and Aghtamar, the Church hierarchy was also removed from Armenia and the majority of Armenians. It, too, advocated conservatism and advised its flock to accept their condition. The Armenian political awakening began in the diaspora and found its way to the agrarian homeland only in the second half of the nineteenth century.

Socioeconomic Conditions in Western Armenia

The Armenian population of western Armenia, unlike that of eastern Armenia, was dispersed on a much larger territory and was separated by numerous Kurdish and Turkish settlements or pasturelands. Certain common features dominated village life in eastern and western Armenia. Like most peasants of that period, the Armenians of eastern Turkey were, until the last quarter of the nineteenth century, generally illiterate. They spoke local dialects of Armenian, Kurdish, or Turkish. Family structure was patriarchal and patrilineal, with property divided equally among the sons. Local traditions and regional customs were strictly observed and except for articles of personal use, such as weapons, tools, and jewelry, most property was shared among the extended family. Houses were small and mud-brick and centered on the *tonir*, or clay-oven that was dug in the ground. The wealthiest and most experienced man was usually elected the village elder. He mediated disputes, administered justice, and distributed the tax load of each extended household. His compensation for this work was in the form of free labor and gifts. Prior to the second half of the nineteenth century, few families, except those claiming noble ancestry, had surnames. After that time individuals took the root of their surname from either the Christian name of the clan's founder, his profession (if he was a craftsman or tradesman), or his birthplace. To this root was added the ending *ian* (also as *yan* or *ean*), *iants*, or *units*.

Aside from speaking a different dialect of Armenian than their eastern countrymen, the residents of western Armenian villages differed most greatly in the configuration of their houses. Ever on guard against Kurdish raids, extended Armenian families lived in close proximity, with houses connected by covered passageways and contiguous roofs. As the photograph of Zeitun illustrates, the western Armenian village could appear to be one unending maze of houses. This sense of physical insecurity also resulted in western Armenian women marrying at a younger age–usually from thirteen to fifteen—and in both men and women seeking to blend in with their Muslim neighbors by wearing clothing similar to theirs. Western Armenian women thus appear to have worn more embroidery and jewelry; in some regions they even wore veils.

The decades of reforms not only did not improve the lot of western Armenians it actually worsened it. The local Turkish or Kurdish chiefs resented any interference by the capital and felt that the reforms threatened their control over their Muslim and Armenian peasants. Armenian village heads and provincial churchmen, encouraged by the reforms, would seek redress by writing petitions. The central government's inevitable inaction, however, would embolden the local *agha, beg,* or *pasha* to retaliate against the Armenians by driving them away from their land. The number of landless Armenians who migrated to the cities increased dramatically after 1856. Many of those who remained were reduced to what can only be described as serfdom or slavery.

The Zeitun Rebellion

Arab, Byzantine, Turkish, Mongol, and Turkmen invasions had decimated the ranks of Armenian feudal lords and military leaders. The fall of the Armenian kingdoms in Armenia and Cilicia had nearly obliterated the remaining power of the princes and nobles. Some had left; others had converted or entered the service of the new rulers of the land. Some nobles, however, had managed to escape to the mountainous valleys of Armenia, notably Karabagh and Zeitun, where they remained autonomous. The Turks had attacked Zeitun, northeast of Cilicia, but its 25,000 inhabitants, ruled by autonomous lords, defended themselves against Turkish incursions and had never been conquered. In the first half of the seventeenth century, Sultan Murad IV (1623-1640) agreed to leave the Zeituntsis in peace, in exchange for their tribute of oil for the lamps of the Hagia Sophia Mosque. No Turkish officials were sent there and the population, some of them armed, maintained their autonomy.

By the mid-nineteenth century, the national awakening in the Balkans and the Russian encroachment into the Black Sea region and Transcaucasia, brought close to half a million displaced Muslims into Anatolia. Having been driven from their homes by Christians, they demanded that the central government find them a place to live. Those coming into the western provinces were settled around Cilicia, while those arriving in the eastern regions found a new home in western Armenia. The central government, which had once more tried to take Zeitun by force but had failed, hoped that the arrival of these groups would aid in curbing Zeitun's growing independence. By settling Circassians and other immigrants in western provinces, they hoped that they would accomplish what the Kurds and Turkmen had done in western Armenia. When that proved unsuccessful, the Turks, in 1862, alarmed by the French intervention in Lebanon a year earlier decided to take control of Zeitun. Claiming that the people of Zeitun had not paid their taxes, a large Turkish army attacked the region. On August 2, 1862 the Armenians defeated the Turkish army inflicting heavy losses, and capturing cannons and ammunition. The Turks then laid siege to Zeitun, hoping to starve it. The Armenians, as the Maronites had done in Lebanon, asked the help of Napoleon III. The French forced the Turks to lift the blockade, but the Turks were permitted to build a fort in Zeitun and station troops there.

The Zeitun rebellion had left its mark, however. Uprisings in Van (1862), Erzerum (1863), and Mush (1864) followed and according to some historians, may have been the first signs of the political awakening of the Armenians in Ottoman Turkey. Between 1862 and 1878 a number of small self-protection bands and societies were formed in Cilicia and Van. The Union of Salvation (1872) and the Black-Cross Society (1878), both established in Van set the stage for the creation of the first Armenian political party.

The Armenian Question

The Armenian Question, according to at least one historian, had its origins in 1071 when the Seljuk Turks defeated the Byzantines in the Battle of Manzikert and became the first foreign group to systematically settle in Armenia. The question was not placed on the international agenda, however, until 1878. Until then the problems of Armenians in Anatolia were unknown in the West and were not included in any discussions concerning the conditions of the Christians living under Turkish rule.

Three years earlier, in 1875-1876, Bosnian and Bulgarian peasants rebelled against Turkish rule and the entire population of several of their villages was massacred in retaliation. Europe and its press demanded an immediate solution for the century-long complaints of the Balkan Christians. The British government was in the hands of the conservatives, led by Benjamin Disraeli, who believed that the Turks, the only bulwark against Russian penetration into the Mediterranean, had to be supported at all costs. Pressures from the liberal opposition led by William Gladstone, as well as mounting world opinion, however, forced Disraeli to call a conference.

In December 1876, the major European powers all gathered in Constantinople to resolve the Eastern Question once again. To their surprise, they were presented with a constitution that had been drafted by the Young Ottomans. Armenians, represented by Grigor Odian, were also involved in creating the document. The new young sultan, Abdul-Hamid II (1876-1909), had signed the constitution. Based on the Belgian constitution of 1830, with some changes to assure the sultan's power, the Ottoman constitution guaranteed civil rights, religious freedom and security of life and property for all. It contained articles for the separation of the legislative, judicial, and executive branches and provided equality for all citizens before the law.

The diplomats, especially the British, felt that such a liberal constitution made any discussion relating to the Balkan Christians superfluous and the conference adjourned. The Bulgarians and other Orthodox or Slavic minorities in the Balkans felt betrayed and the Eastern Question, now labeled the "Eastern Crisis" continued to smolder. Pan-Slavic feelings in Russia were extremely high and encouraged the tsarist government to resolve the issue by war. The Russians calculated that this was the best time to totally nullify the Paris Treaty of 1856. They had already begun to break the terms of that treaty in 1870 when, taking advantage of the Franco-Prussian War, they abrogated the clauses relating to the Black Sea and once again fortified their Black Sea ports. The defeat of France and the emergence of Germany as a new power in 1871 freed Russia to act and in 1872 resulted in the Three Emperors' League, by which Germany, Austria, and Russia loosely agreed to support each other against outside attacks.

The refusal of the Turks to discuss the situation in Bulgaria gave Russia the excuse to enter Moldavia in 1877 and the last Russo-Turkish war of that century began. Once again the war was fought on two fronts, in Eastern Europe and western Armenia. The Armenian hierarchy in Constantinople, who did not trust Russian Pan-Slavism or the Russian Orthodox Church, publicly supported the Ottomans. The Armenian population in western Armenia, however, was weary of the intolerable conditions, and when Kurds, taking advantage of war, once again attacked Armenian villages, the Russian army, led by Armenian generals and accompanied by Russian Armenian volunteers, was welcomed. By 1878, almost all of western Armenia was liberated and the Russian army in Europe was within reach of Constantinople. The Turks agreed to a cease-fire and negotiations began. The Armenian intellectuals of Constantinople, after receiving news of the atrocities committed in western Armenia by Kurds, Circassians and Turkish irregulars, demanded that their leaders end their caution and ask the former Russian ambassador to Constantinople and other Russian officials to include the future of the western Armenians in the forthcoming peace negotiations.

The Treaty of San Stefano (March 3, 1878) formed a totally independent Romania, Serbia, and Montenegro, the latter two receiving additional territories from Bosnia-Herzegovina and Macedonia. A large autonomous Bulgaria, which included most of Macedonia and had access to the Aegean Sea, was also created. As for western Armenia, the Russians annexed Kars, Ardahan, Alashkert, and Bayazid (see map 31). Although the rest of western Armenia was to be returned to the Sultan, article 16 of the treaty provided for Russian troops to remain in the Armenian provinces until the Turkish government carried out the reforms requested by the Armenian inhabitants, and to secure them against Kurdish and Circassian raids.

The British headed by Disraeli and Foreign Secretary Robert Salisbury, and the Austrians headed by Count Andrassy, denounced the treaty and threatened war. Tsar Alexander II troubled by revolutionaries and urged by the German chancellor Otto von Bismarck, who promised to act as the "honest broker," agreed to a European gathering in Berlin within two months. An Armenian delegation, led by the former Patriarch of Constantinople (and later Catholicos), Khrimian, visited the various capitals of Europe to convince the European diplomats to grant western Armenia the same status as Lebanon—that is, a Christian governor, local self-administration, use of revenues for local projects, civil courts and a mixed Armenian and Muslim police force. The great powers, however, spent the time prior to the conference in secret meetings in which the British, Austrians, Russians, and Turks made their own separate agreements. By the time the delegates arrived for the Berlin Congress (June 13-July 13, 1878), the fate of the Balkans and the Armenians was, for all intents and purposes, already decided.

The Treaty of Berlin created a smaller autonomous Bulgaria with no outlet to the Aegean, with most of Macedonia remaining under Turkish rule. Serbia and Montenegro became independent but did not gain much territory. The Serbs were especially stung when Austria was handed a mandate to administer Bosnia-Herzegovina (which remained under the authority of the Sultan) and to garrison the Sanjak of Novi Bazar, a strip of land lying between Serbia and Montenegro. The British were granted Cyprus, an important base in the Mediterranean from where they could keep an eye on the Suez Canal. In exchange, they promised that if the Turks carried out new reforms, they would defend them against any further Russian aggression in Anatolia (that is western Armenia). Granting France the right to occupy Tunis satisfied French ambitions. Romania became independent, but gave up southern Bessarabia to Russia. In Anatolia, the Russians annexed Kars, Ardahan, and Batum, but gave back to the Turks Bayazid and Alashkert, through which the main overland trade route from Iran to the Black Sea port of Trebizond passed (see map 31). Armenian self-rule was not discussed; instead article 61 removed Russian troops and substituted them with a collective European responsibility—without direct supervision—for the implementation of reforms in western Armenia. Khrimian's disappointment was expressed in the famous "iron spoon" speech in which he advocated armed struggle.

Armenian Political and Revolutionary Movements

For the next two years the great powers carried out their responsibility and would occasionally remind the Porte of its promises towards the Armenians. Gladstone, a supporter of the Christians in the Ottoman Empire, became Prime Minister in 1880 and may have pressured the Ottomans to carry out new reforms. Global events soon diverted Europe into other directions, however. Pan-Slavic activities in Austria-Hungary and concerns over a possible Franco-Russian alliance resulted in Germany and Austria coming to terms and favoring the Turks. Tsar Alexander II was assassinated and his son and successor, Alexander III (1881-1894) did not trust the Armenians or other minorities. Moreover, colonial expansion in Africa, Southeast Asia, and China distracted the great powers from the Armenian Question.

In the meantime, the Congress of Berlin had not only disappointed the Armenians, but also had left them in a precarious position. The loyal *millet* was now suspected of pro-Russian feelings.

Kurds and Circassians continued their raids on Armenian villages. The Patriarch tried to ease the situation by declaring his loyalty and reminding the Turks that unlike the Balkan Christians, the Armenians had never wished to separate from the Ottoman Empire. He hoped that the promised reforms would resolve the Armenian Question. Sultan Abdul-Hamid did not accept the Patriarch's assurances. Realizing that the European powers would not intervene, the Sultan encouraged local officials to use a free hand in western Armenia. The petitions of Armenian leaders in the provinces regarding extortion, abductions by the Kurds and Circassians, and the breakdown of law and order were completely ignored by the government. Most Armenians had lost the courage to defend themselves or speak out against injustice. Like the Jews of Russia, they accepted their fate. In addition, Sultan Abdul-Hamid recruited some of the Kurds into irregular cavalry units (known as the *Hamidiye*) to carry out pogroms against the Armenians similar to those against the Jews perpetrated by the Cossacks in Russia. Although the established Armenian leadership did not support Armenian self-protection units, whose anti-clerical and socialistic slogans disturbed the Church and merchant elite, Abdul-Hamid viewed all the Armenians as a threat. He distorted the ideas of the Islamic reformer Jamal al-Din al-Afghani (1838-1897) to his own ends. Whereas al-Afghani, who had visited Constantinople and who had communicated with the Sultan, preached the union of Islamic peoples and values to resist and overthrow Western imperialism, Abdul-Hamid used his position as caliph to unite all Muslims in the empire against Christian revolutionaries in the Balkans and Anatolia.

The disappointment following the Congress of Berlin affected Armenian writers as well. The romantic period was at an end and was replaced by realism. Hakob Baronian (1841-1892) wrote satirical plays, Grigor Zohrab (1861-1915) wrote vivid short stories and Ruben Zartarian (1874-1915) gathered country legends and folk tales. Others from this generation include Siamanto, Varoujan, Medsarents, and Odian. The press followed the movement and in 1884 Arpiar Arpiarian (1852-1908) started *The Orient* as a forum for the realists.

By 1881, realizing that European assurances concerning western Armenia meant little, a number of Armenian leaders ignored the advice of their elders, and, following the resistance movements of the Balkans and the armed struggle of the Armenians in Zeitun, began to organize defense groups in a number of locations. The most famous of these was the Defense of the Fatherland Society of Garin (Erzerum) where armed youth vowed to protect their people. By 1885, the first Armenian political party (the only one formed in Armenia), the Armenakan, was formed by the students of Mkrtich Portugalian, a teacher in Van. Organized by Mkrtich Terlemezian and influenced by the nationalism of Khrimian, the Armenakan platform advocated general education, armed resistance, and the preparation for eventual self-government. Portugalian, who had been expelled from Turkey a few months earlier, founded the newspaper, *Armenia*, in Marseilles that same year.

Portugalian's activities in Europe influenced a number of Russian Armenians studying abroad, who, as will be seen, soon started their own revolutionary organization, the Social Democrat Hnchakian Party, in Geneva. The Armenakans continued their activities in Van and recruited members among the Armenians in Iranian Azerbaijan, the Caucasus and Bulgaria. Neither Portugalian nor the Armenakans advocated independence. They organized armed bands and for the next decade defended the region of Van from Kurdish raids. By the end of the century a small number of Armenakans joined the larger and more organized Armenian political parties, such as the aforementioned Hnchaks and the later Federation of Armenian Revolutionaries, or the Dashnaktsutiun, which had emerged in Tiflis (see chapter 19). The main body of the Armenakans eventually joined the Sahmanadir Ramkavar group (the later Ramkavar party).

The Armenian revolutionaries disagreed on their course of action. The Hnchaks felt that anti-government demonstrations would send a message to the European powers that the Armenians had not forgotten the promises of article 61 of Berlin. The Young Ottomans, who soon established themselves in Geneva as the "Young Turks," did not agree with much of the Hnchak platform, but decided to join with the Armenians in the hope of overthrowing the Sultan and achieving a constitutional government. In 1890 the Hnchaks, challenging their own clerical leaders, organized demonstrations in Erzerum and in the Armenian cathedral of Constantinople in Kum Kapu. Such protests attracted new members, but also resulted in repression and the death of numerous demonstrators and party officials. Armenians in Russia reacted as well, and in the same year a small expeditionary force, apparently sanctioned by the Dashnaks, under the leadership of Sarkis Gougounian, planned a raid on Turkey. Although it failed, the message was clear: Armenians in Russia had not forgotten the Armenian Question either.

In 1894, the Armenian mountaineers of Sasun, frustrated by unfair taxes and services required by Kurdish and Turkish khans and pashas, and encouraged by the Hnchaks, rose in armed rebellion. Although they managed to hold out for a month, promises of amnesty and submission of an official petition to the Sultan induced them to surrender. The agreement was merely a ruse, however, and some 3,000 Sasuntsis were killed. Europe protested but did not act and killings occurred in other regions. In September 1895, the Hnchaks, in order to force the Europeans to act, conducted a huge demonstration in front of the Sublime Porte (known as the Bab Ali demonstration). These ended in terrible bloodshed, with hundreds of Armenians losing their lives. The action, however, forced the British to demand some changes, to which Abdul-Hamid, after some procrastination, agreed.

The Massacres of 1895-1896

The Sultan, however, had no intention of changing his policy toward the Armenians. For the time being Russia, under the new tsar, Nicholas II (1894-1917) had abandoned its active role in the Balkans and Anatolia, while the remaining European powers had other issues to attend to. Their interest in the Balkans and Anatolia could resurface at anytime, however. Faced with the disintegration of his empire in the Balkans, Middle East, and Africa, Abdul-Hamid considered an Armenian national and political awakening in Anatolia especially dangerous. For, if the Armenians succeeded in gaining autonomy or independence, as had the Balkan Christians, the Turks would lose a large part of what, by then, they had come to view as their homeland. Relatively few Turks, after all, had settled in the Arab lands or in the Balkans; the majority had settled in Anatolia. In addition, Anatolia was the Turks' main agricultural and mineral base, and included their principal trade routes. As long as the Armenians accepted an inferior position they could continue to be of service to the empire. Otherwise they would have to be taught to submit.

In October 1895 Turkish and Kurdish forces, with orders from Constantinople, began a systematic attack on Armenian villages and on the Armenian quarters of towns in the six Armenian provinces. The massacres, forced conversions and looting continued until the summer of 1896. Sources estimate that between 100,000 to 200,000

Armenians were killed and over half a million were left in poverty. Hundreds of monasteries and churches were desecrated, destroyed, or converted into mosques and numerous villages were forcibly converted to Islam. Van and Zeitun, where armed Armenians fought back, saw less damage. Throughout all this, the British, French, and Russian envoys protested but refused to act. Except for a handful of armed men, led by popular leaders in Sasun, Bitlis, Van, and Mush who fought back, the majority of the Armenians were too stunned to react. Tens of thousands immigrated to the Arab lands, Europe, and the United States and the political demonstrations evaporated.

The Armenakan and Hnchak top ranks were decimated; the Dashnaks remained the only viable Armenian political organization. European indifference moved the Dashnaks, who up to then had not participated in the public demonstrations organized by the Hnchaks, to act. On August 26, 1896, twenty-six Dashnaks, armed with explosives and led by a very young Babken Siuni, took over the Ottoman Bank in Constantinople and threatened to blow it up. They demanded full amnesty, the restoration of property, immediate implementation of reforms under the supervision of European officials in the six provinces and the introduction of a mixed Muslim-Armenian police force in western Armenia. During the siege ten of the men were killed and the rest, after being assured by Western diplomats that their demands would be given consideration, left the bank and under a safe-conduct guarantee, sailed to Europe. The Turkish reaction was swift: the government instigated riots in Constantinople, in which some 6,000 Armenians were killed. The Turkish response to European protests over this action was denial and blaming the Armenian "terrorists."

The Revolution of 1908

Abdul-Hamid's police, in the meantime, was also active against the Turkish dissidents and intellectuals and arrested a number of their leaders. Between 1891 and 1896, the Young Turks created political cells in Europe. In 1895 another group, the Committee of Union and Progress (*Ittihad ve Terakki Cemiyeti*) was formed with the intention of organizing a coup. They were discovered and most of the leaders were exiled to Europe where they joined the Young Turks. In 1902, the Young Turks joined Armenian Dashnaks, Arabs, Albanians, Jews, and Kurds in the first Congress of Ottoman Liberals held in Paris. Although they agreed to work for a future constitutional state where all nationalities and religions would be accorded equal rights, they disagreed over European intervention on behalf of minorities (Berlin Treaty's article 61). The Armenians continued to demand European intervention and the Dashnaks refused to participate further.

The Japanese victories over Russia and the 1905 Russian Revolution convinced the Turkish, Arab, and Iranian intellectuals that Westernization would put an end to their relative backwardness and make them truly independent states. Meanwhile, the alliance of Armenians and Iranian Azeris in the Iranian Revolution of 1906 brought the Armenians and Turkish revolutionaries closer and they began to plan joint activities against the Sultan. Since earlier attempts by the Armenians to assassinate the Sultan had failed, the Young Turks led by the Committee of Union and Progress moved to Thrace in 1906 to gather support among the officers of the army in Salonika. In 1907, during the second Congress of Ottoman Liberals, initiated by the Dashnaks in Paris, the Armenians and Turks, this time, agreed to work together for the overthrow of Abdul-Hamid and to create a modern state without European help. The Hnchaks, who had refused to attend either gathering, accused the Dashnaks of collaborating with the enemy. A year later, the army in Macedonia, under the command of the Young Turks, marched on Constantinople, deposed Abdul-Hamid (who retained his title of caliph) and established a constitutional government on July 24, 1908.

A few months later, a group of Armenian liberals and some members of the Armenian middle class, inspired by the Ottoman constitution and opposed to terrorist tactics, sought to establish a different kind of political organization. The revolutionaries had already established themselves in Russia, Iran, and Turkey. This left the Armenian community of Egypt as the only powerful Armenian diaspora that had not been affected by revolutionary fervor. Their political and socioeconomic position, as well as the British presence, created an ideal climate for the formation of a new political party that would advocate European liberal traditions and represent the Armenian middle classes of the diaspora. Gathering the remnants of the Armenakans and bringing together those few Hnchaks and Dashnaks who questioned their zealous leaders, these Armenian professionals founded the Armenian Constitutional Democrat Party (*Sahmanadir Ramkavar*) on October 31, 1908 in Alexandria. The party opened a branch in Constantinople, where they attracted many new members and where they later (1921) emerged, under a slightly different name (*Ramkavar Azatakan* or Ramkavar), as a sizable Armenian political organization.

In the meantime, Armenians and Turkish leaders of the capital celebrated the end of Abdul-Hamid and applauded the new era of Armeno-Turkish cooperation. A number of Armenian intellectuals became members of the parliament and a bright future was predicted. Even the Hnchaks, who had refused to cooperate with the Young Turks, decided to refrain from underground activities and to await reforms. The honeymoon lasted less than a year, however. Taking advantage of the revolution, Austria annexed Bosnia and Herzegovina, Bulgaria declared its independence and Crete declared its union with Greece. Reaction in Turkey resulted in a coup and the return of Abdul-Hamid for ten days in April 1909. During those ten days and immediately after the return of the Young Turks, Turkish nationalists and reactionaries killed over 25,000 Armenians in Cilicia. Once order was restored, Abdul-Hamid was exiled and was replaced by his weak brother, Muhammad V (1909-1918).

Although several of the secondary culprits of the massacres were punished, the fact that some Young Turks in Cilicia had approved of and had participated in the terror soured Armeno-Turkish relations. Despite this, the Armenian Patriarchate and the Dashnaks, now the most prominent and visible Armenian political party continued their cooperation with the Young Turks and Armenians enlisted in the Turkish army and fought on behalf of the Turks during the First Balkan War (1912). The leadership of the Young Turks was changing, however. Pan-Turkism, racism and militant nationalism was on the rise and its proponents, such as Zia Gökalp, were now part of the Central Committee of Union and Progress. The goal of pan-Turks was to convert the minorities and to unite the Turkic people of Anatolia, Iran, Transcaucasia, Russia and Central Asia into a pan-Turkic empire. The idea gained more adherents following the departure of hundreds of thousands of Turkish refugees (*muhajirs*) from the Balkans during the 1908-1912 period. Turkish territorial losses in the Balkan wars and the declaration of independence by Albania ended the power of the remaining moderates and liberals in the government. On January 23, 1913, a coup led by the ultra nationalists gave dictatorial powers to a small group led by a triumvirate of Enver Pasha, as Minister of War, Talaat Pasha, as Minister of Interior, and Jemal Pasha, as the Military-Governor of Constantinople. Ignoring the provisions of the constitution, the new leadership ruthlessly suppressed all opposition.

The Genocide

Armenian leaders, fearful of these developments, and faced with the arrival of over 500,000 displaced and overtly anti-Christian Muslim emigrants from the Balkans into western Armenia, once more began to look for outside diplomatic assistance. In the meantime, however, the international political situation had changed drastically. In 1894 Russia made an alliance with France and in 1907 concluded an agreement with Britain by which they delineated zones of influence in Asia, thus forming the Triple Entente. The Central Powers, or the Germans, the Austrians, and vacillating Italians sought their own military and economic alliances against the Triple Entente. The Turks, having lost Britain, their traditional ally, looked toward Germany and were soon purchasing German arms, inviting German military advisors, concluding trade agreements, and planning the Baghdad-Berlin Railway.

By 1913, renewed Armenian political activity, as well as the tense international situation revived the Armenian Question, and Russia urged the powers to convene another conference. The Russian plan was to avoid another war. It had a number of provisions. It put western Armenia under the supervision of a non-Turkish governor; it created a mixed police force; dissolved the *Hamidiye*; ended the settlement of Muslim immigrants from the Balkans in Armenian provinces; provided restitution for recent Armenian economic losses and retained the revenues collected in Armenia for local projects, such as schools. Furthermore, it included Cilicia in this plan. Neither the Armenians nor Russia, however, advocated the separation of western Armenia from Ottoman Turkey.

German and Austrian objections, however, led to a number of compromises and by early 1914 an accord, accepted by the great powers, was signed by Russia and Turkey. The agreement included only a few of the original demands. Turkish Armenia was to be divided into two provinces, supervised by two neutral European governors-general, who would oversee the mixed police force and a number of administrative and fiscal reforms. Cilicia was not included in the plan. By the summer of 1914, Norwegian and Dutch governors had arrived in Turkey and Armenians, although disappointed, hoped that the long overdue reforms would finally be implemented in the six Armenian provinces. Even such mild reforms, however, frightened the Turks, who saw in them a growing autonomy and the eventual independence of western Armenia, as had occurred in the Balkan states.

Meanwhile, on the eve of World War I, a secret Turko-German alliance was negotiated with the understanding that the Germans would aid in the realization of the Pan-Turanic dream. This meant that the Georgians, Russians, and especially the Armenians, the primary obstacle in uniting the Turkish people, had to be eliminated. Their elimination would also enable the Muslim emigrants from the Balkans, to settle in Armenian villages and to recoup whatever wealth they had abandoned in Eastern Europe. Moreover, the Turks felt that in order to create a Turkish bourgeoisie, the Armenian middle class had to be wiped out. Against a stern British warning, Turkey entered the war on the German side in fall of 1914. At the start of the war, Enver Pasha, as a first step in this plan, moved with a large army towards Transcaucasia and Iranian Azerbaijan. The winter campaign of 1914-1915 was a disaster for Enver, whose army suffered terrible losses on both fronts. He left the front and returned to the capital. To save face he blamed the Armenians in Anatolia for his failure. The Central Committee now became very apprehensive about the Russian counteroffensive, which was surely to come after the winter thaw.

Immediately after the failed campaign, in February, Armenian soldiers were disarmed and relegated to work battalions. Armenian citizens, who had been permitted to carry arms following the 1908 revolution, were disarmed as well and many men were taken away to perform the most menial jobs in the army. In March the government decided to suppress or destroy the two main Armenian power centers, Zeitun and Van. The Armenians of Zeitun and a number of other towns in Cilicia were the first to be killed and deported. Although a few resisted and fled to the mountains, most of the population was driven into Syria. Their property was immediately taken over by Muslim emigrants, mostly from Thrace and Bulgaria. The Armenians of Van province were next and by mid-April the Turks succeeded in killing or deporting most of the population of that province. The city of Van, with its 30,000 Armenian majority, was an exception, however. The Armenian quarter barricaded itself and, armed with a few weapons under the leadership of Aram Manukian and Armenak Erkanian, managed to hold out until the arrival of Russian troops in mid-May 1915.

By the end of April the stage was set for the final solution to the Armenian Question. On the night of April 24, 1915, over two hundred Armenian writers, poets, newspaper editors, teachers, lawyers, members of parliament and other community leaders in Constantinople were taken out from their homes at night and later killed. Among them were many of the writers who were born during or after the Armenian literary revival. By the end of the year, some 600 Armenian intellectuals and a few thousand workers had also been arrested and deported into the interior. One of the few noted Armenians to survive was the composer and folk song collector Komitas, who, after witnessing this catastrophe, suffered a breakdown from which he never recovered. Explicit orders were cabled to governors and military commanders of the six Armenian provinces to remove the Armenians by force from their ancestral homeland. The ethnic cleansing followed the same pattern in each province. First, all able-bodied men living in towns or villages were summoned to the municipal headquarters where they were held, or jailed for a short time. They were then taken out of town and shot. The old men, women, and children were then told that they had a few hours or days to leave for new locations. Although some were rounded up in churches, which were then set on fire, the majority, guarded by special brigades composed of Turkish criminals and unemployed ruffians, were taken on long marches, where many died from lack of water, food, or exhaustion. Most of those who survived the march died in the desert camps at Deir el-Zor. Women were raped and old men and boys were burned, maimed or beaten. Kurds and Turks forcibly took many young women as wives or concubines and numerous children were also seized and brought up as Muslims (according to one source more than 250,000 converted). Suicides, torture and murder decimated the ranks of the deportees who were being driven to Aleppo and Mosul. Few reached their destination, and according to most sources more than one million Armenians who lived in the six provinces perished. By 1916 the entire Armenian population of the regions of Van, Mush, Sasun, Bitlis, Erzinjan, Baiburt, Erzerum, Trebizond, Shabin Karahisar, Kharput, Sivas, Ankara, Diarbekir, Marsovan, Urfa, as well as Cilicia was eradicated (see map 32).

Disarmed, outnumbered, surrounded, and without their able-bodied men, the Armenians went to their deaths with minimal resistance. A few individuals managed to fight back or to escape. The six Armenian villages perched on the side of Musa Dagh on the shores of the eastern Mediterranean, realizing the fate of their neighbors, decided to fight. They resisted the efforts of a large Turkish force for forty days and some 4,000 of them were eventually rescued by the French navy. Later, Franz Werfel immortalized their heroic stand in his novel *The Forty Days of Musa Dagh.*

Foreign missionaries shielded some Armenian Catholics and Protestants, but a large number of Armenian converts faced the same fate as their apostolic brothers and sisters. The pleas of many foreign diplomats and missionaries, particularly the American ambassador Henry Morgenthau, who tried to intercede on behalf of the Armenians and to stop the carnage, were ignored. Although German and Austrian officials did not have a part in instigating the genocide, they were well aware of preparations for it and, although they witnessed or received news of the events, refused to do anything decisive about the matter, save for the German command in Smyrna (Izmir). The Armenians of Constantinople and Smyrna were also included in the plan, but except for the several thousand who were arrested early on, they were spared primarily because of the presence of many European consulates and the intercession of American and German diplomats and military personnel. By the time it was over close to 1.5 million people had lost their lives and the Armenian Question in Anatolia had been resolved. The large Armenian community of Smyrna was, along with the Greek, decimated later, in 1922. Meanwhile, the small Armenian enclave in the corner of Cilicia, in the Sanjak of Alexandretta (Iskanderun), which became part of Syria after 1918, left, after the region was returned to the Turks by the French in 1939. Discrimination, harassment, pogroms and arbitrary taxes after WWII reduced the significant Armenian presence in Istanbul through immigration.

In comparing the Armenian Genocide and the Holocaust of the Jews several decades later, a number of common features appear. In both instances a dictatorial party was in control of the state and obedience to the state was an essential part of the national culture. Nationalism and racial homogeneity was advocated and the preparations for the elimination of specific minorities were coordinated, made in advance, and in secret. Deceptive methods were used to prevent resistance and officials who disagreed or hesitated were removed. Special brigades and committees were formed to supervise the plan and the military was used to carry out political decisions. Both Armenians and Jews were singled out as traitors and exploiters and their property was looted or confiscated. They both served as scapegoats for the failures of the dominant group. Medical experiments were carried out on both groups, although fewer Armenians were subjected to that horror. Both groups lost about sixty-five percent of their population. Revisionist historians later denied both events or disputed and minimized the number of victims. A number of Turks and Kurds, like the "righteous gentiles," helped some Armenians to escape by warning, hiding, or letting them go. Those spared in both disasters suffered the guilt of the survivor and their literary responses were very similar. The European victors, as they did in 1945, held trials in Constantinople (in 1918) and pronounced sentences of death or jail on the perpetrators of the genocide.

There are a number of important differences, however. While trains transported European Jews to their death camps, the majority of Armenians were marched to their deaths, often naked, or left to die slowly in desert camps. More importantly, Armenians, unlike the Jews, were uprooted from their 3000-year old homeland. The present government of Germany, unlike that of Turkey, has acknowledged the Holocaust and has paid monetary reparations.

Most Turkish and pro-Turkish American historians, adopting the official Turkish position, have denied the planned extermination of the Armenians, which is accepted by the majority of serious historians as the first genocide of the twentieth century. They assert that Armenian political activities and especially the uprising in Van forced the state to remove the untrustworthy Armenians from the path of the advancing Russian army so that their treachery would not assist the enemy. There was no plan to exterminate the Armenians, they claim; rather they were simply being evacuated from the war zone. They also add that the Armenian population in Turkey, contrary to European and Armenian sources, was not over 2 million, with more than half residing in western Armenia, but was somewhere around 1.3 million, with approximately 650,000 living in western Armenia. They add that although 300,000 Armenians perished at the hand of Kurds or died through unsanctioned actions of outlaws and hastily organized deportations, most died from epidemics, lack of supplies, shelter, and other disasters of war. The same war also killed more than two million Turks, some of whom were killed by Armenian armed bands. Finally, they reject the findings of the post-war tribunals, as well as numerous official reports as biased and anti-Turkish in nature.

Objective sources agree that only a minute percentage of Turkish Armenians offered any help to the Russians; the overwhelming majority remained loyal and some 100,000 enlisted or were drafted into the Turkish army. The revisionist historians ignore the facts that the deportations began earlier than the defense of Van and that Armenians from other regions, far from the war zone, were also deported and killed. The fact that the course of events was almost identical in each hamlet, village, or city in the Armenian provinces, irrefutably points to a well-organized plan. The revisionists also discount reports from German officials in Turkey, who clearly state that Enver Pasha's claim of only 300,000 Armenians dead was inaccurate and that the actual figure, according to their reports, was well over one million. There are thousands of official reports from American, Italian, and other neutral diplomats, as well as by the German and Austrian representatives, who were allies of the Turks. There are also Arab and even Turkish and Kurdish eyewitness accounts. Furthermore, accounts of various journalists, missionaries, and survivors make the genocide undeniable. It is true that more Turks died during World War I, but they died as a result of war and not genocide. Likewise, more Germans died in World War II than did Jews, but of very different causes.

With much of historical Armenia ethnically cleansed of Armenians and a small part of it under anti-nationalist Soviet rule, Armenian national and political aspirations were limited to a few centers in the diaspora. It took fifty years for the Armenians to build the economic and cultural framework in Europe, North America and the Soviet Union (after 1956) and to recover from the shock of their near-annihilation. Meanwhile, having reestablished its ties with France, England, and the United States, the modern Turkish State sought to distance itself from its past and portray itself as the sole Westernized Muslim nation. Its strategic location helped it gain membership in NATO and become an important military ally of the US during the Cold War.

In 1965, on the fiftieth anniversary of the genocide, Armenians everywhere, including Soviet Armenia, demonstrated their frustration and began to demand justice. A number of Turkish diplomats were assassinated by Armenians, who, influenced by national liberation movements around the world, considered terrorism the only way to awaken the conscience of the world. In 1975, a group of young men calling themselves the Armenian Secret Army for the Liberation of Armenia (ASALA) began to operate in Lebanon and cooperated with other national liberation factions. Despite their failure and, according to many, damage to the Armenian image, they succeeded in awakening a number of young Armenians into action. The Dashnaks, who had lost some young members to the ASALA, soon created their own force, the Justice Commandos of the Armenian Genocide, who were even more successful in targeting Turkish organizations and diplomats. The two groups occasionally clashed as well. The Turkish response to these developments was a repeated denial of the genocide by their government and historians.

Turkish and some Western academics, who had received grants from the Turkish government, went so far as to accuse the Armenians of having massacred Turks. Finally the Turks began to spread the notion that the so-called first genocide of the twentieth century offended the memory of the victims of the Jewish Holocaust. The large funds spent by Turkey bore some fruit, for by 1980 what had been previously acknowledged by all as the Armenian Genocide, began to be termed "alleged genocide," or "so-called genocide." The US government, not wanting to damage its relations with Turkey, pressured its allies and the UN not to recognize the Armenian Genocide. Such actions not only rallied the particularly active Armenians, but also brought out those Armenians who had removed themselves from Armenian national affairs. Documents were collected, films were made, books and articles were published, survivors were interviewed and taped, and a number of institutes were founded to fight the Turkish denials. Putting aside their differences, the Armenians began to use their united voices and demanded that their political representatives examine the evidence.

Two decades later their efforts were rewarded when a number of European countries, despite great pressures from Turkey, acknowledged the Armenian Genocide and the US Senate came close in passing such a resolution as well. In addition, the subject of the Armenian Genocide was included in a number of State public school curriculums.

Having failed to erase the truth about the Armenian Genocide, Turkish and some American officials altered their position and pressured Armenian organizations and leaders to partake in a dialogue between select groups of Armenian and Turkish academics. The Turks presented the following compromise: The deportations and killings were not premeditated. Wartime conditions caused some local officials to take matters into their own hands and during the chaos matters got out of hand and some 600,000 Armenians may have died from harsh conditions during the deportations. If one accepts the above, Armenians perished because of war—there was no planned genocide. Pressures from the United States resulted in the creation of a Turkish Armenian Reconciliation Commission

(TARC) as well. It was soon disbanded (recently reorganized) when the Turkish representatives refused to include the genocide on the agenda. There is no question that Armenians and Turks should discuss the events surrounding 1915-1923, but to cast any doubt on the planned genocide, in view of the overwhelming archival documentation around the world, is a flagrant attempt to rewrite history and cannot be accepted. *The Armenian genocide, like the Jewish holocaust, is irrefutable, undeniable, and not open to debate.*

19

Subjects of the Tsar
Armenians in Transcaucasia
(1828-1918)

A T THE CONCLUSION of the Second Russo-Persian War, the Armenians hoped to establish an autonomous state under Russian protection. Tsar Nicholas I rejected the idea, but as a concession to Armenians and their supporters, the khanates of Yerevan and Nakhichevan were, for a short time (1828-1840) combined to form the Armenian *Province (Armianskaia oblast* or *Haikakan marz* (see map 29). The Armenians were soon disappointed, however, for Nicholas and his appointees in the Caucasus were conservatives who generally advocated Russifying the non-Russian areas of the empire and bringing them under the control of the central administration. In 1836 the Russians enacted a set of statutes known as the *Polozhenie*, which sought to oversee the affairs of the Armenian Church far more than the Iranians had ever attempted. A Russian procurator resided at Ejmiatsin to observe the activities of the Church. Whereas, in the past, Armenian religious and secular representatives chose the Catholicos, under the *Polozhenie* two candidates, whose names were submitted to the Tsar for final selection, were nominated. The new catholicos would then swear allegiance to the Tsar. Under the *Polozhenie*, however, the Armenian Church was recognized as a separate entity and retained a degree of autonomy denied the Georgian Church, which became subordinate to the Russian Orthodox Church. The Armenian clergy remained exempt from taxes and Church property was secure. Moreover, the Holy See was given primacy over the Armenian dioceses in Georgia, eastern Caucasus, New Nakhichevan, Bessarabia, and Astrakhan. By 1840, the title of "Armenian Province" was offensive to Nicholas' sense of Russian nationalism and he abolished it. Eastern Armenia was now divided between the two new Transcaucasian provinces. The former territories of the khanates of Yerevan, Nakhichevan, and Ganja became part of the Georgian-Imeretian Province, while Karabagh was included in the Caspian Province (see map 34).

Russian expansion in the nineteenth century added large territories and new ethnic populations to the empire. The main objective of the state was to incorporate these lands and to integrate its people into the Russian administration. The mountain tribes of the Caucasus continued to resist Russian occupation until 1859 and since the region was also a springboard for military campaigns against the Ottoman Turks, Russia appointed military men as the governors of Transcaucasia. Nicholas' administrators were divided into two broad groups, sometimes termed regionalist and centralist. While both advocated Russian rule, the regionalists were more sensitive to local traditions and hoped for a gradual transformation, while the centralists wanted a speedy Russification of all borderlands. Economically, the first group advocated improving the living conditions of the area, while the other urged its exploitation as a colony.

Socioeconomic Conditions: Rise of the Armenian Middle Class

Initially, following the Russian conquest, socioeconomic conditions in eastern Armenia deteriorated. The new administration, unfamiliar with the region, relied heavily on Muslim officials and landlords. Trade declined and taxes were increased. Some Armenians even returned to Iran. The military importance of the Caucasus and the dissatisfaction with and hostility to the Russian administration on the part of the native population, eventually prompted the Tsar to appoint a more capable and sensitive man as the first viceroy of the Caucasus. Count Michael Vorontsov arrived in 1845 and in his nine-year tenure managed to befriend the Georgians, Armenians, and even most Muslims. Realizing that the random territorial divisions had caused dissatisfaction, and in order to establish better control, he partitioned Transcaucasia into four smaller provinces: Kutais, Shemakh, Tiflis, and Derbend. These provinces were then subdivided into counties and districts; most of eastern Armenia fell within the Tiflis Province (see map 35).

Vorontsov lowered tariffs and permitted European commerce to transit through Transcaucasia. Appreciating the Armenian expertise in trade, he granted their merchants and craftsmen special privileges. Armenian businessmen were classified as "respected citizens of the Empire." They were exempted from military service, corporal punishment, and a number of taxes. To better gain the favor of Armenians, Vorontsov, in 1849, detached the regions of Yerevan and Nakhichevan (or the territory of the former Armenian Province) and created a fifth province, the Yerevan Province (see map 36).

Vorontsov's successors continued to reorganize Transcaucasia. In 1862 the Shemakh Province was renamed Baku Province and Derbend became the Daghestan Province. The Armenian district of Lori was severed from the Yerevan Province and became attached to the Tiflis Province. In 1868, taking areas from the Baku, Yerevan, and Tiflis Provinces Russia formed a new province, Elizavetpol (Elizabetpol). Karabagh and Siunik, as well as Ganja became part of the Elizavetpol Province (see map 37). In 1875, a minor change resulted in redistricting the Yerevan Province into seven districts. Following the Russo-Turkish war of 1877-1878, the Russians created two more provinces from western Armenian and western Georgian territories conquered from the Turks. The Batum and Kars Provinces were thus added to the Transcaucasian administration (see map 38). The final change occurred in 1880 when a new district, the Borchalu, was created within the Tiflis Province. The result of this shifting was that some provinces and districts had a mixed Georgian, Armenian, and Turko-Tatar population, a situation that was to have dire consequences in the twentieth century.

The arrival of thousands of Armenian immigrants, the policies of Vorontsov, and the industrialization of some of Transcaucasia's urban centers, created an environment in which the Armenians, with their commercial contacts and talents, performed far better than their Georgian or Turko-Tatar neighbors. In addition, Russian conquests had brought the Armenian communities in the Crimea, Poland, Bessarabia, Russia, Georgia, and eastern Armenia, including the Holy See of Ejmiatsin, under a single state. By the second half of the nineteenth century, an Armenian middle class had emerged and by the end of that century, Armenian tradesmen dominated Tiflis, Baku, Elizavetpol, and other urban centers of Transcaucasia. Like the Armenians in Constantinople, the urban Armenians became the most loyal subjects of the state. Unlike the Armenians in Turkey, however, the urban Armenians of Russia began to view Russian culture as somewhat superior to their own.

More than half of the Armenians of Transcaucasia, however, did not participate in the economic benefits of Russian rule. For the

Armenian peasants, life remained much the same as before, with taxes and duties taking away most of their produce. As in Ottoman Turkey, class differences between urban and rural Armenians were pronounced. Until 1870, the peasants were serfs and much of their land was recognized as the hereditary property of local Muslim and Christian landlords, or belonged to the Church, which together with the State was the largest landowner. The land reform of 1870 did not significantly alter these conditions. Although the peasants were permitted to own land, they had to purchase it from their landlords. Most peasants were too poor to do so and, therefore, there was little improvement in the life of the peasants during the imperial regime.

Immigration from western Armenia and the Russian annexation of Kars and Ardahan, as well as improved economic conditions, resulted in the increase of the Armenian population from half a million in 1840, to over one million in 1897, and slightly under two million in 1917. The Muslims continued to remain a majority in the cities of Nakhichevan and Ordubad. Yerevan only achieved an Armenian majority prior to the First World War. In all the other urban centers of the Yerevan province, Armenians held a solid majority, however. Although the cities of Yerevan and Alexandropol (later Leninakan, present-day Gumri) and the region of Alaverdi attracted some entrepreneurs, who established the wine and cognac industry, foreign trade and copper mines, the Armenian middle class was concentrated, not in the few urban centers of eastern Armenia, but in Tiflis and Baku. Tiflis was the center of the Russian administration of the Caucasus and the Armenians formed the largest ethnic group there. Their middle class dominated trade, banking, bureaucracy, and crafts. Armenian artists like Hakob Hovnatanian (1806-1881) painted numerous portraits of the Russian, Georgian, and Armenian elite of Tiflis. Armenian families with Russified surnames like Tumanovs, Gevorkovs, and Yegiazarovs controlled the leather, tobacco, and textile industries. The mayor of the city and most of the city council was Armenian. It was Baku, however, that attracted new Armenian entrepreneurs. Besides the lure of its trans-Caspian trade with Iran, Central Asia, and Russia, Baku's oil deposits were among the largest in the world. By the twentieth century, Armenian magnates, led by Mantashev, owned thirty percent of the oil in Baku. While the Armenians rose to dominate bureaucracy, banking and industry, the Georgian nobility declined and fell into debt and the Muslim khans lost their political advantages. The differences among the ethnic groups created hostility and envy against the Armenians on the part of their Georgian and especially their Muslim neighbors.

The Armenian Cultural Revival

Urban Russian Armenians, like their counterparts in the Ottoman Empire, were among the first minorities to take advantage of the European influences that had entered Russia during the reign of Catherine the Great and Alexander I. An Armenian printing press was established in St. Petersburg in 1780 and a number of European classics were translated at the end of the eighteenth century. By the second decade of the nineteenth century, Armenians had opened schools in New Nakhichevan and Astrakhan. The famous Lazarev Institute in Moscow, founded in 1815, had a renowned library and its own press. It concentrated on the study of eastern languages and cultures, including Armenian, and educated a number of future Armenian intellectuals. Armenians enrolled in Russian and European academies and a number of them, such as the painter Aivazovsky (1817-1900) achieved great fame. Following the annexation of Georgia, the state opened a Russian school and a Russian Orthodox seminary in Tiflis. This prompted the Armenian Holy See, in 1813, to open a seminary in Ejmiatsin, which, by the end of the century, was transformed into the famous Gevorkian Academy.

In 1824 Archbishop Nerses of Ashtarak, who was instrumental in establishing the seminary at Ejmiatsin and who had left for Tiflis to ·organize the liberation of the remainder of eastern Armenia opened the Nersessian Academy, which became the main Armenian educational center in Transcaucasia. By the mid-nineteenth century, Armenians had some two-dozen schools and a number of presses, including one in Karabagh.

The more liberal reign of Alexander II created new opportunities and enabled urban Armenians to come into contact with political and social developments in Europe and Russia. Like their counterparts in the Ottoman Turkey, a number of Armenian intellectuals sought to educate and to create a sense of nationality among their people. Armenian educators in eastern Armenia, however, faced the same problems and pressures their counterparts were experiencing in western Armenia. Church leaders tried to control the schools and the curriculum. In addition, some Russian officials were suspicious and tried to limit the influence of the West. The better educated, younger or married priests and lay instructors clashed with the establishment when they tried to replace faith and obedience to traditions with reason, science, modern literature, and new ideas about Armenian history. Nevertheless, during the next fifty years this younger generation succeeded in establishing in Russia some 500 schools with 20,000 students and some 1,000 teachers.

The immediate concern of the Russian Armenian intellectuals was the same as those in Ottoman Turkey, how to best educate and reach the majority of their people. A primary stumbling block was that the Church continued to use *grabar*, the classical Armenian language, in all liturgical services and insisted on its use in all Armenian publications. A number of young teachers and journalists felt that Armenians were in need of a living literary language. Like the Armenians in the Ottoman Turkey, the Armenians of Russia decided to adopt a modern standardized means of expression.

Stepan Nazariants (1812-1879) was one of the earliest authors to write in the modern dialect. Khachatur Abovian (1805-1848) and Gabriel Patkanian's (1802-1889) entire literary output was in the vernacular, or *ashkharhabar*, dialect spoken in the Araratian region. Their efforts and those of their students eventually created the modern eastern Armenian literary language used today by the Armenians in Russia, Transcaucasia, and Iran. Abovian had studied at the University of Dorpat (present-day Tartu, Estonia) and returned to Armenia to become a teacher. His novel, *Wounds of Armenia* (*Verk Hayastani*), was a patriotic work that glorified the Armenian language and lamented the foreign domination of his native land. He clashed with both conservative Armenian priests and Russian officials, and mysteriously disappeared in 1848.

Patkanian had been educated in Tiflis by his father, who himself had been educated in Venice by the Mkhitarists. The family moved to Astrakhan where his father taught at the Armenian school. After attending a Russian school, where he learned Russian and French, Patkanian taught at a number of schools in New Nakhichevan and in the Crimea, where he was ordained as a priest. He clashed with the conservative clergy and was exiled to a monastery. In 1846 he was permitted to teach at the Nersessian Academy where he also helped to publish the newspaper *Caucasus* (*Kovkas*). The newspaper, written in classical Armenian, emulated the Russian paper *Kavkaz*, also published in Tiflis. *Kovkas* had historical and biographical articles, as well as translations of European popular novels. By 1850, Patkanian published *Ararat*, the first newspaper in modern eastern Armenian, which was soon closed due to pressure from the Church, as well as the suspicions of the Russian censors. Abovian's and especially Patkanian's influence and teachings were handed down to a new generation, among who were Gabriel's son, Raphael Patkanian (known by the penname Gamar Katipa, 1830-1892) and Gabriel's student, Mikayael Nalbandian (1829-1866). Nalbandian studied theology, as well as Russian and Western languages and literature at the school run by Gabriel Patkanian in New Nakhichevan. He defended his teacher against Church leaders, and for this was forced to go to Moscow. He studied at the Lazarev Institute and Moscow University. The considerable lifting of censorship under Tsar Alexander II allowed Nalbandian and his friend Stepan Nazariants to publish *Aurora Borealis*, a secular and anti-clerical newspaper, in 1858. Extremely anti-Catholic, Nalbandian even criticized the Mkhitarists and their influence on the Armenian cultural revival. Stepan Voskan (1825-1901) and Nalbandian were the first Armenian intellectuals who were truly affected by the European revolutions of 1848 and who advocated that the Church should not dominate the Armenian national revival. Modern national schools, they felt, should be founded to educate those who truly constituted the nation, the common people. Towards the end of his life, Nalbandian visited London, where he met and was influenced by Russian socialists. He was arrested upon his return, exiled to southwestern Russia, and died in 1866.

Although in 1869 a small group of Armenian liberals in Alexandropol formed a society for the liberation of their homeland, Tiflis continued to remain the center of Armenian intellectual activity. Armenian conservatives, under the leadership of the director of the Nersessian Academy, Petros Simonian, published the newspaper *The Bee of Armenia*, which supported the traditional role of the Church as leader of the community. The majority of the Westernized Transcaucasian Armenians, however, embraced the newspaper *The Tiller* (*Mshak*), founded in 1872 by Grigor Artsruni (1845-1892). Artsruni and the editors of a number of other liberal Armenian newspapers in Russia pointed out that Russian rule had not only enabled a cultural revival but had provided the Armenians socioeconomic growth and security from invasion. An Armenian bourgeoisie, they added, had emerged and their children had the opportunity to study in Russia or abroad, join the Russian officer corps, or take part in the administration of the empire.

Armenian Populism, Socialism and Nationalism

Unlike the Armenian intelligentsia in Ottoman Turkey who had studied in Italy, Switzerland, and France and who were influenced by the French revolution, the philosophical ideas of Utopian Socialists, and the Greek and Italian uprisings, Armenians in Russia had studied in Berlin, Leipzig, and St. Petersburg. They, together with the Russian intellectuals, were influenced more by German philosophical ideas. The Russian, and later the Georgian, intellectuals and revolutionaries, however, who were living on their ancestral land, gravitated more toward socialism, while the Armenians, scattered in the Diaspora and, with most of their homeland and half of their people remaining under oppressive Turkish rule, leaned towards nationalism.

During the second half of the nineteenth century, eastern Armenian novelists and poets began to emulate the romanticism of the Western writers by glorifying patriotism, justice, and freedom. The novels of Raffi (Hakob Melik-Hakobian, 1832-1888), Berj Proshiants (1837-1907), Mouratsan (1854-1908), Alexander Shirvanzade (1858-1935), Avetis Aharonian (1866-1948), and the poems of Raphael Patkanian and Smbat Shahaziz (1841-1901) stirred the younger Armenian generation. Like their counterparts in the Balkans, Poland, and Bohemia, they too adopted the concept of rebellion and resistance to foreign domination.

By 1880s Russian Populist ideas of going out among and learning more about the common people, and at the same time educating them and inspiring them with revolutionary ardor, reached Transcaucasia as well. Armenian intellectuals realized that conditions for their fellow Armenians living in eastern Anatolia were far worse than any hardships experienced in Russia. They also realized that the Armenians of Constantinople and Smyrna were too far removed from eastern Anatolia, and, like the Armenian grandees in Baku and Tiflis, had become too cosmopolitan. Like the Russian Populists, these young Armenians felt responsible for their fellow Armenians who suffered so close to them across the border. Giving the motto of the Russian Populists, who advocated "Going to the People," a nationalist turn, the Armenians, adopted the motto of *depi erkire* or "Going to the Homeland."

Armenian Populists did not adopt the peasant socialism or the revolutionary and later terrorist activities of the Russian Populists. Unlike their Russian counterparts, they were willing to accept Russian absolutism if it provided for the liberation of western Armenia. During the Crimean War Armenian volunteer units had joined the Russian army and Armenian officers like Bebutov, Alkhazov, and Loris-Melikov had performed heroically. The Russian occupation of a segment of western Armenia during that war had raised the hope that all of Armenia would be soon under Russian rule. The Russian withdrawal from western Armenia after the Peace of Paris had not diminished that hope. Twenty-one years later, Russia, as we have seen, nullified the humiliating Treaty of Paris and embarked on the third and last Russo-Turkish war of the nineteenth century. Armenian generals Loris-Melikov, Ter-Gukasov, and Lazarev led the Russian armies into western Armenia. Since the Armenians of Transcaucasia were not subject to the draft until 1887, they once again volunteered and fought alongside the Russians to liberate their homeland. The Armenian volunteers felt that they were finally doing something for their people. By 1878 almost all of western Armenia was in Russian hands and Armenians once more began to imagine a united Armenia under Russian protection. During the peace negotiations, eastern and western Armenian religious, military, and business leaders and their Russian supporters used whatever influence they had to include the fate of the western Armenians in the final treaty.

As we have seen, article 16 of the Treaty of San Stefano stated that Russian troops would remain in western Armenia until the political reforms promised by the *tanzimat* were implemented there. Although article 61 of the Berlin Treaty dampened Armenian aspirations, it did allow Russia to annex a chunk of western Armenia and brought some 100,000 Armenians into the Russian Empire. Ignoring the assurances of European diplomats, more than 20,000 additional Armenians left Van, Bitlis, and Erzerum with the evacuating Russian army. Despite the Russian withdrawal from the rest of western Armenia, eastern Armenians saw Loris-Melikov's appointment as Prime Minister of Russia as further assurance that, in time, Russia would succeed in liberating the remainder of historic Armenia.

The assassination of Alexander II brought major changes to Transcaucasia. Alexander III engaged in a policy of Russification and active persecution of non-Russian nationalities. The Russian administration in Transcaucasia decided to target the Armenians. The successful Armenian middle class dominated the urban centers. The economic and, to some extent, the political power of the wealthy merchants and industrialists had created an Armenian elite which was envied and resented by the Russians, Georgians and Turko-Tatars of the region. In 1885 all Armenian schools were closed and replaced by Russian schools. When the Armenians began to organize underground classrooms, the government reopened the schools, but replaced many of the teachers and Russified the curriculum.

The actions of the Russian government drove some Armenians to imitate Russian revolutionaries and to adopt socialism and even anarchism. Six Armenians gathered in Geneva and in 1887 established the Hnchakian Revolutionary Party, later renamed the Social Democrat (Marxist) Hnchakian Party. They published a newspaper, *Hnchak* (*Bell*); a title borrowed from the Russian Social Democratic newspaper (*Kolokol* or *Bell*) printed in Europe. Led by Avetis Nazarbekian and his fiancé Maro Vardanian, the party advocated an independent and socialist Armenia, to be gained through armed struggle. This state would then become part of the future socialist world society.

The Armenians in Russia, in the meantime, were not idle. Revolutionary circles formed in Yerevan, Karabagh, Moscow, St. Petersburg, and Tiflis. The latter became a major center of Armenian revolutionary activities when, under the leadership of Kristapor Mikayelian, it formed a revolutionary organization called Young Armenia and recruited members in Iran and Ottoman Turkey. By 1890, the Armenian revolutionaries decided to create an organization that would unify all Armenian revolutionaries, including the Armenakans and the Hnchaks, into a single political party, with socialism-nationalism as its main platform. Under the leadership of Mikayelian, Simon Zavarian, and Stepan Zorian they formed the Federation of Armenian Revolutionaries (*Hay Heghapokhaganneri Dashnaktsutiun* or Dashnaks) in Tiflis. The Federation, from the very start, faced arguments between its socialist and nationalist factions. The Tiflis leadership was not sufficiently socialist to satisfy the Hnchak founders in Geneva, while the Geneva group was viewed as being more concerned with the success of international socialism than with the liberation of western Armenia.

The Hnchaks tried to recruit members in Russia and Turkey but could attract large numbers only in the more Europeanized circles of Constantinople and Cilicia. Most Armenians did not understand socialism and felt that its ideas could not be put into practice. Populist and nationalist slogans were closer to their heart. A number of compromises were sought, but by 1891 the Hnchak leadership in Geneva, feeling isolated, claimed that they had not agreed to an official union and went their own way. Following the massacres of 1895-96, the Hnchaks themselves split into radical and reformed (moderate) wings. The radical Hnchaks joined the struggle for the proletariat and the world revolution, and attracted members in the urban centers of the Ottoman and Russian Empires, as well as in Europe and the United States. The reformed Hnchaks continued their populist orientation. Some of them were eventually absorbed into the Dashnaktsutiun, which, by subordinating socialism to national issues, managed to unite most Armenians and, despite some divisions involving the degree of socialism of the party, emerged as the most influential Armenian political party. The remaining reformed Hnchaks later joined the Ramkavars.

In 1892, in Tiflis, the Dashnaktsutiun, renamed the Armenian Revolutionary Federation (*Hay Heghapokhagan Dashnaktsutiun*), adopted a platform which called for the creation of a freely-elected government; equality of all ethnic and religious groups, freedom of speech, press and assembly, the distribution of land to landless peasants; taxation based on ability to pay, equal conscription, compulsory education, security of life, and the right to work. The party would defend Armenians by arming the population, creating fighting units, conducting propaganda and espionage, and by killing corrupt officials, traitors and exploiters. The Dashnak program, in many ways, resembled the People's Will faction of the Russian Populist movement. Ironically, while the Marxist Hnchaks called for an independent western Armenia (and eventually eastern Armenia), the more nationalist Dashnaks and their newspaper *Flag* (*Droshak*) advocated autonomy within the framework of Ottoman Turkey.

At the start of the twentieth century there were over one million Armenians in Transcaucasia. Half of them were peasants who lived in the Yerevan province. There were also tens of thousands of Armenians who worked in the oil fields and factories of Baku, Tiflis, and other urban centers. Although the Russian Social Democratic Labor Party had succeeded in recruiting Russian, Georgian and even a few Muslim intellectuals and workers to form Marxist circles and to strike, they had attracted only a handful of Armenians. The Armenian Marxists were soon divided into those who, like Stepan Shahumian, joined the multinational Caucasian Union, followed orthodox Marxism and preached class struggle, and those who formed their own Armenian Social Democratic Workers Organization, referred to as Specifist. The latter maintained that the Armenian situation was different from that of the rest of the workers in Russia. It required specific consideration of a national and cultural self-determination within the Marxist movement.

The split of the Russian Social Democrats into Menshevik and Bolshevik factions, in 1903, affected the Armenian Marxists as well. Some, like Shahumian, followed the Bolshevik path, others agreed with Menshevik ideas, yet others formed separate socialist circles. A small number of Armenians also joined the Socialist Revolutionary Party, a populist group, who, like the Dashnaks, called for the socialization of the land. Unlike the Georgian intelligentsia, who overwhelmingly adopted Menshevik ideas, the majority of Armenians in Russia followed the Dashnak party.

The Armenian Church Crisis and the Armeno-Azeri Conflict (1903-1907)

Although the Dashnak platform advocated revolution and terror, it was against the overthrow of the Russian State and forbade attacking or killing Russian officials. A strong Russia was necessary if it was to aid in the liberation of western Armenia. Events in the first decade of the twentieth century, however, forced the Dashnaks to change their tactics and for the first time to actively oppose the Russian state. On June 12, 1903 Tsar Nicholas II, following the advice of Prince Golitsyn, the governor-general of the Caucasus, abrogated the *Polozhenie* of 1836 and ordered the confiscation of Armenian Church property and the transfer of its schools to Russian jurisdiction. Golitsyn had accurately surmised that by removing the Church and the schools from Armenian control, Russification could progress more swiftly and the Armenian revolutionaries would lose their strength.

The decree, in fact, had the opposite effect. Armenians united behind their Church, and citizens, who had remained outside the political and revolutionary activities, joined the Committee for Central Defense organized by the Dashnaktsutiun. Most other Armenian political parties joined the Committee as well. The Dashnaktsutiun revised its policy, adopted a more socialist outlook, and pledged to defend Armenian rights against the Tsarist State. Catholicos Khrimian of Van (Mkrtich I, known as Khrimian Hairik, 1892-1906), a product of Armenian awakening in Ottoman Turkey, backed the Committee and refused to accept the decree.

The next two years witnessed violent demonstrations, strikes, and various acts of terrorism by Armenians that killed, maimed, or wounded hundreds of Russian officials, including Golitsyn, who was stabbed by three Hnchaks.

On January 9, 1905 there occurred in Russia an event that changed the entire picture. A large group of Russians gathered peacefully in front of the Winter Palace in St. Petersburg to petition the Tsar to alleviate their unbearable economic conditions. They were fired upon and many died or were wounded. "Bloody Sunday" as the event came to be known, began the 1905 revolution. This event, combined with losses in the Russo-Japanese War (1904-1905) and the general economic depression, spread the revolt to every corner of Russia. Faced with a dangerous situation, the Tsar promised the creation of a Duma (representative legislature) and to initiate reforms. He also appointed Count Vorontsov-Dashkov (1837-1916), an astute man and a relative of the first viceroy, to govern Transcaucasia. In August 1905 the Tsar not only rescinded the decree of 1903, but also expressed special affection for his Armenian subjects. The Armenian leaders immediately voiced their total support for the Tsar and the viceroy. Both the Armenian activists and the Dashnaktsutiun had scored a major victory.

The revolution begun in 1905, however, continued its course for another two years. Fearful that the embers of the revolt would spread into Transcaucasia, some Russian officials, in order to distract the Caucasians from the political upheavals in Russia, provoked ethnic and religious conflicts in the region. Socioeconomic hostilities already existed there, and the less prosperous Georgian and Turko-Tatar population, as noted, envied the Armenians. By that time the Georgians had established their own socialist and nationalist parties. The Turko-Tatar population, which was at the lower end of the socioeconomic scale, and which angrily celled themselves as "soulless" (*bijanli*), had also awakened politically, and, influenced by progressive and nationalist ideas among the Russian Tatars, Iranians, and the Ottoman Turks, sought to establish an identity.

On the eve of the new century, pan-Islamic and pan-Turkic ideas began to gain some adherents among the Muslims of Transcaucasia. Although a number of intellectuals favored religious ties to Shi'i Iran, most felt closer to Turkey. Some of their leaders adopted the term Azerbaijani Turk, the name of the people in neighboring Iranian Azerbaijan who spoke the same dialect. A decade later they would declare themselves independent and refer to the lands on which they lived, as Azerbaijan.

Russian administrative divisions, as we have seen, created combined pockets of Armenian and Azeri populations in a number of counties and districts. Encouraged by some Russian officials, spurred by age-old religious and ethnic conflicts, and angered by the economic disparity between them, the charged situation in Russia erupted into civil war between the Armenians and Azeris. The war lasted two years. The Russian army did not intervene to end the conflict until 1907, when the first Russian revolution had finally run its course. Although the war caused thousands of casualties and much property damage on both sides, it had taught the Armenians not to be perennial victims. They realized that they were good fighters and that the Muslims were not invincible. The Azeris, in the meantime, had gained a national consciousness.

The creation of the Russian Duma gave voice to another Armenian political group. Since the Dashnaks and Hnchaks had boycotted the elections, the four Armenians who were elected to the parliament were not members of any political party, but represented the liberal middle class elements of Tiflis, who had made peace with the tsarist officials and had totally rejected the revolutionaries. The Armenians in the First Duma were thus identified with the Russian Liberal Kadet party. By 1907, the Tsar felt strong enough to dissolve the Duma. The Second Duma had five Armenian members all from the Dashnak and Hnchak parties. The Dashnaks had resolved their arguments and had adopted a more explicit socialist platform, and, in 1907, had joined the Second Socialist International. All five Armenian delegates voted with the other radical members of the Second Duma, which was dissolved the same year it convened. The Tsar then changed the election law to favor the supporters of the regime. By the Third and Fourth Duma (1907 and 1912), only one representative from each national group was permitted to sit in the parliament. The Armenians elected Hovhannes Saghatelian, a Dashnak, both times.

Armenian revolutionaries lost their initiative after 1907. The minister of the Tsar, Stolypin, and the secret police began to arrest suspect political leaders. Many were jailed until 1912, when conditions eased and they were finally brought to trial. Defended by Kerensky, the future premier of Russia, most were freed and others received light sentences. Meanwhile the majority of Armenians had come to the conclusion that Russia was their only hope for the liberation of western Armenia. Vorontsov-Dashkov felt that he could use the Armenian middle class to pacify the region and assure its loyalty. Catholicos Gevorg V (1911-1930) petitioned the Tsar not to ignore the fate of the Armenians in Ottoman Turkey. As Turkey moved closer to Germany, Russia, as we have seen, renewed its demands for implementations of reforms in western Armenia.

Russia and the Armenian Question 1914-1918

The outbreak of World War One created great hopes for the Armenians. Assured by the Tsar, the viceroy, and the catholicos, they looked forward to the liberation of their homeland. Some 150,000 Armenians, or approximately ten percent of the Armenians of Transcaucasia, joined the Russian armies. Since the majority of the Russian Armenians were dispatched to the European front, Vorontsov-Dashkov, with the help of the Church and community activists led by Alexander Khatisian, the Armenian mayor of Tiflis, recruited four units from among the Armenian immigrants from Turkey and a small group of Transcaucasian Armenians. Popular commanders such as Andranik, Dro, and Keri led the units. A few months later, volunteers from Europe, Russia, and the United States created three more units.

By mid-1916 the Russian army had occupied most of western Armenia but the Turks had left no Armenians there. Meanwhile, the Russian government had changed its attitude towards the Armenians and western Armenia. The Sykes-Picot plan had partitioned the Ottoman Empire among Britain, France, and later, Russia and Italy. Britain was to get most of the Arab lands; France was to control the regions of Lebanon, present-day Syria, Cilicia, and half of western Armenia. Russia was to receive the province of Trebizond, the rest of western Armenia, and Constantinople (see map 33). Vorontsov-Dashkov was soon replaced and the Armenian press was suppressed. Turkish Armenian refugees were forbidden to return home and the Armenian volunteer units were disbanded and made part of the Russian army.

The Russian army, however, was not successful on the European front. By February 1917, major Russian defeats and a shortage of food resulted in yet another Russian revolution. Kerensky soon led the Provisional Government and the Armenians were assured that the new regime would create an autonomous Armenia under Russian protection. To show its good intentions, the new government began to redraw the map of Transcaucasia. Districts with large Armenian concentrations, such as Karabagh, were to be included in a new Armenian Province. The new representative government also permitted the return of some 150,000 Armenian refugees to rebuild their lives in western Armenia. The administration of Transcaucasia was also transferred to a committee of Armenians, Georgians, and Azeris.

Continued Russian losses and the defeatist propaganda of the Bolsheviks were of grave concern to the Armenians, who knew that a Russian withdrawal from western Armenia would bring Turkish armies to eastern Armenia. Armenian leaders in Transcaucasia, therefore, convened an assembly in Tiflis. Following the example of their Russian counterparts, the few Armenian Bolsheviks boycotted the assembly. Although the Dashnaks had the majority of delegates, the newly formed Armenian People's Party (*Zhoghovrdakan Kusaktsutiun*), a populist party which had replaced the Kadets as representatives of the Armenian liberal middle classes of Transcaucasia, had the second largest number of delegates. The Hnchaks, Socialist Revolutionaries, and nonpartisans had only a handful of representatives. A National Council led by Avetis Aharonian of the Dashnaktsutiun was formed, which, realizing the dangerous situation caused by Bolshevik activity urged the Provisional Government to expedite the release of the Armenian troops fighting in Europe so that they could return to Transcaucasia.

Armenian aspirations were dashed six months later, when the Bolsheviks took power. The October Revolution (October 25, by the Julian calendar, November 7 by the Gregorian calendar), ended the Russian representative government and replaced it with Bolshevik Commissars. Except for Baku, which was controlled by a Bolshevik Commune, chaired by Stepan Shahumian, the rest of Transcaucasia refused to recognize the new government. Instead they formed a federation with its own executive (*Commissariat*) and legislative body (*Seim*) composed of Georgians, Azeris, and Armenians. Although some Georgian and Azeri members contemplated the creation of a separate state, Armenians believed that the restoration of a democratic Russia was their only salvation. They were proven right, for by the end of 1917 the Bolsheviks removed the Russian army from Turkish Armenia and began negotiating for a separate peace with Germany.

The Treaty of Brest-Litovsk, signed between the Bolsheviks and

Germany in early 1918, spelled doom for western Armenia. Although the treaty involved the European front, the Turks pressured the Germans to include territorial gains for them as well. Not only was Russia to withdraw from the lands occupied during the war, but was also forced to return Kars, Ardahan, and Batum, that is regions that Russia had gained in 1878. Lenin, wishing peace at any cost, agreed, and, although the Armenians insisted that the Bolshevik government did not represent the Russian Empire, the Turks advanced to occupy their territorial gains and by mid-April they had pushed the few thousand Armenian and Georgian volunteers back to the pre-1878 borders. In the meantime, civil war began in Russia, and Transcaucasia was left to its own fate.

With the Russian armies gone, Armenian troops and volunteers, led by commanders such as Tomas Nazarbekian, Andranik, and Dro, together with a small Georgian force, were left to defend the front. Knowing that the Azeris would not defend Armenian or Georgian territory, and wanting to test the commitment of the federation's members to defend each other, the Turks proposed to negotiate a peace. They soon found out that the Georgians were willing to sacrifice western Armenia, as long as their territory was not threatened. Outvoted and alone, the Armenians were forced to accept this compromise. A delegation composed of Georgians, Armenians, and Azeris departed for Trebizond to negotiate the handing over of western Armenia. Once in Trebizond, the Georgians and the Armenians learned of the Treaty of Brest-Litovsk and realized that the Turks now demanded the return of Kars, Ardahan and Batum, in addition to western Armenian regions evacuated by the Russian armies. The Georgians hoped to save Batum by sacrificing Kars but the Turks were adamant. The delegation returned to Tiflis and although Azerbaijan refused to contribute troops, the assembly in Tiflis voted for war with Turkey.

The war did not materialize, however. The fall of Batum to the Turks forced the Georgians to accept the provisions of Brest-Litovsk, and together with the Azeri representatives and the disappointed Armenian delegates, declared their independence from Russia and the formation of the Transcaucasian Federative Republic (April 22, 1918). The Georgians claimed the most important administrative posts and ordered the Armenian army to surrender Kars. In order to save eastern Armenia, the Dashnaks, led by Khatisian and Hovhannes Kachaznuni, cooperated with the Georgian Mensheviks and remained in the federation. The representatives of Transcaucasia went to Batum to accept the Brest-Litovsk provisions, but were surprised to learn that the Turks now demanded Akhalkalak and Akhaltsikh, as well as the western half of the Yerevan province. Without waiting for a response, the Turks invaded and took Alexandropol. They then marched towards Tiflis and Yerevan. Germany, fearing a strain in Russo-German relations, told the Turks not to violate the Brest-Litovsk borders and sent a German observer to Batum who reported that the Turks were planning to kill all the Armenians in Transcaucasia and to create a unified Turkish state with Azerbaijan. When German pressures on Turkey proved fruitless, the Georgians once again abandoned the Armenians and put themselves under German protection. In order to do so, they had to withdraw from the federation. On May 26, 1918, the Georgians declared their independence and German flags were hoisted in Tiflis. Two days later, the Azeris declared the independence of Azerbaijan. Since Baku was in the hands of a coalition of Bolsheviks and Dashnaks—strange bedfellows indeed—they selected Elizavetpol (later Kirovabad, present-day Ganja) as the temporary capital and awaited the arrival of Turkish troops to liberate Baku. The Armenians were left on their own and on May 28, the National Council in Tiflis, in order to be able to negotiate with the Turkish delegation in Batum and save what was left of their homeland, had no choice but to declare the independence of Armenia.

20

A Thousand Days
The First Armenian Republic
(1918-1921)

ALTHOUGH the Armenian National Council had assumed dictatorial powers over the Armenian provinces on May 28, 1918, it did not make the declaration public until May 30. Even then, the announcement did not include the term "independence," for no one was sure if there was going to be an Armenia or, if there was, of its exact parameters. The Turkish armies had invaded eastern Armenia two weeks before and had perpetrated massacres in Alexandropol and a number of other towns and settlements. The Turkish forces had encircled the region of Yerevan and the end of historic Armenia was predicted. What saved Armenia was the heroic stand of Armenians of every age and rank, including women and the very old, at the battles of Sardarabad, Kara-Kilisa, and Bash-Aparan. On June 2, the news of Turkish defeats in these encounters and their withdrawal from Yerevan was confirmed; two days later, the Batum agreement was signed between the Armenians and Turks. It was only then that an independent Armenian Republic was informally proclaimed in Tiflis.

Proclaiming a Republic did not create it. While Aram Manukian and General Dro oversaw the defense of Yerevan, the Armenian National Council was in Tiflis, the capital of the newly independent Georgian Republic. The disagreements among the leaders of the different Armenian political parties, all in Tiflis, precluded the establishment of a coalition government until the last day of June, when the continued objections of minor Armenian parties forced the Dashnak-dominated National Council to forgo democratic protocol and to form their own cabinet. The Armenian ruling body, unwelcome in Tiflis, left for Yerevan, which after the loss of

Alexandropol was the only urban center left to the Armenians. On July 19 the Armenian government, led by Prime Minister Hovhannes Kachaznuni, arrived in Yerevan and replaced, the military command of Aram Manukian. The independent Republic of Armenia had formally begun.

The Treaty of Batum had left Armenia a territory of some 4500 square rocky miles (see map 39) and 700,000 inhabitants, of whom 300,000 were hungry refugees from western Armenia and 100,000 were Azeris and Kurds. The industrial center of Alexandropol and the fertile fields of Sharur and Nakhichevan, as well as most of the railroad lines were not included in the Republic. Loss of animals and farming equipment had also decreased agricultural productivity in the region. Yerevan, never a major center of the Russian Empire, was a dusty rural town with a few government offices and almost no industry. Landlocked and surrounded by hostile neighbors, the Republic was also threatened by cholera and typhus epidemics. The majority of Armenian intellectuals, artisans, and entrepreneurs were in Tiflis, Baku, or in Russia. Lack of food, medicine, and the presence of armed bands, who attacked in broad daylight, did not promise a bright future for the new Republic.

Feeling that elections could not take place under such conditions, the enlarged National Council acted as the parliamentary body (*Khorhurd*) instead. Democratic principles were not totally overlooked, however, for although the Dashnaks controlled the cabinet and had the most members in parliament, the other parties were represented and heated debates did occur. The Muslim and Russian minorities had their own representatives. Independence had arrived unexpectedly. Most of the Republic's middle-class leadership had been raised outside historic Armenia and had never even visited Yerevan. The next four months were spent creating some sense out of the chaos, becoming accustomed to living in squalid conditions, and in petitioning Germany to restrain the Turks from further demands.

Meanwhile, Azeri and Turkish forces captured Baku in September and although many Armenians had fled the city, over 15,000 Armenians were massacred. The Turks then entered Mountainous Karabagh and the situation became ominous for that Armenian enclave, as well as for the Armenian Republic. General Andranik and his volunteers in Siunik-Zangezur set off to immediately repel the Turks from Karabagh. Andranik, who had not approved of negotiating with the Turks in Batum, had broken with the Dashnak government, gone to Zangezur, and was in the process of driving the Azeris out of that region. Before anything could be resolved, however, the Turkish capitulation to the Allies brought an end to the world war in Transcaucasia and British forces arrived in Baku.

The Moudros Armistice required the Turks to evacuate their troops from Transcaucasia and Iranian Azerbaijan and to surrender the control of the Straits to the Allies. The Turks withdrew to their pre-war borders, enabling the Armenian forces, under the command of General Dro, to extend the territory of the Republic soon after. With Russia amidst a civil war, the Armenians took Kars and the Georgians Batum, but the districts of Ardahan and Olti, which lay between the two and which were populated mainly by Armenians, were claimed by both Georgia and Armenia. Other territorial disputes discussed below, led to tensions between the two Christian neighbors (see map 40).

The Turkish defeat had a great psychological effect on the Armenians. Many who had been skeptical now realized that the Republic had a chance of survival. A number of Armenian intellectual and financial leaders, who had remained in Tiflis, decided to relocate to Yerevan and to offer their services to the Republic. More importantly, the People's Party, which became the Caucasian equivalent of the Constitutional Democrat Party (Ramkavar) and which represented the middle class, now decided to join the cabinet. The Dashnaks, who needed the expertise of middle-class professionals and who wished to demonstrate to the Allies that Armenia was not governed by radicals, embraced the liberals and gave them half, albeit not the most important, of the cabinet posts.

Despite the hopeful situation, Armenia now had to endure the severe winter of 1918-1919. Lack of bread, fuel, medicine, and shelter caused riots, epidemics, and famine. People ate grass, dead animals, and boiled leather; cases of cannibalism were reported as well. By the time it was over some 200,000 people had died from hunger, frost, and typhus. Aid did finally arrive, however. The American Near East Relief, organized by missionaries and headed by James Barton, raised millions for the "starving Armenians," and by spring, food, clothing and medical supplies began to arrive. More important was the aid given by the United States government. By the end of summer, the American Relief Administration, directed by Herbert Hoover, had sent some 50,000 tons of food, which saved thousands of lives and enabled the Republic to plant crops. The Armenian government was not idle either. It tackled the problem of creating judicial, health, and educational systems, as well as a tax structure and a state budget. The few industries, like the wine and cognac works of Yerevan, and a number of mills were nationalized. Telegraph and rail lines were repaired and new mines were explored.

Three issues remained foremost on the mind of the government: the Paris Peace Conference, which had begun in January 1919, and the territorial disputes with both Georgia and Azerbaijan. The conference in the French capital was to conclude peace terms with the German, Austro-Hungarian and Ottoman Empires, to establish future peace through the creation of a League of Nations, and to hear the claims of various nationalities who, encouraged by points five and twelve, of the Fourteen Points set forth by President Wilson in his address to Congress (January 8, 1918), sought self-determination through autonomy or independence. The Armenian Republic dispatched a delegation headed by Avetis Aharonian. Its mission was to press the Republic's claim to western Armenia or the six Armenian provinces in Turkey, as well as to convince the Allies to grant the Republic an outlet to the Black Sea.

Upon arrival, the delegation met another Armenian group: the Armenian National Delegation headed by Boghos Nubar Pasha, representing the western Armenians, as well as the Armenians of the diaspora. Most members of that delegation belonged to the Constitutional Democrat Party. Boghos Nubar's status among the European statesmen had enabled him to unofficially press a number of Armenian claims. He told Aharonian that Cilicia, with an outlet to the Mediterranean, must be included in the Armenian demands. The two delegations then united and presented a joint petition for an enlarged Armenian Republic stretching from Transcaucasia to the Mediterranean.

There were a number of complications attached to the Armenian claims, however. The Sykes-Picot plan had allocated Cilicia and half of western Armenia to the French. The Russian civil war was far from over and if the Whites were victorious, Russia, according to the same agreement, would end up with Trebizond and the other half of western Armenia. Moreover, Kurdish territorial claims conflicted with Armenian claims. Furthermore, the Turkish army in Anatolia was not disarmed and the small Armenian Republic, with its lack of arms and resources, could not possibly defend an Armenia, which would exceed 100,000 square miles. It would need a mandatory power to assist it in such a transition. Although President

Wilson was disposed to an American mandate, the Armenians had to await the outcome of two events: peace with Germany, which had to be concluded before any other issues could be decided upon; and the approval of the peace settlement and the Covenant of the League of Nations by the US Senate. Some of these obstacles were familiar to the Armenians others were not. Armenia, like most of the smaller nationalities, was not given a seat at the conference and was, furthermore, not privy to the private discussions between David Lloyd George, the prime minister of Britain; Georges Clemenceau, the leader of France; and Vittorio Orlando of Italy.

The French, who were adamant in their desire to punish Germany, to recover territories lost in the Franco-Prussian War, and to receive war reparations, concentrated on the treaty with Germany. The Versailles Treaty was signed on June 28, 1919. A number of regions, which Germany had gained in the eighteenth and nineteenth centuries, were given to Poland and France. The control over some of Germany's industrial regions was temporarily passed to France. Germany lost its colonies, was limited in its armed forces, and was forced to accept the sole blame for the war, which saddled it with astronomical reparation costs. The humiliation embittered the German people, impoverished its economy, gave rise to both left and right wing parties, and put Europe on the road to a second world war.

Having reduced the threat of future German might, France and England were not in a hurry to resolve the partition of the Ottoman Empire. The Sykes-Picot plan had presented them with possibilities for colonial expansion in Asia Minor and the Arab lands. In addition, the British and the French were in an embarrassing situation. The former had given the Jews (in the Balfour Declaration) and the Arabs (through Lawrence of Arabia and others) conflicting and vague promises of a homeland. The Kurds and the "Assyrians" were also promised a degree of self-determination. Both powers had also given the Armenian leadership in Transcaucasia, Europe, and the Middle East their strongest and most sincere vows that the injustices of the past would finally be corrected and the genocide avenged. Armenian blood spilled on behalf of the Allies by the Armenian volunteer units in the Russian, as well as in the British and French armies (the Armenian Legion of some 4,000 troops, which was formed from refugees of Musa Dagh, as well as volunteers from Europe, Middle East, India, and the US and saw action in Palestine and Cilicia) would not be forgotten, they claimed. A large, independent Armenia protected by the Allies was to be their reward. The departure of President Wilson to America to present the European agreement to Congress gave the powers the excuse to stop the peace process with the Ottomans and to iron out these difficulties. The fate of the rest of Europe, as well as Armenia, was to be decided in future conferences and treaties. Armenia and other oppressed nationalities awaited President Wilson's debate with the Senate over the Versailles Treaty, the League of Nations, and the Armenian mandate. In the meantime, political reality began to take precedence over promises, and the Russian civil war raged on.

During the next six months, Europe, while awaiting the American decision, disposed of the Austro-Hungarian Empire by means of the Saint Germain Treaty (September 10, 1919) in which the independence of Poland, Czechoslovakia, and Yugoslavia was recognized, and Austria lost territories to Poland, Italy, and Yugoslavia. The Treaty of Neuilly (November 27, 1919) punished Bulgaria with loss of territory (much of Macedonia and all of Thrace fell within the Greek and Yugoslav states), as well as reparation payments. The Hungarians, racked by economic problems, rebelled against their government and installed a Bolshevik regime under Bela Kun. The short-lived state went to war to keep Hungary intact. It was defeated a few months later and the new government signed the Treaty of Trianon (June, 4, 1920), by which Hungary lost Transylvania and other lands to Romania, Austria, and Czechoslovakia and was saddled with part of the Austro-Hungarian reparations.

Meanwhile, the situation in Transcaucasia was far from calm. The breakup of the region into three independent Republics presented Armenia with its border issues to be resolved. These, as we have seen, had their origins in the nineteenth-century administrative divisions of the Russian Empire. The first was the Armeno-Georgian dispute over the districts of Akhalkalak and Lori, both of which had a solid Armenian majority and were part of historic Armenia, but which had been part of the Tiflis Province and were claimed by Georgia as part of its new Republic. The dispute led to minor military conflicts between the two Christian states, which were resolved by a compromise, whereby Armenia took control of half of Lori, with the other half becoming a neutral zone, and Georgia retained control of Akhalkalak.

The second problem was far more serious, involving territorial disputes between Armenia and Azerbaijan. In Armenian eyes there was little distinction between the Turkic Azeris and the Turks themselves. Azeri cooperation with the Turks during 1917-1918 also contributed to the Armenian Republic's view that Azeri nationalist and pan-Turkic statements were a threat to its existence. Furthermore, the Azeris saw Armenia as a smaller version of the Yerevan province of 1849. Azerbaijan considered itself the successor of the Baku and Elizavetpol provinces; therefore, in its eyes, Karabagh and Zangezur was Azeri territory. They also considered northeastern Armenia and the easternmost parts of Georgia, which had pockets of Turkic people, as part of Azerbaijan. The Azeris also claimed those regions of western Armenia, which were conquered by Russia after 1878. Basically, they envisioned a state from the Caspian to the Black Sea, with a small Armenia locked between it and Turkey. To complicate matters further, there were tens of thousands of Muslims living in the southern part of Armenia, as well as in Yerevan, and hundreds of thousands of Armenians lived in Mountainous Karabagh, Zangezur, and in the cities and suburbs of Baku, and Elizavetpol. During the last days of World War I, Armenian forces under the leadership of General Andranik, as noted, were ready to take Mountainous Karabagh. The war ended and the British asked Andranik to halt his advance and await the Paris Peace Conference. Armenians felt assured that their historic and ethnographic arguments would secure them Karabagh (map 40).

The British command in Baku, however, was pro-Muslim, due to the oil in Baku, which the British began to pump and sell as soon as they landed forces there. In addition, the British Empire had many Muslims who viewed the Sultan as the caliph and expected a generous treatment of the defeated Turks. The British therefore backed the Azeri claims in Karabagh and Zangezur. Zangezur, which thanks to Andranik was fully under Armenian control, expelled the Azeri military and administrative personnel who arrived there, but Karabagh's refusal ended in massacres in a number of Armenian villages and a compromise. The Armenian-populated districts in Karabagh received internal autonomy, but, for the time being, were put under Azeri jurisdiction. From the very start the Azeris violated the agreement and an Armenian rebellion resulted in the burning of Shushi, the capital of Mountainous Karabagh, by the Azeris. The government in Yerevan was not strong enough to intervene and the Karabagh question, together with other territorial questions regarding Armenia, had to await the peace treaties.

At the same time, another problem hampered the internal affairs of the Republic. Although there were a handful of socialists in the government, the political leadership, as stated, was shared by the Dashnaks, who controlled the top cabinet posts and the liberal People's Party, who composed the other half of the cabinet. Each had different philosophies. The People's Party was flexible in structure and advocated a more open government. The Dashnaks were active revolutionaries, who occasionally used what some considered undemocratic methods against both Armenians and non-Armenians. Their party organization, especially their Central Bureau, was more rigid and demanded the full obedience of its members. The intellectual and political leaders of both groups had the welfare of Armenia and the Armenians in mind, but came from different social and economic backgrounds and sought to achieve it by different methods. The former were raised in the liberal traditions of the upper middle classes of Tiflis, Baku, Moscow, and St. Petersburg; while the latter were a product of the lower middle classes, as well as farmers and workers, who were influenced by the revolutionary fervor and national aspirations prevalent in Eastern Europe.

Prior to the spring of 1919, the liberals, whose programs (except for education and charity) were not geared to the uneducated and hungry Armenian crowds of Yerevan, hoped that despite the difficulties of living there, their presence in the government would benefit the Armenian masses by creating jobs and a more representative parliament. After six months, however, signs of strain between the two parties began to appear. The emergence of Boghos Nubar and his pro-liberal delegation in Paris emboldened the liberals in Yerevan, who felt that they had a larger voice than before. The final break came just prior to the first national elections. On the first anniversary of the Republic, Khatisian, speaking for the government, announced the symbolic unification of eastern and western Armenia. The liberal coalition did not comment at that time but, a few days later, resigned from the government, claiming that Boghos Nubar and his party, who represented the western Armenians, were not consulted and that the Dashnaks were once again subverting democratic principles in an attempt to usurp the future government of a united Armenia.

The boycott by the liberals resulted in the overwhelming victory (90 percent of the vote) of the Dashnak party. The minor socialist parties had more constituents in Georgia, Azerbaijan, Russia, and Europe than in Armenia, and together managed to capture the remaining 10 percent. The socialists and liberals began to assert that the whole episode was staged by the Dashnaks to gain control of the Republic. Khatisian, who formed the new government, however, realized that the charge could have major repercussions. In order to diffuse the situation, and out of conviction, he strove to include non-Dashnaks in various posts. He clashed with the Dashnak party Central Bureau, who did not agree with his policy but sought swift changes to strengthen the party and to push the social reforms that would win them the support of the masses. The Bureau chiefs feared that the masses would eventually lose their patience and join the Bolsheviks, whose propaganda and victories in the civil war were beginning to have an effect on the working and poorer classes in Armenia. The main clash between the party and the government came in late 1919 during the party congress. Khatisian maintained that if the party insisted on running the state, there would be no difference between them and the Bolsheviks. The government, he added, had to be independent from the party. The party had to implement its program through their representatives in the legislature. Party veterans, however, insisted that without party control, the state would not be able to survive the difficult days ahead. It was finally decided that members of the Bureau who entered the government would withdraw from active participation in the Central Bureau during their tenure. Although in practice this compromise did not work well, the gesture did avoid an all out confrontation.

The second year of the Republic began on a promising note, with the railway and telegraph back in service and with a slight revival in industry. There were problems with inflation, with the Muslim population, feeding and housing the refugees, and most importantly, the distribution of land to peasants; something the Dashnaks had promised but had not yet implemented. This last item gave the Socialist Revolutionaries ammunition for recruiting some disgruntled peasants and the opportunity to gain more members in the future. A major problem was that the Armenian Republic did not have the infrastructure of Baku or Tiflis. The war, as well as the short Turkish occupation of half of the province, had removed or destroyed animals and equipment. Agricultural projects, plans for dams, schools, veterinary medicine, reforestation, and other items were being set up for the long term and would bear fruit only in the future. Modern courts were being set up and rural self-administration was being organized. There were even efforts to introduce Armenian as the main language of the administration, but since most of the intellectuals used Russian, the government functioned in both languages. Elementary and secondary schools and a state university were opened in a number of urban centers, but a lack of fuel and financial restrictions kept school attendance sporadic. There was optimism, however, and postage stamps and currency were designed and issued. That same year President Wilson dispatched a commission headed by Major-General J. G. Harbord, who spent two months in western Armenia and the Armenian Republic to assess the possibility of a mandate. The commission cited equal arguments for and against an American mandate. They stated that although it was desirable from the humanitarian point of view, the cost would be very large indeed and would involve the United States in a myriad of problems.

As long as the outcome of the Russian civil war was in doubt the European powers refused to recognize Armenia or the other Transcaucasian Republics. At the start of 1920 the defeat of the White armies under General Denikin, made it clear that the Transcaucasian Republics should be recognized as de facto states and be armed to resist the Bolsheviks. Lord Curzon, the foreign secretary of Britain, was in favor of supplying weapons to Armenia, but Winston Churchill of the War Office did not approve, arguing that any such arms would fall into the hands of Bolsheviks, who were sure to win.

In the meantime, the Armenian government had put all its hopes on Europe and the United States. In spring 1920, the United States Senate rejected the Versailles Treaty and the League of Nations. Since the mandates were to be administered by the League, the issue of an Armenian mandate was, for all intents and purposes, dead. Strong support for Armenia in the United States and in the Senate continued, however, and the Armenian Republic and its envoy, Armen Garo (Garegin Pasdermadjian), were officially recognized. Complicating the situation for the Armenians was the fact that the United States had never declared war on Turkey and thus, after Wilson defeat in the Senate, the United States withdrew from discussions on the partition of the Ottoman Empire. The delays in implementing a Turkish settlement proved disastrous for Armenia. During this time, the Turkish nationalists in the interior were organizing strong opposition to the European plans for the partition of Turkey. The Turkish army had not demobilized or disarmed and was being reorganized by Mustafa Kemal (later known as Ataturk) in a capable force. At the same time, European, and later American, businessmen felt that they could reap greater profits from a viable Turkey and it trade routes than with a starving, landlocked Armenia.

Moreover, the colonial offices in Europe continued to consider what the feelings of Muslims in their colonies would be if Turkey, the home of the caliphate was treated as Germany or Austria had been. Britain and France had no conflicting interests in Anatolia, but had major disagreements regarding the Arab lands. Greek and Italian ambitions conflicted in Anatolia, and the Greeks, with British approval, had, in May 1919, landed troops in Smyrna. Since neither the French nor the British had the means or the resolve to attack the Turkish nationalists in faraway Anatolia, they hoped that the Greek invasion would force the Turks to come to terms and accept the European proposals, which were being discussed informally.

Although there was sympathy for the Armenians, time was running out for them. While the Senate was preparing for Wilson's defeat, the European powers finally began the discussion of the peace treaty with the Ottoman Empire in San Remo, Italy. In the meantime, news arrived that Turkish nationalists were killing the Armenians, who had returned to Cilicia in 1918. Outraged by the Greek landing, the Turkish nationalists ignored the decrees from Constantinople and considered themselves the true government of Turkey. The Turkish attacks, the refusal of the French to fight in Cilicia and their eventual return of Cilicia to Turkey in exchange for keeping Syria, would, in the end, spell the death of Armenian Cilicia. Those who were not killed or captured had to once again leave their homes for Lebanon and Syria.

The inability of the Armenians to defend themselves gave the European powers an excuse to take Cilicia and half of western Armenia, that is, the regions which were originally granted the French, out of any future Armenian state. There was still a chance that Constantinople or the Greek armies would convince the Turkish nationalists to agree to a reduced Turkish state. In the meantime, by April 1920, the Allies in San Remo agreed to give Armenia Van, Erzerum, and Bitlis, and an outlet to the Black Sea. The Allies realized that the agreement was a dead letter, for no one in Europe was ready to commit a force to help the Armenians in establishing control over such a large territory. Both the French and the British were now faced with the dilemma of how to fulfill their numerous pledges to the Armenians. Since the Bolsheviks had repudiated the Sykes-Picot plan, the British granted the Armenians the half of western Armenia that was promised to the Russians. The British felt that they had resolved their problem, and hoped that the Greeks and the Transcaucasian Republics would succeed in repelling the Turkish nationalists and the Bolsheviks. Although the United States Senate had basically rejected the European agreements and the question of the League, sympathy for Armenia continued in the Senate. Some historians claim that it was Wilson's rash treatment of the Republican senators and his insistence that his entire proposal be accepted without amendments or reservations, as much as isolationism, that spelled the end of American involvement on behalf of Armenia.

The French and the British, however, continued to hope that Wilson and the United States would still be willing to take the responsibility for Armenia. They asked Wilson to draw the final borders of Armenia, within the guidelines agreed in San Remo. Wilson, hoping that support for Armenia might still reverse the tide in the Senate, accepted. Although he did not submit the final boundaries of Armenia until November (see map 41), on April 18, 1920 the victorious powers announced at San Remo that an agreement was finally reached. Soon after, the Senate totally rejected the idea of an American mandate.

The fall of Adrianople to the Greeks in June 1920 forced Constantinople to accept the conditions of San Remo and three months after San Remo, on August 10, 1920 the Turks, European Allies, and the Armenians, represented by Avetis Aharonian and Boghos Nubar Pasha, signed the Treaty of Sèvres (see map 41). The treaty accepted the future Wilsonian boundary (which was to include the provinces of Van, Bitlis, Erzerum and an outlet to the Black Sea at Trebizond) and promised reparations and the restoration of property to the survivors of the genocide. It also agreed to the return of Armenian women and children who had been taken or adopted by Turks and Kurds. Finally, the treaty recognized the independence of Armenia and promised to punish those responsible for the Armenian genocide. The Armenians, in turn, promised to guarantee the religious and cultural rights of the Muslims who would remain in western Armenia. Thus, twenty-one months after the end of the World War, the conflict was officially over.

By summer 1920, the Armenian Republic had many reasons for hope and fear. In addition to the United States, Armenia was now formally (*de jure*) recognized by Belgium, France, England, Italy, Chile, Argentina, Brazil, and several other states. Armenian passports were considered valid and Armenian diplomats began to work in China, Japan, Ethiopia, Greece, Turkey, Romania, Yugoslavia, Bulgaria, Iran, Iraq, Germany, Belgium, Italy, France and England.

Meanwhile, ominous clouds were forming. Mustafa Kemal, realizing that the agreements in San Remo would mean a weak, truncated Turkish state, announced that the government in Constantinople did not represent the Turkish people and that any agreements it signed were null and void. Since the Allied fleet was in Constantinople, Mustafa Kemal organized a separate government in Ankara. An astute politician, a charismatic and capable leader, and a competent military commander, Mustafa Kemal made it known that he was only interested in keeping the homeland of the Turks, or Asia Minor; in other words, he did not insist on the territorial integrity of the former Ottoman Empire. The Balkans was already divided into independent states and the Arab lands could be severed. British and French governments would thus keep their zones of influence and a strong Turkey would be preferable to them than weak the Transcaucasian states, which could fall prey to Bolshevism. Assured of Allied inaction, Kemal then turned to resolve the Armenian Question and the Greek invasion.

Not able to fight simultaneously on two fronts, Kemal approached the Bolsheviks via Enver Pasha who had fled to Russia and who was working with the Bolsheviks to bring the Russian Muslims to the communists. Kemal assured the Bolsheviks that if they supplied him with arms, grain, and gold, he would bring Azerbaijan, with its numerous Turkish advisors and officers, to their side and would eliminate the "imperialist" Armenians. The Bolsheviks entered Baku at the end of April and were well received by Azeri leaders, who, temporarily forgetting their former nationalistic fervor, portrayed themselves as the representatives of the working class. The fall of Baku forced the Yerevan government to send a mission to Moscow in May to convince the Bolsheviks that an independent and friendly Armenia would be better for Russian interests in the region. In the meantime, the Bolshevik movement had slowly arrived in Armenia and although a small minority, they were vocal and managed to create a minor uprising in May in Alexandropol, demanding the establishment of a Soviet Republic. The reaction of the Dashnaks was swift: some of the Armenian Bolsheviks were executed; the rest fled to Baku. The main result of the short uprising was to end Khatisian's premiership and his policies. The Bureau of the Dashnaktsutiun took over the government with Hamazasp Ohanjanian as premier. After clearing out the Bolsheviks, the Bureau ordered the removal of all Muslims who did not accept the authority of the government. Many Muslims left the southern parts of the Republic and although the socialists did not protest Dashnak policies, these actions alienated the liberals even further. The second anniversary of the Republic was celebrated in quite a different spirit.

There are different interpretations on the events that followed. Sources sympathetic to the Dashnaks claim that the Bolsheviks gave the Armenians false assurances, while awaiting the results of the Soviet-Turkish negotiations in Ankara. Anti-Dashnak sources point out that the Yerevan government was to blame. The majority of the Dashnaks refused to work with Moscow. The Armenian government thus delayed its response to Moscow, forcing the Russians into making a deal with the Turks. Dashnaks counter that any agreement with Moscow would turn the West against them. Since the Treaty of Sèvres was not signed until August, they tried to delay a rapprochement with the Bolsheviks. The Hnchak view points out that the takeover of the Yerevan government by the Dashnak Bureau and the crushing of the young Bolshevik movement in Armenia not only ended any hopes of negotiations with the Bolsheviks, but made them forever distrust Armenian national aspirations.

In the meantime, the Bolshevik and Turkish negotiations continued. Although a number of Bolsheviks insisted that the Turks had to give Armenians some territory from western Armenia, the Turks refused to discuss the issue of borders and insisted that a treaty of alliance be negotiated without reference to borders. Stalin, who did not favor the Armenians, and Lenin, who was concerned about larger matters, agreed. Shortly after the Sèvres treaty, the Russians and Turks made an agreement in Moscow (August 20, 1920). It not only voided all previous treaties made by the imperial government but also stated that any international treaty, such as Sèvres, not accepted by Ankara would not be recognized by Moscow. To show the world their total rejection of Sèvres, the Turks, assured of Russian cooperation and noninterference, American neutrality, and European inaction, attacked Armenia in late September.

By mid-November, the Turks had recaptured the entire region they had controlled prior to their withdrawal in November 1918. The Russians, surprised by the rapid Turkish advance, feared the loss of the Georgian Black Sea ports and the only rail connection to Iran. They approached the Yerevan government and offered to intercede on their behalf. The Turks rejected any Russian interference. The Dashnak Bureau, now blamed for the Turkish victories, gave up the reigns of government to a new cabinet, headed by Simon Vratzian. The cabinet was still dominated by Dashnaks, but had two Socialist Revolutionary members. At the end of November the Bolsheviks entered Armenian territory and insisted that Armenia's salvation lay in becoming a Bolshevik state, denouncing the Treaty of Sèvres, and cutting its ties to the West. The Turks continued their advance and captured Sharur and Nakhichevan. Faced with total annihilation, the Armenian government sent Khatisian to Alexandropol to negotiate with the Turks and appointed a team headed by General Dro to transfer the government to the Bolsheviks. On December 2 Armenia became an "independent" Soviet state and the Bolsheviks promised to restore its pre-September 1920 borders. Contrary to common belief, the Armenian Republic did not completely cease to exist on that date. Although the Republic had changed its political leadership, Dashnaks, as well as other party representatives were guaranteed freedom and continued to serve the state in a number of positions.

On the same day, Turkey demanded that Armenia immediately sign a treaty renouncing Sèvres and all claims to western Armenia, including Kars and Ardahan. In addition Armenia had to accept temporary Turkish jurisdiction in Nakhichevan and Sharur (see map 42). In return the Turks would guarantee the independence of the remaining portion of the Republic. Khatisian, aware of Dro's negotiations with the Bolsheviks, delayed Armenia's acceptance until midnight of December 2. He then signed the Alexandropol agreement in the early hours of December 3. A small part of Armenia was thus saved from Turkish occupation. Since his government no longer existed on December 3, Khatisian calculated that the Bolsheviks would denounce the treaty as null and void and would demand that the Turks return to the former boundaries. At the same time the Dashnaks hoped that if the Bolsheviks did not keep their promises and tried to completely take over the Republic, they could rely on the Turkish guarantee to repulse them. The Armenians thus hoped to use either the Russians or Turks to their benefit. It was a calculated move that ultimately failed.

A few days later, the Red Army, together with zealous young Armenian and non-Armenian Bolsheviks of the Revolutionary Committees arrived in Yerevan and, contrary to the agreement made with Dro, arrested numerous officials and officers. The period known as War Communism, with its harsh requisition, retribution, and attacks on traditional values, had arrived in Armenia and, under the leadership of Sarkis Kasian and Avis Nurijanian, wreaked havoc for the next two months. The Bolsheviks and Turks then moved on to Georgia, the last independent region in Transcaucasia. With the

Red Army gone, the population, fed up with War Communism, angry at the Bolshevik betrayal, and faced with the loss of western Armenia, rebelled in February 1921. Led by Dashnaks and armed non-partisans they ousted the Bolshevik Armenians and set up a National Salvation government with Vratzian as president.

Their victory was temporary, for after the Sovietization of Georgia, the Red Army returned in March and, by the beginning of April, the rebels were forced to withdraw to Zangezur where, under the leadership of Njdeh they fought on, declaring the region as the Independent Mountainous Armenian State (*Lerna-Hayastan*). In the meantime, after the fall of Yerevan to the Red Army in March, the Turks and Russians, without any representatives from Armenia or Georgia, negotiated the fate of Armenia and the rest of Transcaucasia. As far as the Armenians were concerned, the terms followed the general line of the Treaty of Alexandropol, but with some significant changes. Nakhichevan and Sharur would not be returned to Armenia but would become part of Azerbaijan. In order for the Turks to be closer to Nakhichevan (they later exchanged a strip of land with Iran which gave them a common border with Nakhichevan) they demanded the district of Surmalu with Mount Ararat, which had never been part of western Armenia. The Russians, in exchange for Batum and parts of Akhalkalak and Akhaltsikh, which the Turks had occupied, agreed to give up Surmalu and Mount Ararat, the symbol of Armenia, to the Turks. Finally, it was agreed that the treaty would be later signed and ratified by the Transcaucasian Republics. The Treaty of Moscow, signed on March 16, 1921, was the last breath of the first Armenian Republic, some one thousand days after its formal beginning.

21

From NEP to Perestroika
Soviet Armenia or The Second Armenian Republic
(1921-1991)

THE HEART of the former Republic had been saved and was once again under Russian, albeit Soviet, protection and rule. By June 1921 most of Zangezur was either captured or, after being assured by Lenin's representative, the diplomatic Miasnikian, that Armenia would keep Zangezur and the rebels would be granted amnesty, had been pacified. The last Dashnak stronghold remained active in Meghri until July 13, when its members crossed the Arax into Iran. For the next seven decades Armenia was to have only one official party: the Armenian Communist Party. A number of minor socialist parties like the Socialist Revolutionaries, Mensheviks, and Specifists abandoned political activities, were later purged, or joined the Communist Party of Armenia.

A number of parties remained active in the diaspora. The smallest was the Hnchak party. Like European socialists and communists, the Hnchaks had factions who opposed the Soviets, but they ultimately lost and the party firmly supported almost all the policies of the new Soviet Armenia. A group of Armenian socialists, who called themselves the Progressive League (*Harachdimakan*), were not usually in agreement with Moscow, but generally found a common dialogue with the Hnchaks.

A much larger party was the Armenian Democratic Liberal Party (*Ramkavar Azatakan Kusaktsutiun*). Although it was established in 1921, after the Sovietization of Armenia, the party was actually formed by merging the oldest and newest Armenian political groups, that is the Armenakans, reformed Hnchaks, the People's Party, and the Constitutional Democrats. The party was a combination of conservatives, liberals, artisans, professionals, businessmen, and intellectuals. Although liberal and capitalist, the Ramkavars felt that since, for the moment, Soviet Armenia was the only Armenian national state, and since without Russian protection, Armenia, landlocked and surrounded by enemies could not survive, Soviet Armenia, despite being communist, should be supported.

The largest and most active party, the Armenian Revolutionary Federation or Dashnaktsutiun, not only did not support Soviet Armenia, but they felt that the Bolsheviks had betrayed them. They vowed to work with the enemies of the Soviet Union and not to rest until Soviet and historic Armenia was liberated (see chapter 23).

NEP in Armenia

War Communism had turned many supporters of the Bolsheviks against them and on March 15, 1921 Lenin admitted that some Bolsheviks had become over-zealous. A new policy, one that would result in a slower transition to communism was implemented. The policy, termed the New Economic Policy, did not abandon communist goals, but permitted some economic incentives, as well as joint ventures with the West, or State Capitalism.

Bolshevik officials who were more sensitive to local traditions and cultures replaced their zealous comrades. As we have seen, Miasnikian, a man close to Lenin, was dispatched to Armenia as First Secretary of the Party to pacify the region and to gently lead it into the Soviet fold. Lenin wrote that Armenia and the rest of Transcaucasia were to move even more slowly than Russia proper, toward socialism. Miasnikian, a seasoned party member, promised to try and regain some territory in the upcoming negotiations with Turkey, and was successful in pacifying Zangezur, which, with Lenin's backing, remained a part of Armenia. Moscow may have finally realized that Zangezur was the only buffer between Turkey and the Turkic peoples of the Soviet Union.

Since the Transcaucasian states had to ratify the Treaty of Moscow, they met with Russian and Turkish representatives at Kars. The negotiations lasted for almost three weeks and although the Soviet delegation tried to restore at least Ani and Koghb (present-day Tuzlucha) to Armenia, the Turks refused. The Treaty of Kars (October 13, 1921) resulted in the same borders agreed to in Moscow, borders which currently separate Armenia and Georgia from Turkey (see map 43).

Beginning in November 1919 and ending in December 1921,

Turkish forces attacked Armenian and French positions in Marash, Sis, Hadjin, Urfa, and Aintab. The French refused to commit forces to defend Cilicia. First they abandoned half of the region, and at the end of 1921, in exchange for keeping Syria, the French diplomat Franklin Bouillion, handed Cilicia to the Turkish nationalists. Having resolved the Armenian Question in Cilicia and western Armenia, Kemal concentrated all his efforts on the Greek armies in Asia Minor. By the end of 1922 Turkish forces were successful in defeating the Greeks and pushing them out of Asia. The Armenian quarters of Smyrna were burned and the Armenian and Greek population were massacred or fled aboard Western ships to Greece.

The final blow was to come one year later, when the European powers, setting aside their rhetoric, abandoned the Armenians and renegotiated the Treaty of Sèvres. The Treaty of Lausanne (July 24, 1923) did not even mention the Armenian Question. Turkey paid no reparations and was not blamed for any atrocities it had committed during the war. It agreed, however, to protect its Christian minorities—few of who remained in Turkey. The Straits were demilitarized and open to all ships in time of peace and to neutral ships in time of war. Turkey, which was defeated in the World War, nevertheless, with Bolshevik and European assistance and at the expense of Armenia, had regained territories it had lost in 1878.

By 1924 Turkey had abolished the sultanate and caliphate and had become a Republic with Mustafa Kemal as its first president. In just over a decade Mustafa Kemal, now called Ataturk, managed to improve Turkey's image in the West. He introduced the Latin alphabet, Turkified place names, granted women the vote, secularized Turkey, began agricultural and industrial reforms through a five-year plan (loosely based on the Soviet model), and began the negotiations for the return of the Sanjak of Alexandretta (returned by France in 1939).

For the Armenians the uncertainty was finally over. They had managed to retain Zangezur and the presence of the new Soviet State guaranteed Armenian security. As we have seen, more Armenians lived outside Soviet Armenia, most of them in Tiflis, Baku, and in a number of cities in Russia. Economically the most backward of the Transcaucasian Republics, with no major industry, Armenia needed the support of Russia and the help of her two larger neighbors, who controlled all the routes in and out of the landlocked Republic.

Armenia was pressured to form a union with Georgia and Azerbaijan. Stalin, the commissar in charge of the Soviet nationalities, wanted to combine Transcaucasia into one unit, and to attach it politically and economically to Moscow. Georgia resisted such ties but in the end, realizing it would remain alone, agreed, especially since the border disputes between the Republics had to be resolved. All three were rewarded in a fashion: Armenia received Lori, but Georgia received Akhalkalak; Armenia retained Zangezur, but Azerbaijan received Karabagh and Nakhichevan. As a concession to protests from Armenian communists, Mountainous Karabagh (Nagorno-Karabakh in official Soviet terminology) was classified as an autonomous region within Azerbaijan, and Nakhichevan was made an autonomous Republic subordinate to Azerbaijan (see map 44). Nakhichevan, which for centuries had been an integral part of Persian and Russian Armenia, was severed from Soviet Armenia. Karabagh with its solid Armenian majority, which was part of historic Armenia and had been a bastion of pro-Russian and anti-Muslim activities since the eighteenth century, remained outside the borders of Soviet Armenia as well.

In spring 1922 the three Republics formed a federal union, which gave them some autonomy vis-a-vis Moscow. Although Stalin was not satisfied with this arrangement and wanted their total subordination, Lenin insisted that the Republics retain a degree of autonomy. By fall of that year the USSR (Union of the Soviet Socialist Republics) was created. The Transcaucasian Federal Union was dissolved and a Transcaucasian Federated Republic took its place. Russia (which also included Turkestan, or the five present-day Muslim republics of Central Asia) Ukraine, Belorussia, and Transcaucasia formed the USSR. Each republic had its own constitution, modeled after that of the Russian Republic. Local communist parties became subordinate to the party chiefs (Central Executive Committee) in the Kremlin, which, in turn, controlled the Presidium. The budget of individual republics was part of the all-union budget. Foreign policy, foreign trade, civil and criminal legislation, education, health services and the army were unified for the entire USSR. In the case of Transcaucasia, the federation decisions were subordinate to Moscow's. Armenia, as the junior member of the federation, had to occasionally give in to its stronger neighbors, but Miasnikian's closeness to Lenin's and Stalin's representative in Transcaucasia, and Georgia's resistance to Moscow, gained Armenia some leverage.

The years of NEP had a great effect on Armenian economy and

culture. One of Lenin's major decisions prior to his illness was the concept of "nativization"(*korenizatsiia*), which was to encourage the various nationalities to administer their own republics. All local newspapers, schools, and theaters would use the native language of the republic. The language and culture of each republic was to be supported by the state. Lenin surmised that this was the only way to bring the republic's intellectuals into the party and to convince the nationalities that Russian chauvinism was a thing of the past and that communism would treat all equally.

Armenians from other regions were encouraged to immigrate. Armenian intellectuals from Tiflis and Baku, faced with the cultural "nativization" of Georgia and Azerbaijan, moved to Yerevan. Immigrants from Europe and the Middle East arrived as well. Yerevan's population doubled and some industry began to be developed, although the population of Armenia remained predominantly agrarian. For the first time Armenian became the official language of the republic. All illiterate citizens up to age fifty had to enroll in schools and learn their own language. Special schools were created to produce teachers. Schools were opened in the cities and villages and a State University was founded in Yerevan. A science institute was established and after more than five hundred years, Armenian once again was used in scientific publications and lectures. The many dialects of the immigrants and locals created a problem, hence the dialect spoken in Yerevan became the standard literary language and a simplified orthography was devised as well. Historians, linguists, composers, painters, sculptors, novelists, and poets, such as Leo, Adjarian, Abeghian, Spendarian, and Sarian, came to Armenia and were given state support for pursuing their art on their native soil. A conservatory of music, national theater, and a film studio were established as well. Religion was not condemned but anti-religious propaganda was rigorously advocated by the state. The urban population, still small, was less religious than the peasant masses. Although the catholicos recognized the Soviet Armenian Republic, there was an uneasy relation between the Church and the leaders of the Armenian Communist Party. Finally, the traditional role of women was changing, much to the chagrin of most Armenian men. Abortion, divorce, and a female presence in the work force were introduced. Nationalism and anti-Soviet sentiments were not tolerated, but "nativization," and the departure of Muslims to Azerbaijan, created a more homogenous Armenia. The Armenian language, literature, and arts continued to unite and revitalize the nation within the limits imposed by communism. Between 1920 and 1937 Armenian writers and poets such as Tumanian, Isahakian, Derian, Armen, Yesayan, Mahari, Totovents, Alazan, Zorian, Bakunts, Demirjian, and Charents managed to combine socialism with their nationalist temperament and to revive the eastern Armenian literary tradition of Abovian and Raffi.

In the meantime, political changes were occurring in Armenia. At the end of 1923 the Dashnaktsutiun officially ended its presence in Armenia and its members, together with independent socialists, were thrown out of the Communist Party and government posts; some were arrested as well. Ashot Hovhannesian succeeded Miasnikian, who died in a plane crash in 1925. Haik Hovsepian replaced him in 1927. He lasted only a year and was replaced by Haigaz Kostanian, who held power for two years. The frequent changes reflected the power struggle in the Kremlin.

Stalin and the Armenians

In Russia, the three years following Lenin's death in 1924 witnessed the rise of Stalin and the demise of Trotsky. Meanwhile, NEP had not produced its desired effect. Industry was not growing sufficiently and low agricultural prices were forcing the peasants to hold back their produce. By fall 1928, food shortages in the cities put an end to the arguments of those who favored the continuation of NEP. Stalin, who had aligned himself with Bukharin, a NEP supporter, in order to destroy Trotsky, Kamenev and Zinoviev, now rid himself of Bukharin. As Stalin consolidated his power, people loyal to him were promoted, the rest demoted or removed. In spring 1929 Stalin's Socialism in One Country, as an alternative to NEP, and his five-year plan to industrialize Russia were put into motion. In order to support rapid industrialization, the peasants had to join collective farms and give up their grain and animals to the state. The result was peasant resistance. Farmers killed their animals and destroyed their crops rather than surrender them. Close to one million animals were killed in Armenia alone. In the long run, resistance was futile and after threats, arrests and executions, as well as such measures as the state-organized famine in the Ukraine, Armenian peasants, like all others, were collectivized. The harsh conditions on the farms and in the villages forced many to the cities and a new working class emerged. Industry burgeoned under heavy state sponsorship and central economic planning. The entire economy was under state control. Armenia's working classes grew and soon made up one-third of the population. The peasants rose in the party ranks as well and the whole nature of the party began to change. The next step was to purge anyone who questioned or opposed the new order. Old communists were replaced with Stalin's proteges and henchmen. In 1930 Stalin made Aghasi Khanjian the head of the Armenian Communist Party.

Khanjian's efforts on behalf of Armenia and his concern over the loss of Karabagh made him a popular leader, but made him unpopular with Beria, the powerful Georgian leader, a close friend of Stalin and the unofficial watchdog in Transcaucasia. In 1936 Khanjian was called to Tiflis and there "committed suicide." Khanjian was replaced with Haik Amatuni, who purged Armenia of Khanjian's supporters. A year later, Amatuni and his group were purged for not being diligent enough in cleansing Armenia of the enemies of communism. Mikoyan and Beria now arrived in Yerevan and appointed Grigor Harutiunian from Tiflis, a henchman of Beria, to head Armenia. Almost the entire cadre of Armenian top rank communists, as well as many intellectuals, were arrested, executed, or exiled to Siberia. Among them were Kasian, Nurijanian, Hovsepian, Amatuni, Yesayan, Bakunts, Totovents, Mahari, and Charents. By 1939 the purges were over and Stalin and the secret police (NKVD) had eliminated all opposition. The older Marxist generation of mostly non-working class intellectuals was replaced by a younger generation, either working class or career bureaucrats. They were loyal to Stalin and remained in power until the late 1970s. The state had eliminated all resistance and had a monopoly over every aspect of the political, socioeconomic and cultural life of its citizens.

Another blow to Armenia, as well as to other nationalities, was the end of "nativization." Russian became compulsory for all students. Students were encouraged to enroll in the new Russian schools that had opened in Armenia. Anyone wishing to be promoted or to advance in Moscow felt that attending an Armenian school would lead to a professional a dead end. Russian words replaced certain Armenian terms as well. Nationalism was condemned and replaced with Soviet patriotism, itself a form of Russian nationalism. The popular novels of Raffi were condemned as nationalistic. According to one scholar, the purges totally halted the eastern Armenian literary revival. The Church was not spared either, for anti-religious activities increased and when Catholicos Khoren I (1933-1938) was reportedly strangled in Ejmiatsin, no new Catholicos was elected (until 1945). Abstract art was also condemned and Socialist Realism became the norm for all the arts. In time Russians took over some of the top positions in government and began viewing themselves and being viewed as superior to non-Russians.

The Second World War brought many changes to Armenia. The Nazi danger forced Stalin to reconcile with the Church and seek the support of all nationalities to save their collective homeland. The works of Raffi were once again published, churches and the printing press at Ejmiatsin were opened and a new seminary was permitted to train priests. Some priests were allowed to return from Siberia as well. Nazi atrocities frightened people into forgetting the abuses of the past and rally around the state. The fear of Turkey led Armenians to reject any other possible action. Turkey was flirting with the Nazis and von Papen's missions to Ankara were not ignored. Most able-bodied Armenian men were at the front, as was the Red Army, and there would be little protection against an attack from Turkey. The memories of similar circumstances during World War One were still alive.

A small group of Dashnaks in Eastern Europe, on their own initiative, joined the Nazis (not out of sympathy for Hitler, but against Communist Russia) to liberate Armenia. The majority of Armenians in the USSR and the diaspora, however, were opposed to Hitler and joined the American armed forces, the French Resistance, and particularly the Red Army, where half a million Armenian troops engaged in the heaviest battles, produced sixty generals, and four out of the ten marshals of the Soviet Union, including Marshal Bagramian. Armenian losses approached 175,000 in a war, which, according to new data, took some 30 million Soviet lives. By the end of the war a new Catholicos, Gevorg VI (1945-1954), who, as a bishop, had cooperated with the Soviets in the war effort, was elected and allowed to live in Ejmiatsin. The Church and the state started a repatriation campaign. Many Armenians in the diaspora, especially the Ramkavars and Hnchaks, supported the return to the homeland. The repatriation brought over 100,000 Armenians, mostly from Greece and the Middle East. Most of these were the immigrants who had been displaced during the 1915-1922 period. The local population, who resented sharing the little that was left after the war, did not particularly welcome their arrival in a socialist state, which was devastated after the war. They were condescendingly referred to as *aghbar* (which can best be rendered as "the poor relations"). By 1948, with the advent of the Cold War, their inability to adapt themselves to Soviet-style living and thinking made them suspect and many were exiled to Siberia.

Stalin raised the Armenian Question again. He demanded the return of Kars and Ardahan, or as he viewed them, the Russian territories gained in 1878 and lost in 1921. Turkey, which had good relations with the Soviets until the mid-1930s, began a rapprochement with the Nazis in the late 1930s and, after the war, was internationally isolated. Stalin's motive had nothing to do with the Armenians, for reportedly the territory was to be added to the Georgian Republic. Rather, the Armenian Question was merely used as a cover for Stalin's expansionist policy in the Middle East (also manifested in the Soviet actions in supporting Iranian Azerbaijani communists in 1945-1946). Moscow thus sanctioned the repatriation of Armenians and the publication of works on the Armenian genocide. The policy forced Turkey to seek aid from the United States. Turkey was brought into the Western Alliance and eventually joined NATO and the Armenian Question was shelved. Kremlin's policy towards the Armenians changed as well. Repatriates were suspect and books on the genocide were banned. By 1950 communism in China and the Korean War had put an end to cooperation with the former Allies and had increased the Cold War mentality. As in the ancient, classical, and medieval periods, Armenia was once again caught between two super-powers. In the event of war, American missiles in western Armenia (eastern Turkey) would be deployed against eastern Armenia and vice-versa. Contact between Armenia and the diaspora virtually ceased and Stalin began to tighten the reigns on any expressions of national culture. Raffi was again banned and modern writers and composers, such as Aram Khatchaturian, were told that their works were too nationalistic and lacked a working class spirit. A new purge removed suspected "Dashnaks" from Armenia to Central Asia.

Stalin's policies had a major socioeconomic impact on Armenia. As industry was encouraged, peasants began to arrive in the cities and the urban population increased. Armenia slowly changed from a peasant economy into an industrial one, a process that continued until the late 1970s. Yerevan changed as well. The dusty town was transformed into a major urban center. Designed by city-planner and architect Tamanian, boulevards were laid out and an opera, museums, national archives, and government buildings and boulevards were constructed, many from the red, red-orange, yellow, and lilac-colored volcanic tufa stone which gives Yerevan its distinctive look.

The planned Soviet economy was designed to sustain the mutual interdependence of the republics by assigning the production of specific products to each region. Armenia and other small republics were to feel the full impact of these measures upon their independence four decades later.

Khrushchev and the Armenians

Stalin's death in 1953 opened a new era for Armenia and the rest of the Soviet Union. The first step towards this was to remove the pervasive control of the secret police. Beria was shot and the top NKVD henchmen in the Soviet Union, including Armenia, were removed. Suren Tovmasian became the new head of the Armenian Communist Party and held power until 1960. Tovmasian was a part of Stalin's bureaucracy and thus little changed politically in Armenia during his tenure. On the social and cultural levels changes did occur, however. Nikita Khrushchev's attack, backed by Anastas Mikoyan, a top-ranking member of the politburo, on Stalin's cult and crimes, enabled the rehabilitation of dead communists such as Khanjian and Charents, the release of thousands from the Siberian gulag, and the republication of Raffi and Patkanian. Stalin's body was removed from Lenin's tomb on Red Square; his large statue in Armenia was toppled and eventually replaced by one of Mother Armenia. The party once again accepted Armenian language and culture and a new policy of "nativization" emerged. Armenians from other parts of the USSR came to Yerevan, as did a number from Iran. Political conditions improved for the former repatriates and some were even permitted to emigrate.

Khrushchev's changes in the economic sector were significant for Armenia as well. Large collective farms were divided into smaller ones. Armenia was permitted to plant other crops besides grain. Tobacco, vegetables, grapes and other fruits, more suitable to Armenia's soil and climate were planted. Local ministries responsible to Moscow were given more decision-making authority and better-educated managers. For decades the Soviet consumer had sacrificed material goods for the industrial growth and defense of the country. The peasants and workers of all nationalities craved relief from these deprivations. In the Khrushchev era consumer goods began to appear and farmers were permitted to cultivate small plots for their own personal use. The production of livestock and various irrigation projects increased Armenia's agricultural output. A lack of land, however, meant that Armenia's farms produced less than its neighbors' and that Armenia had to rely on other republics for its food. Armenia's strength was in the industrial sector, which surpassed that of Georgia and Azerbaijan. Soviet Armenia had, started with 80 percent of its population engaged in agriculture and seven decades later ended with close to 80 percent of its population living in urban centers and engaged in heavy industry, management, and services. Khrushchev's efforts to dismantle the Stalin bureaucracy and launch experiments in the economic and political sectors began a power struggle in the early 1960s. Iakov Zarobian, who was not associated with the old regime, was put in charge in Armenia. There now rose a new group of intellectuals and managers who although subordinate to Moscow, frequently had the welfare of Armenia uppermost in their minds. A new kind of nationalism, a certain pride of Armenian abilities, skills, and achievements had emerged by 1965. This was to have a major cultural and political effect on Armenians over the next two decades.

Brezhnev and the Armenians

The ouster of Khrushchev in 1964 moved the Soviet Union into a long period of stagnation. Reforms and experimentation abruptly halted and under the leadership of Leonid Brezhnev, many Stalinist bureaucrats or *apparatchiks* were slowly brought back to the Kremlin as well as to the rest of the country. In 1966, Anton Kochinian, a typical party functionary, was put in charge of Armenia. The door opened by Khrushchev, the demand for consumer goods and artistic freedom, as well as national pride, could not now be completely shut. Rather, Brezhnev's system began an era of "benevolent neglect." Local party bosses, all loyal to Moscow and proteges of Stalin's bureaucrats; were allowed greater autonomy in running the affairs of their republics. As long as the production quotas were fulfilled and there was no turmoil, the center rarely interfered in local matters. As a concession to Armenian national sentiments and the more emancipated intelligentsia, party leaders slowly permitted the construction of monuments to the heroes of Sardarabad, the victims of the genocide, General Andranik and Vardan Mamikonian. Numerous books on Armenian history and literature were printed. The Armenian genocide and the history of the 1920s were discussed far more openly than before, albeit, still with some restrictions. A new generation of writers and artists such as Baruir Sevag, Gevorg

Emin, Hovhannes Shiraz, Minas Avetisian, and Hagop Hagopian began a new era in Armenian arts and literature. In the 1970s a Soviet census revealed that over 99 percent of Armenians in the Republic considered Armenian, rather than Russian, their national language. Even the Kurds, Assyrians and Azeris living in Armenia spoke Armenian. No other republic had as high a percentage of inhabitants who considered their national language as their primary mode of communication. By the 1970s Armenians constituted 90 percent of the population of the Republic, a higher percentage than any other ethnic group living in their own republic. The troubling fact remained, however, that despite this, Armenians, after the Jews, were still the most dispersed nationality in the USSR. Only two-thirds of the Armenians of the USSR lived in Armenia, with the remaining one-third, primarily in Georgia, Azerbaijan, and Russia. Hence, while Armenians in Armenia were glowing with national pride, outside the Republic, many Armenians were becoming Russianized.

Tourism became a significant part of Soviet Armenia's economy. Armenians from the diaspora were encouraged to come to the homeland and see its progress first hand. Hotels and museums were opened and exchange programs were established. A special Committee for Cultural Relations with Armenians Abroad was formed and symbolically housed in the building of the last independent Dashnak government in Yerevan. Even Dashnaks were welcome to come to see the great changes for themselves. Armenian textbooks were printed for Armenian schools in the diaspora and sent free of charge, as were newspapers, periodicals and other books printed in Yerevan.

Industry continued to make major inroads in Armenia and more people moved to the cities. The Medzamor nuclear plant was built in the 1970s to satisfy the need for heat and electricity not only in Armenia but also in Georgia and Azerbaijan. As Armenian industrial output increased and surpassed that of Georgia and Azerbaijan, so did its pollution and the damage to its environment. Mount Ararat, shrouded behind a brown veil of smog, could rarely be seen from Yerevan and cancer was on the increase. Every major river in Armenia was declared ecologically dead and poorly planned projects resulted in the lowering of Lake Sevan's water level.

Another distressing development fostered by Brezhnev's policy of benevolent neglect was the cliques and power bases formed by the local communist bosses. Corruption became rampant and a second economy developed a black market that catered to those who could afford foreign goods or needed favors. Absentee workers appeared on payrolls and some individuals held more than one job. Stealing supplies and goods from the government became commonplace. Inferior structures were built and inferior products made simply to satisfy quotas. Cement and steel was diverted from schools and other state buildings to private houses and paint, doors, windows, toilets and other items were stolen and sold or used by private contractors. The party bosses, for personal benefits and promotions, approved projects that were economically or ecologically detrimental to Armenia. Speculation and bribery became commonplace. An individual's network of relations and contacts became far more important than training, knowledge, or talent. Even universities were not immune and professors were known to give high grades in exchange for goods. Those intellectuals and entrepreneurs who could not function under Yerevan's cliques migrated to other republics where their abilities were rewarded and where they achieved high positions in local administrations. At the same time this freer atmosphere also created a new intelligentsia, who despised the prevailing situation and who felt that the corruption, emigration of talented individuals, pollution and general loss of ethics had put Armenia on the road to disaster. Corruption in Transcaucasia and Central Asia surpassed that found in all other republics and eventually reached such proportions that the Kremlin could not ignore it.

Anti-Soviet activities on the part of a few dissidents resulted in the removal of Kochinian in 1974 and brought in Karen Demirjian, who was educated in Russia and whose job was to "clean up" the Republic. Demirjian cracked down on corruption and began major projects, like the subway, sports complex, and the new airport. Demirjian's promises and activities raised the hopes of honest intellectuals and they now demanded concrete changes. A number were given a role in the administration and an uneasy alliance began. The Soviet system was too entrenched, however, and the Demirjian government was criticized for moving too slow for some Armenians.

In 1978, during the debate over a new Soviet Constitution, thousands of Armenians unsuccessfully petitioned Moscow for the separation of Mountainous Karabagh and Nakhichevan from Azerbaijan. At the same time, when Moscow considered changing part of the constitution and removing the use of native languages as the official languages of the republics, Armenians, together with the Georgians, protested vehemently and defeated the proposition. Armenian words soon began replacing Russian official terms. Armenian nationalism had resurfaced, but, unlike nationalism in the Baltic republics and Georgia, it was not directed against the Russians but against the Turks, and as long as it was not too overt, the Demirjian government allowed its expression. April 24 became an official day of mourning and several books about conditions in Karabagh and the destruction of Armenian monuments in Nakhichevan were published. The Armenian Question was also raised unofficially in some circles. The Church under Catholicos Vazgen I (1954-1994) became more active and the Catholicos visited many communities in the diaspora. In Armenia, new churches were built, old churches and historical monuments restored, and liturgical works appeared. Armenian priests from abroad came to study at Ejmiatsin and Armenian men and women from the diaspora, mostly from the Middle East, especially those with Hnchak and Ramkavar affiliations, arrived to study at Yerevan University. The Demirjian years (1974-1988) are today viewed as the golden era of Soviet Armenia.

Political Dissidence in Soviet Armenia

What most Armenians in the diaspora were not aware of was the beginning of a dissident movement in Armenia, which had manifested itself as early as 1967. Tired of communism and dissatisfied with the futile and sometimes self-serving activities of the Armenian political parties in the diaspora, a group of young Armenians formed a secret party in Armenia, ironically on the 50th anniversary of the Bolshevik Revolution. The National Unity Party demanded the return of Nakhichevan, Mountainous Karabagh, and western Armenia and the creation of an independent democratic state. In 1974 it managed to illegally publish one issue of a journal and stage a protest where its members burned Lenin's picture on the main square in Yerevan. Kochinian was blamed for not suppressing the movement and was dismissed and the secret police arrested some of the Armenian activists.

The group soon split into two factions. One, led by Stepan Zatikian, advocated terrorism against the Soviet regime and reportedly placed a bomb in the Moscow subway. Some of its members were arrested and executed. The other, composed of moderates became active as a human rights group, monitoring civil rights on behalf of the Helsinki Accord of 1975. It demanded a degree of self-determination and the freeing of Karabagh from Azeri control, an end to corruption and industrial and nuclear pollution. Karabagh remained the most volatile issue, however. With 80 percent of its population Armenian, it remained under Azeri jurisdiction, which, contrary to their promise of autonomy, had bound it to Baku. Some 125,000 Armenians were, for all intents and purposes, cut off from their culture. The refusal of Yerevan, Baku, or Moscow to act on the Karabagh question solidified Armenian opposition.

Gorbachev and the Armenians

Brezhnev's death in 1982 ushered in an era of unprecedented change. Yuri Andropov, the head of the KGB, replaced Brezhnev and began tightening state control over the society and attempted a serious crackdown on corruption. Upon his death in 1984, his successor, Konstantin Chernenko, who was elected by the older members of the Central Committee, made a half-hearted attempt to reverse Andropov's disciplinary measures. It was too late, however, for the country was lagging behind the West economically and technologically. A new educated leadership, who had traveled or studied abroad, felt that the whole fabric of Soviet society had to change if it was to compete successfully against the West in the twenty-first century. Chernenko's death, a year later, presented an opportunity for the new intelligentsia to assert itself. Mikhail Gorbachev, who had the support of the new generation of communist leaders, was elected to lead the country along a very different path. Gorbachev, a "new communist," planned a complete revamping of the Soviet system. He proposed to reconstruct the economic system (*perestroika*), permit free social expression (*glasnost*) and initiate political decentralization (*demokratizatsiia*). Although he opposed the separation of the minorities from the USSR, Gorbachev did promise greater political and cultural autonomy to them.

In early 1988, Armenians in Mountainous Karabagh, encouraged by Gorbachev's declarations and prompted by a number of statements made by Armenian leaders in Armenia and Russia, demonstrated peacefully and demanded to be made part of Armenia. On February 20, the Karabagh Soviet voted overwhelmingly to transfer the region to Armenia. The same day a huge demonstration followed in Yerevan. In the next few days more demonstrations were held in Yerevan and Stepanakert, the Soviet era capital of Mountainous Karabagh. Neither the Moscow nor the Yerevan hierarchy responded. The response came from Azerbaijan, when, during the last three days of February, the Azeris in Sumgait, an industrial town north of Baku were permitted to carry out a pogrom in which they killed, raped, maimed, and burned hundreds of Armenians and destroyed their property. The pogrom encouraged by Baku and conducted in full sight of the police, bore shades of the 1895-1896 massacres. Moscow's inaction regarding Sumgait infuriated the Armenians throughout the Soviet Union and turned them against Gorbachev. For the first time in many decades, Armenian nationalism, although primarily against the leadership in the Kremlin, had become anti-Russian in tone. There were unsubstantiated reports that these incidents were welcomed by Gorbachev who wished to discredit the corrupt apparatus in Transcaucasia and Central Asia, which was firmly entrenched and opposed his reforms.

In mid-1988 Demirjian was replaced with Suren Harutiunian, who had served in Moscow and who was unaffiliated with the so-called Mafia in Yerevan. Harutiunian was viewed as just another communist serving a system that had lost its credibility with the Armenian public. By the end of the year the Armenian intelligentsia was split: some of them asked the crowds to calm down and to rely on Gorbachev's reforms to bring about gradual change. They stated that the traditional Armenian doctrine was to rely on Russia. Others, led by the Karabagh Committee, the Union for National Self-Determination, the National Union, all based in Yerevan, and the Crane Committee in Karabagh, realizing that Moscow was not going to consider any historical, demographic, cultural, and even legal arguments in favor of uniting Karabagh with Armenia, demanded more immediate changes, but not secession. Following violent clashes between Soviet troops and demonstrators in Yerevan, Harutiunian lost whatever support he may have had. Although Moscow admitted that Azeris had violated the constitutional rights of the Armenians in Karabagh, and that representatives from Moscow would be dispatched to assess the situation, the rejection by the Supreme Soviet of Karabagh's request to join Armenia increased the tensions. Mass rallies and strikes took place in Yerevan and counter demonstrations in Baku. By the end of 1988 the government imposed a daily curfew throughout Armenia. As the communist government lost credibility, the Karabagh Committee gained respect and in effect became a second government.

At noon, on December 7, 1988 a terrible earthquake struck northwest Armenia killing over 25,000 people and leaving hundreds of thousands injured and homeless. Gorbachev was in New York. His immediate return, and the international press coverage that followed, brought world attention to Armenia. The Karabagh Committee, led by Ashot Manucharian, Levon Ter Petrosian and Vazgen Manoukian, challenged the authority of the state by organizing its own relief effort and despite the catastrophe, continued to demand a resolution to the Karabagh problem. Its eleven members were arrested on orders from Moscow, martial law was declared, and Gorbachev, as well as the Catholicos and a number of Armenian intellectuals urged calm and promised to look into the situation in Karabagh.

In January 1989 Moscow did send Arkady Volskii, who took over the administration of Karabagh from Azerbaijan. In the meantime, Gorbachev was faced with a dilemma. If he sided with more radical reformers, like Boris Yeltsin, the ex-party chief in Moscow, he would be forced to establish a more democratic state and decrease the power of the party. Such an action would inevitably lead to complete independence for some republics, particularly the Baltic States. If he sided with the conservatives, he would have to enforce party discipline, maintain the status quo, and crack down on nationalist dissidents. The struggle divided the USSR. Although the new elections had brought more liberals into the Supreme Soviet, Gorbachev was still forced to maintain a delicate balance among those who wanted faster change, those who preferred a slower pace, and those who opposed any change at all.

By May 1989 Moscow realized it had no choice but to release the members of the Karabagh Committee, who were viewed as national heroes. In the meantime, a general strike in Karabagh aggravated the Azeri rail blockade of Armenia, delayed supplies for earthquake reconstruction, and caused some food and fuel shortages. Meanwhile, the Armenians of Azerbaijan (some 250,000) began to immigrate to Russia and Armenia. By fall, the various Armenian dissidents and national groups formed the Armenian National Movement (ANM) or Hayots Hamazgayin Sharzhum. For the next five months, the National Movement, led by the scholar Levon Ter Petrosian, and the communists, led by Harutiunian, coexisted. By the summer of 1989 the idea of independence became more and more popular. Some Soviet Armenian dissidents, as well as the Dashnaktsutiun in the diaspora, advocated the restoration of historic Armenia (which included Karabagh, Nakhichevan, and western Armenia). Other Armenians continued to insist that Armenia's salvation lay with the Russians and that pan-Turkism was a greater threat.

The leadership of the Armenian National Movement led by Ter Petrosian did not agree. They viewed the question of the restoration of western Armenia, and even Nakhichevan, as unrealistic and untimely. Armenia could not achieve such a goal without the support of a major power, which historically had proven as disastrous. Karabagh was different, however, they maintained. The Armenians of Karabagh, not the Armenian Republic had demanded self-rule. This was not a territorial issue but a self-determination issue. Volskii had to consider the wishes of the Armenian Council of Karabagh, which represented the people. In the meantime, Azerbaijan continued its demands for the ouster of Volskii and the restoration of Azeri control over Karabagh. In November the Supreme Soviet voted in favor of Azerbaijan and returned Karabagh to Azeri control.

By the end of 1989 the fall of East European regimes encouraged clashes between nationalists and communists in Azerbaijan and Georgia, and began serious secessionist activities in the Baltic republics. Moscow's pro-Azeri stand began a secessionist movement in Armenia as well. The Azeri nationalist leaders could not, or did not, control the masses in Baku and Ganja, and in January 1990 mobs organized pogroms, which killed and maimed Armenians and looted their property in those cities. Russia sent troops to Baku and the remaining Azerbaijani Armenians had to leave all their belongings and flee to Russia or Armenia. Armenians responded by attacking Azeri farmers who lived in Armenia and forced tens of thousands to leave for Azerbaijan. Both sides thus found themselves with numerous refugees. All efforts at negotiations failed and the situation was becoming out of control.

Moscow, fearing Azeri nationalism and Islamic resurgence, far more than Armenian frustrations, used the civil violence in Baku to install Ayaz Mutalibov, a communist, as the new president of Azerbaijan. During the next four months Azerbaijan received Moscow's blessing to crush Armenian resistance in Karabagh. Russian forces were deployed to remove Armenians from their villages and to resettle Azeris in their place.

Armenia's total loss of faith in Moscow resulted in major gains for Armenian National Movement candidates in the May elections. The Soviet Armenian flag was replaced with the tri-color of the former independent Republic and May 28 became the national day of the Armenian Republic. The Kremlin reacted by giving Baku more control over Karabagh and by sending tanks to Yerevan. The Armenian capital and its residents were in a state of shock. The action backfired, and by August, Levon Ter Petrosian was elected as head of the Armenian parliament. He then announced that in a year's time Armenia would have a referendum on the issue of independence. Ter Petrosian was careful to avoid confrontation, however. The use of the term "issue of independence" as opposed to "independence," as well as Ter Petrosian's careful conformity with the by-laws of the Soviet Constitution meant that Armenia was the only state in the Union that adopted a democratic and free multiparty election. Such an election required two-thirds of the vote for secession from the USSR. Many Western observers felt that the government of Armenia, by meticulously following every condition, had prudently created a situation, which stopped Gorbachev from sending Russian forces, as he had done in Lithuania. It would also obligate the world to recognize Armenia's independence if the referendum went against Moscow.

The Armenian communists were now totally discredited and the National Movement quickly took control of Armenia. Unlike the 1918-1921 period, there was no internal strife during the transition. Despite Moscow's efforts to create conflict in order to justify its military presence, Armenian communists surrendered their posts without a struggle and the new parliament did not take advantage of its opportunity to retaliate against the former leaders. No other former republic can boast of such an orderly transition.

Ter Petrosian's early months as the head of parliament were spent in disarming those Armenians who, frustrated by the Azeri blockade and the forced deportation of Armenians from Karabagh, had not only taken over police stations and army barracks, but had also sought an open conflict with Azerbaijan.

During the first eight months of 1991 the Azeris, helped by the Russian army, weapons, and equipment, subjected the Armenians of Karabagh to ferocious bombings and attacks, which, according to a British journalist and historian, resembled Nazi reprisals in occupied Europe. Never, since the anti-Armenian measures of 1903-1907, had there been such violent anti-Armenian feeling on the part of the Russian government. Soviet helicopters and tanks killed, disarmed, and removed Armenians from the Shahumian and Hadrut regions of Karabagh. Numerous villages were depopulated and Azeris even bombed the cities of Goris, Ghapan, Sisian, and Meghri in Zangezur, inside the Armenian Republic. The world press, the United Nations, and the major powers stood silent while Armenian men, women and children were surrounded and bombed in Karabagh. Meanwhile, relief for refugees from Azerbaijan, Karabagh, and the earthquake zone was hampered by the Azeri blockade. Conditions in Armenia reminded some of the situation in 1920, when the first Republic was under siege.

Gorbachev, meanwhile, tried to save the Soviet Union by creating a treaty that would bind the former republics to Russia. But only the Slavic and Muslim republics were ready to sign it. Armenia, Georgia, Moldavia, and the Baltic republics refused. Armenia paid a high price for its refusal, for Russia continued to aid Azerbaijan and the blockade of Armenia tightened. Since Armenia had exported most of its industrial products to Russia and had imported much of its food from its neighbors, it now had to face shortages. In spring, Georgia declared its independence and Azerbaijan followed that summer. Armenia was once again left alone to decide its course.

Before the new Union treaty could be signed, however, the communist hard-liners, who did not wish to see a fractured Soviet Union, carried out a coup on August 1991. Although Azerbaijan's president Mutalibov welcomed the coup, and Georgia's new leader, Zviad Gamsakhurdia, remained uncommitted, Armenia categorically refused to recognize the coup. It is ironic that Armenia, despite all of Gorbachev's anti-Armenian policies, retained its democratic principles and supported Russia's legal president against the hard-liners. The coup did not succeed and on September 20 the national referendum in Armenia overwhelmingly (99 percent) voted for independence. On September 21, 1991, the Armenian parliament by a vote of 213 to 0 declared a sovereign state and seceded from the Soviet Union and two days later, on September 23, Armenia declared its independence. A new Armenian Republic was born. The next step was to elect a new government.

22

The New Diaspora
The Armenian Global Community in the Twentieth Century

B Y THE END of the nineteenth century, the Armenian communities outside the Ottoman and Russian Empires, Iran and
Egypt had either assimilated or had lost their economic and
political influence and were generally reduced to insignificant clusters in a number of urban centers. The massacres of 1895-1896 and
the anti-Armenian policies of Sultan Abdul-Hamid forced many
Armenians to emigrate from Anatolia. Some joined the communities
in Europe and the Middle East, while others journeyed to the
Americas. The Armenian Genocide created thousands of refugees
who eventually settled both in the old and new worlds. Although a
significant number went to the Armenian Republic in 1918-1919,
some, as we have seen, fled in 1920-1921, or were deported by Stalin in 1936-1939. A second wave of approximately 100,000
repatriates arrived in Soviet Armenia in 1945-1948 and a third,
much smaller group between 1953-1965. By 1985, however, nearly
half of the post-war repatriates had emigrated to the West. Revolutions and civil wars in Asia and North Africa throughout the four
decades following the Second World War resulted in the diminish-
ing of the Armenian communities there and the growth of the
Armenian diaspora in Europe, Australia, and the Americas. The
economic hardships following the fall of the Soviet Union has
forced the migration of some one million Armenians to Russia,
Europe, North America, and Australia. The historical events of the
last one hundred years have thus resulted in a pattern whereby new
Armenian immigrants have rejuvenated the earlier diaspora by reviving their Armenian identity. At present Armenians, together with
the Jews, are the only people that have more members living in the
diaspora than in their own country. It is estimated that out of the

more than seven million Armenians in the world only two and a half million live in the Armenian Republic. Like the Jews, Armenians are to be found in almost every country of the globe. The following survey will examine most of these communities.

EASTERN EUROPE

The large Armenian communities of Eastern Europe discussed in chapter 17 faced great pressures after the Counter-Reformation and slowly but surely assimilated. By the twentieth century the number of Armenians in Eastern Europe had dwindled from over half a million to barely 40,000, most of whom were products of intermarriages and had little or no knowledge of their Armenian heritage.

Poland

The center of the largest Armenian community in the late medieval period, the Polish-Armenian community had greatly diminished prior to World War II. It was concentrated in the city of Lvov, where an Armenian cathedral and an Armenian priest served the needs of the community. Most of the Polish Armenians had converted to Catholicism. In 1938 the Catholic Armenian archbishop died and, soon after, World War II decimated much of the Armenian community (both Catholic and Apostolic) in Poland. Following the war, Lvov, the main Armenian center, became part of Ukraine.

The Armenian ties with Poland persisted, however. Armenian students from the Soviet Union and Soviet Armenia, attracted by the relatively free atmosphere in communist Poland, married Poles and settled in Warsaw. Following the collapse of the communist system, illegal Armenian immigrants flocked to Poland and today there are over 100,000 Armenians living in half a dozen cities across the country, including Gdansk, Warsaw, and Krakow. Many are street vendors, while others have opened small coffee shops and bars. The large numbers has attracted the attention of the Catholic Church and a fifteenth-century Catholic church in Gliwice has recently been converted into an Armenian Catholic church. This sole Armenian church, of either denomination, is served by an Armenian-speaking Polish priest. The large Armenian presence in Poland will undoubtedly spur new cultural and religious centers and may start a new Armenian diaspora.

Ukraine

Lvov, part of Soviet Ukraine since 1945, as well as the Crimea has not forgotten the historical presence of the Armenians in their communities (see chapter 17). Since the collapse of the Soviet Union, Armenians from other parts of Russia, as well as Armenia, have relocated to the Ukraine, where there are currently 150,000 Armenians. The Armenian community of Lvov, some 3,000 strong, is in the process of regaining possession of the Armenian cathedral, closed by the communists in 1946. Ejmiatsin has appointed a primate to the Ukraine and a religious revival has begun. The Armenian presence is even stronger in the Crimea, particularly in Feodossia, which has some 10,000 Armenians. Seven Armenian churches built between the twelfth and fifteenth centuries, are reminders of the powerful Armenian trading activities in the region (see chapter 17). The Aivazovsky Museum in Feodossia houses paintings of the famous Armenian artist. Armenians also live in other parts of the Crimea. There are currently over 7,000 Armenians in Simferopol, who plan to construct an Armenian church to replace the one bulldozed by the communists. The Armenians of Yalta, also 7,000-strong worship at their large stone church constructed in the early twentieth century. The church, which was neglected during the Soviet era, is currently being renovated. The Armenians in the Crimea, numbering at 25,000, are at the forefront of the economic revival of the region.

The largest Armenian centers in the Ukraine are Odessa and Kiev. Odessa, a great port and cosmopolitan city on the Black Sea, has attracted Armenians from Russia and Armenia and has currently over 30,000 Armenians. A new church was recently built to replace the old Armenian church razed during the communist period. The rest of the Armenians in the Ukraine are concentrated in Kiev, Kherson, and Sevastopol.

Hungary

The Armenians of Hungary were, prior to the 1990s, the least active community in Eastern Europe. Most did not speak Armenian. A small Armenian Catholic Mkhitarist church in Budapest was, and is, the only Armenian house of worship in the country. A number of Hungarian Armenians studied in Soviet Armenia and upon return took various official posts maintaining their Armenian roots as best as they could. The situation changed when after the fall of communism, Hungary, in 1994, not only gave minorities the right to set up self-governments, but also allocated special funds for that purpose. Four years later the Armenians became one of the thirteen recognized minority groups in the country. Soon after, the Armenians of Budapest set up a weekly radio hour, a bimonthly television program, and a bilingual newspaper. One of the main goals of the Armenian leadership is to familiarize the Hungarians with Armenian history and culture. In addition to books, film festivals and other cultural activities, the Armenians have succeeded in publicizing the fact that three of the thirteen heroes who fought against the Austrians in the 1848-1849 were Armenian (see chapter 17). There are currently over 12,000 Armenians, a few recent arrivals from Armenia, in Budapest, Veszprém, and Székesfehérvár,

Moldova

Despite its long history in what was Bessarabia (see chapters 16 and 17), the large Armenian community, founded by Catherine the Great in the eighteenth century, paid a heavy price during the upheavals that engulfed that region. The breakup of the Russian Empire gave Bessarabia back to Romania. The Stalin-Hitler pact brought the region under Soviet rule for a short time. Germany occupied it during Hitler's invasion of the Soviet Union. After the war, the Soviets annexed the region and made it the Republic of Moldavia. The fall of the Soviet Union encouraged the Moldavians (some 60% of the population) to proclaim the region as the independent Republic of Moldova. The large Russian and Ukrainian minority (some 30% of the population), fearing that the Moldovians would seek reunion with Romania, took up arms and, after a civil war, broke away and formed the Trans-Dniester Republic.

By the early 1990s, the Armenian community, some of whose ancestors came there during the eighteenth century, others who had settled there in the Soviet period, had been reduced to less than 5,000, mainly in Chisinau (the former Kishinev), Beltsy, and Grigoriopol, this last falling within the Trans-Dniester region. The situation changed drastically when some 25,000 Armenians arrived from Azerbaijan, New Nakhichevan, and Karabagh. The community has awakened and has taken control of the Armenian churches, which had ceased functioning during the Soviet period. Clubs, associations, and other cultural events are slowly starting up and the Armenians may yet revive this once-powerful community.

Bulgaria

The Armenian community of Bulgaria received many refugees from the political upheavals in neighboring Russia and Turkey in the years 1915-1922. Most settled in Sofia, Plovdiv, and Burgas. The 30,000-strong community was on the road to economic revival, when World War II halted its progress. Following the war, communists closed most of the private enterprises owned by these Armenians. Some Bulgarian Armenians left for the Americas, while large numbers repatriated to Soviet Armenia. From 1946 until 1991, the Armenians of Bulgaria were supervised by the communist Yerevan Association, a government-funded organization which published the *Yerevan* newspaper. The fall of communism has energized the 20,000-strong Armenian community. Armenian refugees from the former Soviet Union have found Bulgarian flea markets in Russe profitable and are increasing the size of the community. Two new newspapers, one in Plovdiv, the other in Burgas, have emerged and the Armenian school in Plovdiv (started in the nineteenth century) has reopened. There are currently seven Armenian churches in Bulgaria and the shortage of Armenian clerics has become a serious issue.

Romania

The Armenian community of Romania was also rejuvenated by the wave of refugees from Turkey during the years 1915-1922. They settled in Bucharest, Constanza, Suceava, Bacau, Gherla, Piteshti, Tulca, and Botoshani. It soon numbered 60,000. Some like their compatriots from Bulgaria, Greece, Syria, Egypt, and Lebanon left for Armenia in 1946. Many more left for the United States following the establishment of communism in 1947. The nationalization policy left many Armenians without their private businesses. Numerous wealthy Armenian industrialists lost everything. Although only some 4,000 Armenians remain in Romania, they are represented in parliament. The Armenian museum in Bucharest houses important material going back to the fall of Ani in the eleventh century. The Armenian church (rebuilt on the site of an older church in 1911-1915) and the Armenian cemetery (1856) in Bucharest, as well as 21 other Armenian churches, built between the fourteenth and eighteenth centuries, demonstrates the strong Armenian historical presence in Romania despite its present numbers.

Czech Republic

There are over 13,000 Armenians in the Czech Republic. Almost all of them came after the collapse of the Soviet Union. Many were young men looking for employment or artists and craftsmen selling their wares in the streets. A community has slowly risen and an Armenian school and restaurant have recently opened in Prague. Some have found employment in Radio Free Europe-Radio Liberty, which, together with Voice of America, continue to broadcast despite the collapse of totalitarian regimes in Eastern Europe.

Albania

The Armenians of Albania settled there mostly in the 1920s and 1930s. Their education gave them an advantage over the generally uneducated public and they established a middle class community in the capital, Tirana. The communist takeover in 1945 resulted in the loss of property and even jail for many Armenians. Prior to 1985, the few hundred Armenians of Albania lived a life of total isolation. The policies of Enver Hoxa kept Albania detached not only from the West, but also from every other communist nation. The collapse of communism has forced the 150 Armenians left in Albania to seek political asylum in Germany and Italy.

Greece

Prior to 1895 there were only some 500 Armenians in all of Greece. A large part of this group resided in Thessaloniki. Originally from Mush they were hired (in 1872) by the Germans to build a railroad connecting that city to Istanbul and for other projects and did not return. More arrived after the massacres of 1895-1896 and some joined the Greeks in the First Balkan War against the Turks. The largest Armenian group arrived after 1922, following the expulsions of the Christians from Smyrna (Izmir). Some 150,000 Armenians, including 17,000 orphans came to Greece. Economic conditions in Greece were not good. Half a million of Greek refugees had poured in from Smyrna. Most Armenians did not wish to stay and in 1924 some 100,000 left for other states. The German occupation did not improve the life of the 60,000 Armenians, who had just begun to re-build their shattered lives. After World War II, thousands left for Armenia, North America, Australia, and Europe and there were barely 10,000 Armenians left in Greece. Although small the community became more educated and affluent. The collapse of communism has brought Armenians from Russia, Armenia and Georgia and the community now numbers over 25,000. A number of churches, including an Armenian Evangelical church, and clubs serve the Armenians in Greece, most of who live in Athens. The excellent diplomatic relations between Greece and the Armenian Republic has enabled the community to commemorate the Genocide and to play a more active role in Greek politics.

Cyprus

The Armenian Community of Cyprus is also the product of refugees who arrived during the 1895-1922 years. In 1926 the Melkonian Educational Institute was founded to educate and shelter the orphans of the Genocide. During the Lebanese civil war, the Melkonian had many students from that war-torn country. Today a large number of its students are Armenians from Bulgaria. The 1974 Turkish invasion of Cyprus seriously affected the Armenian community, because most of the Armenian quarter of Nicosia, with its clubs, school, and church, fell into the Turkish-occupied sector. The same was unfortunately true of Famagusta, whose Armenian church and monastery of Surb Makar have been left in ruins and converted to a store. The Cyprus community, which had over 15,000 members before the invasion, has been reduced to only 2,000, with the rest emigrating to the West.

WESTERN EUROPE

The Armenian communities of Western Europe had also declined by the end of the nineteenth century. The arrival of refugees from Turkey, the Middle East, and the former Soviet Union, expanded some established centers and has created new ones as well.

Italy

Besides the Armenian Catholic priests at San Lazzaro, there were only a dozen Armenian families in Italy prior to the twentieth century. The large Armenian presence recorded in chapter 14 had disappeared. The Genocide brought a few hundred Armenians; some from Rhodes, to Italy and the community grew to about 2,000 by the end of that century. At present there are two main Armenian centers in Italy, Milan and Venice. Milan's community is the largest, most affluent and active in Armenian cultural presentations. Armenian artists, architects, manufacturers, and journalists have introduced Armenia and its culture to the Italian citizens. Venice, because of the presence of the Mkhitarists at the island of San Lazzaro and their (now closed) Murad-Raphaelian school on the main island, remains the historical center of Armenians in Italy (see chapter 17).

France

France received a great number of Armenian refugees and orphans following the Lausanne treaty in 1923. This was due to the shortage of laborers following the decimation of able-bodied Frenchmen during World War I. Over 200,000 Armenians settled in Marseilles, Valence, Grenoble, Lyons, Nice, Paris, and other cities prior to World War II. Armenians served in the French army and in the Resistance movement during the German occupation. New immigrants, many of who had studied French, arrived from the Arab world (following the 1956-1958 revolutions), Turkey (after the 1955 problems), Lebanon (after the civil war started in 1974), and Iran (after the 1979 Islamic Revolution).

By the end of the century, the French community became the most active Armenian community in Europe, and, despite great pressures from Turkey, France has recognized the Armenian Genocide. There are over 300,000 Armenians in France. Armenians can be found in every major profession, including fashion, law, politics, research on AIDS, education, cinema, and music. Some thirty-five Armenian churches, twenty of them Apostolic, serve the Armenians. Armenian newspapers, organizations, schools, and institutions of higher learning thrive as well, including the Mkhitarist School in Sèvres. The French-Armenian community has produced artists such as Verneuil, Grégoire Aslan, Aznavour, Carzou, and Jansem and scholars such as Sirarpie Der Nersessian. The widely respected scholarly journal *Revue des Etudes Armeniennes* is published in Paris and the Nubarian Library houses a great collection of Armenian books and newspapers.

Belgium

The Armenian community of Belgium experienced Europe's world wars firsthand. During the First World War, many Armenians, who were still Turkish citizens, left Belgium for Holland to escape the German onslaught and for fear of being sent back to Turkey to be drafted. Most returned after the war and a chair in Armenian studies was established in the University of Brussels in 1931, with the famed professor Nicholas Adontz as its first chair holder. Armenians arrived in Belgium in sizable numbers after World War II. They soon controlled the cigarette production industry in Belgium. Unlike other Armenian communities, the Belgian Armenians have stayed out of Armenian internal political divisions. The 5,000-strong community has received new immigrants from Iran, Lebanon, Armenia, and in 1985 they accepted 1,500 Armenians living in two Kurdish villages (Sirnak and Silope) in eastern Turkey. The Armenians of Belgium are a cohesive group with members in the legal and diamond professions. In fact, there are some fifty Armenian diamond dealers in Antwerp's diamond district. The Armenian church in Brussels, as well as the Armenian Social Center has become the gathering point of new immigrants from Armenia.

The Netherlands

The Armenian community in the Netherlands had all but disappeared when a few Armenian families arrived there in the early 1950s from Indonesia, after its independence from the Netherlands. Others came there during the 1970s and 1980s following the Lebanese Civil War, the Islamic Revolution in Iran, and the Gulf War. Armenians from Turkey, especially from the Kurdish village of Sirnak also found a new home in the Netherlands. New Armenian immigrants have arrived from Russia and Armenia as well. An Armenian Cultural Center has been founded and the Armenian church in Amsterdam, which had been sold to Catholics in 1828, was repurchased in 1987. There are currently some 8,000 Armenians in the Netherlands, some of them illegal immigrants or refugees. Despite the small number of Armenians, the Netherlands has an Armenian Studies Program in the famed University of Leiden.

A number of new communities have appeared in Western Europe as a result of political upheavals in the Middle East and are growing steadily due to recent Armenian emigration from the former Soviet Union. Six churches and a number of cultural centers serve the 50,000 Armenians who live in these communities. The most significant of these are in Austria, England, Germany, Sweden, and Switzerland. There had been a few Armenians in Austria as early as the seventeenth century and an Armenian reportedly established the first coffeehouse in Vienna. A number of Armenians from the Polish army had settled in Vienna after they helped to repulse the Turks in 1683. The arrival of the Mkhitarists in 1811 opened the doors to a small number of students from Russia and Turkey. The Armenian presence in Sweden goes back to the nineteenth century when an Armenian chapel was built by an Egyptian Armenian outside Stockholm. There are some 9,000 Armenians in Sweden. Most are refugees from Armenia and the turmoil in the Middle East. The majority of them reside in Stockholm and Upsala. England received a few Armenian merchants from the sixteenth to the eighteenth centuries who in 1780, set up an Armenian press in London. Others arrived after the First World War. The main numbers came after 1980 and included many Armenians from Iran. The community has recently initiated various cultural activities. Geneva is the only city in Switzerland that has a significant Armenian presence. The Armenians of Switzerland, despite their small numbers, are active politically and culturally. The Armenians in Germany, residing mostly in the northern part, are all refugees or illegal workers from Armenia. New Armenian clusters have appeared in other European cities as well.

THE ARAB WORLD

The Armenian communities in the Middle East experienced their greatest change in the last one hundred years. The Armenian communities in the Arab world received a large percentage of the refugees and survivors of the massacres and Genocide. The European mandates enabled the Armenians to make advances in the economic and administrative sectors and to establish cultural and political associations.

Egypt

As noted in chapter 15, the Armenians of Egypt enjoyed a strong presence in that country in the nineteenth century and the Nubarian family in particular enjoyed special privileges. The departure of the AGBU and the British did not adversely affect the Armenian community of Egypt. The role of the Armenians in the Egyptian government, as well as prosperous Armenian businesses, helped that country remain a major Armenian center, where numerous schools, churches, and newspapers guided the 40,000 Armenians living in Cairo and Alexandria. The political changes in Egypt following the military uprising in 1952 and the economic policies of President Nasser after 1956 forced the emigration of many Armenians to Europe, Australia, and the United States. At present there are only some 5,000 Armenians left in Egypt, primarily in Cairo and Alexandria. Despite the decline of its Armenian community, Egypt remains an important and active Armenian cultural center. Three Armenian newspapers, two schools, four sports clubs, and a large church, continue the Armenian historical presence in Egypt. Diplomatic ties between Egypt and the Armenian Republic are very friendly and the Armenians have not been subjected to the anti-Christian violence faced by the Copts.

Palestine, Israel, Jordan

The Armenian communities of Palestine and Jordan, which were never large, also attracted some refugees from Turkey who laid the foundations for new centers in Jerusalem, Haifa, and Amman. The short-lived security during the British Mandate soon gave way to Arab-Jewish strife. Following the establishment of the State of Israel in 1948 and the Arab-Israeli wars, many Armenians emigrated to Europe, United States, and more peaceful centers in the Middle East. The majority of the Armenians of that region are primarily involved in the religious and scholarly activities surrounding the Armenian Patriarchate of Jerusalem. The major problem facing the Armenians in Israel is to resist the encroachment of Zionists upon Armenian properties, especially by the right-wing Sharon government.

Syria

Most of the Armenian survivors of the massacres and Genocide settled in Syria, mainly in Aleppo. The new arrivals were aided by Armenian and American missionary and philanthropic organizations and succeeded in invigorating the earlier settlements and creating one of the most active Armenian communities in the twentieth century. In many ways the Armenian schools, churches, centers, and hospitals in Syria, especially in Aleppo and its environs, became the inspiration and models for the Armenian communities of Beirut, Baghdad, Jerusalem, and Amman during the second half of the twentieth century. Until the end of the Second World War, the region was under British and French mandates. Fortunately the area did not become a theater of war during the Second World War and actually benefited from the war materiel and personnel, which were concentrated there to repulse the Germans from North Africa. Armenians, Assyrians, Christian Arabs, and a number of non-Sunni Muslim sects such as the Druzes, 'Alawis, and Isma'ilis, were favored by and cooperated with the Europeans. Syria's independence in 1944 did not threaten the well being of the Armenian community, which continued to grow to some 75,000. The revolution of 1958, however, and the creation of the United Arab Republic with Egypt, as well as the military coup of 1963, not only hurt Armenian businesses, but also restricted Armenian cultural activities. Some immigrated to Lebanon, others to the United States. Fortunately for the Armenians, Syria soon abandoned the political and economic programs of Egypt and starting in 1971 President Hafez al-Assad reformed the extreme policies of the Ba'th Party and created a more tolerant Syria. Here, social programs and businesses have striven to sustain the large population growth of the country. The 'Alawis are in charge of major government posts and the Armenians are treated well. In Aleppo alone there are some 40,000 Armenians who utilize Armenian centers, ten schools, a hospital, and organize numerous community-sponsored events. The community in Damascus has also grown in the last quarter of a century and new Armenian businesses have managed to stop the flow of emigration. In fact some Armenians from Lebanon, Iraq, and Kuwait, who have fled turmoil in those countries, have settled, temporarily or permanently, in Damascus. Syria, with over 100,000 Armenians has, at present, the largest Armenian community in the Arab world. Various bilateral agreements and warm political relations between Syria and the Armenian Republic have helped the Armenians of Syria maintain a strong presence.

Lebanon

The Armenians of Lebanon were, for a time, the most important Armenian community outside of the Soviet Union and the United States. The core of the modern community arrived as a result of the massacres and Armenian Genocide in Turkey. By 1926 there were some 75,000 Armenians in Lebanon and the Lebanese Constitution granted them and other minorities civil rights, which, in time, enabled the Armenians to elect their own members of parliament. The country's geographic location and the security offered by the French, as well as its Christian-dominated government attracted more Armenians there and in 1930 the Catholicosate of Cilicia moved to Antelias, outside of Beirut. Armenian Catholic and Evangelical Churches also established centers in Beirut. In 1939 the Sanjak of Alexandretta, which included Musa Dagh, was transferred to Turkey. As a result 30,000 Armenians moved into Syria and Lebanon. The Armenians of Musa Dagh settled in the highlands of Anjar. Armenians rose swiftly to economic and social prominence, and Lebanon's liberal government made it possible for all Armenian political parties to establish themselves. During the short-lived Lebanese civil strife of 1958 the Armenians split and sided with both factions. By 1974 there were over 200,000 Armenians, who had two-dozen churches, some seventy schools, including institutions of higher learning, such as the Haigazian College, founded in 1955 by the Armenian Missionary Association of America and the Union of the Armenian Evangelical Churches in the Near East. In addition there were more than fifty athletic, patriotic, and benevolent organizations, and numerous literary and cultural periodicals and newspapers. The Lebanese Civil War (1974-1989) took its toll and although Armenians remained neutral and some of their community infrastructure remained undamaged, thousands left for safer shores, especially the United States. Some 75,000 have remained and thanks to their neutrality and the efforts of their leaders, have played a role in the Syrian-backed National Accord Document, and are once again enjoying the benefits of Lebanon's unique situation. Diplomatic ties between Lebanon and the Armenian Republic are extremely cordial. Forty-seven Armenian schools and numerous associations and organizations, including an Armenian Fund for

Economic Development are putting the community on the road to recovery with members in parliament and the central government.

Iraq

Most of the Armenians of Iraq arrived after WWI and established communities in Baghdad, Mosul, and Basra. Armenians were engaged in private businesses, worked in technical, administrative and financial positions for the British Petroleum Company, or participated in the trade between the Persian Gulf and the Mediterranean. They were also instrumental in the introduction of the Communism. Even after Iraq achieved its independence in 1932, the British presence did not end and the Armenians continued to enjoy the benefits of Iraq's economic rise, especially since, unlike the Assyrians and Kurds, they did not engage in anti-government and nationalist activities and were viewed as loyal citizens. Armenian organizations, churches, and schools served the 35,000 Armenians in that country. The revolution of 1958 and the subsequent radical policies of the Ba'th Party forced the migration of many Armenians from Iraq to Lebanon, Kuwait, United States, and the Gulf States. During the Iran-Iraq War (1980-1988) many Armenians were drafted and died (as were Armenians drafted by Iran). The difficult political and economic conditions, combined with the disastrous effects of the Gulf War on Iraq, spelled the doom of the Armenian community there. Many emigrated or have temporarily abandoned the unstable situation. Fewer than 10,000 Armenians remained in Iraq. The 2003 US invasion of Iraq will probably reduce the Armenian community even further.

Persian Gulf States

The Armenian communities in the Persian Gulf States began their existence well after World War II. Most came from Iran, Lebanon, Syria, and more recently from Armenia. Today there are some 1,500 Armenians in the United Arab Emirates. Unable to become citizens despite their economic successes, they enjoy total freedom as managers, jewelers, engineers, merchants, and mechanics. An Armenian school has some 100 students enrolled in weekend programs. Weekly Armenian services are conducted in one of the local churches and a priest from Antelias supervises the spiritual needs of the community. There are also Armenians in Bahrain and Qatar, but their numbers are too small to form an actual community. The largest community in the Persian Gulf was that of Kuwait, which mushroomed during the economic boom of that country. Arab nationalism and compulsory military service in Egypt and Syria drove young Armenian men to Kuwait. An Armenian church and a school soon created a viable community. Lack of citizenship did not stop the Armenians in excelling in auto repair, plumbing, electrical, and other services. Prior to the Iraqi invasion, there were over 12,000 Armenians in Kuwait, with 700 students enrolled in the Armenian school. The Iraqi invasion occurred in the summer, when many Armenian families and their children were away in Syria or Lebanon. Most did not return, while others fled. A year later (1991) there were only 500 Armenians left. Today, there are some 2,500 Armenians and the community is slowly reviving. The Armenian school, which after the war had only 90 students, has currently over 300 students.

NON-ARAB MUSLIM STATES

Turkey

The Genocide, as we have seen, destroyed western Armenia and numerous other Armenian centers in Turkey. What was left of the Armenian community in Turkey was concentrated primarily in Istanbul. The anti-Armenian policies following World War II (the 1945 property tax [*varlik vergisi*] on minorities and the mob attacks on Armenian and Greek shops in Istanbul and Izmir in 1955) forced some to emigrate. The remaining Armenians, however, learned to improvise and keep their identity as best as they could. Armenian schools were not permitted to talk about the Genocide or other national issues. Some Armenians changed their last names to the more Turkish-sounding *oglu* ending. Conditions improved greatly after 1956. Armenians orphans were gathered from the interior and brought to Istanbul. Armenians continued their economic and cultural activities without any sanctioned discrimination. Today, the Armenian community, some 60,000, has numerous organizations and associations, over thirty active churches, twenty schools, two sport associations, nine choirs, and a large hospital. It is interesting that the Armenian community of Istanbul does not view itself as a diaspora. Since the Armenians already had a large community in Istanbul prior to the arrival of the Turks in 1453. The major problem of the Armenians in Turkey is that they have no seminary to prepare new priests and no institution of higher learning. Despite having some 5,000 Armenian students in their twenty schools, they cannot hire teachers from abroad and cannot send their graduates to Armenian universities or learning centers in the Middle East or Italy. Armenian schools can only teach Armenian six hours a week; the rest of the curriculum is in Turkish taught primarily by Turkish teachers. Most Armenians prefer to speak Turkish and some intermarriages between Armenians and Turks have occurred. The Armenian Patriarchate of Istanbul as well as the Armenian Patriarch retain their prestige, both in the diaspora and in Turkey and are frequently visited by or visit Turkish government officials. However, Armenian political activities in Europe and North America, as well as the Karabagh conflict have generated numerous violent acts against Armenian churches and cemeteries there.

Iran

By the twentieth century, Iran, like Egypt, was a major center of Armenian life in the Middle East. As we have seen, by the end of the nineteenth century, there were some 100,000 Armenians in Iran. The proximity of the Armenians in Iranian Azerbaijan to Transcaucasia and eastern Anatolia brought them under the influence of the political activities of Russian and Turkish Armenians. Armenakan, Hnchak and Dashnak cells opened in Tabriz and Salmas and a number of Armenian revolutionaries sought refuge from the tsarist and Turkish police there. The massacres of 1895-1896 brought Armenian refugees to northwestern Iran. The Revolution of 1905 in Russia had a major effect on northern Iran and, in 1906, Iranian liberals and revolutionaries, joined by many Armenians, and demanded a constitution in Iran. Although the Shah signed the document, his successor dissolved the *majlis* or parliament and it was only in 1909 that the revolutionaries forced the crown to give up some of its prerogatives. The role of Armenian military units under the command of leaders such as Yeprem Khan and Keri, in the Iranian Constitutional Movement is well documented.

Thousands of Armenians escaped to Iran during the Genocide. The Turkish invasion of Iranian Azerbaijan during the First World War devastated a number of Armenian communities in that region, such as Khoi. The community experienced a political rejuvenation with the arrival of the Dashnak leadership from Armenia in 1921.

The establishment of the Pahlavi dynasty began a new era for the Armenians. The modernization efforts of Reza Shah (1924-1941) and Mohammad Reza Shah (1941-1979) gave the Armenians ample opportunities for advancement. Armenian contacts with the West and their linguistic abilities gave them an advantage over the native Iranians. They soon gained important positions in the arts and sciences, the Iranian Oil Company, the caviar industry, and dominated professions such as tailoring, shoemaking, photography, auto-mechanics, and as well the management of cafes and restaurants. Immigrants and refugees from Russia continued to increase the Armenian community until 1933. World War II gave the Armenians opportunities to increase their economic power. The Allies decided to use Iran as a bridge to Russia. Western arms and supplies were shipped through Iran and some Armenians, who knew Russian, played a major role in this endeavor. The Hnchaks, especially, were active and the Iranian Communist Party had an Armenian contingent. The majority of the Armenians remained loyal to the Dashnaks, while the minority, who had communist sympathies, either went underground or left with the Iranian Socialists when they fled to Russia in 1946. In 1953 the Iranian and few Armenian communists made a brief comeback during the Mossadeq period, but the return of the Shah, once again decimated their ranks. Most Armenians, under Dashnak leadership, however, had remained neutral or loyal to the regime and were rewarded by the Shah. For the next quarter of the century Armenian fortunes rose in Iran, and Tehran, Tabriz, and Isfahan became major centers with over 300,000 Armenians. The Shah trusted and liked his Armenian subjects and Tehran, like Beirut, became a major center of Armenian life.

Armenian churches, schools, cultural centers, sports clubs and associations flourished and Armenians had their own senator and members of parliament. Thirty churches and some four-dozen schools and libraries served the needs of the community. Armenian presses published numerous books, journals, periodicals, and newspapers. The better-educated upper classes, however, were fewer in number and, compared to their counterparts in Lebanon, were relatively unproductive culturally.

Although the Islamic Revolution has ended the second golden age of the Armenian community in Iran, the community has not lost its prominence altogether. Ayatollah Khomeini's restrictions, the Iran-Iraq War, and the economic problems resulting from Iran's isolation forced the exodus of over 100,000 Armenians. The current government is more accommodating and Armenians, unlike the Kurds and Iranian Azeris, have their own schools, clubs, and maintain most of their churches. The fall of the Soviet Union, the common border with Armenia, and Armeno-Iranian diplomatic and economic agreements have opened a new era for the Iranian Armenians.

AFRICA

Outside Egypt, whose Armenian community was discussed above, the Armenians in Africa came to that continent primarily after the First World War. Although a small number settled in Sudan and in South Africa, most chose Ethiopia as their new home. The Ethiopian Armenians gained favor with Emperor Haile Selassie and an Armenian, Kevork Nalbandian, even composed the former national anthem of Ethiopia. Armenian businessmen started mills, tanneries, shoe factories, and printing presses. In 1934 a large church was constructed in Addis Ababa and a year later an Armenian school was opened there as well. The community was never large and at its height had only some 1,500 members, some of them of mixed Ethiopian-Armenian parentage. The military revolution, as well as the civil war (1974-1991), nationalized Armenian businesses and reduced the community to some 150 members, with most others emigrating to the United States, Australia, and Canada. The Armenian school has only eleven Armenian students, six of whom are of mixed parentage, while the church, without a priest, functions with the help of an archdeacon. The Ararat Armenian Community Club and Restaurant, however, is very popular with diplomatic circles and its income helps sustain the church and the school.

The Armenian community of Sudan was centered in Khartoum where it built a church. The civil war in Sudan, which began in the late 1980s, ended the viability of that community. The Armenians in South Africa settled mostly in Johannesburg. The turmoil in South Africa has encouraged most to emigrate to the United States, Canada, or Australia.

SOUTH ASIA

The Armenian community in India declined after India became a colony of the British crown. Although some wealthy Armenian merchants such as Galstaun and Chater erected buildings, parks, and left sizeable endowments, most, including Chater, left the region. The turbulence during World War I and World War II and the partition of India reduced the number of Armenians further. By the second half of the twentieth century, Delhi, Agra, Chinsurah, Dhaka, and Surat had no Armenians. Madras and Bombay struggled to maintain small Armenian communities. The large Armenian church in Bombay (built in 1796) was demolished and a new modest church, as well as a commercial building named "Ararat" was constructed on the site in 1957. Calcutta, with its Armenian College (established in 1821), the Davidian Girls School, and the Armenian Sports Club remained the only viable Armenian community. Lack of students forced the two schools to combine into the Armenian Academy. Its British curriculum attracted some boys from Iran and Lebanon and by the early 1960s its student body boasted over 200. Economic opportunities in Australia, as well as intermarriage continued to erode the number of Armenians in India, however. By the end of the century, there were only three Armenians in Madras and four Armenians in Bombay, while the Armenian Academy in Calcutta had only six students. At present, despite the presence of half a dozen of churches, there are barely 200 Armenians of mixed parentage in India, most of them in Calcutta, and none in Bangladesh. The recent activities of the present Armenian government has started a student exchange program with India and the presence of an Armenian embassy in New Delhi may rejuvenate the remaining Armenians in India.

THE FAR EAST

In the 1920s, Armenians who had fled the Russian Revolution, civil war, and the Bolsheviks, began to arrive in Harbin, in the Chinese province of Manchuria, and in Shanghai. An Armenian Church was constructed in Harbin and Armenian merchants and artisans opened businesses in China and Southeast Asia. The Armenians worked closely and occasionally intermarried with the Europeans of China. The Second World War devastated the remaining Armenian centers in the region. The Japanese rounded up all Europeans in China, Burma, Indonesia, Philippines, Malaysia, and Singapore, including the Armenians. Those who survived the ravages of the war were soon faced with the discriminatory policies of the nationalist or communist governments that followed the de-colonization of South and Southeast Asia. Most immigrated to Australia or South America. Out of the once-successful community, less than 150 Armenians remain in Malaysia, Singapore and Hong Kong. Bangkok, however, has recently attracted new Armenian immigrants.

AUSTRALIA

The major upheavals in South Asia forced the Armenians of that region to leave in droves and seek refuge in Australia, where a number of them had already immigrated during the 1920s. Political changes and economic hardship in Eastern Europe and the Middle East brought more immigrants to Australia (and a few to New Zealand). The Australian government policy for diversity has enabled the Armenian community to enter into various professions and have a voice in community politics and funding. Immigrants from the former Soviet Union have swelled the numbers of Armenians in Australia to 50,000. Most reside in Melbourne and Sydney, where churches, clubs, and newspapers have fostered a professional and vibrant community.

SOUTH AMERICA

The Armenian community of South America, like that of Australia, arose in the early twentieth century by immigrants from South Asia. A number also came from Turkey. The majority went to Argentina, Brazil, Venezuela and Uruguay. Unlike their compatriots who had emigrated to Europe or other parts of Asia, Armenians in the Americas had no previous connections, commercial or cultural, to aid them in acclimatizing to such a different culture. But, by the 1940s each of these countries had Armenian teachers, engineers, doctors, and lawyers. In addition, Armenian craftsmen opened their own businesses and, thanks to the economic boom in the region, became affluent. Their economic successes prompted other Armenians to relocate there from Greece, the Middle and Far East, and recently from the Armenian Republic. By the end of the twentieth century there were over 20,000 in Brazil, and 15,000 in Uruguay, concentrated Sao Paulo and Montevideo, respectively. The numbers are somewhat deceiving, however, for with the exception of the Argentine Armenians, the Armenians of South America are not a cohesive community. A dozen churches (including Catholic and Evangelical), a number of schools, newspapers, and clubs and organizations have been established, but assimilation is taking its toll and economic hyper-inflation, as well as political instability, have resulted in some emigration to North America.

The Armenian community in Argentina is by far the largest and most cohesive Armenian community in South America. The Argentinean government encouraged immigration and by the mid-1940s there were some 20,000 Armenians in Argentina. All Armenian political parties, as well as the AGBU and regional unions established branches in Buenos Aires, Schools and churches were built and a community center was constructed on Acevedo Street (currently Armenian Street). Armenians took advantage of Argentinean educational rights and social mobility and rose to prominent positions in every profession, including music, medicine and journalism. By the end of the century the Armenian population approached 100,000 with several Armenian schools accommodating over 2,000 students.

NORTH AMERICA

The United States

Sources mention that in the first half of the seventeenth century, an Armenian called Martin, who was originally from New Julfa, came to Virginia via Amsterdam. The genesis of the Armenian community in the United States, however, began more than two centuries later. After American missionaries established schools in Turkey in the second half of the nineteenth century, they enabled some Armenians to come to the United States and attracted more Armenian immigrants to the "promised land." A small group of Armenians thus settled on the East Coast and built a church in 1891 in Worcester, Massachusetts. America was too far and too expensive for most to reach, however, and it was only after the massacres of 1895-1896 that a large contingent of Armenian men, realizing they had little to lose, took a risk and traveled to America. By 1900 some 15,000 had arrived. Most settled in Boston and Watertown. Between 1900 and 1916 some 70,000 Armenians immigrated to the United States. Statistics indicate that the great majority of them were men under 45, who were skilled and literate and who had left their wives and families to seek their fortune. Before the closing of the gates in 1924, some 23,000 additional Armenians arrived in North America. Altogether over 100,000, the overwhelming majority from Turkey, settled in the United States

In 1948 a few thousand Armenians arrived from Europe under

the Displaced Persons Act. Known as D.P.s, they included Armenians who had fled western Russia with the retreating German armies. More Armenians arrived in the late 1950s and early 1960s, following the political problems in the Middle East.

The early immigrants to the United States had settled in the urban and industrial centers of the East Coast, primarily in New York, Massachusetts, Connecticut, and New Jersey, with a few settling in the mid-western cities of Detroit, Chicago, and Cleveland. Others settled in Texas and Utah. The only Armenians who did not follow this pattern were those who, at the end of the nineteenth century, settled in the San Joaquin Valley in Central California. Here, they engaged in farming and grape growing particularly around Fresno. For the next half a century Fresno Armenians suffered terrible discrimination. Signs saying "No Armenians Allowed" appeared in store windows and real estate offices. The Fresno community, nevertheless, expanded until the Depression when San Francisco and Los Angeles began to attract new immigrants. Until the 1960s the East Coast and the Midwest received the largest percentage of Armenian immigrants. As customary with other immigrant groups, the first two generations worked very hard to establish themselves in the new land. Some tried to assimilate as soon as possible, while others clung to their traditions. They saved money to bring their families over and to open small businesses. Their literacy and skills meant that they would move upward whenever possible. Discrimination, which was great in some places and at certain times, did not deter the Armenians, who had lived through much worse.

By the third generation American Armenians had produced numerous doctors, lawyers, engineers, and academics, as well as very successful entrepreneurs. Armenian politicians, sports figures, composers, actors, artists and authors such as Alan Hovhannes, Rouben Mamoulian, Arshile Gorky and William Saroyan created a sense of pride among the new generation of American Armenians. Successful Armenian businessmen like Alex Manoogian, Kirk Kerkorian, the Hovnanians, and others, donated millions for the establishment of community centers and schools.

In the 1970s and 1980s some 80,000 Armenians from Soviet Armenia, some of who had repatriated there in the late 1940s, taking advantage of détente and relaxed emigration laws created primarily for Russian Jews, came to the United States. In addition Armenians fleeing the civil war in Lebanon, the fundamentalist Islamic Revolution in Iran, and the Iran-Iraq War, relocated there as well. The 1988 earthquake and the deteriorating conditions in Armenia and in the former Soviet Union have brought thousands more to the United States. There are Armenian communities in every major state including Oregon, Seattle, Tennessee, Florida, Wisconsin, and Virginia. The great flood of Armenian immigrants in the last three decades, however, has preferred the West Coast, especially California. The greater Los Angeles area, in particular, is home to over 300,000 Armenians.

There are at present over 1 million Armenians in the United States. With well over 100 churches, numerous schools, associations, academic programs, cultural societies, magazines, newspapers, as well as influential organizations, the Armenians of the United States are a force to be reckoned with. Armenian political action committees, scholars, and professionals have succeeded in reversing Turkish efforts at denying the Armenian Genocide. They are also pressing the United States, a staunch supporter of Turkey, to officially recognize the Armenian Genocide

Canada

Among the Armenians who left the Ottoman Empire for the United States in the late nineteenth century, were a few who settled in Canada, mainly in the area of southern Ontario. Following the massacres of 1895-1896, more Armenians arrived in the region and by 1930 an Armenian church was built in St. Catherines. Other Armenians settled in the Quebec region. Most of the early arrivals were Protestant or Catholic Armenians. In 1908 Canada closed its borders to Armenians, who were classified as "Asiatics." Some refugees and orphans were allowed to get through after the Genocide, but the community did not exceed 4,000.

In 1948, thanks to the efforts of the Canadian-Armenian Congress, the ban was lifted and thousands began to arrive from war-torn Europe. Soon after the political upheavals in the Middle East brought thousands more arrived from Egypt, Lebanon, Syria, Palestine, and Iran. Armenians entered every major profession and the community became a force in the Canadian political and cultural life. Artists like the famous photographers Karsh and Cavouk, the filmmaker Atom Egoyan, and the Zoryan Institute represent the vibrant community which numbers over 55,000 residing mainly in Toronto and Montreal, with smaller groups in Calgary, Vancouver, Edmonton, Ottawa, and Kitchener. Sixteen churches, fourteen cultural centers, and seven schools serve the needs of this growing community.

THE FORMER SOVIET UNION

Russia

The Armenian presence in pre-Revolutionary Russia was discussed in chapters 16 and 19. Few Armenians—most of them military or government officials—had moved to Russia prior to 1960s. Most married Russian women and became Russified. Between 1960 and 1990, however, thousands of Armenian settled in Moscow, Leningrad (St. Petersburg), Irkutsk, Khabarovsk, Novossibirsk, Sochi, Saratov, Rostov-on-Don (New Nakhichevan) Krasnodar (Ekaterinograd), and other urban centers. Young Armenian professionals sought careers in diplomatic, military, economic, and scientific circles of the Russian Republic. The highly educated Armenians could and did compete for jobs in the main Republic of the Soviet Union. In addition to these, thousands of Armenians drifted to Moscow and Leningrad where, as illegal residents, they tried to make a living selling wares in the open markets, as well as the black market.

The fall of the Soviet Union caught many off guard. Russia granted citizenship to everyone who had lived legally in Russia prior to February 6, 1992. Although many Armenians took advantage of the law, thousands did not or could not. The terrible economic conditions in Armenia forced hundreds of thousands Armenians to seek jobs in Russia. It is difficult to estimate the number of permanent or temporary Armenian residents in Russia. Many sources claim that there are currently some 2 million or more Armenians in Russia. Moscow has more than 650,000; Rostov has 200,000, some 300,000 live in St. Petersburg, 100,000 in Sochi, 50,000 in Krasnodar, and the rest are in Siberia as well as the other urban centers of Russia. Given these statistics, there are as many Armenians in Russia as there are in the Armenian Republic. The large influx has rejuvenated the Armenian centers of the past. Armenian churches and other eighteenth-century buildings, which had been confiscated, closed or in ruin, are now restored and functioning in St. Petersburg, Moscow, and Rostov/New Nakhichevan. New churches have been built in Krasnodar and Sochi. Like in the past, the influential Armenian community of Russia continues to play a major role in maintaining the generally pro-Armenian policy of Russia.

Transcaucasia, Baltic States, Central Asia

The collapse of the Soviet Union left large ethnic blocs—including the Armenians—who found themselves in countries which were not their own. Armenians had enjoyed a comfortable life-style in the various republics of the USSR, especially in Uzbekistan, Azerbaijan, Georgia, Latvia, Lithuania, and Estonia (the Armenians of Russia and Ukraine were discussed above). New national policies openly excluded or politely discouraged anyone but local ethnic groups from participating in the political life of the new nations. Many Armenians were not granted citizenship in the new states. Although the Armenians, most of who were professionals, have managed to maintain their presence and their jobs in some regions, in other areas they have faced tremendous problems and, in some cases, death.

The terrible pogroms of the Armenians in Baku and Sumgait and the desecration of the Armenian church in Baku ended the Armenian presence in Azerbaijan, which had boasted the third largest Armenian community in the former USSR). The political upheavals and war in Georgia have greatly reduced the once large Armenian community, the second largest in the former USSR. Armenian newspapers, theaters and churches have become targets of periodic harassment.

The Baltic States of Estonia, Latvia, and Lithuania had attracted Armenian professionals and soldiers during the Soviet era. Estonia had some 2,000 Armenians before 1991. More arrived after the collapse of the USSR looking for jobs in the scientific sector. The Armenian community numbers some 3,000 and has recently leased an old Lutheran church to serve the spiritual needs of the community, almost all of who reside in the capital, Tallinn.

A number of Soviet Armenian soldiers had been posted to Latvia. They married and remained in the capital, Riga. More Armenians, attracted by the relative freedom of the Baltic States arrived there in the 1980s. Artists and technicians found Latvia a haven and the community grew slowly. More Armenians have arrived after independence and have begun small business ventures. An Armenian school and a church serve the 3,000 Armenians of Latvia.

The Armenians of Lithuania also came after World War II. They settled and married local women. Many more arrived after the earthquake of 1988 and the collapse of the Soviet Union. Despite major difficulties, most of which have involved legal residency status; the 3,000 Armenians reside in the capital of Vilnius.

The Armenian presence in Central Asia goes back to the era of the Silk Road. Tamerlane (Timur) forced Armenian artisans to Samarkand, most of who assimilated. By the end of the 19th century, there were some 5,000 Armenians in the region. Most were involved in trade, cotton growing, and mining. There were soon eight Armenian churches and a number of schools in Central Asia. The Russian revolution ended the prominence of the Armenians and destroyed all the churches. New Armenians began arriving in Central Asia during World War II, when they were evacuated from the warzone in Russia. Others were exiled there during the purges, but more arrived after 1956. By 1980 the highly educated Armenians enjoyed a very high living standard in the Muslim republics, especially in Uzbekistan. Armenians were employed in major positions within the government, the scientific community, and the tourist industry. Thousands of Armenians arrived in Uzbekistan from Azerbaijan and Karabagh in the late 1980s and throughout 1990s. The Armenian community, more than 40,000, has its base in Tashkent and Samarkand (with its Armenian church). Armenians are welcome in Uzbekistan and are employed as managers, engineers, doctors, lawyers, and judges.

23

Internal Conflicts
Diasporan Parties and Organizations
(1921-2003)

THE ESTABLISHMENT of Soviet Armenia resulted in bitter political divisions among the Armenian political parties, all of whom, except the Armenian Communist Party, established organizations outside the homeland. The Dashnaks, who were the most powerful diaspora party, made an all-out effort to assume the leadership outside Armenia. They rejected Soviet Armenia and continued to demand a free and independent Armenian state, one that encompassed the territory of historical Armenia. The Hnchaks generally supported the Soviet Union and refrained from making overt nationalistic statements. The Ramkavars, having no viable political platform, decided to accept the *status quo* in Armenia, and sought to preserve the Armenian identity in the diaspora through cultural activities.

After the Sovietization of Armenia, the Hnchaks and the Ramkavars accused the Dashnaks, especially their Central Bureau, of having ruled the Armenian Republic like a dictatorship. Dashnak policies and intractability, they asserted, not only had resulted in the loss of the Republic, but in the loss of additional territories to the Turks and Azeris. The Hnchaks and Ramkavars separated themselves from the history of the first Republic. They rejected the red, blue, and orange tricolor flag of the Republic as the emblem of the Dashnak party and accepted the flag of Soviet Armenia. At the same time, the Dashnaks claimed sole possession of the flag and the historical record of the first Republic. The Dashnaks accused the Hnchaks of being Bolshevik lackeys and the Ramkavars of being out of touch with the masses and the realities of Armenian history. They portrayed the Ramkavars as liberal businessmen who, ignoring the struggle for the independence of historic Armenia, concentrated their efforts on social and cultural activities geared to upper middle class Armenians.

A closer examination reveals that all sides ignored many facts in this polarization. Until the middle of 1920 the government of Armenia, except for top cabinet posts, included non-Dashnaks among its members. The tricolor was not a party flag but the symbol of the Republic. Realizing that Bolshevik ideology, as it was preached at the time, had no room for Armenian nationalism, the Dashnaks put all their hopes in the Allies and President Wilson. In addition, the Dashnaks believed that the Allies could and would enforce the Treaty of Sèvres, while the Bolsheviks, who were not party to the treaty and were negotiating with Turkish nationalists, would reject it. Their ultimate disappointment was one shared by all Armenians. On the other hand, the Hnchaks and, especially, the Ramkavars, rather than being out of touch, were simply pragmatic and created the possibility of a dialogue with the Bolsheviks which, at times, enabled the diaspora to provide crucial assistance to Soviet Armenia. In addition, the liberal yet cautious policies of the Ramkavars directed their middle class wealth to causes that culturally benefited the large Armenian diaspora.

The assassination of Archbishop Levon Tourian on December 24, 1933 in New York by members of the Dashnak party split the diaspora even further. Other developments, however, such as Moscow's invitation to diaspora Armenians to repatriate to Soviet Armenia and the Soviet efforts to regain Kars and Ardahan, encouraged unity. The repatriates, however, were not welcomed, and in fact, often exiled. Kars and Ardahan remained part of Turkey. The disappointing results of both of these endeavors and the ensuing Cold War once again split the diaspora along party lines. Armenian communities in the non-communist diaspora declared themselves either sympathetic to or opposed to Soviet Armenia. As the United States and its allies organized to limit the expansion of communism, they attracted, financed, and at times recruited national groups such as Armenians, Poles, Ukrainians, Croats, Latvians, Estonians, and Lithuanians.

The Dashnaks, despite their revolutionary and socialist background, and because of their opposition to the Soviet Armenian government, gained the trust of the West, while the West and their anticommunist allies suspected the Hnchaks. The Ramkavars were caught in the middle. They were accused by the Dashnaks of supporting Soviet Armenia and were, at times, suspected by the

American government. Defending their policy, the Ramkavars argued that their support of Soviet Armenia was based not on ideology but on patriotism and cultural ties to the fatherland. Although the Armenians in Eastern Europe and East Asia did not have to face this rift, the large and politically active Armenian communities in the Arab world, Iran, and North America were particularly affected by the post-war ideological conflict.

With the death of the Catholicos of the Holy See of Cilicia in 1952, the Dashnaks helped elect a candidate who favored their principles. When the Catholicos of Ejmiatsin, influenced by Soviet Armenian officials and the anti-Dashnak parties in the diaspora, refused to recognize the election, the Church split as well. This ecclesiastical division polarized the diaspora communities even further. Armenian groups fought, betrayed, and occasionally killed each other in Iran in 1953 and Lebanon in 1958, with the Armenian Hnchaks and communists supporting the anti-Shah and anti-Maronite factions, and the Dashnaks joining the pro-Western coalitions. The Cilician See, meanwhile, began to extend its jurisdiction beyond Lebanon, Syria, and Cyprus and founded separate prelacies in communities where the Dashnaks had gathered support, especially, in Iran, Greece, Canada, and the United States.

Although weak politically, the Ramkavars, by 1960 had managed to gain major positions at the Armenian General Benevolent Union (AGBU) and its worldwide network of schools. Their contacts with Soviet Armenia also gave them a major voice in those diaspora churches that were controlled by Ejmiatsin.

By the mid-1960s the Armenians had established themselves in every corner of the globe and the ideological differences, although great, were no longer the only cause of concern. Secure and accepted by their host countries, other issues occupied the communities, particularly, the fear of assimilation and frustration with the Turkish denial of the Armenian Genocide. Armenians in the Muslim world found it relatively easy to maintain their culture, but in the Christian world, especially in Europe and North America, Armenians were intermarrying in large numbers, a phenomenon which some referred to as the "White Massacre." Armenians in America, in particular, considered themselves Americans and had no desire to repatriate to Armenia, even a free one. They had changed from being Armenian to feeling Armenian. Traditional Armenian values were being challenged throughout the diaspora as well. Divorce rates were on the increase and the young were not interested in traditions that they viewed as foreign. Like most Jews prior to the creation of modern Israel, the Armenians began to see the diaspora as a permanent situation. The Soviet Union appeared there to stay and the United Nations was not going to reopen the Armenian Question; worst of all, the Turkish government maintained its silence or outright denial of the atrocities perpetrated against the Armenians. However, in 1965, on the 50th anniversary of the Genocide and again following the 1988 earthquake most Armenians in the diaspora set aside the divisions of the past and political and church factions began to cooperate informally.

Independence caught the diaspora Armenians, especially their political parties, off guard. Uncertainties and debates soon followed the initial euphoria. With an independent Republic the entire role of the diaspora had to be reexamined. Although some immediately rushed to support the new Republic with all their financial resources, others complained that such efforts were draining funds and were detrimental to important projects and activities in the diaspora. The churches connected with the Cilician See had now to justify their continued existence and pressures for an ecclesiastical union began to surface. Finally, the very existence of diasporan political parties became superfluous. The Dashnaks, the largest and most active, and the Hnchaks, the smallest and least active party in the diaspora, were especially at a loss. With the demise of the Soviet system, the latter party had lost credibility, but since its membership had become almost hereditary, they continued their political activities. The former, however, had a serious dilemma. For seventy years the raison d'être of the Dashnak party had been the attainment of a free, non-communist Armenia. Armenia was finally free, but it was not the Dashnaks who had accomplished that task.

The Ramkavars and the Hnchaks soon fell in line with the new government in Armenia. The politically active Dashnaks felt slighted. After seventy years of effort, they wished to be embraced by the new Armenian State and be given positions of importance in the government. Having received a very small vote in the 1991 election (see chapter 24), the Dashnaks began to oppose the government. They criticized Armenia's efforts in Karabagh and its non-belligerent tone toward Turkey. The party, soon banned in Armenia, continued its attacks in their press. Armenian economic and political woes and mistakes gave the Dashnaks ample fuel to rebuke Armenia. The ban was lifted several years later and the Dashnaks have since toned down their criticisms (see chapter 24).

Since none of the diasporan political parties have any significant influence in Armenia, all three have continued to function in the diaspora. This is a unique occurrence and to many, illogical, given the existence of a free and independent Armenia. Such action has caused some members to leave the parties or to split from what they see as a fossilized leadership that refuses to give up power. That part of the Armenian Church in the diaspora, which is led by the Catholicosate of the Great House of Cilicia in Antelias, Lebanon, has also maintained what it considers its historic separate status. The Armenian Patriarchs of Jerusalem and Istanbul have, at times, also refused to fully cooperate with Ejmiatsin.

As with all national institutions existing abroad, the diasporan parties have never relied on public elections. Their leaders are elected by relatively small inner circles and do not have to answer to a larger constituency. The Armenian press in the diaspora, with few exceptions, is also financed by the three political organizations and follows party lines. Ironically, the diasporan parties and press are very similar to the defunct Soviet system and do not know how to function in a democracy. One hopes that one does not have to wait for another calamity to finally witness the unification of Armenian political and religious institutions.

The Armenian General Benevolent Union

As noted, Egypt, with its strong Armenian community, was the guiding head of the Armenians in the Arab world. At the start of the twentieth century the Egyptian Armenians found a new leader, Boghos Nubar, the son of Nubar Pasha. Boghos had studied agriculture and engineering in Switzerland and France. Upon his return, he had served as the director of the Egyptian railways and had supervised the government's irrigation plan for the Sudan. He had become a banker and corporate officer in a number of companies and, like his father, was granted the title of pasha.

The massacres of the Armenians in 1895-1896 in Turkey and especially the Armeno-Azeri clashes in Transcaucasia, beginning in 1905, had a sobering effect on the Armenian middle class of Egypt. Liberals and disenchanted socialists felt that there was a need for a worldwide Armenian philanthropic organization. On Easter day (April 15), 1906, ten Armenian professionals met at Boghos Nubar's mansion in Cairo and drafted the by-laws of the Armenian General Benevolent Union.

Although initially there were some plans for the AGBU to also act as a political assembly, the idea was immediately abandoned. The AGBU's mission was to help the Armenians in historic Armenia by establishing or subsidizing schools, libraries, workshops, hospitals, and orphanages. It was to provide the peasants with land, seeds, animals, and tools and to assist in time of fire, famine, earthquakes, and other natural or man-made disasters. The aid was for all Armenians, regardless of religious or political affiliation. By 1913 the AGBU had 142 chapters in Europe, America, Africa, and the Ottoman Empire. During the Genocide it lost all of its eighty chapters in Ottoman Turkey. The first decade after the First World War was spent locating orphans and creating orphanages and hospitals. Refugees had to be sheltered and when the Near East Relief withdrew from Arab lands, the AGBU and other Armenian organizations replaced it. As the Bolsheviks consolidated their power in Armenia, it became increasingly difficult for outside organizations to work there, and although the AGBU managed to help Armenia, it now concentrated its philanthropy in the diaspora.

At the end of the British protectorate of Egypt in 1922 the AGBU headquarters first moved to Paris and, after the World War II, to the United States, where it grew considerably. It has now more than two-dozen schools, as well as chapters in Argentina, Australia, Austria, Belgium, Brazil, Cyprus, Bulgaria, Canada, Egypt, England, Ethiopia, France, Greece, Holland, Iran, Italy, Lebanon, Switzerland, Syria, Uruguay and over twenty chapters in the United States.

Ramkavar party members, as noted, managed to gain several top positions in the organization and began diverting the AGBU toward their political agenda. Despite the fact that the Ramkavar leadership transformed the AGBU into a large grass root organization that served many Armenians, the Union, by the 1980s had lost much of its bipartisan goals, was viewed by many as a Ramkavar organization, and was attacked by the Dashnaks. The terrible earthquake in Armenia and its economic woes after independence reawakened the AGBU to its original mandate. Most of the top leaders were replaced and the new board tried, although not completely, to distance itself from the Ramkavar Party. The AGBU has become one of the most important organizations in rebuilding Armenia. With an annual budget of over 30 million dollars, the AGBU sponsors numerous activities, including the American University of Armenia, the Armenian Philharmonic, soup kitchens, scholarships, hospitals, and a variety of other charitable and industrial projects.

Literary Activity in the Diaspora

The Armenian Genocide, as we have seen, wiped out almost the entire cadre of Armenian intellectuals in Turkey. What had taken a century to develop was destroyed in a month. A small group managed to survive, however, and, according to one expert, formed a transition literary generation. France and the Middle East became the new home of western Armenian literature. By 1930 a group of young men such as Shahnur, Topalian, Shushanian, Beshiktashlian, Aharon, Sarafian, and Nartuni created a new circle in Paris and published the review *Menk*. Their poems, short stories, novels, and essays did not dwell on the past and predicted a bright future. World War II, however, soon ended this short-lived revival. A number of writers, such as Shant, Oshagan and Tekeyan chose the Middle East as their new home. Shant wrote romantic plays and became an educator. Oshagan returned to Constantinople in 1920 (still under European supervision) and together with Tekeyan, Zarian and others, issued a literary manifesto and started the literary journals *Bartsravank*, *Mehyan*, and the newspaper *Chatakamart* with the goal of reviving Armenian literary activities. In 1922 the Turkish nationalists took control of Constantinople and the circle was disbanded. Tekeyan and Oshagan left Turkey and traveled in Europe, and eventually settled in the Middle East. Tekeyan settled in Cairo and Oshagan in Jerusalem. Tekeyan's works analyzed modern Armenian literature, while Oshagan's writings, according to one scholar, were really literary responses to the catastrophe of the Genocide. They and others had their works printed in various journals in Beirut (*Ahekan*, *Akos*), Aleppo (*Nayiri*), Boston (*Hayrenik*), and New York (*Nor Gir*). A number of Western Armenian authors, such as Yesayan, Totovents, and Mahari immigrated to or sought refuge in Soviet Armenia. The first two lost their lives during the Stalin purges of the 1930s (which also took the lives of Charents and Bakunts) and the latter died as a result of severe criticism and persecution. Lacking public and state support, Western Armenian literary output has been minimal. Soviet Armenian restrictions on diaspora literature did not helped matters either. Whether the current freedom in Armenia will spark a literary revival in the diaspora remains to be seen.

24

The Growing Pains of Independence
The Third Armenian Republic
(1991-2003)

THE ELECTION campaign in the newly formed Republic of Armenia was peaceful but was marked by heated debate. Levon Ter Petrosian's vision of an independent Armenia did not not coincide with that of some of his countrymen, who vehemently disagreed with his policies on the many critical issues facing the country particularly his willingness to come to some sort of a compromise on Karabagh. A number of former Karabagh Committee members resigned from the government, left the Armenian National Movement, formed separate factions, or declared their own candidacy for the presidency. An earlier dissident party, the National Self-Determination Union and its leader, Paruir Hairikian, stated that Armenia had to cut all its ties with the Soviet Union after the upcoming election.

The 1991 election in Armenia was also of vital importance to the future of the Armenian political parties in the diaspora. To demonstrate their viability, all three diaspora parties immediately registered for the upcoming presidential elections. The Ramkavars, who had always cooperated with the government in Armenia, endorsed the candidacy of Levon Ter Petrosian. The Hnchaks, desperate to have a voice in the new government, backed Ter Petrosian as well. The Dashnaks, basically agreed with Hairikian's platform, but in a calculated move, presented their own candidate, the venerable actor Sos Sargisian.

On October 16, 1991 barely a month after independence, Armenians went to the polls. Levon Ter Petrosian, representing the Armenian National Movement (ANM), won 83 percent of the vote. The other candidates had a poor showing indeed, with the National

Self-Determination Union and Dashnak candidates together managing only 12 percent (with the Dashnaks getting only 4.4 percent of the vote), and the various other parties and individuals totaling 5 percent. Neither the Dashnaks nor the communists could accept their defeat, and ironically, found common cause against Levon Ter Petrosian's government. The former had lost its preeminence and the latter its privileges. Receiving a clear mandate did not mean that the government of Levon Ter Petrosian would be free from internal or external pressures. The major internal problem was the virtual blockade of Armenia by Azerbaijan and the plight of the hundreds of thousands of Armenian refugees from Azerbaijan and the earthquake zone. Other domestic issues involved the implementation of free market reforms, the establishment of democratic governmental structures, and the privatization of land. The external concerns involved future relations with Russia, Turkey, Georgia, and Iran. In addition, Gorbachev's post-coup efforts to maintain a restructured Soviet Union meant that the West would not recognize the new Republic right away. The immediate concern, however, was the conflict with Azerbaijan over Mountainous Karabagh and the political uncertainties in Georgia, which contained 400,000 Armenians. In some ways the scenario of 1918 was repeating itself.

Meanwhile, Gorbachev continued to support Azerbaijan in order to pressure Armenia to join his new union. Ter Petrosian's first job was to calm Moscow's concern about future Armenian relations with Russia. A day after the elections, faced with numerous Azeri attacks on Karabagh and Armenia, he signaled his willingness to come to some understanding with Moscow. Still refusing to join a political union, Armenia nevertheless signed the economic treaty, which created a free trade zone and an agreement to coordinate food, industrial, and energy supplies. Gorbachev had gained some leverage and, in exchange, offered to mediate a cease-fire in Karabagh. Azerbaijan, advancing on all fronts in Karabagh and assured that Armenia and Karabagh would soon come to their knees, refused to accept the invitation. Ter Petrosian had scored a political victory, however. He had indicated that, despite its independence, Armenia was not severing its ties to Moscow. He also demonstrated to the West, and to many Armenians in the diaspora, that his government was not impulsive, but was willing to move cautiously and gradually towards resolving conflict.

Ter Petrosian's next step was to assure Turkey that Armenia had no territorial claims against it and that it desired neighborly diplomatic and economic relations. The same message was sent to Georgia, Iran, and Azerbaijan. Rather than espousing an ideologically dogmatic and biased outlook, Armenia was to have a pragmatic and flexible foreign policy. As far as Karabagh was concerned, Armenia once again reiterated that the conflict was not between Armenia and Azerbaijan, but between the Armenian enclave of Mountainous Karabagh and Baku. It was a question of human rights and self-determination, which had to be resolved by direct communication.

In the long run, Armenian efforts to establish political and economic relations with Turkey did not materialize. The Turks not only maintained their blockade of Armenia but also insisted that the issue of Karabagh had to be resolved before anything else could be discussed. The Azeri blockade had resulted in food and fuel shortages and, since 1989, had virtually halted supplies for earthquake reconstruction. The closing down of the Medzamor Nuclear Energy Plant in 1989 meant that Armenian citizens, including the many refugees, would have to face another difficult winter. The political and economic situation in Russia and Georgia indicated that Armenia, aside from the trickle of foreign aid, had to rely mainly on its own efforts. Ter Petrosian's policy vis-à-vis Turkey was severely criticized by the Dashnaks, while the Hnchaks and communists criticized his lukewarm relations with Moscow.

Gorbachev still hoped to salvage the former USSR and proposed the creation of a Union of Sovereign States. He received a verbal agreement from the leaders of seven republics, which included Azerbaijan, but excluded Armenia, Georgia, the Baltic States, and, most importantly, Ukraine. Azerbaijan's president, Mutalibov, continued to cooperate with Gorbachev and received Russian military aid to squeeze Karabagh into submission. In early November 1991, Azerbaijan shut its gas pipelines into Armenia. At the same time Turkey became the first country to recognize the Republic of Azerbaijan. By the end of November, emboldened by its military and political successes, Azerbaijan's parliament, urged by its National Front, which had gained many supporters, abolished Karabagh's autonomous status and voted to take direct control of the enclave. The State Council in Moscow realized that such an action would not only force Ter Petrosian to abandon his moderate position, but would elicit a strong reaction from the European Parliament, which had been sympathetic to Armenia. Ignoring Gorbachev's idea of a buffer zone, the Russian State Council ordered Azerbaijan to repeal its decision. Mutalibov, who feared the National Front, urged the parliament to change its mind. Turkey, who did not want a renewed Russian presence in the region, also advised the National Front to back down and Iran offered to reconcile the two sides.

In the meantime, Georgia was also being punished for refusing Gorbachev's offer to join the Union of Sovereign States. Gamsakhurdia, the popular intellectual dissident, who had been jailed by the communists and who had become president of Georgia in spring 1991, faced major problems with the Muslim enclave of Southern Ossetia, which had declared its desire to join Northern Ossetia in the Russian Republic. Ossetia had begun its separatist movement in 1990 but had been admonished by Moscow, which counted Georgia among its union members. In 1991, a year later, however, independent Georgia's actions resulted in Russian military aid to the Ossetians, who began a war against Georgia. Gorbachev, who was discouraging the Armenian separatist movement in Karabagh, was encouraging the same type of movement in Southern Ossetia. Gamsakhurdia's extreme nationalism and heavy-handed rule did not help matters and actually antagonized other Muslim minorities, like the Abkhazians. Eventually his low regard for democratic principles sparked a rebellion by the National Guard, which, by the end of the year, had put Gamsakhurdia in a precarious position.

Events moved faster than anyone had predicted, however. Gorbachev's plan for the Union of Sovereign States never materialized. On December 1, 1991 Ukraine voted for independence and on December 8, the leaders of Russia, Ukraine, and Belarus set up a commonwealth which invited other former Soviet republics to join as independent states. Yeltsin had outmaneuvered Gorbachev. Armenia immediately announced that it would join the commonwealth and on December 21, together with eight other former republics, including Azerbaijan, formally applied to join the Commonwealth of Independent States (CIS). In March 1992 it officially became a member of the CIS. In May of that year Armenia had also joined the CIS Defense Treaty.

On December 25, 1991 Mikhail Gorbachev resigned as president and the Union of Soviet Socialist Republics was officially dissolved. On January 6, 1992, Nagorno-Karabakh declared its independence. The change in Russian leadership, not welcomed in Azerbaijan, was greeted with great enthusiasm in Armenia. Mutalibov was a hard-line communist, who was willing to obey Moscow's bidding as long as it kept him and his clique in power and supported Azerbaijan's efforts to destroy the Armenian movement in Karabagh. With Gorbachev's exit he joined the CIS and tried to ingratiate himself to Yeltsin, but his past actions, especially his support for the August coup and his treatment of ethnic Russians in Baku, made him unpopular.

The demise of the USSR once again forced Armenia out into the international arena. On March 2, 1992, Armenia was recognized as a sovereign state and became a member of the United Nations. Armenian diplomatic missions were hastily opened in countries where there was an Armenian community to give financial and practical aid to the new diplomats. Soon after, passports, stamps, and eventually a new currency were introduced. Street and place names were also changed. Although the refugee situation, food, medical, fuel shortages, the Azeri blockade, the civil unrest in Georgia, a hostile Turkey and the emergence of partisan politics, reminded many of the 1919-1920 era, there were significant differences. Russia, with all its problems, was not amidst a civil war. Armenia had a more organized and more representative government, was protected by the UN Charter, and had a better infrastructure than the first Republic.

With Gorbachev's exit, Russian troops were withdrawn from Karabagh. The Karabagh Armenians began to fight back and, a year later, had not only recaptured most of the enclave, but had taken Kelbajar, which was outside the region (see map 44). The Azerbaijan Popular Front, which, like the Armenian right, had advocated a total break with Russia, and had demanded closer ties with Turkey, began to gain new followers in the government. The Azerbaijani parliament refused to ratify the CIS treaty and forced Mutalibov's resignation. A caretaker government of National Front and communist ministers tried to govern until the new presidential elections in late spring. Two months later, however, the communist-dominated parliament, fearing the loss of power, voted to restore Mutalibov, who immediately declared a state of emergency and canceled the forthcoming elections. Riots by armed supporters of the National Front forced him to flee a day later and in early June, a leader of the National Front, Abulfez Elchibey, an academic, won the election and became the new president of Azerbaijan. His absolute refusal to join the CIS and his closeness to Turkey not only worried Russia, but Iran, as well.

Meanwhile, Gamsakhurdia could not contain the rebellion against him and, in early January 1992, fled Tbilisi. Eduard Shevardnadze, who had been the communist chief of Georgia for thirteen years (1972-1985), and who had later been part of Gorbachev's cabinet and foreign minister of the USSR, returned to Georgia. His refusal to join the CIS gave the Abkhazian minority an opportunity to declare that it wanted to join the CIS. Moscow, in order to reassert itself in the region and to halt Turkey's influence, gave some aid to the Abkhazians, who managed to resist the Georgians and repel the Georgian army. By fall 1993, Georgia had decided that it was prudent to join the CIS and to begin negotiations with Abkhazia.

In the meantime, Elchibey's nationalist policies and pro-Turkish attitudes had alienated not only Russia and Iran, but had initiated a separatist movement by the Lezgis and the Taleshis, the former, Sunnis and the latter, of Iranian stock. Armenia, as a member of CIS, could rely on Russia far more than Azerbaijan, which was not a member. By summer of 1993, the Armenians of Karabagh had taken over Shushi, as well as the entire corridor between Armenia and Karabagh (see map 44). The Azeri army and the opposition decided to remove Elchibey. At this juncture Heydar Aliyev, the former communist chief of Azerbaijan (1969-1987) and member of the Politburo in Gorbachev's time, took advantage of the situation. He had bided his time in Nakhichevan where he had established closer ties with Turkey. Two bridges were put across the Arax, connecting Nakhichevan to Turkey; the Turkish president had visited the region, had promised economic aid, and had warned Armenia not to attack Nakhichevan. By late summer Aliyev, favored by Moscow over Elchibey, was at the helm of the Republic and the democratically elected Elchibey had sought refuge in Nakhichevan. In early fall, Azerbaijan became a member of the CIS and by October 1993 Moscow was once again the main broker in the Caucasus. With Moscow's leverage in the Caucasus reinstated, Russia's role had changed to that of a mediator and big brother. Unlike in the past, however, it did not make any statements on territorial integrity of the ex-Soviet republics. It seemed that Moscow preferred the war of attrition.

Meanwhile, the severe blockade of Armenian continued. The GNP fell by 60 percent between 1991 and 1993. Fuel and gas were especially in short supply. The winter of 1992-1993, in particular, was very harsh. The nuclear plant of Medzamor remained shut and schools, offices, factories and hospitals had to close due to lack of heat and electricity. Many books and trees were sacrificed to keep warm. Aid from the United States, Europe, and the Armenian diaspora was of great assistance, but the mortality rate among children and the old was high. The birth rate fell as well. Better organization, foreign aid, as well fuel from Iran and Turkmenistan, alleviated the energy crisis and the problems of 1992-1993 did not reoccur.

By 1994 Armenia had done well on the diplomatic front and had established additional missions in Asia, Europe, and the Americas. A shaky cease-fire agreement was observed in Karabagh as well. The struggle in Karabagh had cost 20,000 lives but had managed to capture Aghdam and Fizuli (see map 44). A continuing problem facing the new state were some 300,000 refugees from the ethnic cleansing in Azerbaijan, the civil war in Georgia, and those who had lost their homes and belongings in the 1988 earthquake. The continued Azeri and Turkish blockade severely hampered any economic recovery; only imports from Russia, Iran and foreign aid kept the economy moving at a very slow pace. By the end of 1994 over 500,000 Armenians (some of them refuges from Georgia and Azerbaijan) had temporarily or permanently left for Russia or other regions of the former USSR, North America, Australia, and Europe.

In order to be eligible to receive loans from the International Monetary Fund, Armenia continued its policy of privatization. Expansion of price liberalization and the halting of state subsidies continued at a fast pace. In 1995 40% of the GDP was owned by the private sector. Prices for essential food items, however, had increased by 25%, the price of bread had risen eleven times, and the cost of electricity was six times higher.

Difficult economic conditions strengthened the opposition parties and created new coalitions by former members of the Armenian National Movement Party. The Communist Party of Armenia, the National Progress Organization, the Democratic Party of Armenia, the National Democratic Union, the National Self-Determination Movement, and the Armenian Revolutionary Federation accused the government of violating human rights. Physical attacks on and arrests of opposition leaders, as well as the banning of the Dashnak party and its newspapers added fuel to the accusations. Despite a 28 million dollar loan from the World Bank, the reconstruction of the earthquake zone moved at a snail's pace and 450,000 residents continued to live in temporary housing, six years after the devastating earthquake. The opposition parties united into the National Coalition Alliance and held a number of large anti-government rallies during 1995.

The situation in Karabagh, meanwhile, had improved greatly. Despite sporadic shelling of border villages by the Azeris, the cease-fire agreement of 1994 held and Armenian and Azeri leaders met in a number of meeting organized by the Organization on Security and Cooperation in Europe (OSCE) as well as Russia. The Armenian government despite its historical ties to Russia tried to run an independent course. Armenians feared that a major civil unrest in Russia would seriously affect landlocked Armenia. Yeltsin's problems in Chechnia and Georgia's problems with its Muslims and separatists kept Armenia alert. The Yerevan government was well aware of similar conditions that had finished off the first Armenian Republic. Sensing that US policy favored Turkey and Azerbaijan, Armenia cautiously made new overtures to Russia and signed an agreement allowing the Russian military to lease a base in Armenia for 25 years. Russian units were soon guarding the Armenian border with Turkey.

The two major events of 1995, however, were the reopening of the Medzamor Nuclear Plant and the election of a new Catholicos. Despite protests from environmentalists, the Medzamor plant began partial operations and supplied the much-needed electricity for the country. The frequent blackouts in Yerevan were finally over. In April 1995, Karekin II, Catholicos of the Great House of Cilicia was elected (took the name Karekin I) to replace the late Vazgen I as the 131st Catholicos of All Armenians. It was rumored that the government, led by President Ter Petrosian exerted tremendous pressure to have Karekin elected. The election was certainly a great coup for the ANM. The Cilician See controlled important diocese in the Middle East, and had a significant following in the large Armenian diaspora in Europe and the Americas. Calls for the union of the two Churches began immediately. Armenia was now an independent state and its Catholicos was the former leader of the opposing See. The Dashnaks and the communists were now portrayed or seen as forces of division, while the ANM became the advocate of unity and cooperation. The parliamentary elections of July 1995 kept the ANM in control. The new constitution of Armenia, which granted the president more power, was also approved by 68% of the voters. The opposition accused the government of fraud and election tampering. The government responded by arresting a number of opposition leaders and conducting searches in their headquarters. After five years in office, Ter Petrosian announced that he would be running for president once again in 1996. The GNP has grown at an average of six percent (and continued to do so until 1998), and the president took credit for it. He ran under the banner of the Republic bloc, which represented the ANM and a few smaller allied political groups, which included the Ramkavars. Six other candidates participated in the presidential election of September 1996. They represented the National Democratic Union, the Communist Party, the Union of National Unity, the Democratic Party of Armenia, the National Self-Determination Union, the Scientific-Industrial and Civic Union, and the Artsakh-Hayastan Movement.

Ter Petrosian's platform included the strengthening of democratic institutions, continued elimination of corruption and crime, the strengthening of the army and intelligence agencies, the acceleration of economic reforms with supplemental increases in wages and the creation of a national social security system. He also called for increasing cooperation with Russia, Georgia and Iran, as well as establishing more stable relations with Azerbaijan and Turkey. Most important, however, was his promise to find a compromise solution to the Karabagh conflict and to improve relations with the substantial Armenian diaspora throughout the world. He added that Armenians sincerely wished to end the long and costly Karabagh conflict, which had slowed down the economic recovery. Armenia was willing to give back all the territory it had captured outside Mountainous Karabagh, save the Lachin corridor, in exchange for serious guarantees and a special autonomous status for Karabagh.

By September the candidates from the Democratic Party and the National Self-Determination Union, as well as Artsakh-Hayastan Movement withdrew from the election and supported Vazgen Manoukian, the candidate of the National Democratic Union for president. The banned Dashnaks also fell in with Manoukian. Manoukian's platform called for the full independence of Karabagh, new parliamentary elections and a new constitution, which would give the legislative and judicial branches more power vis-à-vis the strong executive branch.

The election results gave Ter Petrosian a victory with 51 percent of the vote in his favor. Manoukian received 37 percent of the vote, while the communists had a surprising strong third finish. Once again the opposition accused the ruling party of massive frauds in the counting of the ballots. Foreign observers cited some irregularities but concluded that they did not significantly affect the outcome. Continued rallies, riots and some shootings resulted in arrests and the ban on all public gatherings for a short time. Ter Petrosian appointed a new cabinet headed by Armen Sarkissian and calm returned to Yerevan.

One of the important events of 1996 was the opening of the bridge spanning the Arax into Iran. Armenia had now a highway from Meghri to northern Iran, its second largest trading partner after Russia. Natural gas, textiles, and foodstuff began to arrive in larger quantities from Iran. Armenia opened more diplomatic missions in Europe and Asia and applied for membership to the World Trade Organization (WTO). Discussion with Azerbaijan resulted in an exchange of prisoners and talks with Turkey increased the possibility of opening a border between the two states. By 1997 Armenia, despite some criticism, was doing well. Armenia's human rights record was better than that of Azerbaijan or Georgia. Its economy grew slightly, privatization continued and inflation dropped dramatically to 20 percent. Unemployment was still a major problem and drug addiction and AIDS had increased. Nevertheless, according to a survey by the UNDP (United Nations Development Program), some 700,000 Armenians had left the country since its independence.

The resignation of Armen Sarkissian due to ill health was a blow for Ter Petrosian. Sarkissian was responsible for the rapprochement between the government and the opposition, as well as the diaspora leaders. The president of Karabagh, Robert Kocharian, was named the new Prime Minister of Armenia. Kocharian immediately met with the opposition leaders, including the Dashnaks, and promised a program of national unity. Meanwhile Armenia and Russia signed a bilateral treaty of close economic and military cooperation. At the same time, Armenia asked NATO to be included in its Partnership for Peace program.

Two issues dominated the second half of 1997. Lifting the ban on the Dashnaks and rumors that the government was prepared to give up Karabagh and make it subordinate to Azerbaijan. The plan forwarded by the OSCE's Minsk Group proposed the withdrawal of Armenian forces from Karabagh before talks on the final political status of the enclave. The refusal to disclose the details of the proposed peace plan for Karabagh only intensified the rumors. The so-called Karabagh party in the parliament, known as *Yerkrapah* (Defenders of the Land), were war veterans who had been elected to the parliament and who enjoyed the support of Vazgen Sargisian, the Minister of Defense. By January 1998 a major split occurred between Levon Ter Petrosian and members of his own cabinet over Karabagh. Prime Minister Kocharian, Defense Minister Vazgen Sargisian, and the Interior and National Security Minister Serge

Sargisian insisted that a confederation model was the only solution for the Karabagh conflict. Karabagh and Azerbaijan would enjoy equal status over the region. Other supporters of the president including Foreign Minister Arzoumanian soon resigned. The president, his family, and close associates were also accused of profiting from shady deals and corruption.

Meanwhile the economic crisis in Russia (1998) struck Armenia's largest trading partner and defense spending had risen to nine percent of the budget between 1993 and 1998. On 3 February 1998, Levon Ter Petrosian, fearing a total destabilization of the state, resigned. Robert Kocharian became acting president, pending new elections. Kocharian partially lifted the ban on the Dashnaks and its leaders supported his candidacy in the upcoming election. Kocharian also reversed Ter Petrosian's policy of preventing Armenians in the diaspora from holding dual citizenship. The now popular Demirjian, who led Soviet Armenia for 14 years, announced his candidacy as well. In November 1988, the OSCE proposed the creation of a "common state" that would nominally preserve Karabagh as a part of Azerbaijan but give it extensive powers of self-government. Azerbaijan rejected this plan.

Kocharian's platform was to strengthen industry, create more jobs, increase foreign investment and crack down on the black market and tax evasion. He promised to increase wages, reform the social security and pension systems and introduce free health care for the needy. Closer ties with Russia were advocated and the question of the Armenian Genocide was revived once more. The election results gave Kocharian over 38 percent of the vote, Demirjian received over 30 percent, Vazgen Manoukian of the National Democratic Union received 12 percent and the communist candidate 11 percent. Once again charges of irregularities were made, but the outside observers decided that although flawed it had not affected the overall election results. Since no candidate had received more than 50 percent a run-off election was scheduled in two weeks. The second round of elections gave Kocharian 60 percent and Demirjian 40 percent of the vote. The new president formed his cabinet under Prime Minister Armen Darbinian. The ban against the Dashnaks was completely lifted and Kocharian included them into the government. Soon after Kocharian attended the Black Sea Economic Cooperation Organization, which stressed the need for free trade and greater economic relations between member states, which included Turkey and Azerbaijan. By summer 1998 the economy had grown by 6.4 percent. Foreign investments, especially by Armenians from the diaspora, increased. The rumors of the betrayal of Karabagh were largely over and the rivalry between the political parties had subsided considerably.

By the end of 1998 a number of political murders, as well as accusations of elitism and rule by a small clique, had tarnished Kocharian. Manoukian and Demirjian added their criticism. Even the Dashnaks voiced their concern over the problems. Kocharian soon realized that he did not even control his original base of Karabagh. Arkady Ghukassian, his choice for the president of Karabagh, had little influence over his own parliament, which was controlled by Defense Minister Samvel Babayan. The parliamentary elections of May 1999 reshaped the balance of power. The Unity Coalition led by Vazgen Sargisian and the People's Party of Armenia led by Karen Demirjian won the elections and left Kocharian without any control over the parliamentary majority. Vazgen Sargisian, who became Prime Minster, removed Serge Sargisian, a Karabaghi, and the closest ally of Kocharian from his post of Minister of the Interior. Karen Demirjian, meanwhile, became the speaker of Parliament. Sargisian managed to help Ghukassian gain a firm control over Karabagh and start democratic reforms. Samvel Babayan lost his post as Defense Minister and became the chief of the army of Karabagh. Upon assuming control of the government, Sargisian immediately vowed to attack tax evasion, corruption, and the shadow economy. He also clashed with Kocharian over educational deferments granted students who were eligible for the draft. Aliyev and Kocharian now launched direct bilateral talks on Karabagh and a possible settlement began to emerge, wherein Karabagh would be *de facto* independent within Azerbaijan—a kind of common state. By September 1999 there was great hope in Armenia that the political conditions had finally stabilized and the economy was on a serious rebound. The only sad note was the death of Catholicos Karekin I and the disunity among the Armenian churchmen. The leaders from the diaspora did not wholly approve of the front-runner Archbishop Karekin Nersissian of Yerevan, who was favored by the Armenian government, as well as the Armenian population of Armenia and Russia. Most, however, felt that conditions demanded a Catholicos from the homeland and Karekin's efforts on behalf of his flock had brought much-needed aid.

As the delegates were busy voting for the new Catholicos, the optimism of many Armenians was shattered when on October 27, five terrorists entered the building of the National Assembly of Armenia and killed Vazgen Sargisian, Karen Demirjian, two deputy speakers, two ministers, and four deputies. Defense Minister Vagharshak Harutiunian emerged as a leader with a cool head. His firm and steady action prevented the army from removing the government. He also assured that the Armenian forces were on the alert against possible invasions from Turkey or Azerbaijan. He became a buffer between Kocharian and the generals. Soon after, he was instrumental in dismissing Babayan after the latter reportedly ordered an armed assault on Arkady Ghukassian, the president of Karabagh. In order to retain unity, as well as the integrity of the main parties, Kocharian appointed Aram Sargisian, the brother of the slain Vazgen as Prime Minister, and Stepan Demirjian, the son of the slain Karen, as the chairman of the People's Party. The talks with Aliyev on the status of Karabagh were postponed. Archbishop Karekin was elected the new Catholicos (became Karekin II) and his first official duty was to officiate at the funeral of the nine dead politicians.

The new millennium witnessed the worldwide celebration of the 1700th anniversary of Christianity in Armenia. A new cathedral, named after Gregory the Illuminator, was completed in time to coincide with the 10th anniversary of the Republic (September 23, 2001). Pope John Paul II visited Armenia and spoke about the "Great Crime" (the Genocide). The period also saw a number of European states acknowledging the Genocide. Kocharian's political fortunes, however, decreased and his government was accused of corruption on an unprecedented scale. Although the economy improved somewhat after 2001, the question of Karabagh was still unresolved and emigration, albeit at a slower pace, continued unabated. Meanwhile, democratic, constitutional, economic, and legal reforms were urgently needed to attract foreign capital. Kocharian tried to regain the trust of the public by halting emigration, and stemming corruption and nepotism. Meanwhile, Stepan Demirjian and other candidates voiced their willingness to challenge Kocharian in the next presidential election. The election of 2003 was marred by irregularities, arrests, and killings. It handed Kocharian another term and resulted in major protests throughout Yerevan.

Present-day Armenia (see map 45), twelve years after independence, is like a ship amidst a storm. Sources estimate that another 500,000 people have left the country. Altogether over one million Armenians have left their homeland. Some claim that there are now more Armenians living in Russia than in Armenia. The population is estimated to be barely over 2 million. The present government's main objective has been to ensure the integrity of the state against Azeri or Turkish attacks. Armenia is especially concerned about the pressure, which the American and European oil companies are exerting on their governments to back Azeri demands in Karabagh. Rumors of a possible swap of the Lachin corridor for a similar corridor in Meghri to connect Azerbaijan to Nakhichevan and Turkey have unsettled the Armenians in Armenia and the diaspora. Such a plan would be suicidal, for it would not only close the only Armenian connection to a friendly state, but would connect Turkey to all the Turkic peoples in the Caucasus and Central Asia. The United States, Europe, and the United Nations are ignoring the fact that Nakhichevan and Karabagh were always a part of Armenia. They also forget the Treaty of Sèvres (1920) and ignore the fact that the Treaties of Moscow and Kars (1921), which separated Mt. Ararat, Kars, Ani, and Ardahan from Armenia, were basically illegal. Armenia and Russia are too weak, and have to rely on American and European aid. Recent American pronouncements in support of Azerbaijan and the various Turkic regimes in Central Asia, following the terrorist attacks of September 11, 2001, are additional sources of apprehension. The recent coup in Georgia, the death of Aliyev, and US treats to Syria and Iran are also causes for concern. The West, as in the post-World War I period, may once again abandon the Armenians. This explains Armenia's heavy reliance on Russia, the employment of Russian defense units, and the purchase of MiG-29s. It also illustrates the need for a military pact with Greece and friendly relations with China, Iran, Syria, and the former Iraqi government, the last three all Turkey's neighbors.

Armenia is a small, landlocked, resource-poor country, surrounded by a number of hostile and powerful neighbors. Its only assets are the entrepreneurial spirit of its people, their high level of education, the promising talent of its scientists, and its diverse and prosperous diaspora. Armenia will emerge from its current situation by building formidable defenses (maybe even nuclear weapons, modeled after Israel), a viable economy, and by establishing a state perceived as the legitimate guarantor of the rights and duties of its people. Much remains to be done. One hopes that history has taught Armenia and its people that vigilance, moderation, and caution must replace blind faith and dogma.

Plates

IRAN & OTTOMAN EMPIRE	WESTERN/CENTRAL EUROPE	RUSSIA & EASTERN EUROPE	SOUTH & EAST ASIA	AFRICA & THE AMERICAS
Bayazid I (1481-1512)	High Renaissance in Italy (ca. 1500-1530)	Basil II (1504-1533)	Ming Dynasty continues in China (to 1644)	Songhai Empire continues in the Sudan (to 1591)
Isma'il I (1501-1524) est. Safavid Dynasty	Henry VIII (1509-1547)	Sigismund I (1506-1548)	Portuguese trade monopoly in East Asia (1500-1600)	Slave Trade (ca. 1500-1870) Eleven million Africans brought to the New World
Shi'ism state religion in Iran (ca. 1510)	Francis I (1515-1547)	Pskov conquered (1510)		
Selim I (1512-1520)	Concordat of Bologna (1516)	Smolensk conquered ((1514)	Portuguese in Goa (1510)	
Battle of Chaldiran (1514)	Charles V (1519-1556)	Battle of Mohacs (1526)	Malacca falls to Portuguese (1511)	Portugal in East Africa (1500-1600)
Ottoman and Safavid wars in Armenia, deportation and scorched-earth policy (1514-1590)	Church of England (1534) Luther's 95 Theses (1517) Loyola est. Jesuits (1534)	First siege of Vienna (1529) Ivan IV (1533-1584) Sigismund II (1548-1571) Fall of Kazan (1552)	Babur founds Mughal Dynasty (1526) Christian missionaries active in Japan and China (1550-1650)	Balboa sights Pacific Ocean (1513) Magellan rounds South America (1520)
Ottomans conquer Syria & Egypt (1516-1517)	Council of Trent (1545-1563)	North Cape Route discovered (1553)		Cortez ends Aztec Empire (1521)
Suleiman I (1520-1566)	Schmalkaldic Wars (1546-1547)	Fall of Astrakhan (1556)	Akbar (1556-1605)	Pizarro ends Inca Empire (1533)
Tahmasb I (1524-1576)	Peace of Augsburg (1555)	Oprichnina founded (1565)	Portugal in Macao (1557)	Sa'idid Dynasty in Morocco (1554-1659)
Etchmiadzin sends mission to the West to liberate Armenia (1547-1562)	Philip II (1556-1598) Elizabeth I (1558-1603)	Union of Lublin (1569) Russian expansion to Siberia (1581-1598)	Spain occupies the Philippines (1564) Toyotomi Hideyoshi (1585-1598)	St. Augustine colony in North America (1565)
Peak of Ottoman power (ca. 1550)	St. Bartholomew's Day Massacre (1572)	Livonian War ends (1582)	Plague in China (1586-1589)	Islamic state of Kanem-Bornu in Central Sudan (1575-1846)
Selim II (1566-1574)	Adoption of Gregorian Calendar (1582)	Moscow becomes a patriarchate (1589)	Unification of Japan (1590)	
Battle of Lepanto (1571)	Spanish Armada (1588)	Uniate Church est. in Ukraine (1595)	China and Japan fight in Korea (1592-1598)	
Murad III (1574-1595)	Henry IV (1589-1610) est. Bourbon House	Boris Godunov (1598-1605)	Hideyoshi bans Christianity in Japan (1597)	
'Abbas I (1587-1629)	Gustavus Adolphus (1594-1632)	Times of Troubles (1598-1613)		
Iran relinquishes eastern Anatolia to the Ottomans (by 1590)	Edict of Nantes (1598)			

Table 11: 1500-1600

IRAN & OTTOMAN EMPIRE	WESTERN/CENTRAL EUROPE	RUSSIA & EASTERN EUROPE	SOUTH & EAST ASIA	AFRICA & THE AMERICAS
Ottoman power challenged (ca. 1600-1700)	Thirty Years' War (1618-48)	Romanov Dynasty est. (1613)	Battle of Sekigahara (1600)	British est. Jamestown (1607)
'Abbas' deportations of Armenians to Iran (1603-4)	Richelieu (1624-42)	Alexis (1645-76)	Dutch East India Co. (1602)	Champlain est. Quebec (1608)
New Julfa est. (1605)	Frederick William of Prussia (1640-88)	Revolt of Stenka Razin (1670-71)	Tokugawa Shogunate (1603-1867)	Mayflower lands at Plymouth (1620)
Murad IV (1623-49)	English Civil War (1642-49)	Armenians granted trade privileges in Russia (1667)	Jahangir (1605-27)	Dutch found New Amsterdam (1624)
Safi I (1629-42)	Louis XIV (1643-1715)	Church reforms by Nikon,	East India Co. (1609)	Portuguese in West Africa (ca. 1630)
Zuhab Treaty (1639)	Mazarin (1643-61)	Schism and the rise of Old	Shah Jahan (1627-58)	Montreal est. (1642)
'Abbas II (1642-66)	Peace of Westphalia (1648)	Believers (1667)	Korea under China (1627)	New England Confed. (1643)
Catholicos Hakob (1655-80)	Cromwell (1653-58)	Andrusovo Treaty (1667)	Dutch take Java (1628)	Dutch settle in Cape Town (1651)
Köprülü viziers (1656-91)	Colbert (1661-83)	Jan Sobieski (1674-96)	Japan expels Europeans (1637)	Portuguese take Brazil (1654)
Decline and fall of Safavid Dynasty (1666-1732)	Second siege of Vienna (1683)	2nd Battle of Mohacs (1687)	Dutch in Indonesia (1641)	British take Jamaica (1655)
Safi II (1666-94)	Edict of Nantes revoked (1685)	Peter the Great (1689-1725)	Manchus est. Ch'ing Dynasty (1644-1911)	Peter Stuyvesant surrenders New Amsterdam (New York) to Britain (1664)
Russo-Turkish War (1677-81)	War of the League of Augsburg (1688-97)	Treaty of Nerchinsk (1689)	Aurengzeb (1658-1707)	Westminster Treaty (1674)
Ahmad II (1691-95)	Glorious Revolution (1688)	Azov and Kamchatka taken (1696)	Britain gets Bombay (1661)	La Salle claims Louisiana for France (1682)
Hosein I (1694-1722)	Bill of Rights (1689)	Battle of Zenta (1697)	Aurengzeb bans Hinduism (1669)	
Russo-Turkish War (1695-6)	Charles XII (1697-1718)	Peter's first trip to Europe (1697-98)	Maratha state (1674-1750)	
Mustafa II (1695-1703)	Treaty of Ryswick (1697)	Streltsy revolt (1698)	Dutch in Canton (1683)	
Karlowitz Treaty (1699)			British est. Calcutta (1690)	

Table 12: 1600-1700

IRAN & OTTOMAN EMPIRE	WESTERN & CENTRAL EUROPE	RUSSIA & EASTERN EUROPE	SOUTH & EAST ASIA	AFRICA & THE AMERICAS
Decline of Ottoman Empire (ca. 1700-1800)	War of the Spanish Succession (1701-13)	Battle of Narva (1700) St. Petersburg founded (1703)	Decline of Mughals (ca. 1700-1800)	Rise of Ashanti Empire on Gold Coast (ca. 1700-50)
Russo-Turkish War (1710-11) Passarowitz Treaty (1718)	British take Gibraltar (1704) England & Scot. Union to form Great Britain (1707)	Great Northern War (1709-21) Battle of Poltava (1709)	Mohammad Shah (1719-48) China controls Tibet (1720) Treaty of Kyakhta (1727)	Benjamin Franklin (1706-90) German immigration to North America begins (1709)
Fall of Isfahan (1722) Russo-Iranian War (1722-23) Armenians of Karabagh led by David Beg resist Ottoman attacks (1724-34)	Peace of Utrecht (1713) Rise of Prussia under King Frederick William I (1713-40)	Death of Ori (1711) St. Petersburg capital of Russia (1713) Peter's second trip to Europe (1716)	Ch'ien Lung (1736-96) Sack of Delhi by Nader Shah (1739)	John Paul Jones (1747-92) French-Indian War (1756-63) British take Quebec (1759) End of Funj Sultanate in eastern Sudan (1762)
Turko-Iranian War (1734-35) Treaty of Rasht (1732) Catholicos Abraham Kretatsi (1734-37)	Louis XV (1715-74) Walpole P. M. of Britain (1720-43) War of the Austrian Succession (1740-48)	Peace of Nystad (1721) Holy Synod est. (1721) Russo-Turkish accord (1724) Anna (1730-40)	Ahmad Shah Durrani of Afghanistan (1747-73) Battle of Plassey (1757) Clive gov. of Bengal (1758) China occupies eastern Turkestan (1758)	Stamp Act (1765)
Treaty of Ganja (1735) Nader Shah Afshar (1736-47) Russo-Turkish War (1736-9) Belgrade Treaty (1739)	Frederick the Great (1740-86) Maria Theresa (1740-80) Maria Theresa accepts crown of Hungary (1741)	War of the Polish Succession (1733-35) Bering Straits discov. (1741) Elizabeth (1741-62)	English oust French from India (1761) British take Madras (1766) First Mysore War (1767-69)	Mason-Dixon Line drawn (1766) Boston Tea Party (1773) American War of Indep. (1775-83)
Turko-Iranian treaty (1747) Karim Khan Zand (1750-79) Catholicos Simeon (1763-80) Russo-Turkish War (1768-74) Küchük Kainarja Treaty (1774)	Seven Years' War (1756-63) George III (1760-1820) Peace of Paris (1763) Louis XVI (1774-92)	Russo-Austrian accord (1746) Catherine the Great (1762-96) First partition of Poland (1772)	W. Hastings in India (1772-85) Ram Mohan Roy (1772-1833) Maratha War (1779-82) Second Mysore War (1780-84)	Declaration of Independence (1776)
Aqa Mohammad Qajar (1779-97)	Joseph II (1780-90) Pitt the Younger, P. M. of Britain (1783-1801)	Pugachev revolt (1772-74) Cossacks submit (1775) Crimea annexed (1783)	Cornwallis Gov.-Gen. of India (1786-93) White Lotus Rebellion (1789)	US Constitution (1789) Washington president (1789-97)
Catholicos Ghukas (1780-99) Russo-Turkish War (1787-92) Treaty of Jassy (1792) Selim III (1789-1807)	French Revolution (1789-91) France a republic (1792) Reign of Terror (1793-94) The Directorate (1795-99)	Russo-Swedish War (1787-90) Second partition of Poland (1793)	Third Mysore War (1790-92) Hyderabad Treaty (1798) Wellesley Gov.-Gen. of India (1798-1805)	Canada Constitution (1791) Bill of Rights (1791) San Lorenzo Treaty (1795)
Sack of Tiflis (1795) Fath 'Ali Shah (1797-1834) French in Egypt (1798)	Napoleon's Consulate (1799)	Third partition of Poland (1795) Paul (1796-1801)	Kingdom of Mysore loses its sovereignty (1799)	Adams president (1797-1801)

Table 13: 1700-1800

IRAN & OTTOMAN EMPIRE	WESTERN & CENTRAL EUROPE	RUSSIA & EASTERN EUROPE	SOUTH & EAST ASIA	AFRICA & THE AMERICAS
Decline of Ottoman Empire accelerates (ca. 1800-1912)	Napoleon emperor (1804)	Annexation of Georgia (1801)	East India Co. in Singapore (1819)	Washington D.C. capital (1800)
Catholicos Arghutian (1800)	Tilsit Treaty (1807)	Alexander I (1801-25)	British take Burma (1824-26)	Jefferson president (1801-9)
Catholicos David (1801-7)	Napoleon abdicates (1814)	First Russo-Iranian War (1804-1813)	British take Mysore (1830)	Louisiana Purchase (1803)
Catholicos Daniel (1801-9)	Congress of Vienna (1814-15)	Gulistan Treaty (1813)	First Opium War (1839-42)	Slave importation prohibited (1808)
Muhammad 'Ali (1804-48)	Holy Alliance (1815)	Serbs gain partial autonomy (1817)	Hong Kong taken (1841)	Madison president (1809-17)
Hosein Qoli Khan (1807-27)	Metternich System (1815-48)	Nicholas I (1825-55)	Treaty of Nanking (1842)	Revolts against Spain in Latin America (1810-25)
Mahmud II (1808-39)	Troppau Confer. (1820-21)	Decembrist revolt (1825)	Treaty of Lahore (1846)	Treaty of Ghent (1814)
Catholicos Yeprem (1809-31)	Louis Philippe (1830-48)	Anglo-Russ. Treaty (1825)	Perry in Japan (1854)	Monroe president (1817-25)
End of Janissaries (1826)	Victoria (1837-1901)	Second Russo-Iranian War (1826-1828)	Treaty of Peshawar (1855)	Monroe Doctrine (1823)
Unkiar Skelessi Treaty (1833)	Communist Manifesto (1848)	Turkmenchai Treaty (1828)	Sepoy Mutiny (1857-58)	Adams president (1825-29)
Al-Afghani (1839-97)	Revolutions of 1848-49	Armenian Province (1828-40)	The British Raj (1858-1947)	Jackson president (1829-37)
Abdul-Mejid I (1839-61)	Franz Joseph I (1848-1916)	Russo-Turkish War (1828-29)	Treaty of Tientsin (1858)	Death of Bolivar (1830)
Tanzimat Era (1839-76)	Napoleon III (1852-70)	Adrianople Treaty (1829)	Treaty of Peking (1860)	Alamo (1836)
Straits Convention (1841)	Unification of Italy (1859-70)	Greece independ. (1829)	Shogunate ends (1868)	Van Buren president (1837-41)
Catholicos Nerses (1843-57)	Bismarck in power (1862-90)	Romania autonomous (1829)	Gandhi (1869-1948)	W. Harrison president (1841)
Nasr ad-Din Shah (1848-96)	First Socialist International (1864-1871)	Serbia autonomous (1830)	Compulsory military service in Japan (1872)	Tyler president (1841-45)
Anglo-Iranian War (1856-57)	Unification of Germany (1866-71)	Vorontsov viceroy of the Caucasus (1845-54)	Famine in Bengal (1873)	Polk president (1845-49)
Isma'il Pasha (1863-79)	Franco-Prussian War (1870-71)	Crimean War (1853-56)	Korea indep. (1876)	Liberia indep. (1847)
Young Ottomans formed (1865)	Vatican state est. (1871)	Alexander II (1855-81)	First Kaffir War (1877)	Taylor president (1849-50)
Suez Canal opens (1869)	Paris Commune (1871)	Peace of Paris (1856)	Satsuma revolt stopped (1877)	Fillmore president (1850-53)
Patriarch Khrimian (1869-73)	Third Republic (1871-1914)	Herzen's "Bell" (1857-1867)	Victoria procl. Empress of India (1877)	Pierce president (1853-57)
	Second Disraeli ministry (1874-1880)	Emancipation of serfs (1861)	Gandamak Treaty (1879)	Buchanan president (1857-61)
British control Suez (1875)	Second Gladstone ministry (1880-1885)	Sale of Alaska (1867)	First Indian National Congress meets (1886)	Lincoln president (1861-65)
Ottoman Constitution (1876)		Three Emperors' League (1872)		Civil War (1861-65)
Abdul-Hamid II (1876-1909)		Russo-Turkish War (1877-78)		

Table 14: 1800-1918

British occupy Egypt (1882)	Parnell imprisoned (1881-82)	San Stefano Treaty (1878)	French in Indochina (1887-1954)	Emancipation Proclamation 1863
Armenakan party formed in Van (1885)	Congress on Africa (1884)	Populist movt. (1878-1884)	First general election in Japan (1890)	Gettysburg Address (1863)
Young Turks formed in Geneva (1891)	Boulanger Affair (1887-89)	Berlin Congress (1878)		Arch. Maximillian (1863-67)
Catholicos Khrimian (1892-1907)	Kaiser William (1888-1918)	Bulgaria autonomous (1878)		Johnson president (1865-69)
Union and Progress formed (1895)	Second Socialist International (1889-1914)	Alexander III (1881-94)		13th Amendment (1865)
Armenian massacres (1895-96)	Suicide at Mayerling (1889)	Hnchak Party formed (1887)		Dominion of Canada (1867)
Patriarch Ormanian (1896-1908)	Irish Home Rule rejected by Lords (1893)	Dashnak Party formed (1890)		Grant president (1869-77)
Crete revolt (1905)	Empress Elizabeth assassinat. (1898)	S. Witte (1892-1903, 1905-6)		Porfirio Diaz (1877-1911)
AGBU formed (1906)	First Hague Peace Conf. (1899)	Franco-Russ. Treaty (1893)		Hayes president (1877-81)
Iranian Revolution (1906)	King Umberto I assassinated (1900)	Nicholas II (1894-1917)		Scramble for Africa (1880-1900)
Young Turks move to Salonika (1906)	King Alexander and Queen Draga assassinated (1903)	Socialist Rev. Party (1901)		Garfield president (1881)
Turkish Revolution (1908)	Russ. Social Democratic Party split into Bolshevik and Menshevik factions (1903)	Trans-Siberian railroad completed (1903)		C. Arthur president (1881-85)
Sahmanadir Ramkavar Party formed (1908)		Anti-Armenian measures (1903-1905)	Sino-Jap. War (1894)	Gordon killed by Mahdi in Khartoum (1885)
Armenians massacred in Cilicia (1909)	King Carlos I assass. (1908)	Russo-Jap. War (1904-5)	Port Arthur leased to Russia (1898)	Cleveland president(1885-89)
World War I (1914-1918)	Austria annexes Bosnia (1908)	Phleve assassinated (1904)	Britain leases Kowloon (1898)	B. Harrison president (1889-93)
Armenian Genocide(1915-22)	Arch. Ferdinand assassinated in Sarajevo (1914)	Revolution of 1905	Boxer Rebellion (1900-1901)	Cleveland president (1893-97)
Sykes-Picot plan (1916)	World War I (1914-1918)	Armeno-Azeri conflict (1905-7)	Commonwealth of Australia (1900)	Hawaii annexed by US (1893)
Arab revolt (1916-1917)		Vorontsov-Dashkov viceroy of Caucasus (1905-16)	Muslim League formed (1906)	Spanish-American War (1898)
Balfour Declaration (1917)		First Duma (1906)	"Open Door" agreement (1907)	Boer War (1899-1902)
		Anglo-Russ. Accord (1907)	Japan annexes Korea (1910)	Sudan Convention (1899)
			Chinese Republic (1911-49)	T. Roosevelt president (1901-1909)
		World War I (1914-1917)		Taft president (1909-13)
		February Rev. (1917)		Wilson president (1913-21)
		October Rev. (1917)		Panama Canal opens (1914)
				US enters WW I (1917)

Table 14: 1800-1918, *Continued*

TRANSCAUCASIA	RUSSIA	THE MUSLIM WORLD	EUROPE & THE UNITED STATES	AFRICA, ASIA, LATIN AMERICA
1918	**1918**	**1918**	**1918**	**1918**
Battle of Sardarabad	Bolsheviks dissolve Duma	Turkish armies collapse in Palestine	Wilson's 14 Points	Montagu's Report on Indian Constitutional Reform
Georgia, Armenia, Azerbaijan declare independence	Brest-Litovsk Treaty	Moudros Armistice	WW I ends	Mexico nationalizes oilfields
Batum Agreement	Capital moved to Moscow	Muhammad VI (to 1922)	Czechoslovakia, Poland, Austria, Yugoslavia formed	
Andranik in Zangezur	Red Army formed		**1919**	
Kachaznuni leads Arm. govt.	Japanese in Siberia		Armenian delegations in Paris	
Fall of Baku, Armenians massacred	Assassin. attempt on Lenin		Hoover heads US Relief	
Turks leave Transcaucasia, British land in Baku	Civil War (to 1920)		Prohibition Amendment	
1919	Tsar and family murdered	**1919**	Paris Peace Conference	**1919**
Famine in Armenia	Death of Plekhanov	King-Crane Commission	First League of Nations meets	Amritsar Massacre
Armenian delegation led by Aharonian leaves for Paris	First Constitution	Italians land in Anatolia	Mussolini founds Fascists	German African colonies fall to France & Britain
American relief arrives	**1919**	Greeks land in Asia Minor	Bela Kun's govt. in Hungary	Govt. of India Act passed
Armeno-Georgian territorial dispute	Third International (to 1943)	Mustafa Kemal defies Allies (to 1922)	Versailles Treaty	Rowlatt Act passed
Armeno-Azeri territorial dispute	Red Army takes Crimea	Wafd Party in Egypt	St. Germain Treaty	War with Afghanistan
Khatisian leads Arm. govt.	Red Army takes Ufa	Sa'ad Zaghlul deported	Curzon apptd. Foreign Sec.	Korea rebels against Japan
Harbord Commission	War with Finland (to 1920)	Turk. nationalist conferences in Erzerum and Sivas	Immigration curtailed in US	Death of Botha
1920	Red Army takes Omsk	French repress Arab nationa-lism in M. E. & N. Africa	Neuilly Treaty	Jan Smuts P.M. of South Africa (to 1924)
Armenia recognized	Red Army takes Kharkov	**1920**	Wilson leaves Paris	**1920**
Baku falls to Bolsheviks	Kolchak defeated	Allies occupy Constantinople	Stambuliski rules Bulgaria	Communist and nationalist movements in South Asia
Bolshevik demonstr. in Arm.	Denikin fights on	Provisional govt. in Ankara	US Senate considers joining League of Nations	
Ohanjanian leads Arm. govt.	Nationalization and foreign trade monopoly	Treaty of Sèvres	**1920**	Gandhi emerges as India's leader (to 1948)
Vratzian leads Arm. govt.	**1920**	Turks attack Armenia	US votes against League	
Bolsheviks in Yerevan	Odessa captured	Turko-Bolshevik accord	San Remo Conference	German colonies fall to Japan
Alexandropol Treaty	Denikin and Warngel defeated	Faisal king of Syria	Trianon Treaty	Civil War in China (to 1926)
	End of Civil War	French and British mandates	19th Amendment	
	War Communism (to 1921)		League moves to Geneva	
	Famine (to 1922)		Govt. of Ireland Act passed	
	War with Poland (to 1921)			
	Allied forces withdraw			

Table 15: 1918-1921

ARMENIA & THE USSR	THE MUSLIM WORLD	EUROPE	THE AMERICAS	AFRICA/ASIA/AUSTRALIA
Treaty of Moscow (1921)	Reza Khan's coup (1921)	German mark falls (1921)	Harding president (1921)	First Indian parliament (1921)
NEP (1921-1927)	Faisal I (1921-33)	Mussolini march on Rome (1922)	Teapot Dome scandal (1923)	US-Jap. Naval Agr. (1922)
Treaty of Kars (1921)	Palestine mandate (1922)	Irish Free State (1922)	Coolidge president (1923-29)	Gandhi jailed (1922)
Miasnikian (1921-25)	Turkish republic (1922)	Beer Hall Putsch (1923)	Pan-American Treaty (1924)	Earthquake in Japan (1923)
Anglo-Soviet trade (1921)	Abul-Mejid II (1922-24) as Caliph only	Zinoviev Letter scand. (1924)	Immigration Bill (1924)	Hertzog P.M. S. Africa (1924)
Rapallo Treaty (1922)	Lausanne Treaty (1923)	Locarno Confer. (1925)	FBI under J. Edgar Hoover (1924-72)	Hirohito emperor (1926-89)
USSR formed (1921)	Ankara capital (1923)	Pilsudski's coup (1926)	Inter-American Treaty of Arbitration (1929)	Parliament in Canberra (1927)
Death of Lenin (1924)	Transjordan indep. (1923)	German economic collapse (1927)	H. Hoover president (1929-33)	Chiang Kai-shek (1928-49)
Britain recog. USSR (1924)	Kemal president (1923-38)	Kellog-Briand Pact (1928)	Dunning tariff (1930)	Emp. Haile Selassie (1930-74)
Hovhannesian (1925-27)	Qajar dynasty ends (1924)	Lateran Treaty (1929)	Smoot-Hawley tariff (1930)	Jap. seize Manchuria (1931)
CPSU expels Trotsky (1927)	Caliphate abolished (1924)	Allied troops leave Rhineland (1930)	Veterans Compensation Act (1931)	Gandhi arrested (1932)
Stalin in power (1928-53)	Reza Shah Pahlavi (1925-41)	German banks closed (1931)	Stimson Doctrine (1932)	Japan withdraws from League of Nations (1933)
Hovsepian (1928)	Ibn-Saud (1926-1953)	Gömbös in Hungary (1932)	Federal Reserve est. (1932)	Philippines indep. (1933)
First 5-Year Plan (1928)	Republic of Lebanon (1926)	Hitler chancellor (1933)	U.S. RFC est. (1932)	Washington treaties renoun. by Japan (1934)
Trotsky leaves USSR (1929)	Turkey adopts Latin alphabet and secular state (1928)	Reichstag fire (1933)	F. D. Roosevelt president (1933-1945)	Siam's Rama VIII (1935-46)
Kostanian (1929-30)	Passfield White Paper (1930)	Stavisky scandal (1933)	20th Amendment (1933)	Italy invades Ethiopia (1935)
Collectivization in full force (1930)	Const. named Istanbul (1930)	First concentration camps in Germany (1933)	US off gold standard (1933)	China-Japan war beg. (1936)
Khanjian (1930-36)	Saudi Arabia (1932)	Hitler-Mussolini meet (1934)	U.S.AAA & FERA est. (1933)	All-India Congress Party wins elections (1937)
Second 5-Year Plan (1932)	Iraqis kill Assyrians (1933)	S.A. purged by S.S. (1934)	TVA est. (1933)	Konoye P. M. of Japan (1937)
Famine in USSR (1932)	Balkan Pact (1934)	Dollfuss assassinated (1934)	Chicago World's Fair (1933)	Panay incident (1937)
Catholicos Khoren I (1933-38)	Kemal named Atatürk (1935)	Hitler as Führer (1934-45)	PWA est. (1933)	US-Jap. tensions rise (1939)
USSR joins League (1934)	Persia named Iran (1935)	Nazis repudiate Versailles Treaty (1935)	US recog. USSR (1933)	World War in the Pacific (1940-45)
Kirov assassinated (1934)	Arab High Committee (1936)	Laval P.M. of France (1935)	US Securities Act (1933)	Japanese victories (1941-42)
Purges and trials (1934-38)	Montreux Con. (1936)	Rome Pact (1936)	21st Amendment (1933)	US troops in N. Africa (1942)
Stakhanov year (1936)	Saadabad Pact (1937)	Rome-Berlin Axis (1936)	U.S. FFMC est. (1934)	Casablanca Conf. (1942)
New USSR Const. (1936)	Royal Comm. on Palestine recomm. two states (1937)			Atom bombs dropped (1945)
Amatuni (1936-37)	Sidqi assassinated (1937)			
Third 5-Year Plan (1938)				
Harutiunian (1938-1953)				

Table 16: 1921-1991

ARMENIA & THE USSR	THE MUSLIM WORLD	EUROPE	THE AMERICAS	AFRICA/ASIA/AUSTRALIA
Stalin-Hitler Pact (1939)	Inönü (1938-1965)	Edward VIII abdicates (1936)	CWERA est. (1934)	Vietnam Republic est. (1946)
Eastern Poland annex. (1939)	Alexandretta to Turk. (1939)	Spanish Civil War (1936-39)	Social Security Act (1935)	Chinese civil war beg. (1945)
Molotov (1939-1957)	Von Papen in Turkey (1940)	Anti-Comintern Pact (1936)	Huey Long assass. (1935)	India indep. (1947)
War with Finland (1939-40)	War in North Africa (1940-3)	Chamberlain P.M. (1937)	Wealth Tax Act (1935)	Gandhi assass. (1948)
Baltic Rep. Annex. (1940)	Moh. Reza Shah (1941-79)	Anschluss (1938)	U.S. Neutrality Act (1937)	Chinese People's Rep. (1949)
Trotsky assassinated (1940)	Tehran Conference (1943)	Munich Confer. (1938)	US recog. Franco (1939)	Nationalist China formed in
Russo-Jap. neutrality (1941)	Arab League founded (1945)	Sudetenland taken (1938)	US economic boom begins	Formosa (Taiwan) 1949
Nazi invasion (1941-44)	Pakistan created (1947)	Franco (1939-75)	(1939)	Nehru president (1949-64)
USSR accepts Atlantic	Arabs reject division of	Anglo-Polish Treaty (1939)	U.S. OPA est. (1941)	Korean War (1950-53)
Charter (1941)	Palestine (1947)	W.W. II (1939-45)	Jap. attk. Pearl Harbor (1941)	Honolulu Conf. (1952)
Siege of Moscow ends (1942)	Israel created (1948)	Churchill elected P.M. (1940)	U.S. Savings Bonds (1941)	Mau Mau act in Kenya (1952)
Fall of Sevastopol (1942)	Transjordan named Hashemite	Hess flies to England (1941)	Jap. in US interned (1942)	Kenyatta arrested (1953)
Patriarchate re-established	Kingdom of Jordan (1949)	Jewish Holocaust (1942-45)	Gen. McArthur Chief Com.	Dien Bien Phu taken (1954)
(1943)	Israel admit. to UN (1949)	Allies land in Sicily (1943)	in Far East (1942)	Burma-Jap. Treaty (1954)
Siege of Stalingrad ends	Mossadeq in Iran (1951-53)	D-Day (1944)	Dumbarton Oaks Conf. (1944)	US-Nat. China Pact (1954)
(1943)	King Abdullah assass. (1951)	Hoxha in Albania (1944-85)	Eisenhower supreme comm.	Collectives in China (1955)
Moscow Conference (1943)	Turkey in NATO (1951)	Potsdam Conference (1945)	in Europe (1944-1952)	Great Leap Forward (1958)
Siege of Leningrad ends	Rev. In Egypt (1952)	Tito (1945-1980)	Truman president (1945-52)	Reforms in Congo (1959)
(1944)	King Hussein (1952-)	Italy a republic (1946)	UN Conf. in S.F. (1945)	US present in Vietnam (1963)
Yalta Conference (1945)	Germany agrees to pay comp.	Benelux union est. (1947)	UN World Bank est. (1945)	Kenya indep. (1963)
War against Japan (1945)	to Israel (1952)	Czech. Comm. State (1948)	NY est. UN headquart. (1946)	Tanzania formed (1964)
Cath. Gevorg VI (1945-54)	Republic of Egypt (1953)	Berlin airlift (1948-49)	Churchill's Iron Curtain	Zambia formed (1964)
Fourth 5-Year Plan (1946-51)	Shah leaves Iran (1953)	Rep. of Ireland (1949)	Speech (1946)	Rhodesia indep. (1965)
Treaties with Finland, Italy,	Nasser (1954-1970)	Fed. Rep. of Germany (1949)	Peron (1946-55, 1973-74)	Indira Gandhi (1966-77)
Bulgaria, Hungary and	Israel-Jordan border clashes	Dem. Rep. of Germany (1949)	Marshall Plan (1947)	Malawi republic (1966)
Romania (1947)	increase (1955)	W. Ulbricht (1950-71)	Taft-Hartley Act (1947)	Milit. coup in Ghana (1966)
Break with Tito (1949-55)	Baghdad Pact (1955-59)	Elizabeth II (1952-)	Cold War begins (1948)	Cult. Revolution (1966-76)
Fifth 5-Year Plan (1951)	Sudan indep. Republic (1956)	Commonwealth Conf. (1953)	NATO signed (1949)	Pueblo incident (1968)
General Party Congr. (1952)	UN truce between Israel, Leb.	Zhivkov in Bulg. (1954-89)	Sen. McCarthy's anti-	Death of Ho Chi Minh (1969)
	Syria, Jordan (1956)		Communist camp. (1950-4)	

Table 16: 1921-1991, *Continued*

Death of Stalin (1953)	Israel invades Sinai (1956)	Vienna Treaty (1955)	McCarran Act (1950)	US bombs Cambodia & Laos (1971)
Malenkov (1953-56)	US aid to Israel (1956)	Invasion of Hungary (1956)	22nd Amendment (1951)	Gen. Idi Amin (1971-79)
Tovmasian (1953-60)	Pakistan Islamic Rep. (1956)	J. Kádár (1956-88)	Eisenhower pres. (1953-60)	Indo-Pakistani war (1971)
Catholicos Vazgen I (1954-94)	Nasser takes Suez Can. (1956)	Gomulka (1956-70)	Rosenbergs executed (1953)	Bangladesh formed (1972)
20th Party Congress, Stalin's crimes exposed (1956)	Br. & Fr. Attack Egypt (1956)	Cardinals Wyszynski and Mindszenty released (1956)	Potomac Charter (1954)	Ceylon Republic, renamed Sri Lanka (1972)
Khrushchev (1956-64)	Egypt retains Canal (1957)	Rome Treaty (1957)	Hammarskjöld in UN (1953)	Tanaka P.M. of Japan (1972)
Sputnik launched (1957)	Martial law in Jordan (1957)	Common Market (1958)	Bus boycott in Ala. (1955)	Marcos declares martial law in Philippines (1972)
Gromyko (1957-1985)	Israel withdraws from Sinai (1957)	De Gaulle (1956-70)	AFL & CIO merge (1955)	Nixon in China (1972)
Geneva & Disarm. Confer. fails (1960)	UAR (1958-61)	Cyprus a republic (1960)	M. L. King leads desegrega-tion movt. (1956-68)	Japan regains Okinawa (1972)
Zarobian (1960-66)	Revolution in Iraq (1958)	Berlin Wall Crisis (1961-2)	Eisenhower Doctrine (1957)	End of Vietnam War (1973)
Currency reform (1961)	Aswan Dam loan from USSR (1958)	Profumo crisis (1963)	AFL/CIO expels Teamsters (1957)	Famine in Africa (1974)
First man in space (1961)	Ayub Khan (1958-69)	Wilson elected P.M. (1964)	Alaska 49th state (1958)	Ethiopian Civil War begins (1975)
Rift with China (1963)	Lebanese conflict (1958)	Ceausescu (1965-1989)	Castro takes Cuba (1959)	Khmer Rouge take Cambodia (1975)
Atom. Test ban discus. (1963)	CENTO (1959)	France leaves NATO (1966)	Khrushchev in US (1959)	Communists take over South Vietnam (1975)
Brezhnev (1964-82)	Milit. coup in Turkey (1960)	Greek military coup (1967)	Hawaii 50th state (1959)	Mayaguez incident (1975)
Mikoyan retired (1965)	Milit. coup in Syria (1961)	Protests in Warsaw (1968)	U-2 incident (1960)	Pathet Lao in Laos (1975)
Economic pact w/Italy (1966)	Ben Bella (1962-65)	Czech. invaded (1968)	Kennedy-Nixon debate (1960)	N. Mariana Islands become US Commonwealth (1975)
Kochinian (1966-74)	UAR & Iraq union (1963)	Prot. and Cath. conflict in N. Ireland begins (1969)	Kennedy president (1961-63)	Chiang Kai-shek dead (1975)
Dipl. break with Israel (1967)	Saudi King Faisal (1964-75)	G. Pompidou elec. (1969)	Bay of Pigs (1961)	Fraser P.M. Australia (1975)
Kiev summit (1968)	Arafat leads Al-Fatah (1964)	W. Brandt elec. (1969)	R. Trujillo assass. (1961)	Vietnam united (1976)
Treaty of friendship with W. Germany (1970)	Revolution in Algeria (1965)	E. Heath elec. (1970)	Cuban Missile Crisis (1962)	Seychelles indep. (1976)
Demonstrations in Yerevan (1974)	Israel-Jordan clashes (1966)	Gierek (1970-1980)	U-Thant in UN (1962)	Port. Timor becomes part of Indonesia (1976)
Demirjian (1974-88)	Six-Day War (1967)	E. Honecker (1971-1989)	Civil Rights marches (1963)	Milit. coup in Thailand (1976)
Russ. Helsinki group arrested (1977)	Coronation in Iran (1967)	British direct rule on N. Ireland (1972)	Johnson president (1963-68)	Riots in South Africa (1976)
Brezhnev assumes title of president (1977)	Arafat chairman PLO (1969)	Two Germanies est. diplomat. relations (1973)	Malcolm X shot (1965)	
New Soviet Const. (1978)	Golda Meir (1969-74)	H. Schmidt elec. (1974)	Watts riot (1965)	
	Sadat (1970-81)	Turkey invades Cyprus (1974)	Anti-war protests beg. (1966)	
	Milit. coup in Turkey (1971)	Greece restores dem. (1974)	25th Amendment (1967)	
	Arab-Israeli clashes (1972)		Che Guevara killed (1967)	

Table 16: 1921-1991, *Continued*

ARMENIA & THE USSR	THE MUSLIM WORLD	EUROPE	THE AMERICAS	AFRICA/ASIA/AUSTRALIA
Treaty with Vietnam (1978)	Iran nationalizes oil (1973)	Portugal restores dem. (1974)	Martin L. King assass. (1968)	Death of Mao (1976)
Afghanistan invaded (1979)	Arab-Israeli War (1973)	Juan Carlos I (1975-)	R. Kennedy assass. (1968)	Gang of Four arrested (1976)
Sakharov banished (1980)	Oil embargo (1973-74)	Helsinki accords (1975)	Nixon president (1969-74)	War in Angola (1976-88)
Andropov (1982-84)	Rabin (1974-77)	Pope John Paul II (1978-)	Moon landing (1969)	Fukuda P.M. of Japan (1976)
Korean airline shot over USSR (1983)	Golan Heights truce (1974)	M. Thatcher elected (1979)	Chicago Eight trial (1969)	Djibouti indep. (1977)
Chernenko (1984-85)	Nixon in Middle East (1974)	Mountbatten assass. (1979)	Allende in Chile (1970-73)	US-China est. full diplom. relations (1978)
Sakharov hunger strike (1984)	US halts aid to Turkey (1975)	Birth of Solidarity (1980)	Kent State killings (1970)	Botha P.M. S. Africa (1978)
Gorbachev (1985-91)	Saudi King Khalid (1975-82)	Mitterand elected (1981)	Pentagon Papers (1971)	Vietnam invades Cambodia (1979)
Gorbachev-Reagan summit (1985)	Suez reopened (1975)	A. Papandreou elected (1981)	26th Amendment (1971)	Indira Gandhi (1980-84)
Glasnost/Perestroika (1987)	Lebanese Civil War (1975-89)	Jaruzelski in power (1981-89)	Waldheim in UN (1971)	Zimbabwe Indep. (1980)
Baltic and Karabagh movements begin (1988)	OPEC raises oil prices (1975)	Assas. attempt on pope (1981)	Watergate Affair (1972-75)	ANC more active (1981-93)
Harutiunian (1988-1990)	Begin (1977-83)	H. Kohl elected (1982)	SALT I (1973)	B. Aquino assass. (1983)
Earthquake in Armenia (1988)	Milit. coup in Pakistan (1977)	ECSC issues document (1983)	Nixon resigns (1974)	Golden Temple killing (1984)
Gorbachev president (1988)	Sadat in Israel (1977)	J. Popieluzko killed (1984)	Ford president (1974-76)	Rajiv Gandhi (1984-91)
Soviet open elections (1989)	Milit. coup in Afghan. (1978)	Gibraltar-Spanish border opened after 16 years (1985)	US Bicentennial (1976)	Hong Kong accord (1984)
Soviets leave Afghan. (1989)	Camp David Accord (1978)	Anglo-Irish Agreement (1985)	J. Carter president (1977-80)	C. Aquino pres. (1986)
Yeltsin leaves CPSU (1990)	Islamic Rev. in Iran (1979)	K. Waldheim elected (1986)	Panama Canal Treaty (1977)	Tokyo Summit (1986)
Mutalibov (1990-91)	Milit. coup in Turkey (1980)	O. Palme assass. (1986)	SALT II Treaty (1979)	Sanctions on S. Africa (1986)
Elchibey (1991-92)	Iran-Iraq War (1980-88)	V. Havel elected (1989)	Sandinistas (1979-90)	Macao accord (1987)
Gamsakhurdia (1991-92)	Iran releases hostages (1981)	Dem. in Poland (1989)	Grain embargo on Sov. (1980)	Tamil revolt Sri Lanka (1987)
Attempted coup (1991)	Mubarak (1981-)	Berlin Wall down (1989)	Reagan president (1981-88)	Strikes in S. Africa (1988)
CIS formed (1991)	Saudi King Fahd (1982-)	Ceausescu killed (1989)	Falkland Islands War (1982)	F. W. De Klerk (1989-94)
Armenia member CIS (1991)	Özal (1983-93)	Dem. In Hungary (1989)	Grenada invaded (1983)	Martial law in Tibet (1989)
USSR ends (1991)	Peres (1984-90)	German unification (1990)	Star Wars proposed (1983)	Tianamen Sq. killing (1989)
Armenia independent (1991)	Milit. coup in Sudan (1985)	L. Walesa elected (1990)	Irangate scandal (1986)	Revolt in Liberia (1990)
	US bombs Libya (1986)	European Union (1991)	INF Treaty (1988)	Emperor Akihito (1990-)
	Intifada begins (1988)	Yugoslav breakup and factional war begins (1991)	Bush president (1989-92)	Civil War in Chad (1990)
	B. Bhutto (1988-1990)		Panama invasions (1989)	
	Gulf War (1990-91)		Malta Summit (1989)	

Table 16: 1921-1991, *Continued*

ARMENIA SINCE INDEPENDENCE

1991-Levon Ter Petrosian elected President
1991-American University of Armenia established
1992-Karabagh declares its independence
1992-US opens embassy in Armenia
1992-Armenia member of the UN
1992-Shushi liberated-Lachin corridor connects Karabagh to Armenia
1992-1993-Severe lack of heat and electricity during the winter
1993-Karabagh Armenians take Kelbajar, Aghdam, and Fizuli
1994-Cease-fire in Karabagh
1994-Death of Catholicos Vazgen I.
1994-Russian military bases in Armenia
1995-Karekin II, Catholicos of Cilicia, elected Supreme Catholicos at
     Ejmiatsin as Karekin I.
1996-Ter-Petrosian re-elected as President
1997-Bilateral treaty on economic and military cooperation with Russia
1997-Kocharian named Prime Minister
1998-Ter-Petrosian resigns
1998-Robert Kocharian becomes President
1998-Ban on the Dashnak party lifted
1998-Diaspora Armenians granted dual citizenship
1999-Death of Catholicos Karekin I
1999-Karekin II, Archbishop of Ararat, elected Catholicos
1999-Assassination of Armenian government leaders in parliament
2000-Mkhitarists of Venice and Vienna united
2001-1700th anniversary of Christianity in Armenia
2001-Pope John Paul II visits Armenia
2001-Opening of Cathedral of St. Gregory the Illuminator in Yerevan
2001-Pope beatifies Ignadios Maloyan, Armenian Catholic Archbishop of
     Mardin, martyred in 1915
2003-Kocharian re-elected as President

Table 17: Armenia 1991-2003

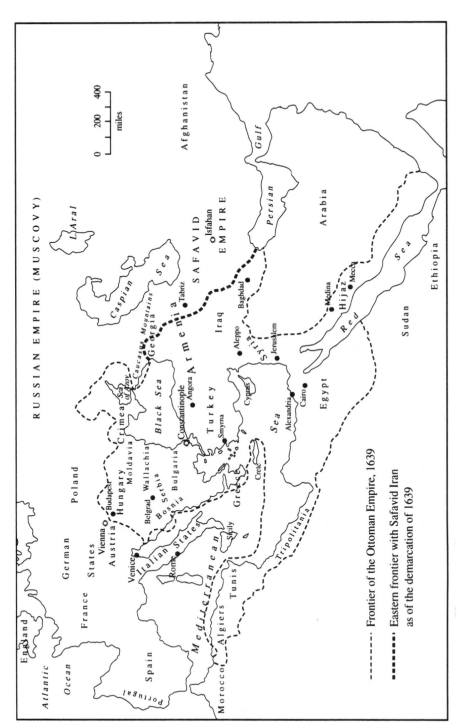

Map 20: The Ottoman Empire in 1639

RUSSIAN EMPIRE (MUSCOVY)

Atlantic Ocean

England

France

Spain

Portugal

German States

Poland

Austria

Vienna

Hungary

Budapest

Italian States

Venice

Rome

Sicily

Moldavia

Wallachia

Serbia

Bosnia

Belgrad

Bulgaria

Greece

Crete

Mediterranean Sea

Morocco

Algiers

Tunis

Tripolitania

L. Aral

Caspian Sea

Crimea

Sea of Azov

Black Sea

Turkey

Constantinople

Angora

Smyrna

Cyprus

Sea

Alexandria

Cairo

Egypt

Caucasus Mountains

Georgia

Armenia

Tabriz

SAFAVID EMPIRE

Isfahan

Afghanistan

Persian Gulf

Arabia

Red Sea

Medina

Mecca

Hijaz

Iraq

Baghdad

Aleppo

Syria

Jerusalem

Sudan

Ethiopia

miles

0   200   400

- - - - - - Frontier of the Ottoman Empire, 1639

▪▪▪▪▪▪ Eastern frontier with Safavid Iran
as of the demarcation of 1639

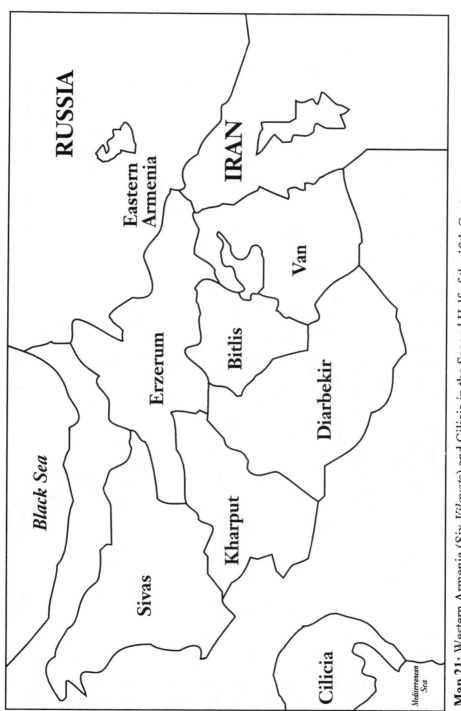

Map 21: Western Armenia (Six *Vilayets*) and Cilicia in the Second Half of the 19th Century

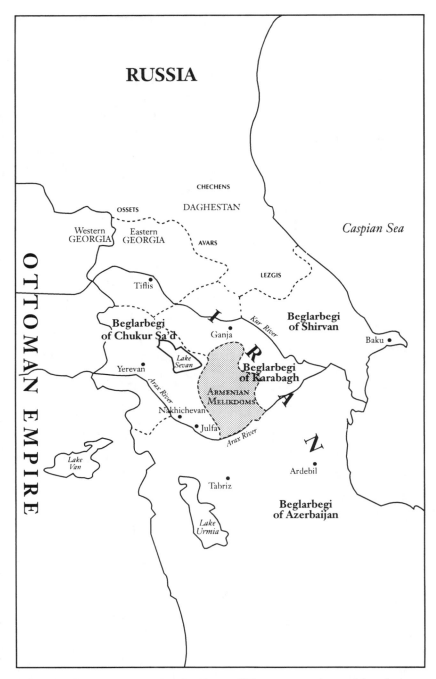

Map 22: Eastern Armenia, the Rest of Transcaucasia, and Iranian
Azerbaijan in the Late 17th and Early 18th Centuries

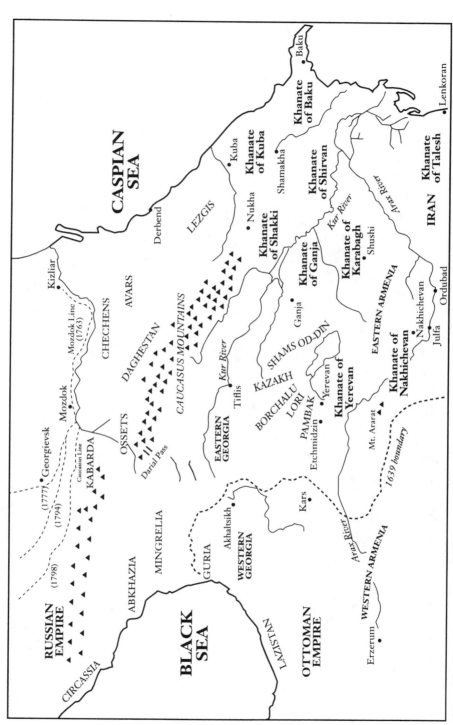

Map 23: The Caucasus in the Late 18th Century

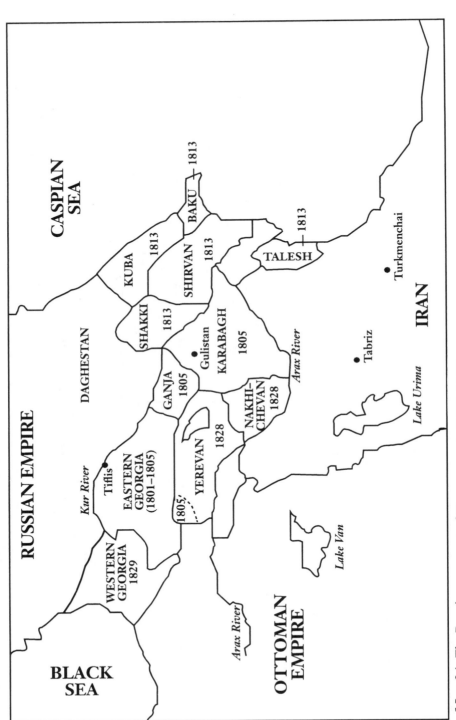

Map 24: The Russian conquest of Transcaucasia (1801-1829)

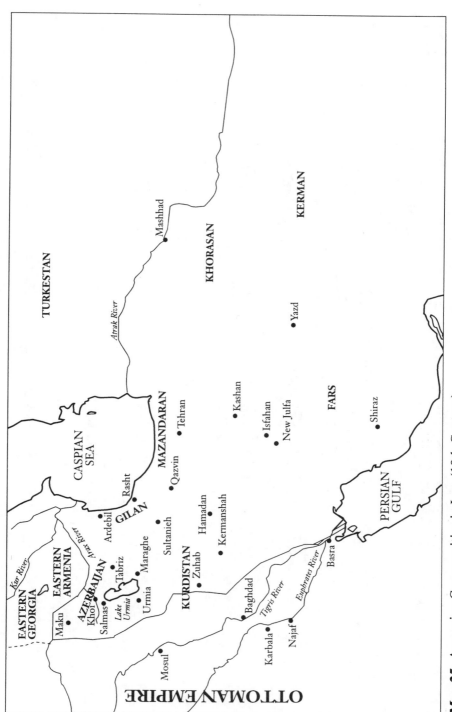

Map 25: Armenian Communities in Iran (19th Century)

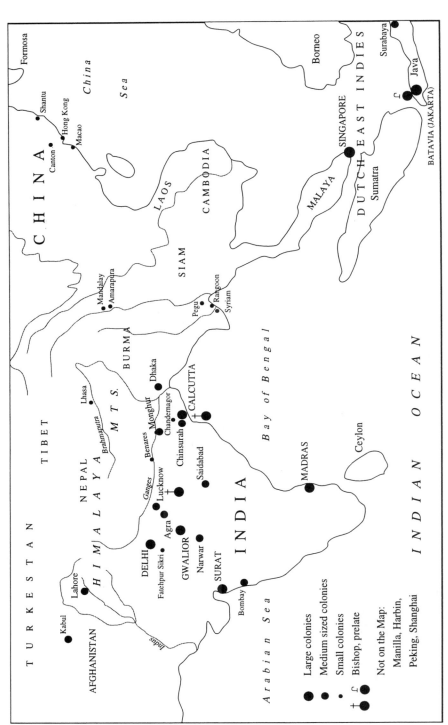

Map 26: Armenians and Southeast Asia (19th Century)

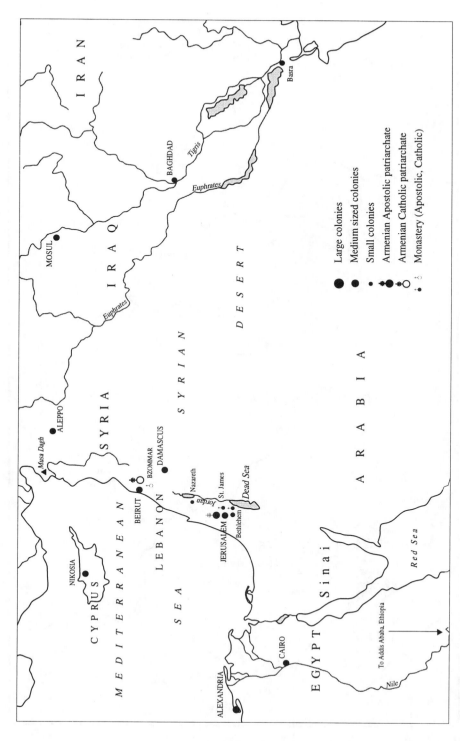

Map 27: The Armenian Diaspora in the Arab World (19th Century)

Map 28: Armenian Centers in Russia in the Eighteenth Century

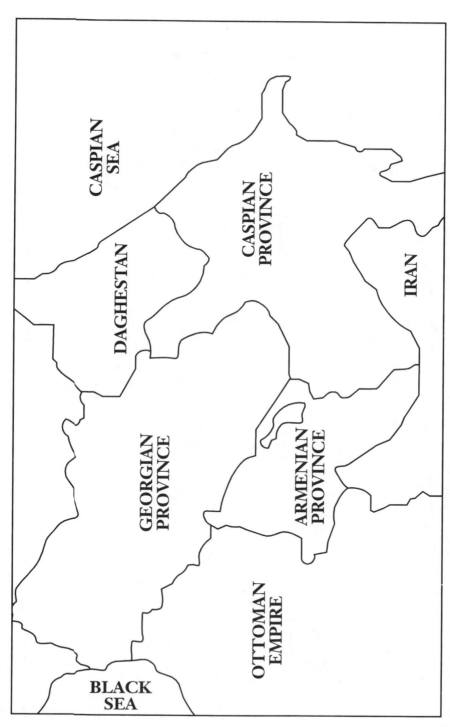

Map 29: The Armenian Province (1828-1840)

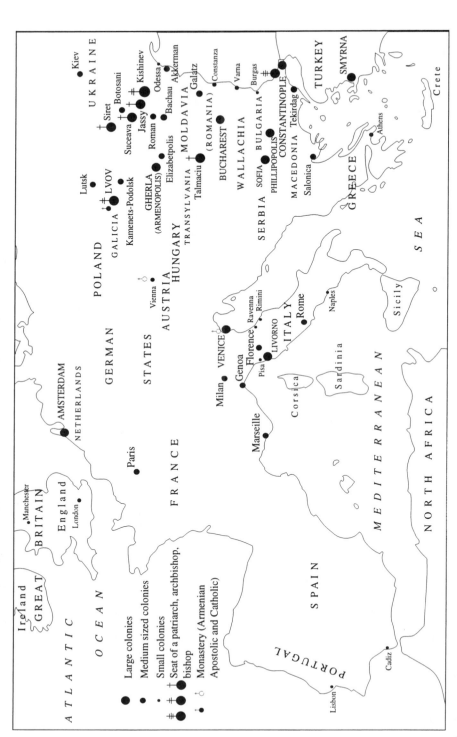

Map 30: The Armenian Diaspora in Eastern and Western Europe (19th Century).

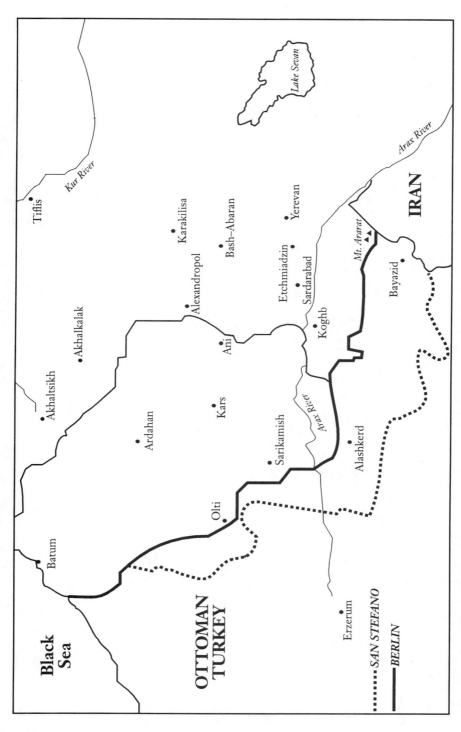

Map 31: The Russo-Turkish Border after the San Stefano and Berlin Treaties (1878)

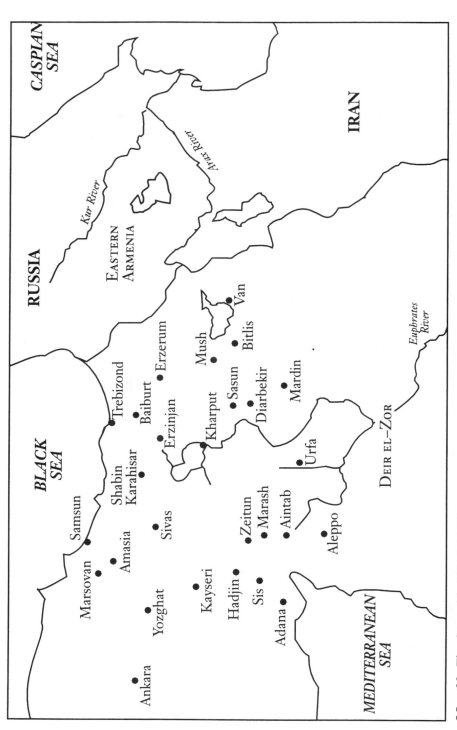

Map 32: The Genocide (1915-1922)

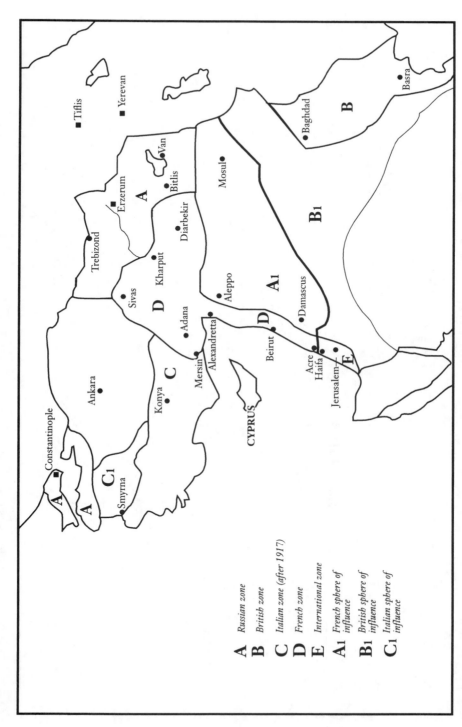

Map 33: The Sykes-Picot Plan for the Partition of the Ottoman Empire (1915-1916)

A   Russian zone
B   British zone
C   Italian zone (after 1917)
D   French zone
E   International zone
A1   French sphere of influence
B1   British sphere of influence
C1   Italian sphere of influence

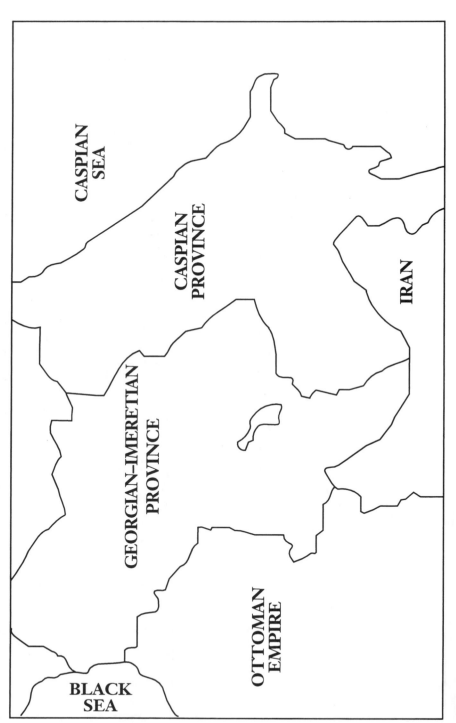

Map 34: Transcaucasia (1840-1845)

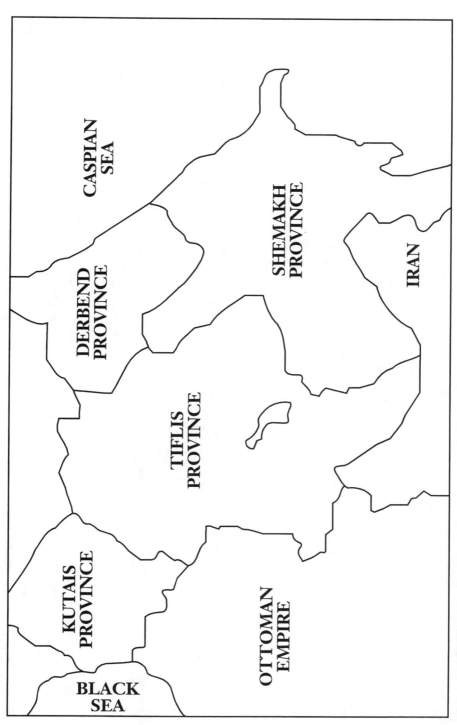

Map 35: Transcaucasia (1845-1849)

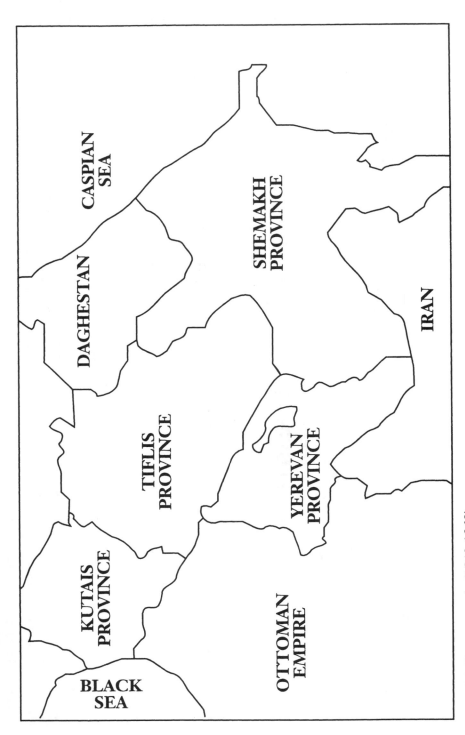

Map 36: Transcaucasia (1849-1868)

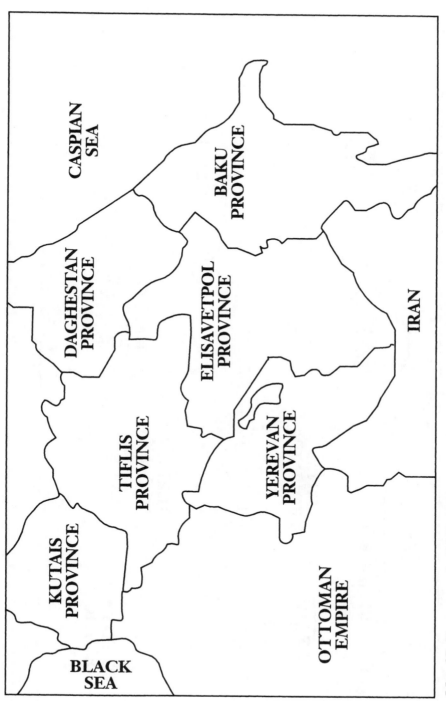

Map 37: Transcaucasia (1868-1878)

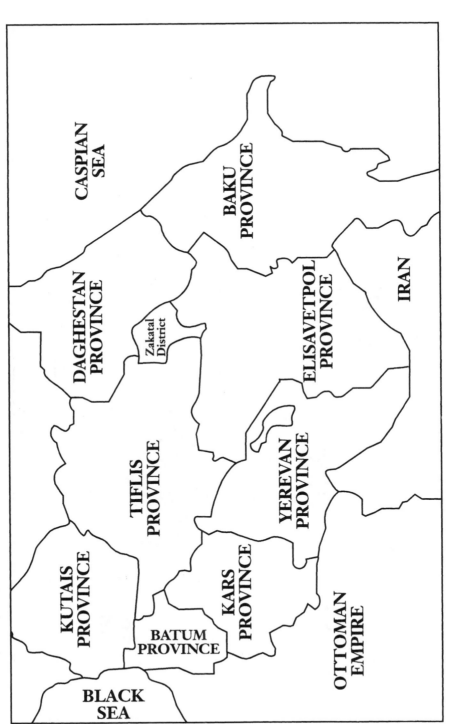

Map 38: Transcaucasia (1878-1918)

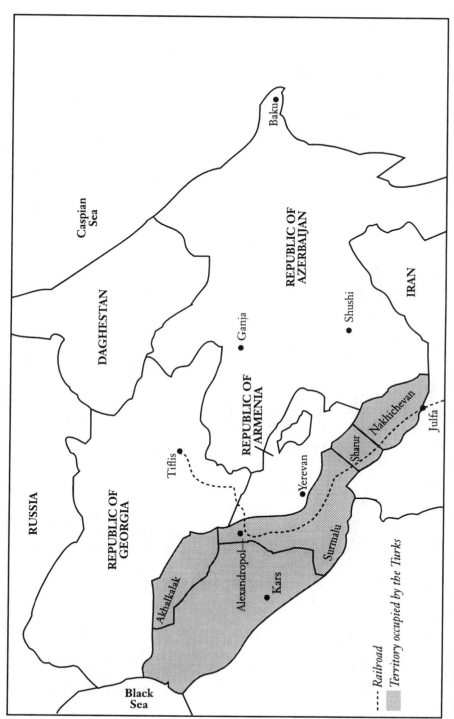

Map 39: The Armenian Republic after the Batum Treaty, June 1918

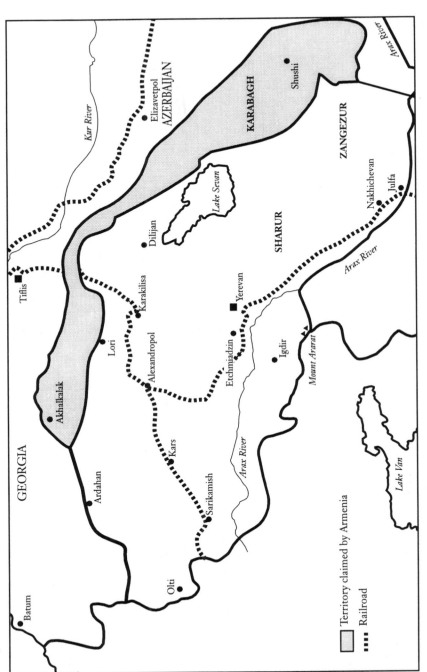

Map 40: The Armenian Republic, September 1920

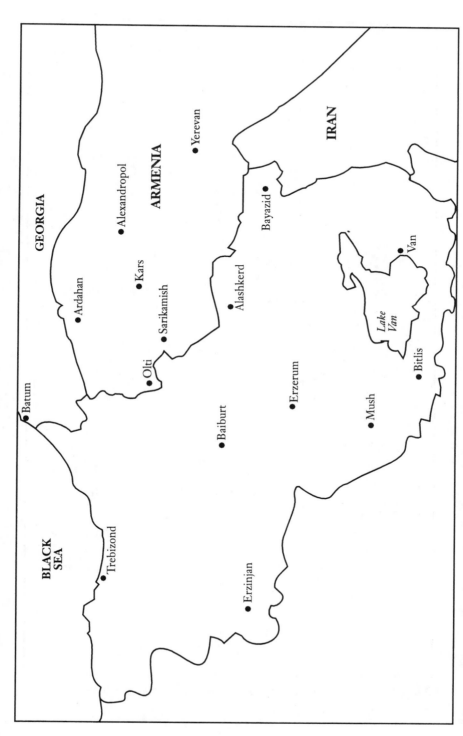

Map 41: Wilson's Armenia for the Treaty of Sèvres, 1920

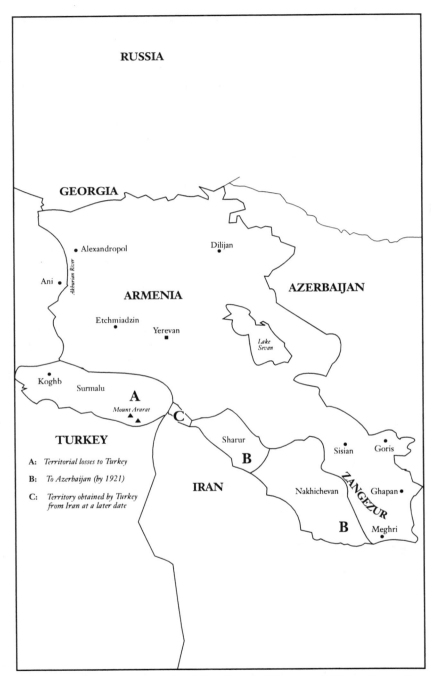

Map 42: The Armenian Republic after the Treaty of Alexandropol
(December 1920)

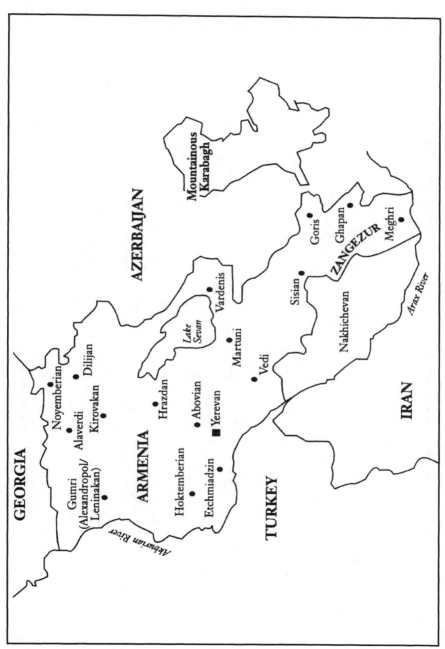

Map 43: Soviet Armenia, Nakhichevan and Karabagh (1921-2003)

Map 44: Mountainous Karabgh (1923-2003)

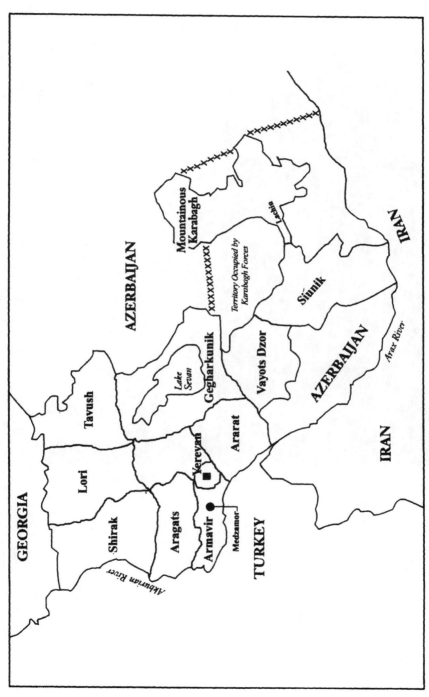

Map 45: Administrative Districts of Present-day Armenian Republic.

38. Armenian Patriarchate, Istanbul

39. Mkhitarist Center, San Lazzaro, Venice, Italy

40. Mkhitarist Center, Vienna, Austria

41. View of New Julfa, Iran

42. Armenian Cathedral, New Julfa, Iran

43. Armenian Church, Madras, India

44. Armenian Church, Calcutta, India.

45. Armenian Church, Singapore

46. Armenian Church, Yangoon (Rangoon), Myanmar (Burma)

47. Armenian Church, Dhaka, Bangladesh

48. Armenian Church, Cairo, Egypt

49. Armenian Church, Addis-Ababa, Ethiopia (AGBU)

50. The Storming of the Yerevan Fortress, October, 1827

51. Armenian Church, New Nakhichevan, Rostov-on-Don, Russia

52. Armenian Church, St. Petersburg, Russia

53. Lazarian Institute, Moscow, Russia

54. Armenian Church, Tbilisi, Georgia

55. Samuel-Murad Armenian School, Sévres, France

56. Murad Raphaelian School, Venice, Italy

57. Armenian Church, Amsterdam

58. Armenian Bible, Amsterdam 1664

59. Armenian Church, Budapest, Hungary (AGBU)

60. Armenian Church, Bucharest, Romania (AGBU)

61. Armenian Church, Sochi, Russia (AGBU)

62. Armenian Church, Russe, Bulgaria (AGBU)

63. Armenian Church, Moldova (AGBU)

64. Armenian Church, Crimea, Ukraine (Mutafian)

65. Melkonian School, Cyprus (AGBU)

66. Armenian Church, Baghdad, Iraq

67. Armenian Church, Samarkand (AGBU)

68. View of Zeitun (ALMA)

69. Cathedral of St. Gregory the Illuminator, Yerevan

70. Modern Yerevan

Select Bibliography and Suggested Readings

General Reference

Abrahamian, A. G. *A Concise History of the Armenian Diaspora,* 2 vols. (in Armenian). Yerevan, 1964-1967.

Academy of Sciences of Armenia, *History of the Armenian People* (8 vols. in Armenian). Yerevan, 1971-1984.

Bardakjian, K. *A Reference Guide to Modern Armenian Literature, 1500-1920.* Detroit, 2000.

Bosworth, C. E. *The Islamic Dynasties.* Edinburgh, 1967.

Cambridge History of Iran (7 vols.) Cambridge, 1968-1991.

Cambridge Ancient History (12 vols.) Cambridge, 1971-1992.

Cambridge Medieval History (9 vols.) Cambridge, 1911-1967.

Cambridge Modern History (14 vols.) Cambridge, 1967-1971.

Cambridge History of Islam (2 vols.) Cambridge, 1970.

Dédéyan, G. ed., *Histoire des Arméniens.* Toulouse, 1982.

Encyclopedia of Islam.

Encycopaedia Iranica.

Hacikyan, J. ed., *The Heritage of Armenian Literature,* vols. 1-2. Detroit, 2000, 2003.

Hakobian, T. Kh. *Armenia's Historical Geography* (in Armenian). Yerevan, 1968.

_____. *History of Yerevan,* vols. II-IV: 1500-1917 (in Armenian). Yerevan, 1959-1981.

_____, et. al. eds. *Dictionary of Armenian Place Names* (in Armenian), 5 vols. Yerevan, 1986-2001.

Hewsen, R. *Armenia: A Historical Atlas.* Chicago, 2001.

Hovannisian, R. G. ed., *The Armenian People: From Ancient to Modern Times,* 2 vols. New York, 1997.

Leo, *History of Armenia,* vols. I-V (in Armenian). Yerevan, 1966-1986.

Manandian, H. *A Critical Study of the History of the Armenian People,* 3 vols. (in Armenian). Yerevan, 1946-1952.

Miansarof, M. *Bibliographia Caucasica et Transcaucasica.* Amsterdam, 1967.

Nersessian, V. *Armenia* (Bibliographical Guide). Oxford, 1993.

Pasdermadjian, H. *Histoire de l'Arménie depuis les origines jusqu 'au traité de Lausanne.* Paris, 1949.

Salmaslian, A. *Bibliographie De L'Arménie.* Yerevan, 1969.

Thomson, R. *A Bibliography of Classical Armenian Literature to 1500.* Brepols, 1995.

The following are the best reference books on Armenian art and architecture and the source of some of the plates used in this book:

Ancenay, M. & Buss, W. *Arménie*, Bologna, 1998.
Armenian Churches. Ejmiatsin, 1970.
Armenian Khatchkars. Ejmiatsin, 1973.
Bauer, E. *Armenia: Past and Present*. New York, 1981.
Der Nersessian, S. *Armenian Art*. London, 1978.
Donabedian, P. & Thierry, J. *Armenian Art*. New York, 1989.
Novello, A. L. *The Armenians*. New York, 1986.

Armenian History-Literature (in English translations)

Agathangelos. *History of the Armenians* (Thomson). Albany, 1976.
Aristakes Lastivertc'i. *History* (Bedrosian). New York, 1985.
Kirakos Gandzakets'i. *History of the Armenians* (Bedrosian). New York, 1986.
Bishop Ukhtanes of Sebastia, *History*, 2 vols. (Arzoumanian). Ft. Lauderdale, 1985-1988.
Daredevils of Sassoun (Surmelian). New York, 1964.
David of Sassoun (Shalian). Athens, Ohio, 1964.
Egishe Vardapet. *History of Vardan and the Armenian War* (Thomson). Cambridge, Mass., 1982.
Ghazar P'arbec'i. *History* (Thomson). New York, 1991.
Ghewond Vardapet. *History* (Arzoumanian). Philadelphia, 1982.
Hovhannes Draskhanakertetsi. *History of Armenia* (Maksoudian). Atlanta, 1987.
Koriun. *Life of Mashtots* (Norehad). New York, 1964.
Matthew of Edessa. *Chronicle* (Dostourian). London, 1993.
Moses Khorenatsi. *History of the Armenians* (Thomson). Cambridge, Mass., 1978.
Nerses Shnorhali. *General Epistle* (Aljalian). New Rochelle, 1996.
P'awstos Buzand. *The Epic Histories* (Garsoian). Harvard, 1989.
Psuedo-Yovhannes Mamikonean. *History of Taron* (Avdoyan). Atlanta, 1993.
Sebeos. *History* (Bedrosian). New York, 1985.
T'ovma Metsobets'i. *History of Tamerlane and his Successors* (Bedrosian). New York, 1987.
The Fables of Mkhitar Gosh (Bedrosian). New York, 1987.
The Georgian Chronicle (Bedrosian). New York, 1991.
Tovma Artsruni. *History of the House of the Artsrunik'* (Thomson). Detroit, 1985.
The Passion of St. Shushanik (Maksoudian). New York, 1999.

Pre-Urartian Period and the Urartian Kingdom

Azarpay, G. *Urartian Art and Artifacts: A Chronological Study.* Berkeley, 1968.
Burney, C. and Lang, D.M. *The Peoples of the Hills: Ancient Ararat and the Caucasus.* New York, 1972.
Gamkrelidze, T.V. and Ivanov, V.V. *Indo-European and Indo-Europeans: A Reconstruction and Historical Typological Analysis of a Proto-Language and Proto-Culture,* 2 vols. (in Russian). Tbilisi, 1984.
Kavoukjian, M. *Armenia, Subartu and Sumer.* Montreal, 1987.
Mallory, J.P. *In Search of the Indo-Europeans.* London, 1989.
Piotrovskii, B.B. *Urartu: The Kingdom of Van and its Art.* New York, 1967.
_____. *The Ancient Civilization of Urartu: An Archeological Adventure.* New York, 1969.
Renfrew, C. *Archeology and Language: The Puzzle of Indo-European Origins.* Cambridge, 1988.

Medes, Achaemenids, Yervandians, Seleucids, Artashesians, Parthians, Arshakians, and Sasanians

Bedoukian, P. *Coinage of the Artaxiads of Armenia.* London, 1978.
Debevoise, N.C. *A Political History of Parthia.* Chicago, 1938.
Bury, J.B. *History of Greece to the Death of Alexander.* London, 1955.
Dodgeon, M.H. & Lieu, S.N. *The Roman Eastern Frontier and the Persian Wars, AD 226-363.* London, 1991.
Frye, R. *The Heritage of Persia.* London, 1962.
Garsoian, N. "Byzantium and the Sasanians" in *Cambridge History of Iran* (Vol. 3, pt. 1).
_____. *Armenia between Byzantium and the Sasanians.* London, 1985.
_____. *The Paulician Heresy.* The Hague, 1967.
_____. ed., *East of Byzantium: Syria and Armenia in the Formative Period.* Washington, D.C., 1982.
Herodotus, *The History* (trans. G. Rawlinson). New York, 1943.
Lang, D.M. "Iran, Armenia and Georgia," in *Cambridge History of Iran* (vol. 3 pt 1).
Manandian, H. *Tigrane II et Rome* (Lisbon, 1963).
_____. *The Trade and Cities of Armenia in Relation to Ancient World Trade* (English translation and commentary by N. Garsoian). Lisbon, 1965.
Olmstead, A. T. *History of the Persian Empire.* Chicago, 1948.
Plutarch, *Lives* (Dryden trans.), 6 vols. New York, 1898.

Rostovtzeff, M.I. *Social and Economic History of the Roman Empire,* 2 vols. Oxford, 1957.

_____. *Social and Economic History of the Hellenistic World,* 3 vols. Oxford, 1941.

Russell, J. *Zoroastrianism in Armenia.* Cambridge, Mass., 1987.

Starr, G. *A History of the Ancient World.* New York, 1974.

Strabo, *The Geography* (trans. H. L. Jones), 8 vols. London, 1961.

Toumanoff, C. *Studies in Christian Caucasian History.* Georgetown, 1963.

Xenophon, *Anabasis* (The Persian Expedition) [trans. R. Warner]. London, 1975.

Georgia and Caucasian Albania

Allen, W.E.D. *A History of the Georgian People.* New York, 1971.

Lang, D.M. *The Georgians.* New York, 1966.

Movses Daskhurantsi, *The History of the Caucasian Albanians* (trans. C.J. Dowsett). London, 1961.

The Armenian Church and the Christian Churches of the East

Arberry, A.J. ed., *Religion in the Middle East,* 2 vols. Cambridge, 1969.

Azarya, M. *The Armenian Quarter of Jerusalem.* Berkeley, 1984.

Gonzalez, L. *A History of Christian Thought,* 2 vols. New York, 1971.

Maksoudian, K. *Chosen of God: The Election of the Catholicos of All Armenians.* New York, 1995.

Ormanian, M. *The Church of Armenia.* New York, 1988.

_____. *Azgapatum* (in Armenian) Constantinople & Jerusalem, 3 vols. 1912-1927. Additional volumes prepared by Rev. Arzoumanian, New York, 1995-1997.

Sarkissian, K. (Archbishop). *The Council of Chalcedon and the Armenian Church.* New York, 1975.

Tanner, N.P. *Decrees of the Ecumenical Councils,* 2 vols. Georgetown, 1990.

Thomson, R. *The Teaching of St. Gregory.* Cambridge, Mass., 1970.

Byzantium and the Armenians in the Byzantine Empire

Adontz, N. *Armenia in the Period of Justinian: The Political Conditions based on the Naxarar System* (translated with commentary by N. Garsoian). Lisbon, 1970.

Charanis, P. *The Armenians in the Byzantine Empire.* Lisbon, 1963.
Der Nersessian, S. *Armenia and the Byzantine Empire.* Cambridge, 1965.
Ostrogorsky, G. *History of the Byzantine State.* New Brunswick, 1969.
Runciman, S. *Byzantine Style and Civilization.* Penguin, 1975.
_____. *Byzantine Civilization.* Cleveland, 1967.
Vasiliev, A.A. *History of the Byzantine Empire,* 2 vols. Madison, 1952.

Arabs, Islam and the Bagratunis

Hourani, A. *A History of the Arab Peoples.* Cambridge, Mass., 1991.
Lane-Poole, S. *A History of Egypt in the Middle Ages.* New York, 1969.
Minorsky, V. *A History of Sharvan and Darband in the 10th-11th Centuries.* Cambridge, 1958.
_____. *Studies in Caucasian History.* London, 1953.
Ter-Ghewondyan, A. *The Arab Emirates in Bagratid Armenia* (translated with Commentary by N. Garsoian). Lisbon, 1976.
Toumanoff, C. "Armenia and Georgia," in *Cambridge Medieval History* (vol. 4 pt. 1).

Crusades and Cilician Armenia

Atamian-Bournoutian, A. "Cilician Armenia," in vol. 1 of Hovannisian's *The Armenian People.*
Bedoukian, P. *Coinage of Cilician Armenia,* New York, 1962.
Boase, T.S.R. ed., *The Cilician Kingdom of Armenia.* Edinburgh, 1978.
Der Nersessian, S. "The Kingdom of Cilician Armenia," in vol. 2 of Setton *History of the Crusades.*
Edwards, R. *The Fortifications of Armenian Cilicia.* Washington D.C., 1987.
La Chronique Attribuée au Connétable Smbat (Translated by Gerard Dédéyan), Paris, 1980.
Maalouf, A. *The Crusades Through Arab Eyes.* New York, 1984.
Runciman, S. *A History of the Crusades* (3 vols.), New York, 1964.
Hetoum, *A Lytell Cronycle* (Translated by Richard Pynson). Toronto, 1988.
Mikaelian, G. *History of the Cilician Armenian State* (in Russian), Yerevan, 1952.
Mutafian, C. *La Cilicie au carrefour des empires,* 2 vols. Paris, 1988.
Rudt-Collenberg, W. H. *The Rupenides, The Hethumides and Lusignans. The Structure of the Armenian-Cilician Dynasties.* Paris, 1963.

Setton, K. M. ed., *A History of the Crusades* (6 vols.). Madison, 1969-1990.

Stewart, A.D. *The Armenian Kingdom and the Mamluks*. Leiden, 2001.

Armenia from the Eleventh to the Sixteenth Centuries

Barthold, W. *Turkestan Down to the Mongol Invasion*. London, 1968.

Bedrosian, R. *The Turco-Mongol Invasions and the Lords of Armenia in the 13-14th Centuries* (Ph.D. diss. Columbia, 1979).

Cahen, C. *Pre-Ottoman Turkey*. New York, 1968.

Grousset, T. *The Empire of the Steppes*. New Brunswick, 1970.

Inalcik, H. *The Ottoman Empire: The Classical Age, 1300-1600*. London, 1973.

Juvaini. *The History of the World Conqueror* (trans. Boyle), 2 vols. Manchester, 1958.

Morgan, D. *Medieval Persia, 1040-1797*. London, 1988.

Rashid al-Din. *The Successors of Genghiz Khan* (trans. Boyle). New York, 1971.

Sanjian, A. *Colophons of Armenian Manuscripts 1301-1480*. Harvard, 1969.

Saunders, J.J. *History of the Mongol Conquests*. London, 1971.

Spuler, B. *The Mongols in History*. New York, 1971.

Vryonis, S. *The Decline of Medieval Hellenism in Asia Minor and the Process of Islamization from the Eleventh to the Fifteenth Century*. Los Angeles, 1971.

Wittek, P. *The Rise of the Ottoman Empire*. London, 1971.

Woods, J.E. *The Aqquyunlu: Clan, Confederation, Empire: A Study in 15/9th-Century Turko-Iranian Politics*. Minneapolis, 1976.

Armenians in the Ottoman Empire

Anderson, M.S. *The Eastern Question, 1774-1923*. New York, 1966.

Arpee, L. *The Armenian Awakening: A History of the Armenian Church, 1820-1860*. Chicago, 1909.

Artinian, V. *The Armenian Constitutional System in the Ottoman Empire, 1839-1863*. Istanbul, 1988.

Berkes, N. *The Development of Secularism in Turkey*. Montreal, 1964.

Braude, B. & Lewis, B. eds., *Christians and Jews in the Ottoman Empire*, 2 vols. New York, 1982.

Bryson, T. A. *American Diplomatic Relations with the Middle East, 1784-1975*. Metuchen, N.J., 1977.

Daniel, R.L. *American Philanthropy in the Near East, 1820-1960*. Athens, Ohio, 1970.

Davison, R. *Reform in the Ottoman Empire, 1856-1876*. Princeton, 1963.

Etmekjian, J. *The French Influence in the Western Armenian Renaissance*.

New York, 1964.

Hamilton, W. *Researches in Asia Minor, Pontus, and Armenia.* Zurich, 1984.

Inalcik, H. & Quataert, D. *An Economic and Social History of the Ottoman Empire, 1300-1914.* Cambridge, 1994.

Islamoglu-Inan, H. *State and Peasant in the Ottoman Empire.* Leiden, 1994.

Jelavich, B. *The Ottoman Empire, the Great Powers and the Straits Question, 1870-1887.*

_____. *History of the Balkans, Vol. 1: Eighteenth and Nineteenth Centuries.* Cambridge, 1993.

Kasaba, R. *The Ottoman Empire and the World Economy: The Nineteenth Century.* Albany, NY, 1988.

Krikorian, M. K. *Armenians in the Service of the Ottoman Empire, 1860-1908.* London, 1977.

Lewis, B. *The Emergence of Modern Turkey.* Oxford, 1969.

Lewis, R. *Everyday Life in Ottoman Turkey.* London, 1971.

Lord Kinross, *The Ottoman Centuries: The Rise and Fall of the Turkish Empire.* New York, 1977.

Lynch, H.F.B. *Armenia: Travels and Studies,* vol. 2. London, 1901.

Mardin, S. *The Genesis of Young Ottoman Thought: A Study in the Modernization of Turkish Political Ideas,* Princeton, 1962.

Marriott, J.A.R. *The Eastern Question: A Study in European Diplomacy.* Oxford, 1951.

Oshagan, V. *The English Influence on West Armenian Literature in the Nineteenth Century.* Cleveland, 1982.

Salt, J. *Imperialism, Evangelism and the Ottoman Armenians 1878-1896* London, 1993.

Sarafian, K. *History of Education in Armenia.* La Verne, Ca., 1978.

Shaw, S. *Between Old and New: The Ottoman Empire under Sultan Selim III, 1789-1807.* Harvard, 1971.

Stavrianos, L. S. *Th Balkans since 1453.* New York, 1966.

Tootikian, V. *The Armenian Evangelical Church.* Detroit, 1982.

Armenians in Iran

Arakel of Tabriz, *History* (in Armenian). Vagharshapat, 1896.

Baghdiantz-McCabe, I. *The Shah's Silk for Europe's Silver.* Atlanta, 1999.

Bournoutian, G. *The Khanate of Erevan under Qajar Rule, 1795-1828.* Costa Mesa, Ca. 1992.

_____ *A History of Qarabagh: An Annotated Translation of Mirza Jamal Javanshir Qarabaghi's Tarikh-e Qarabagh.* Costa Mesa, Ca. 1994.

_____ .*The Chronicle of Abraham of Crete.* Costa Mesa, Ca., 1999.

_____ .*History of the Wars, 1721-1738.* Costa Mesa, Ca., 1999.

_____.*The Journal of Zak`aria of Agulis*. Costa Mesa, Ca., 2003.
_____."The Armenian Community of Isfahan in the Seventeenth
    Century," (2 parts), *Armenian Review* 24-25 (1971-1972).
_____. "Armenians in Nineteenth Century Iran," in *The Armenians
    of Iran*, Chaqueri ed.
Chaqueri, C. ed. *The Armenians of Iran*. Harvard, 1998.
Davrizhetsi, A. *History* (in Russian). Moscow, 1973.
Garoyants, N. *Iranian-Armenians* (in Armenian). Tehran, 1968.
Ghougassian, V. *The Emergence of the Armenian Diocese of New Julfa in
    the Seventeenh Century*. Atlanta, 1998.
Gregorian, V. "Minorities of Isfahan: The Armenian Community of
    Isfahan, 1587-1722," *Iranian Studies* 7 (1974).
Herzig, E. "The Deportation of the Armenians in 1604-1605 and Europe's
    Myth of Shah 'Abbas I," in *History and Literature in Iran,* C. Melville
    ed. Cambridge, 1990.
_____. The Armenian Merchants of New Julfa, Isfahan (Ph.D. Diss.,
    St. Anthony's College, 1991).
Ra'in, I. *Iranian-e Armenians* (in Persian). Tehran, 1970.
Ter Hovhanian, H. *History of New Julfa* (in Armenian). New Julfa, 1980.
Zak`aria of Kanaker, *Chronicle* (in Armenian). Vagharshapat, 1870.

Armenians on the Indian Subcontinent

Emin, J. *Life and Adventures of Joseph Emin 1726-1809,* 2 vols. Calcutta,
    1918.
Khachatrian, H. "Shahamir Shahamirian's Views on Natural Law,"
    Armenian Review 42 (1989).
Seth, M.J. *Armenians in India.* Calcutta, 1983 (first published in 1937).
Tololyan, M. "Shahamir Shahamirian's Vorogait Parats, (Snare of Glory),"
    Armenian Review 42 (1989).

Armenians in the Arab World

Arberry, A. J. ed., *Religion in the Middle East,* vol. I. Cambridge, 1969.
Azarya, V. *The Armenian Quarter of Jerusalem.* Berkeley, 1984.
Dadoyan, S. *The Fatimid Armenians*, Leiden, 1997.
Lutfi Al-Sayyid, A. *Egypt and Cromer: A Study in Anglo-Egyptian
    Relations.* London, 1968.
Nubar Pacha, *Memoirs de Nubar Pacha.* Beirut, 1983.
Polk, W. & Chambers, R. eds., *Beginnings of Modernization in the Middle
    East.* Chicago, 1968.
Rose, J. *Armenians of Jerusalem.* London, 1993.
Sanjian, A. *The Armenian Communities in Syria under Ottoman Dominion.*
    Harvard, 1965.
Tibawi, A. *A Modern History of Syria, including Lebanon and Palestine.*

New York, 1969.

Yapp, M. E. *The Making of the Modern Near East, 1792-1923.* London, 1987.

Ye'or, B. *The Dhimmi: Jews and Christians under Islam.* London, 1985.

European Travel Accounts on Armenians in Iran and Turkey

Vartoogian, J. *The Image of Armenia in European Travel Accounts of the 17th century.* (Ph.D. diss., Columbia, 1974).

Ghazarian, V. ed. *Armenians in the Ottoman Empire.* Waltham, Mass. 1997.

Armenians in Russia and Transcaucasia:

A Critical Examination of Armenian Catholic Communities in Transcaucasia. New York, 1994.

Allen W.E.D. & Muratoff, P. *Caucasian Battlefields: A History of the Wars on the Turco-Caucasian Border, 1828-1921.* London, 1953.

Allen, W.E.D. ed., *Russian Embassies to the Georgian Kings 1589-1605,* 2 vols. Cambridge, 1970.

Atamian, A., *The Archdiocese of Naxijevan in the 17th Century* (Ph.D. diss. Columbia, 1984).

Atkin, M. *Russia and Iran, 1780-1828.* Minneapolis, 1980.

Baddeley, J. *The Russian Conquest of the Caucasus.* London, 1908.

Bryce, J. *Transcaucasia and Ararat.* London, 1896.

Bournoutian, G. *Armenians and Russia, 1626-1796: A Documentary Record,* Costa Mesa, Ca., 2001.

_____. *Russia and the Armenians of Transcaucasia, 1797-1889: A Documentary Record,* Costa, Mesa, Ca., 1998.

_____. *The Khanate of Erevan under Qajar Rule, 1795-1828.* Costa Mesa, Ca., 1992.

_____. "The Ethnic Composition and the Socio-Economic Conditions in Eastern Armenia in the First Half of the 19th Century," in *Transcaucasia: Nationalism and Social Change.* Ann Arbor, 1983 (ed. Suny).

_____. "Eastern Armenia from the Seventeenth Century to the Russian Annexation," in *The Armenian People,* vol. II. (ed. Hovanissian).

_____. "The Russian Archives and Armenian History," in *Journal of the Society for Armenian Studies* (10, 2000).

Gregorian, V. "The Impact of Russia on the Armenians and Armenia," in *Russia and Asia,* W. S. Vucinich, ed., Stanford, 1972.

Lang, D.M. *The Last Years of the Georgian Monarchy, 1658-1832.* New York, 1957.

Hovannisian, R. *Armenia on the Road to Independence, 1918,* Berkeley, 1969.

Lynch, H.F.B. *Armenia: Travels and Studies,* vol. 1. London, 1901.

Rhinelander, A. L. *The Incorporation of the Caucasus into the Russian Empire: The Case of Georgia, 1801-1854* (Ph.D. diss., Columbia, 1972).

_____. *Prince Michael Vorontsov: Viceroy to the Tsar,* Montreal, 1990.

Suny, R. *Looking toward Ararat,* Bloomington, 1993.

Villari, L. *Fire and Sword in The Caucasus,* London, 1907.

Von Haxthausen, A. *Transcaucasia.* London, 1854.

Armenians in Europe and the Americas

Adalian, R. *From Humanism to Rationalism: Armenian Scholarship in the Nineteenth Century.* Atlanta, 1992.

Amadouni, G. *L'Eglise Armenienne et la Catholicite.* Venice, 1978.

Bakalian, A. *Armenian-Americans, From Being to Feeling Armenian,* New Brunswick, N.J., 1993.

Barkhudarian, V. *History of the Armenian Community of New Nakhichevan* (in Armenian) Yerevan, 1967.

Grigorian, V. ed., *Documents of the Armenian Court at Kamenets-Podolsk* (in Armenian). Yerevan, 1963.

Mikaelian, V. *History of the Armenian Community of the Crimea,* 2 vols. (in Armenian) Yerevan, 1964-1970.

Mirak, R. *Torn Between Two Lands: Armenians in America 1890 to World War I.* Harvard, 1983.

Oles, M. *The Armenian Law in the Polish Kingdom (1356-1519).* Rome, 1966.

Papazian, K. & Manuelian, P. *Merchants from Ararat.* New York, 1979.

Schutz, E. *An Armeno-Kipchak Chronicle on the Polish-Turkish Wars in 1620- 1621.* Budapest, 1968.

Ter-Oganian, L. & Raczkowska, K. *Armenians in Poland: A Bibliography* (in Polish). Warsaw, 1990.

The Armenian Question and Its Final Solution

Akcam, T. *Turk Ulusal Kimligi ve Ermeni Sorunu.* Istanbul, 1992.

Anassian, H. *The Armenian Question and the Genocide of the Armenians in Turkey: A Brief Bibliography of Russian Materials.* Los Angeles, 1983.

Astourian, S. "The Armenian Genocide: An Interpretation," *The History Teacher,* 23 (2, 1990).

Aharonian, K. *A Historical Survey of the Armenian Case.* Trans. K. Maksoudian, Watertown, 1989.

Bardakjian, K. *Hitler and the Armenian Genocide.* Cambridge, Mass., 1985.

Bliss. E.M. *Turkey and the Armenian Atrocities.* Fresno, Ca. 1982.

Buxton, N&H. *Travels and Politics in Armenia.* London, 1914.

Charney, I., ed. *Genocide: A Critical Bibliographic Review.* London, 1991

Dadrian, V. *The History of the Armenian Genocide.* Providence, 1995.

_____. *German Responsibility in the Armenian Genocide*, Watertown, Mass, 1998.

Dasnabedian, H. *History of the Armenian Revolutionary Federation. Dashnaktsutiun 1890-1924.* Milan, 1988.

Davis, L.A. *The Slaughterhouse Province: An American Diplomat's Report on the Armenian Genocide, 1915-1917.* New Rochelle, N.Y., 1989.

Derogy, J. *Resistance and Revenge.* New Brunswick, N.J., 1990.

Dobkin, M. *Smyrna 1922: The Destruction of a City.* Kent, Ohio, 1988.

Hoogasian Villa, S. & Matossian, M.K. *Armenian Village Life Before 1914.* Detroit, 1982.

Hovannisian, R. *The Armenian Holocaust: A Bibliography Relating to the Deportations, Massacres, and Dispersion of the Armenian People, 1915-1923.* Cambridge, Mass., 1978.

_____. ed. *The Armenian Genocide in Perspective.* New Brunswick, N.J., 1986.

_____.ed., *The Armenian Genocide: History, Politics, Ethics.* New York, 1992.

_____. *Armenia on the Road to Independence, 1918.* Berkeley, 1969.

Kazanjian, P. *The Cilician Armenian Ordeal.* Boston, 1989.

Keyder, C. *State and Class in Turkey.* London, 1987.

Kirakossian, J. *The Armenian Genocide: The Young Turks Before the Judgment of History.* Madison, 1992.

Langer, W. *European Alliances and Alignments, 1871-1890.* New York, 1939.

_____ *The Diplomacy of Imperialism, 1890-1902,* 2 vols. New York, 1935.

Lepsius, J. *Armenia and Europe.* London, 1897.

_____. *Deutschland und Armenien 1914-1918.* Potsdam, 1919.

Marashlian, L. *Politics and Demography: Armenians, Turks, and Kurds in the Ottoman Empire.* Cambridge, Mass., 1991.

Martin, E. *The Hubbards of Sivas: A Chronicle of Love and Faith.* Santa Barbara, Ca., 1991.

Melson, R. *Revolution and Genocide: On the Origins of the Armenian Genocide and the Holocaust.* Chicago, 1992.

Miller, D. & Touryan-Miller, L., *Survivors: An Oral History of the Armenian Genocide.* Berkeley, 1993.

Morgenthau, H. *Ambassador Morgenthau's Story.* New York, 1919.

Mukhtarian, O. & Gossoian, H. *The Defense of Van.* Michigan, 1980.

Nalbandian, L. *The Armenian Revolutionary Movement: The Development of Armenian Political Parties through the Nineteenth Century.* Berkeley, 1963.

Nassibian, A. *Britain and the Armenian Question, 1915-1923.* London, 1984.

Nichanian, M. *Writers of Disaster.* Princeton, 2002.

Peroomian, R. *Literary Responses to Catastrophe: A Comparison of the Armenian and the Jewish Experience.* Atlanta, 1993.

Rifat, M. *The Dark Folds of the Ottoman Revolution.* Beirut, 1968.

Sachar, H.M. *The Emergence of the Middle East, 1914-1924.* New York, 1969.

Sarkissian, A.O. *History of the Armenian Question to 1885.* Urbana, Ill., 1938.

Seton-Watson, R. *Britain in Europe, 1789-1914.* Cambridge, 1938.

Stuermer, H. *Two War Years in Constantinople.* New York, 1990.

Tarzian, M. *The Armenian Minority Problem.* New York, 1922.

Ter Minassian, A. *Nationalism and Socialism in the Armenian Revolutionary Movement (1887-1912).* Cambridge, Mass., 1984.

Ternon, Y. *The Armenians: History of a Genocide.* Delmar, N.Y., 1981.

Toriguian, Sh. *The Armenian Question and international Law.* La Verne, Ca., 1988.

Tozer, H. *Turkish Armenia.* London, 1881.

Trumpener, U. *Germany and the Ottoman Empire, 1914-1918.* Princeton, 1968.

Ussher, A. *An American Physician in Turkey.* Boston, 1917.

Walker, C. *Armenia: The Survival of a Nation.* New York, 1990.

Wegner, A. *Die Verbrechen der Stunde-die Verbrechen der Ewigkeit.* Hamburg, 1982.

Werfel, F. *Forty Days of Musa Dagh.* New York, 1934.

Yeghiayan, V. trans. *The Case of Soghomon Tehlirian* (court proceedings). Los Angeles, 1985.

Zürcher, E.J. Turkey: *A Modern History.* New York, 1993.

Documents on the Armenian Genocide

Adalian, R. ed., *Guide to The Armenian Genocide in the U.S. Archives, 1915-1918.* Alexandria, Virginia, 1994.

Sarafian, A. ed., *United States Official Documents on the Armenian Genocide (3 vols. to date)* Watertown, Mass., 1993-1995.

The Treatment of Armenians in the Ottoman Empire: Documents Presented to Viscount Grey of Fallodon. London, 1916.

The Armenian Genocide: Documentation edited by Institut fir Armenische Fragen, vols. I, II, VIII. Munich, 1987-1991.

Revisionist Works by Turkish and American Authors

Documents on Ottoman-Armenians, 2 vols. Ankara, 1983.
Ottoman Archives: The Armenian Question (3 vols. to date). Istanbul, 1989.
Ercan, Y. ed., *The Armenians Unmasked.* Ankara, 1993.
Karpat, K. *Ottoman Population, 1830-1914: Demographics and Social Characteristics.* Madison, 1985.
Lowry, H. *The Story Behind "Ambassador Morgenthau's Story.* Istanbul, 1990.
McCarthy, J. *Muslims and Minorities: The Population of Ottoman Anatolia and the End of the Empire.* New York, 1983.
Shaw, S.&E. *History of the Ottoman Empire and Modern Turkey,* vol. 2. New York, 1977.
Sonyel, S.R. *The Ottoman Armenians: Victims of Great Power Diplomacy.* London, 1987.
Uras, E. *The Armenians in History and the Armenian Question.* Istanbul, 1988.
Simsir, B.N. *British Documents on Ottoman Armenians, 1856-1890,* 2 vols. Ankara, 1982-1983.

The First Armenian Republic

Afanasyan, S. *L'Arménie, 1 'Azerbaïjan et la Géorgie. De l'indépendence á l'instauration du pouvoir soviétique, 1917--1923.* Paris, 1981.
Baldwin, O. *Six Prisons and Two Revolutions, 1920-1921.* Garden City, N.Y, 1925.
Barton, J. *Story of Near East Relief 1915-1930.* New York, 1930.
Evans, L. *United States Policy and the Partition of Turkey 1914-1924.* Baltimore, 1965.
Gidney, J. *A Mandate for Armenia.* Kent, Ohio, 1967.
Helmreich, P. *From Paris to Sèvres: The Partition of the Ottoman Empire and the Peace Conference of 1919-1920.* Columbus, Ohio, 1974.
Hovannisian R., *The Republic of Armenia,* 4 vols. Berkeley, 1971-1996.
Howard, H. *Turkey, the Straits and US Policy.* Baltimore, 1974.
Kazemzadeh, F. *The Struggle for Transcaucasia, 1917-1921.* New York, 1951.
Kayaloff, J. *The Battle of Sardarabad.* The Hague, 1973.
_____. *The Fall of Baku.* Bergenfield, N.J., 1976.
Kerr, S. *The Lions of Marash: Personal Experiences with American Near East Relief.* Albany, N.Y., 1973.
Nansen, F. *Armenia and the Near East.* New York, 1928.

Suny, R. *The Baku Commune, 1917-1918: Class and Nationality in the Russian Revolution.* Princeton, 1972.

Swietochowski, T. *Russian Azerbaijan, 1905-1920.* Cambridge, 1985.

＿＿＿＿＿＿＿. *Russia and Azerbaijan.* New York, 1995.

Trask, R. *The United States Response to Turkish Nationalism and Reform, 1914-1939.* Minneapolis, 1971.

Soviet Armenia and the Third Armenian Republic

Aspaturian, R. *The Union Republics in Soviet Diplomacy.* Geneva, 1960.

Bournoutian, G. "Rewriting History: Recent Azeri Alterations of Primary Sources Dealing with Karabakh," in *Journal of the Society for Armenian Studies* [JSAS](6, 1992-1993).

＿＿＿＿＿＿. "The Politics of Demography: Misuse of Sources on the Armenian Population of Mountainous Karabakh," in *JSAS* (9, 1999).

Chorbajian, L, Donabedian, P, Mutafian, C. *The Caucasian Knot: The History and Geo-Politics of Nagorno-Karabagh.* London, 1994.

Denber, R. ed., *The Soviet Nationality Reader*, Boulder, Co., 1992.

Goldenberg, S. *Pride of Small Nations.* London, 1994.

Hajda, L. & Beissinger, M. eds., *The Nationalities Factor in Soviet Politics and Society.* Boulder, Co., 1990.

Karklins, R. *Ethnic Relations in the USSR.* Boston, 1986.

Libaridian, G. *Armenia at the Crossroads: Democracy and Nationhood in The Post-Soviet Era.* Watertown, Mass., 1991.

＿＿＿＿＿＿*The Challenge of Statehood: Armenian Political Thinking since Independence.* Watertown, Mass., 1998.

Matossian, M. *Impact of Soviet Policies in Armenia.* Leiden, 1962.

Mouradian, C.S. *De Staline á Gorbachev: Histoire d'une Republique Soviétique: L'Armenie.* Paris, 1990.

Norehad, B. *The Armenian General Benevolent Union,* New York, 1966.

Parliament of the Republic of Armenia, *Decision '91. Armenia's Referendum on Independence, September 21, 1991.* Yerevan, 1991.

Rost, Y. *Armenian Tragedy: An Eyewitness account of Human Conflict and Natural Disaster in Armenia and Azerbaijan.* New York, 1990.

Shahmuratian, S. ed., *The Sumgait Tragedy: Pogroms against Armenians in Soviet Azerbaijan.* New Rochelle, N.Y. 1990.

Simon, G. *Nationalism and Policy Toward the Nationalities in the Soviet Union.* Boulder, Co., 1991.

Smith, G. ed., *The Nationalities Question in the Soviet Union.* London, 1990.

Tillet, L. *The Great Friendship: Soviet Historians on the Non-Russian Nationalities.* Chapel Hill, 1969.

Verluise, P. *Armenia in Crisis.* Detroit, 1995.

Walker, C. ed., *Armenia and Karabagh.* London, 1991.

Wright J, et al. eds. *Transcaucasian Boundaries*. New York, 1995.

Art, Music, Architecture, Language and Culture

Ayvazian, A. *The Historical Monuments of Nakhichevan*. Detroit, 1990.
Avedissian, O. *Peintres et Sculpteurs Arménians*. Cairo, 1959.
Akopian, G. *Miniatures of Vaspurakan*. Yerevan, 1989.
Armenian Artists. New York, 1993.
Armenian Miniatures. 2 vols. Yerevan, 1969 and 1987.
Der Hovanessian, D. & Margossian, M. eds. *Anthology of Armenian Poetry*. New York, 1978.
Der Nersessian, S. *The Armenians*. New York, 1970.
_____. *Armenian Manuscripts in the Walters Art Gallery*. Baltimore, 1973.
_____ *Miniature Painting in the Armenian Kingdom of Cilicia*, 2 vols. Washington, D.C., 1993.
Der Nesessian, S. & Mekhitarian, A. *Armenian Miniatures from Isfahan*. Brussels, 1986.
Durnovo, L. A. *Studies in the Fine Arts of Medieval Armenia* (in Russian). Moscow, 1979.
Ermakov. D. I. *Armenia, 1910* (photos). Rome, 1982
Guevorkian, A. *Crafts and Mode of Life in Armenian Miniatures,* Yerevan, 1978.
Kendel, B. & Thomson, R. *David the Invincible: Definitions and Divisions of Philosophy*. Pennsylvania, 1983.
Keshishian, J. *Inscribed Armenian Rugs of Yesteryear*. Sterling, 1994.
Mathews, T. and Wieck, R. eds. *Treasures in Heaven: Armenian Illuminated Manuscripts*. New York, 1994.
Mutafian. C. *Le Royaume Arménien de Cilicie*. Paris, 1993.
Nersessian, V. *Essays on Armenian Music*. London, 1978.
Novouspensky, N. *Ivan Aivazovsky*. St. Petersburg, 1995.
Russell, J. *Yovhannes T`lkuranc`i and the Mediæval Armenian Lyric Tradition*. Atlanta, 1987.
Samuelian, T. ed. *Classical Armenian Culture*. Pennsylvania, 1982.
Samuelian, T. & Stone, M. *Medieval Armenian Culture*. Pennsylvania, 1984.
Sanjian, A., ed. *David Anhaght*. Atlanta, 1986.
Sanjian, A. & Mathews T. *Armenian Gospel Iconography: The Tradition of the Glajor Gospel*. Washington, D.C., 1991.
Soviet Armenian Art (in Russian). Moscow, 1978.
The Inscribed Rugs of Armenia. Kimbell Art Museum, 1984.
Weitenberg, J.S., ed. *New Approaches to Medieval Armenian Language and Literature*. Amsterdam, 1995.

INDEX